COPING WITH LACK OF CONTROL IN A SOCIAL WORLD

Coping with Lack of Control in a Social World offers an integrated view of cutting-edge research on the effects of control deprivation on social cognition. The book integrates multi-method research demonstrating how various types of control deprivation, related not only to experimental settings but also to real-life situations of helplessness, can lead to a variety of cognitive and emotional coping strategies at the social cognitive level. The comprehensive analysis in this book tackles issues such as:

- Cognitive, emotional and socio-behavioral reactions to threats to personal control
- How social factors aid in coping with a sense of lost or threatened control
- Relating uncontrollability to powerlessness and intergroup processes
- How lack-of-control experiences can influence basic and complex cognitive processes

This book integrates various strands of research that have not yet been presented together in an innovative volume that addresses the issue of reactions to control loss in a socio-psychological context. Its focus on coping as an active way of confronting a sense of uncontrollability makes this a unique, and highly original, contribution to the field. Practicing psychologists and students of psychology will be particularly interested readers.

Marcin Bukowski, Lecturer and Researcher, Institute of Psychology, Jagiellonian University, Poland.

Immo Fritsche, Professor of Psychology, Leipzig University, Germany.

Ana Guinote, Professor of Psychology, University College London, UK.

Mirosław Kofta, Professor of Psychology, University of Warsaw, Poland.

Current Issues in Social Psychology

Series Editor: Arjan E. R. Bos

Current Issues in Social Psychology is a series of edited books that reflect the state of the art of current and emerging topics of interest in basic and applied social psychology.

Each volume is tightly focused on a particular topic and consists of seven to ten chapters contributed by international experts. The editors of individual volumes are leading figures in their areas and provide an introductory overview.

Example topics include: self-esteem, evolutionary social psychology, minority groups, social neuroscience, cyberbullying and social stigma.

Self-Esteem
Edited by Virgil Zeigler-Hill

Social Conflict within and between Groups
Edited by Carsten K.W. De Dreu

Power and Identity
Edited by Denis Sindic, Manuela Barret and Rui Costa-Lopes

Cyberbullying: From theory to intervention
Edited by Trijntje Völlink, Francine Dehue and Conor Mc Guckin

Coping with Lack of Control in a Social World
Edited by Marcin Bukowski, Immo Fritsche, Ana Guinote, and Mirosław Kofta

COPING WITH LACK
OF CONTROL IN
A SOCIAL WORLD

*Edited by Marcin Bukowski, Immo Fritsche,
Ana Guinote, and Mirosław Kofta*

Routledge
Taylor & Francis Group

LONDON AND NEW YORK

First published 2017
by Routledge
2 Park Square, Milton Park, Abingdon, Oxon OX14 4RN

and by Routledge
711 Third Avenue, New York, NY 10017

Routledge is an imprint of the Taylor & Francis Group, an informa business

© 2017 selection and editorial matter, Marcin Bukowski, Immo Fritsche,
Ana Guinote & Mirosław Kofta; individual chapters, the contributors

British Library Cataloguing-in-Publication Data
A catalogue record for this book is available from the British Library

Library of Congress Cataloging-in-Publication Data
Names: Bukowski, Marcin, editor. | Fritsche, Immo, editor. | Guinote, Ana,
 1963– editor.
Title: Coping with lack of control in a social world / edited by Marcin
 Bukowski, Immo Fritsche, Ana Guinote & Miroslaw Kofta.
Description: 1 Edition. | New York : Routledge, 2016. | Series: Current
 issues in social psychology | Includes bibliographical references and
 index.
Identifiers: LCCN 2016015428 | ISBN 9781138957923 (hardback) |
 ISBN 9781138957930 (paperback) | ISBN 9781315661452 (ebook)
Subjects: LCSH: Control (Psychology) | Social psychology.
Classification: LCC BF611 .C677 2016 | DDC 155.9/2—dc23
LC record available at https://lccn.loc.gov/2016015428

ISBN: 978-1-138-95792-3 (hbk)
ISBN: 978-1-138-95793-0 (pbk)
ISBN: 978-1-315-66145-2 (ebk)

Typeset in Bembo
by Apex CoVantage, LLC

CONTENTS

CONTRIBUTORS

Dan L. Ames, University of California, Los Angeles, USA

Markus Barth, University of Leipzig, Germany

Marcin Bukowski, Jagiellonian University, Poland

Soledad de Lemus, University of Granada, Spain

Cydney H. Dupree, Princeton University, USA

Susan T. Fiske, Princeton University, USA

Immo Fritsche, University of Leipzig, Germany

Katharine H. Greenaway, The University of Queensland, Australia

Ana Guinote, University College London, UK and Leadership Knowledge Centre, Nova School of Business and Economics, Portugal

Joseph Hayes, Acadia University, Canada

Eva Jonas, University of Salzburg, Austria

Philipp Jugert, University of Leipzig, Germany

Aaron C. Kay, Duke FUQUA School of Business, USA

Mirosław Kofta, University of Warsaw, Poland

Małgorzata Kossowska, Jagiellonian University, Poland

Izabela Krejtz, SWPS University of Social Sciences and Humanities, Poland

Joris Lammers, University of Cologne, Germany

Ian McGregor, University of Waterloo, Canada

Christina Mühlberger, University of Salzburg, Austria

Katerina Petkanopoulou, University of Granada, Spain

Michael C. Philipp, Massey University, New Zealand

Mike Prentice, University of Salzburg, Austria

Rosa Rodríguez-Bailón, University of Granada, Spain

Marzena Rusanowska, Jagiellonian University, Poland

Bastiaan T. Rutjens, University of Amsterdam, The Netherlands

Klara Rydzewska, SWPS University of Social Sciences and Humanities, Poland

Sindhuja Sankaran, Jagiellonian University, Poland

Grzegorz Sedek, SWPS University of Social Sciences and Humanities, Poland

Sandra Sittenthaler, University of Salzburg, Austria

Russell Spears, Groningen University, The Netherlands

Sheridan A. Stewart, Stanford University, USA

Janine Stollberg, University of Leipzig, Germany

Katherine R. Storrs, The University of Queensland, Australia

Daniel Sullivan, The University of Arizona, USA

Jillian K. Swencionis, Princeton University, USA

Maïka Telga, University of Granada, Spain

Jolien van Breen, Groningen University, The Netherlands

Guillermo B. Willis, University of Granada, Spain

COPING WITH LACK OF CONTROL IN A SOCIAL WORLD

An introduction

Marcin Bukowski, Immo Fritsche, Ana Guinote
and Mirosław Kofta

The need for personal control is one of the most critical dimensions of people's lives. Losing a job, having health problems, experiencing the death of a loved one are just some of the most vivid situations that make us realize the deleterious consequences of losing control over our lives. Whereas some of these instances involve people's independent ability to achieve what they want, such as performing well on a task or protecting their health, many instances of having or losing control are inherently linked to the social context. As a highly interdependent social species, humans' personal control, be it of a large or small scope, variety and intensity, might be jeopardized in nearly all social contexts: at school, in the family, at work, or in political life.

At the same time, being united in collectives or groups has helped humans develop a tremendous mastery of their physical environments (e.g., living in communities regardless of weather conditions, travelling to the moon) and a possibility to study the foundations of their very existence. Ironically, these collective vehicles of human agency can also be seriously threatened. Put differently, the complexity of human relations and personal motives can affect people's sense of control in multiple ways. Individual actors and groups can increase one another's sense of control (e.g., by facilitating joint projects or providing strength in numbers), decrease control (e.g., by inducing powerlessness or social inequalities that force membership in disadvantaged groups) or restore control (e.g., when, after control loss, friends and members of groups provide a sense of safety or security). Given the importance of the social context for individual control, several questions arise, such as: What are the antecedents of control gains and losses in social contexts? How does lacking control shape the ways individuals think, feel, and act? And what are the coping mechanisms deployed by individuals when control is lost? The aim of this book is to address these issues. By providing a concerted effort to understand control in social contexts, this book aims to contribute to a better understanding of one of the fundamental human needs – the need for control – and its role in the dynamics of social relations and human social cognition.

Past and present of control research

What is personal control?

Personal control has been defined as the extent to which a person can produce desired outcomes and prevent undesired ones (Antonovsky, 1979; Gurin, Gurin, & Morrison, 1978; Skinner, 1996). When people think that they can achieve such desired ends, they have *personal control*, also labeled sometimes as *perceived control* or *sense of control* (Abeles, 1991; Gurin & Brim, 1984). In this understanding, control involves the self as agent, who is focused on introducing changes in the social or physical environment with her/his behaviors as the means to achieve this goal (Skinner, 1996). This basic definition emphasizes effectiveness in dealing with the environment, changing the surroundings to fit the needs of the individual (Rothbaum, Weisz, & Snyder, 1982). In this sense, personal control resembles the notion of general self-efficacy (Bandura, 1997) and refers to such constructs as need for autonomy, competence, or mastery as different possible sources of motivation for personal control. Nowadays, however, psychologists prefer a broader conceptualization of this construct. They believe that people can restore or maintain control not only through direct action tendencies but also in indirect ways, when they accommodate to environmental constraints in order to satisfy their needs (Landau, Kay, & Whitson, 2015; Rothbaum et al., 1982).

What happens when control over the environment is threatened? Most probably, people become involved in restoration or repair of control, which could manifest in efforts to change the environment, but also, as recently stressed, in attempts to adjust the self to the environment if the latter is seen as unchangeable (Landau et al., 2015; Rothbaum et al., 1982; Thompson, Sobolew-Shubin, Galbraith, Schwankovsky, & Cruzen, 1993). As this volume demonstrates, people's struggles with perceived lack of control result in an impressive diversity of responses, ranging from action, approach tendency, and engagement, through compensatory reinterpretations of situations and the self, to withdrawal, avoidance, helplessness, and relinquishment of control.

Originally, inspired by learned helplessness theory, research on the psychological consequences of uncontrollability focused on exploring mental deficits induced by lack of control, and on the implications this knowledge has for understanding depressive disorders (Hiroto & Seligman, 1975; Seligman, 1975). Quite early, however, Wortman and Brehm (1975) realized that – depending on the severity and duration of control deprivation – either coping or withdrawal/escape (helpless-like) responses become more likely. Further research, in line with Wortman and Brehm's intuitions, revealed the whole complexity of human psychological response to loss of control. Nowadays, students of control deprivation no longer portray people as passive victims of uncontrollability, but as active agents trying to regain threatened control by whatever means available. Of course, as will be shown, researchers would not deny that control deprivation may result in helplessness and depression. However, the evidence discussed in this book shows that getting into a state of mental passivity and withdrawal from active coping is the last, rather than the first, human psychological response to loss of control. Even a longstanding threat to control (such as when realizing the inevitability of one's own death) may still lead to compensatory or symbolic responses. Also, researchers assume that, in order to explain which particular response to lack of control emerges, one must take into consideration the specificity of mediating cognitive, emotional, and motivational processes.

Social dimensions of coping with lack of control

How do we cope with lack of control? This crucial question has already been addressed by research rooted in clinical, developmental, personality, or motivational psychology (Brehm, 1966; Burger, 1992; Langer, 1975; Mikulincer, 1994; Skinner, 1995). For a long time, however, this research line addressed the individual person and the interplay of internal cognitive, affective, and motivational processes engendered by threat to control. Even though it is true that personal control, as well as control deprivation, is experienced by the individual, in this book we turn readers' attention to the fact that personal control is deeply embedded in the social context. The social environment seems to be a critical factor that allows us to understand the emergence of uncontrollability perceptions and their subsequent management. The current book examines how the social context can affect one's sense of personal control, as well as how losing personal control affects how individuals feel, think, and act in relation to their social environment. In particular, we focus on threatened personal control, and the role other people and groups play in arousing feelings of control loss as well as in the ways of coping with these feelings.

Control in a social world

We believe that an important gap in earlier research on control deprivation was that it failed to consider the social context (with the notable exception of studies on powerlessness; e.g., see Guinote, 2010; Smith, Jostman, Galinsky, & van Dijk, 2008; Weick, Guinote, & Wilkinson, 2011; Wilkinson, Guinote, Weick, Molinari, & Graham, 2010). However, within the past two decades a growing body of research unravels the importance of social determinants and consequences of perceived lack of control (e.g., Fiske & Dépret, 1996; Fritsche et al., 2013; Kay, Gaucher, Napier, Callan, & Laurin, 2008; Landau et al., 2015; Pittman & D'Agostino, 1989; Whitson & Galinsky, 2008). This research shows that lack of personal control has profound implications for people's social cognition and behavior. The experience of personal control is affected not only by social comparisons with more or less powerful others (Festinger, 1954), but also by the fact that humans are highly interdependent, and dependency creates the seeds for control gains and loss (Emerson,

1962; Fiske & Berdahl, 2007). These recent advancements in social psychological research highlight a number of dimensions in which the social context can be relevant for the study of personal control, its loss and its restoration. All these dimensions are carefully analyzed in this book.

First, the cognitive, affective, and motivational effects of control loss on how we perceive and understand other people are studied. Following experience of control loss, our perceptions of people substantially change. Partly, this change is due to purely cognitive demands that control-depriving situations impose on our minds (e.g., control deprivation results in mental overload and deficit of free cognitive resources, see Kofta & Sedek, 1998). At the same time, it is a well-established finding within the literature on motivated social cognition that in cognitively demanding circumstances people are likely to process information in a strategic way, aimed at restoring their deprived needs (Fiske & Taylor, 2008; Kunda, 1999). In this book, we bridge those two perspectives by examining what situational factors related to control loss can inhibit or enhance strategic and goal-directed cognition and action.

This leads us to the second social dimension for personal control: strategic perception of other people and social groups driven by the motive to restore or compensate for a threatened sense of control. As has been recently demonstrated, a variety of strategies allows perceivers to regain control, such as self-definition in terms of agentic ingroups (Fritsche et al., 2013; Greenaway et al. 2015), or to compensate for control loss, such as heavy reliance on order-providing beliefs and ideologies (social, religious), search for individual or collective allies, but also blaming powerful, individual, or collective enemies (Kay et al., 2008; Rutjens, van Harreveld, & van der Pligt, 2013; Sullivan, Landau, & Rothschild, 2010; Whitson & Galinsky, 2008).

A third important dimension on which the interaction between the social context and a sense of personal control is analyzed in this book relates to the notion of social power. The experience of control deprivation emerges not only as a consequence of one's own deficient abilities and lack of competence in fulfilling personal goals, but also due to the fact that other people (e.g., superordinates, members of a higher status group) have social power over one's life. More and more studies consistently show that being in a subordinate position dramatically changes the way we think and act (e.g., makes us reluctant to use categorical perception, makes us endorse more egalitarian values and life goals than powerful counterparts, etc.; Guinote, Cotzia, Sandhu, & Siwa, 2015).

Thus, in our book we take a socio-motivational perspective and highlight the fundamental role of thinking about other people, and about oneself in reference to them, as a way of dealing with lack of control. This does not mean that the impressive tradition of research on control deprivation as an individual experience will be ignored. Instead, the chapters in this volume are deeply rooted in previous, experimental research on control motivation by examining how cognitive and affective changes induced by uncontrollability can influence the way we think about others and emotionally react to them. In particular, we will review new findings suggesting that, when deprived of personal control, people deliberately or automatically seek out effective cognitive and behavioral strategies that help them to regain control and feelings of mastery. Human actions aimed at restoring personal control will be analyzed from the agentic point of view, emphasizing the active role of the person in the coping process when faced with uncontrollability (see, e.g., Kofta, Weary, & Sedek, 1998). However, we will also show how such coping efforts – particularly when repeatedly failing to restore control – might in fact result in growing cognitive and affective malfunctioning and behavioral disruption.

Book contents

In this volume, we are particularly interested in studying complex and dynamic reactions to control loss in various social contexts, related to interpersonal as well as intergroup processes. This perspective allows us to bring basic research on control motivation in touch with such important social instances of uncontrollability as being confronted with unexpected and highly threatening events in the social world (e.g., unemployment, terrorist attacks, etc.), lacking social power, being a member of a low-status and/or stigmatized group, living in poverty, experiencing helplessness in the course of school learning, being subordinate in an organization, or being a target of discrimination (de Lemus, Spears, van Breen, & Telga, Chapter 9, this volume; Fiske, Ames, Swencionis, & Dupree, Chapter 10, this volume; Guinote & Lammers, Chapter 11, this volume; Rydzewska, Rusanowska, Krejtz, & Sedek, Chapter 4, this volume; Mühlberger, Jonas, & Sittenthaler, Chapter 13, this volume; Sullivan & Stewart, Chapter, 6, this volume). Our social world creates a nearly infinite number of occasions in which personal control might be threatened or totally eliminated.

Analyzing experiences of control loss in social settings not only allows us to identify the real-life context in which it typically emerges and reconstruct the experience dynamics, but also to recognize the ways of coping typical for those settings. Interestingly, people's responses to control loss in social contexts may themselves change the social context, such as, for instance, increasing people's inclination to social conflict when powerful enemies or conspirational actors are blamed for misfortunes (Sullivan & Stewart, Chapter 6, this volume) or when people praise their ingroups while derogating (e.g., ethnic) outgroups (Stollberg, Fritsche, Barth, & Jugert, Chapter 8, this volume). At the same time, personal control loss seems to drive people's readiness to build up friendship networks (Guinote & Lammers, Chapter 11, this volume), to be an active part in collective endeavors or social movements (Stollberg et al., Chapter 8, this volume) or to resist social inequality (de Lemus et al., Chapter 9, this volume). Moreover, placing both appraisals of and responses to lacking control in real-life social contexts helps us to better understand the critical moderators that determine the strategy of coping people are likely to choose.

In this book, we focus on three main thematic areas. Firstly, we explore cognitive, emotional, and socio-behavioral reactions to perceived uncontrollability (i.e., the effects of various states of uncontrollability on cognitive performance and social information processing strategies). Then, we focus on various socially grounded responses to control deprivation, such as compensatory or active coping, both serving the functions of control maintenance or restoration (the effects of control loss on perceiving others and thinking about individuals and groups are mainly considered in this part). Finally, we relate the notion of uncontrollability to issues of powerlessness and intergroup cognition by studying how powerless or subordinate people think about others and what emotions guide their thoughts and actions (i.e., the role of group membership and identification in combating feelings of uncontrollability and uncertainty, but also the social implications of uncontrollability and powerlessness are examined in this part).

Let us now briefly introduce the major ideas and findings discussed by the authors in this volume. In the first section – *Cognitive, emotional, and socio-behavioral reactions to uncontrollability* – the types of basic psychological responses people exhibit after being control deprived are discussed.

In the first chapter, entitled "From coping to helplessness: Effects of control deprivation on cognitive and affective processes", Bukowski and Kofta analyze various types of cognitive and emotional reactions to lack-of-control experiences. The authors propose that coping and helplessness perspectives can no longer be seen as competitive views of reactions to control loss, but actually address different stages of confrontation with uncontrollability (coping in early stages, helplessness in the late stage). They argue that impairment of information processing after exposure to uncontrollability is, paradoxically, due to the fact that people are cognitively active (continue problem-solving attempts in an objectively uncontrollable situation). Prolonged, intense, cognitive coping aiming at control restoration can result in growing behavioral uncertainty (i.e., uncertainty about how to act) and cognitive deficits at a basic, attentional level of information selection, as well as at a more complex, reasoning level of information integration into meaningful mental models.

Greenaway, Philipp and Storrs, in the second chapter, entitled "The motivation for control: Loss of control promotes energy, effort, and action", review up-to-date research that provides evidence for enhanced motivation to restore control following relatively short-lasting exposure to control deprivation. Individuals become initially energized by loss of personal control but after an extended period of exposure to control-depriving situations people can become listless and passive, as described by early work on learned helplessness. Greenaway and colleagues also point out some important social consequences of the finding that loss of control facilitates effortful pursuit of personal goals: in such circumstances, people increasingly focus on achieving their personal goals at the expense of social goals (such as keeping or building positive interpersonal or intergroup relationships). Thus, in some circumstances, goal competition between one's own and social goals, induced by loss of control, might lead to increased prejudice towards outgroups and other forms of social aggression.

Kossowska, Bukowski, and Sankaran in Chapter 3 – "Ironic effects of need for closure on closed-minded processing mode: The role of perceived control over reducing uncertainty" – analyze circumstances in which people who are chronically motivated to reduce uncertainty and use closed-minded, effortless cognitive strategies become prone to apply more open-minded and effortful ways of thinking. The authors argue that perceived control over reducing uncertainty plays a key role in determining the way people will react to situations that disconfirm their expectations (about themselves or about the world). Kossowska et al. demonstrate that when people are highly motivated to reduce uncertainty (i.e., have high need for closure), but feel that they cannot reduce it (i.e., have no control) they might abandon their dominant, effortless cognitive strategies and achieve certainty via more effortful and deliberative information-processing strategies. This extends previous research that deemed the latter strategies to be typical for people with low need for closure.

Chapter 4, entitled "Uncontrollability in the classroom: The intellectual helplessness perspective", by Rydzewska, Rusanowska, Krejtz, and Sedek addresses the issue of uncontrollability and intellectual helplessness in an applied, educational context. Their research shows that faulty teaching promotes development of intellectual helplessness, and that the phenomenon itself is context-dependent (e.g., helplessness in math classes appears to be unrelated to helplessness in native language classes). Importantly, its detrimental effects on math achievement remain significant after controlling for math anxiety. Also, these studies show that even chronically helpless students are not totally passive, but frequently engage in active "survival strategies", which only simulate understanding of the lesson content (such as acquiescing when new material is presented, or talking at high speed about everything that pops to mind in response to the teacher's question).

In the next section, *Socially grounded responses to control deprivation: From compensation to active coping*, the role of the social context (other individuals, ingroups, and outgroups) as a resource that can help people to cope with a situation that threatens personal control is discussed.

In Chapter 5, "Compensatory control theory and the psychological importance of perceiving order", Rutjens and Kay focus on the function of compensatory control. In contrast to the majority of researchers viewing compensatory control strategies as indirect ways of satisfying a basic need for personal control, the authors argue that compensatory control efforts following personal control threat (e.g., through endorsement of external agents of control such as God or government) ultimately help to regain order and meaning in the perceived world. To support their view, the authors refer to several findings from their own laboratory showing that: (a) personal control and perceived external control (e.g., of powerful social and spiritual agents) operate in a hydraulic fashion; (b) priming randomness increased both motivation to exert personal control and belief in a controlling God; (c) affirmation of order (that does not involve external agents) appears to be sufficient for downregulating threats to control.

In Chapter 6, entitled "Perceived uncontrollability as a coping resource: The control-serving function of enemies and uncertainty", Sullivan and Stewart discuss the meaning and adaptive functions of control-related experiences from the perspective of cultural-existential psychology. They assume that, following threat, people either engage in denial, or in projection of anxiety onto the external world (e.g., by searching for an external source of their misfortunes). In contrast to existing literature, which focuses on the compensatory role of benevolent external agents, the authors argue that making malevolent agents (e.g., personal and political enemies, conspiring groups) salient might also regain a sense of personal control. This happens because identifying a particular focal enemy allows people to reduce anxiety resulting from perceptions of the world as a source of a multitude of unpredictable and uncontrollable hazards (and so helps to impose meaning and structure). The authors review several studies from their own and other laboratories in support of this view.

Hayes, Prentice and McGregor in Chapter 7, "Giving in and giving up: Accommodation and fatalistic withdrawal as alternatives to primary control restoration", discuss the interplay between primary and secondary control, mostly in the context of the fundamental Piagetian distinction between assimilation and accommodation. They propose that secondary control might be a highly effective, avoidance-oriented resolution of threatened primary control, its essence being a change in one's own beliefs and knowledge structures in accordance with situational demands (accommodation process). They present evidence that – following mortality salience – participants with low (but not high) self-esteem accommodated their beliefs in accord with evidence inconsistent with their worldview. However, accommodation going too far (resulting in changing a person's core, not only her or his peripheral beliefs) appeared to be no longer effective in coping with the terror of death.

In Chapter 8, entitled "Extending control perceptions to the social self: Ingroups serve the restoration of control", Stollberg, Fritsche, Barth, and Jugert point to the fact that people develop not only personal but also group identities (Tajfel & Turner, 1979). When deprived of personal control, an individual may therefore regain a sense of an agentic self by pursuing shared ingroup goals and defining the self in terms of an agentic ingroup. Instead of representing a case of vicarious (secondary) control, they argue, ingroup identification, ingroup bias, and conformity with ingroup norms may in fact be expressions of primary control efforts at the group level. The authors discuss how mechanisms of secondary vicarious control through external agents (Kay et al., 2008) can be empirically distinguished from processes of extended primary control through the ingroup. They conclude that, so far, the present findings do not allow for a clear-cut judgment of which specific process – compensatory control or group-based control – is involved, calling for future research.

De Lemus, Spears, van Breen, and Telga in Chapter 9, "Coping with identity threats to group agency as well as group value: Explicit and implicit routes to resistance", focus on the psychological roots of social resistance, understood as a group's opposition to societal circumstances that perpetuate social disadvantage and low status of group members. The authors argue that threats to social identity cannot be reduced to questioning group value (as many social psychologists seem to assume), because they simultaneously threaten collective agency (ability of the group to change their fate). Low ingroup status implies lack of power and collective self-efficacy, that is to say, deprivation of control at the group level. But at a more subjective level, group members are able to exert psychological control as a resistance strategy. Therefore, threats to group identity (e.g., when stereotypical expectations as to a woman's traditional, inferior social role are made salient) could provoke resistance not only at the explicit level (e.g., support for collective actions), but also implicitly (e.g., activating ingroup bias). The authors describe a series of experimental studies supporting their predictions about implicit resistance, and discuss them in terms of their implications for group agency.

In the last section of the book, called *Uncontrollability, powerlessness, and intergroup cognition*, the ways people psychologically cope with lack of control are analyzed in the context of outcome dependency, power, or economic and social status relations.

Fiske, Ames, Swencionis, and Dupree in Chapter 10, entitled "Thinking up and talking up: Restoring control through mindreading", address the hypothetical role of predictability and controllability motives in outcome-dependency contexts. The authors analyze asymmetrical dependency, with special focus on the psychology of those subordinated (with relatively low status and power). In an impressive series of studies, the authors show that being subordinated results in more vigilance to a high-status (power-holding) person and better encoding of diagnostic (inconsistent) information, processes presumably in service of regaining predictability and control over the partner's behavior. However, when no control restoration is possible, then people switch to defensive distortion: they tend to discount negative information about the power-holders and focus on their benign, positive traits.

In Chapter 11, "Accentuation of tending and befriending among the powerless", Guinote and Lammers focus on how powerless people cope with lack-of-control experiences in various social contexts. Typically, the powerless, in contrast to the dynamic powerful, are seen as socially inactive. However, the authors show that the psychological state of powerlessness triggers multifaceted and dynamic social strategies that serve the adaptation of individuals. That is, the powerless turn to others in order to form stronger social bonds, increase their communal focus, and display more prosocial behavior, are more generous, and show more adherence to social norms. The authors conclude that the priorities of the powerless are to achieve a detailed and complex understanding of the social world, to help others, and to create socially shared beliefs that ensure fairness. Here, the search for communion and social coordination are the coping mechanisms that can help an individual to restore control.

In Chapter 12, "The emotional side of power(lessness)", Petkanopoulou, Willis, and Rodríguez-Bailón focus on the emotions of powerless people and their social functions. The authors argue that emotions mainly serve two broad social functions that are crucial for people's interactions: a social distancing function and an affiliative function. Whereas some emotions, such as sadness, shame, and guilt, help people to get closer to others and affiliate with them, others, such as anger and pride, create social distance and promote competition for status. Powerlessness is most commonly associated with the experience and expression of affiliative emotions, such as sadness and guilt. However, as shown by the authors, when power differences are illegitimate, then powerless individuals can also display social distancing emotions such as anger. Their function in this case is to regain relative power or status. Eventually, approach-related emotions like anger could also lead powerless people to enhance their personal sense of control.

Mühlberger, Jonas, and Sittenthaler in Chapter 13, entitled "Uncontrollability, reactance, and power: Power as a resource to regain control after freedom threats", begin with the observation that individuals who lack control try to regain it by relying on diverse strategies that often have a defensive nature. Further, they propose that power can be conceptualized as a resource that enables people to regain control because it provides a sense of efficacy, freedom, and control. In other words, individuals who are threatened by control loss but feel powerful manage to free themselves from the negative effects of this threat and engage in information processing relevant to their desired goals. The authors present research from their own lab, revealing that if people's sense of control is threatened but they still feel powerful and have the necessary resources to attain their goals, they are able to refrain from behaving in a defensive and hostile way and instead adapt to the new situation in a more flexible manner.

Summing up, this volume brings together different perspectives on the issue of how people cope with feelings of uncontrollability in their social lives. The variety of theoretical approaches and empirical findings seems to build a coherent picture of a person who, when faced with his or her own inability to control important aspects of the environment, seeks effective social and cognitive strategies that either help to compensate or to regain a sense of control through the self. We hope that this book not only lets us better understand how social-psychological factors determine the way people cope with lack of control, but also reveals how people's desire for control shapes their social environments.

Acknowledgments

We would like to thank the authors of this volume for their commitment, hard work, and most importantly, their thought-provoking and inspiring contributions. We are also thankful for the financial support of the Polish National Science Centre (grants DEC-2011/01/D/HS6/00477 and DEC-2014/15/B/HS6/03755) and the Dedalus Trust (grant 520180 F67), which enabled this joint project and editorial work.

References

Abeles, R. (1991). Sense of control, quality of life, and frail older people. In J. Birren, J. Lubben, J. Rowe, & D. Deutschman (Eds.), *The concept and measure of quality of life in the frail elderly* (pp. 297–314). San Diego, CA: Academic Press.
Antonovsky, A. (1979). *Health, stress and coping.* San Francisco: Jossey-Bass.

Bandura, A. (1997). *Self-efficacy: The exercise of control*. New York: Freeman.

Brehm, J. (1966). *A theory of psychological reactance*. New York: Academic Press.

Burger, J. M. (1992). *Desire for control: Personality, social, and clinical perspectives*. New York: Plenum.

Emerson, R. M. (1962). Power-dependence relations. *American Sociological Review, 27*, 31–41.

Festinger, L. (1954). A theory of social comparison processes. *Human Relations, 7*, 117–140.

Fiske, S. T., & Berdahl, J. (2007). Social power. In A. Kruglanski & E. T. Higgins (Eds.), *Social psychology: Handbook of basic principles* (2nd ed., pp. 678–692). New York: Guilford.

Fiske, S. T., & Dépret, E. (1996). Control, interdependence, and power. Understanding social cognition in its social context. In W. Stroebe & M. Hewstone (Eds.), *European Review of Social Psychology* (Vol. 7, pp. 31-61). New York: Wiley.

Fiske, S. T., & Taylor, S. E. (2008). *Social cognition: From brains to culture*. New York: McGraw-Hill.

Fritsche, I., Jonas, E., Ablasser, C., Beyer, M., Kuban, J., Manger, A. M., & Schultz, M. (2013). The power of we: Evidence for group-based control. *Journal of Experimental Social Psychology, 49*, 19–32.

Greenaway, K. H., Haslam, S. A., Cruwys, T., Branscombe, N. R., Ysseldyk, R., & Heldreth, C. (2015). From "we" to "me": Group identification enhances perceived personal control with consequences for health and well-being. *Journal of Personality and Social Psychology, 109*, 53–74.

Guinote, A. (2010). The situated focus theory of power. In A. Guinote & T. Vescio (Eds.), *The social psychology of power* (pp. 141–176). New York: Guilford Press.

Guinote, A., Cotzia, I., Sandhu, S., & Siwa, P. (2015). Social status modulates prosocial behavior and egalitarianism in preschool children and adults. *PNAS, 112*, 731–736.

Gurin, P., & Brim, O. G. (1984). Change in self in adulthood: The example of sense of control. In P. B. Baltes & O. G. Brim (Eds.), *Life-span development and behavior* (pp. 282–334). San Diego: Academic Press.

Gurin, P., Gurin, G., & Morrison, B. M. (1978). Personal and ideological aspects of internal and external control. *Social Psychology, 41*, 275–296.

Hiroto, D. S., & Seligman, M. E. P. (1975). Generality of learned helplessness in man. *Journal of Personality and Social Psychology, 31*, 311–327.

Kay, A. C., Gaucher, D., Napier, J. L., Callan, M. J., & Laurin, K. (2008). God and the government: Testing a compensatory control mechanism for the support of external systems. *Journal of Personality and Social Psychology, 95*, 18–35.

Kofta, M., & Sedek, G. (1998). Uncontrollability as a source of cognitive exhaustion: Implications for helplessness and depression. In M. Kofta, G. Weary, & G. Sedek (Eds.), *Personal control in action: Cognitive and motivational mechanisms* (pp. 391–418). New York: Plenum Press.

Kofta, M., Weary, G., & Sedek, G. (1998). *Personal control in action: Cognitive and motivational mechanisms*. New York: Plenum Press.

Kunda, Z. (1999). *Social cognition: Making sense of people*. Cambridge, MA: MIT Press.

Landau, M. J., Kay, A. C., & Whitson, J. A. (2015). Compensatory control and the appeal of a structured world. *Psychological Bulletin, 141*, 694–722.

Langer, E. J. (1975). The illusion of control. *Journal of Personality and Social Psychology, 32*, 311–328.

Mikulincer, M. (1994). *Human learned helplessness: A coping perspective*. New York: Plenum Press.

Pittman, T. S., & D'Agostino, P. R. (1989). Motivation and cognition: Control deprivation and the nature of subsequent information processing. *Journal of Experimental Social Psychology, 25*, 465–480.

Rothbaum, F., Weisz, J. R., & Snyder, S. S. (1982). Changing the world and changing the self: A two-process model of perceived control. *Journal of Personality and Social Psychology, 42*, 5–37.

Rutjens, B. T., van Harreveld, F., & van der Pligt, J. (2013). Step by step: Finding compensatory order in science. *Current Directions in Psychological Science, 22*, 250–255.

Seligman, M. E. P. (1975). *Helplessness: On depression, development, and death.* San Francisco: Freeman.

Skinner, E. A. (1995). *Perceived control, motivation, and coping.* Newbury Park, CA: Sage Publications.

Skinner, E. A. (1996). A guide to constructs of control. *Journal of Personality and Social Psychology, 71*, 549–570.

Smith, P. K., Jostman, N., Galinsky, A. D., & van Dijk, W. W. (2008). Lacking power impairs executive functions. *Psychological Science, 19*, 441–447.

Sullivan, D., Landau, M. J., & Rothschild, Z. K. (2010). An existential function of enemyship: Evidence that people attribute influence to personal and political enemies to compensate for threats to control. *Journal of Personality and Social Psychology, 98*, 434–449.

Tajfel, H., & Turner, J. C. (1979). An integrative theory of intergroup conflict. In W. G. Austin & S. Worchel (Eds.), *The social psychology of intergroup relations* (pp. 33–47). Monterey, CA: Brooks/Cole.

Thompson, S. C., Sobolew-Shubin, A., Galbraith, M. E., Schwankovsky, L., & Cruzen, D. (1993). Maintaining perceptions of control: Finding perceived control in low-control circumstances. *Journal of Personality and Social Psychology, 64*, 293–304.

Weick, M., Guinote, A., & Wilkinson, D. (2011). Lack of power enhances visual perceptual discrimination. *Canadian Journal of Experimental Psychology, 65*, 208–213.

Whitson, J. A., & Galinsky, A. D. (2008). Lacking control increases illusory pattern perception. *Science, 322*(5898), 115–117.

Wilkinson, D., Guinote, A., Weick, M., Molinari, R., & Graham, K. (2010). Feeling socially powerless makes you more prone to bumping into things on the right and induces leftward line bisection error. *Psychonomic Bulletin and Review, 17*, 910–914.

Wortman, C. B., & Brehm, J. W. (1975). Reponses to uncontrollable outcomes: An integration of reactance theory and the learned helplessness model. In L. Berkowitz (Ed.), *Advances in experimental social psychology* (Vol. 8, pp. 277–336). New York: Academic Press.

PART 1

Cognitive, emotional, and socio-behavioral reactions to uncontrollability

1

FROM COPING TO HELPLESSNESS

Effects of control deprivation on cognitive and affective processes

Marcin Bukowski and Mirosław Kofta

Author note

Work on this chapter was supported by grants awarded by the Polish National Science Centre (NCN) to Marcin Bukowski (DEC-2011/01/D/HS6/00477) and to Mirosław Kofta (DEC-2014/15/B/HS6/03755).
We would also like to thank Janina Pietrzak for her valuable help with language editing.
Contact: marcin.bukowski@uj.edu.pl

1. Facing uncontrollability: Helplessness or coping?

Individual strivings to exert, maintain, or restore a sense of personal control over the environment have long been considered to be a core and basic type of motivation (Bandura, 1977; Burger, 1992; DeCharms, 1968; Skinner, 1996; White, 1959). Early research on the control motive in humans was particularly focused on how control deprivation affects cognitive and emotional functioning (e.g., Hiroto & Seligman, 1975; Seligman, 1975). In his seminal work, Seligman (1975) proposed that prolonged and stable experiences of uncontrollability (operationalized as response-outcome non-contingency) result in the learned helplessness syndrome, including cognitive deficits (understood as the inability to detect new contingencies), a depressed mood, and the inability to pursue important goals. Since then, numerous studies have shown that a lack of contingency between action and outcome results in deterioration of performance and affective disruption (e.g., Hiroto & Seligman, 1975; Kofta & Sędek, 1989; Tennen, Drum, Gillen & Stanton, 1982). Extending Seligman's original framework, Sedek and Kofta (1990; see also Kofta & Sedek, 1998) developed the idea that prolonged, inefficient investment of cognitive effort is a critical aspect of uncontrollable situations, leading to the emergence of cognitive exhaustion. In this mental state, a person shows cognitive deficits in problem solving and avoidance learning associated with a negative mood. Inspired by this theoretical idea, subsequent studies investigated these cognitive deficits at the levels of basic processes of selective attention, as well as of reasoning and the formation of meaningful mental models (Kofta, 1993; Kofta & Sedek, 1998; Ric & Scharnitzky, 2003; von Hecker & Sedek, 1999). Several cognitive malfunctions observed in this line of experimental research appear to be shared by people suffering from clinical depression or with elevated depressive mood (e.g., von Hecker & Sedek, 1999; Kofta & Sedek, 1998; McIntosh, Sedek, Fojas, Brzezicka-Rotkiewicz, & Kofta, 2005). Also, very much in line with these findings, Hertel and her colleagues (e.g., Hertel, 2000; Hertel & Hardin, 1990; Hertel & Rude, 1991) showed that memory malfunctioning in depressive patients is not due to limited cognitive resources, but to lack of cognitive initiative, i.e., deficits of focal attention to relevant stimuli. Once attention-directing stimuli were introduced to experimental instructions, memory deficits of depressive participants disappeared.[1]

In contrast to research rooted in the learned helplessness/depression tradition, in other theoretical frameworks, lack of personal control is frequently seen as a challenge, mobilizing people to regain control (Brehm, 1966; Pittman & Pittman, 1980; Wortman & Brehm, 1975). In this line of studies, rather than viewing humans as victims of uncontrollability, researchers consider people to be active agents who cope with loss-of-control experiences to regain control and fulfill their needs. Brehm's reactance theory (1966) assumed that threat to freedoms activates a motivational process called reactance, which drives people to engage in behaviors aimed at the restoration of those threatened freedoms. Further research on reactance motivation revealed that moderate levels of uncontrollability evoke negative emotional states (such as anger) but simultaneously increase motivation to succeed and improve performance (Brehm & Brehm, 1981; Miron & Brehm, 2006; Wortman & Brehm, 1975). When discussing the nature of the mobilization phase of the response to loss of control, we will analyze in this chapter various ways of coping with uncontrollability. Undoubtedly, one of the most important distinctions is that between problem-focused and emotion-focused coping (Lazarus & Folkman, 1984; see also Skinner, 1996). Some strategies employed to manage uncontrollability are aimed at changing the situation, whereas others aim at dealing with one's own emotional reactions to it. In the domain of research on learned helplessness, a fine-grained analysis of various coping strategies was done by Mikulincer (1994), who makes a distinction between several strategies of coping with control loss, including problem solving, reappraisal, avoidance, and reorganization (revision of self-schemas).

Control-regaining efforts also manifest at the level of social information processing: control deprivation has been shown to increase the tendency to be more accurate in judgments and to use a more systematic processing style (Pittman & Pittman, 1980). Pittman and D'Agostino's (1989) explanation was that control deprivation experiences call into question the adequacy of one's beliefs and understanding of the way things work. In response, control motivation grows and changes the mode of information processing so as to support restoration of control. Overall, the findings from this line of research suggest that lacking control can improve cognitive performance (or at least, can provoke processes that immunize us against the deleterious effects of uncontrollability). We will refer to these findings in more detail further on (Bukowski, de Lemus, Lupiáñez, Marzecová, & Gocłowska, 2016; Mikulincer, Kedem, & Zilcha-Segal, 1989; Ramirez, Maldonado, & Martos, 1992).

Other lines of research that also conceptualize loss of control as a challenge are increasingly popular in the area of intergroup and political cognition. The first line shows that the experience of control loss is likely to instigate compensatory processes (secondary control) that help to restore the threatened sense of control by regaining a perception of structure, order, coherence, and meaning in the surroundings. This process allows researchers to account both for illusory patterning of phenomenological field and for various types of cognitive shortcuts and biases, such as belief in conspiracies or superstitions, that emerge after loss-of-control experiences (Fast et al., 2009; Kay et al., 2010; Sullivan et al., 2010; Whitson & Galinsky, 2008). The second line shows that lack of control can also stimulate people to endorse and support ingroups, and this process might lead to ethnocentric as well as pro-social consequences (Fritsche, Jonas, & Kessler, 2011). The group-based control model (Fritsche et al., 2013), assuming that threats to personal control promote actions at the collective level aimed at the restoration of primary control (see also: Stollberg, Fritsche, Barth, & Jugert, Chapter 8, this volume), constitutes yet another way of explaining how people react to control loss.

Thus, four different lines of theorizing and research – reactance theory, control motivation framework, compensatory control, and group-based control models – commonly assume that a person deprived of control is actively searching for meaningful causal relations and contingencies in the environment in order to regain a sense of control.

The question arises how to come to terms with apparently conflicting views on the consequences of control deprivation: one pointing to helplessness (demobilization) effects, the other to coping (mobilization) effects. We propose that these seemingly incompatible approaches can be combined into a coherent theoretical model. Drawing on the seminal work of Wortman and Brehm (1975), we take a dynamical approach to control deprivation and assume that short exposure to uncontrollability is likely to provoke various types of coping attempts, whereas only long-term uncontrollability results in disengagement and helplessness. Also, we assume that initially adaptive changes in cognitive responding engendered by lack of control (e.g., switching to a more flexible and open-minded information-processing style) can ultimately lead to cognitive and emotional deficits when control-restoration attempts, even if repeated, appear futile. Finally, we postulate that the major process accounting for both coping activity and – after enduring contact with uncontrollable situations – cognitive and behavioral deterioration is mounting behavioral uncertainty – the direct consequence of long-lasting, inefficient attempts to cognitively cope with an uncontrollable situation.

In this chapter, we will first analyze how lack of control affects cognition. To do that, we introduce the notion of behavioral uncertainty as a major process accounting for shifts away from active coping with uncontrollable situations to mental and behavioral disengagement and decreased mood, observed after prolonged confrontation with uncontrollability. Further on, we analyze how coping with behavioral uncertainty manifests at different levels of information processing (information selection, cognitive structuring, causal knowledge formation). Importantly, we look at these processes in the context of different phases of control deprivation (their consecutive emergence depending on the length, intensity, and stability of the loss-of-control experience). Finally, we consider how uncontrollability affects emotional processes and how these processes in turn modify the course of information processing and (inter)group judgment.

2. Control-deprivation effects on cognition and affect

When confronted with an uncontrollable situation in an important domain, people seem likely to engage in intense cognitive effort, because they try to understand what is going on ("Why can't I do it?") and generate various hypotheses about how to solve the problem. We propose that the most immediate consequence of a lack-of-control experience is increased behavioral uncertainty. This hypothetical process may explain both vigorous attempts to restore control during early confrontation with uncontrollability, as well as deterioration of performance and decreased mood, emerging after prolonged control loss.

Behavioral uncertainty

Uncertainty is a multifaceted concept; the experience of uncertainty may emerge in relation to the world or to the self, may be permanent or transient, may refer not only to something in the future but also to something that already happened (e.g., Hogg, 2000; Swann, 2012; Weary & Edwards, 1996). Behavioral uncertainty, we propose, is experienced when a person strives toward a goal but appears unable to reach it despite repeated attempts. Such behavioral uncertainty has three distinct features: first, it refers to action in the near future; second, as long as a person is in an uncontrollable situation, it cannot be reduced despite trying; third and perhaps most importantly, it tends to gradually increase over the course of prolonged exposure to uncontrollability.

How and why does it emerge? Some degree of uncertainty accompanies any goal-oriented, novel behavior (we must find or construct an adequate action program to reduce initial uncertainty about how to achieve a goal before we move to successful action, see e.g., Gollwitzer & Kinney, 1989). An inherent feature of an uncontrollable situation is, however, lack of contingency between behavior and outcome (e.g., Kofta & Sędek, 1989; Maier & Seligman, 1976). As a consequence, systematic and valid feedback to the generated hypotheses is unavailable. It immediately follows that, if a situation is objectively uncontrollable, one cannot predict the consequences of whatever action he or she is actually considering, resulting in increased uncertainty (Kofta & Sedek, 1998, 1999; Sedek & Kofta, 1990; Sedek, Kofta, & Tyszka, 1993).

To cope with a continuing lack of control, people generate new hypotheses but can neither prove nor reject any, thus increasing the entropy of the hypotheses set (e.g., Kofta & Sedek, 1999). Moreover, given that the situation remains uncontrollable, any seemingly adaptive shift to new cognitive strategies (e.g., a switch from a default heuristic to a systematic information-gathering strategy, see Pittman & D'Agostino, 1989) results in a further increase of behavioral uncertainty. Finally, when lack of control continues despite a person's attempts to regain control, the generation and application of mental models is heavily impaired (e.g., von Hecker & Sedek, 1999). Mental models – flexible theories of a situation generated on-line – are uncertainty-reducing mental instruments (e.g., Gentner & Stevens, 1983; Johnson-Laird, 1983; Kofta, 1993). Therefore, impaired mental modeling will further increase the perceived unpredictability of the world, and high, irreducible uncertainty is going to be highly aversive. So, it does not seem very surprising that, after prolonged exposure to uncontrollability, people disengage from active coping, that is, stop investing mental energy in problem-solving attempts and show symptoms of cognitive exhaustion and learned helplessness.

In order to cope with behavioral uncertainty (as with any other type of uncertainty), a person has to efficiently manage inconsistent and often conflicting pieces of information. To better understand the specific nature of behavioral uncertainty resulting from control deprivation experiences, let us distinguish two levels of cognitive processing. At the first level, uncertainty may accompany basic attentional processing involved in filtering and selection of goal-relevant information. At the second level, uncertainty concerns the contingency between goals (intentions) and actions (plans and their execution: e.g., uncertainty increases along with the number of simultaneously held hypotheses).

In addition, a person in an uncontrollable situation might be increasingly uncertain of his or her self-perceived ability to cope with control loss. However, when a person cannot find a problem solution despite trying, and behavioral uncertainty increases – ability uncertainty will ultimately decrease (i.e., the person comes to the conclusion that "I do not have the abilities that are necessary to solve the problem"). The latter self-inference seems critical for the aforementioned withdrawal from behavioral and cognitive coping observed after prolonged exposure to uncontrollability.

Let us now turn to the question of how behavioral uncertainty, emerging from lack-of-control experiences, manifests at two basic levels of information processing: attentional selection to goal-relevant information and the perception of causal relations in the environment.

Uncontrollability and cognitive control

How does uncontrollability affect the attentional processes of information search, selection, and inhibition of distractors? Previous research has revealed that uncontrollability experiences lead to performance impairment on subsequent tasks and to lowered mood (Hiroto & Seligman, 1975; Kofta & Sedek, 1999). High levels of uncertainty appear to be a valid mediating variable between uncontrollability experiences and subjective symptoms of cognitive difficulties, which are related to decreased performance levels in a variety of cognitive tasks (Kofta & Sedek, 1999; Sedek & Kofta, 1990).

At the level of basic attentional processing, exposure to lack of personal control leads to decreased selectivity in filtering input data (Kofta & Sedek, 1998) and relaxes attentional constraints, resulting in broadened, less selective information intake (Minor, Jackson, & Maier, 1984). Research performed using a dual-task paradigm showed that control deprivation affects attentional selection processes (Kofta & Sedek, 1998). In this study, participants were pre-exposed to the *Informational Helplessness Training* (exposure to unsolvable tasks without feedback; Sedek & Kofta, 1990) and subsequently asked to perform a dual task, in which the primary task was a letter-recognition task and the secondary task required keeping a horizontal line within given boundaries. The findings revealed a decrease of primary-task performance in the dual-task condition only for the group with uncontrollability pre-exposure. Interestingly enough, a main effect of uncontrollability on an increased number of false alarms was found, independently from task condition (Sedek & McIntosh, 1996). This result suggests that impaired filtering of information might be the main mechanism responsible for deficits in performance in more difficult task conditions.

More recently, Bukowski and colleagues (2015) showed that stable uncontrollability experiences decrease the efficiency of executive attention. In this research, impact of lack-of-control experiences was studied on attentional control, defined in terms of Posner's Attentional Networks Theory as the ability to resolve conflicts or interferences and regulate ongoing actions, thoughts, and feelings (Petersen & Posner, 2012; Posner & Rothbart, 2007). Whereas the function of the executive network is related to attentional control, the orienting network allows people to selectively orient attention to sensory events, while (phasic) alerting is responsible for achieving and maintaining an alert state. An ANTI-Vigilance procedure was applied in order to additionally measure attentional vigilance and to determine whether the predicted effects of control deprivation are indeed specific to executive attention or reflect a more general impact on a broader range of attentional processes. Across two experiments, the authors found that experimentally induced experiences of uncontrollability (via exposure to a series of unsolvable tasks) have a negative impact on attentional control, strengthening the conflict effect (as seen in increased reaction times to incongruent as opposed to congruent stimuli). Additionally, it was found that uncontrollability can lead to a less selective orienting strategy (i.e., an increased orienting of attention to all types of stimuli that might help to reduce cognitive conflict). Importantly, this tendency reduced the ability to disengage attention from invalid cues. The results obtained for the vigilance measure confirmed the hypothesis that the tendency to rely on invalid cues and the existence of stronger conflict effects might be related to a less selective response strategy in general. The authors conclude that this strategy can heavily impair the operation of the goal-driven attentional system (Bukowski et al., 2015).

Of considerable interest, the detrimental effects of uncontrollability experiences on attentional orienting and vigilance were pronounced when lack of control was induced by means of exposing participants to unsolvable tasks without feedback, a procedure that was shown to induce irreducible uncertainty (Kofta & Sedek, 1999). In this case, broader attentional effects could be observed in comparison to a procedure that applied explicit and non-contingent feedback (the procedure used by Hiroto & Seligman, 1975, to induce uncontrollability). Why did this occur? It seems that a lack of feedback for behavior (when exposed to unsolvable tasks) creates a strong state of uncertainty, stemming from the fact that people do not know whether the inability to solve the task results from their own lack of competence (i.e., internal factors) or the difficulty of the task (i.e., external factors). Therefore, a broader range of attentional processes, apart from executive functions, is affected (Bukowski et al., 2015).

In sum, both lines of research, one exploring dual-task performance and the other exploring efficiency of attentional networks, support the idea that uncontrollability affects selective attention, reducing the efficiency of executive control processes and promoting diffused and dispersed attentional processing (Bukowski et al., 2015; Kofta & Sedek, 1998). Additionally, it seems justified to argue that deficits that emerge after control deprivation in filtering relevant from irrelevant information are due to decreased efficiency of goal-driven, top-down attentional control. From a broader perspective, this loosening of goal-driven control for the sake of stimulus-driven, bottom-up attentional control might be considered to be a highly adaptive response pattern, since it allows for changing the current action plan when it appears inefficient: broadened attention allows finding new, more effective ways of operating, which will presumably be helpful in control-restoration strivings. However, this attentional strategy may decrease the ability to pursue one definite goal, resulting in an increased uncertainty about which information is goal-relevant and which irrelevant. As a result of this process, behavioral uncertainty seems to grow.

On a more general level, one can say that people experiencing irreducible behavioral uncertainty switch to a less efficient and more dispersed processing and performance mode, which might reveal an adaptive way of adjusting to prolonged uncontrollability (McIntosh et al., 2005). This different processing mode might be characterized by a broadened but also dispersed focus of attention and higher sensitivity to different sources of information, goal-relevant as well as goal-irrelevant, resulting in increased behavioral uncertainty. We believe, however, that, in order to better understand the adaptive or coping-based nature of such responses, it is important to take into consideration the dynamics of control deprivation and restoration. We will explore this issue further on in this chapter.

Uncontrollability and cognitive structuring

So far, we have discussed the effects of uncontrollability on basic cognitive processes of attentional control. Now we address the issue of how uncontrollability affects more integrative cognitive processing that encompasses structuring of information, perceptions of causality, and creation of explanatory knowledge structures such as mental models.

Let us assume that uncontrollability experiences inform the acting person that his or her knowledge structures about causal relations in the environment need to be revised. Consistent with this claim, previous research has shown that after experiencing lack of control, people increase their attributional activity and search for new explanations that help them to understand why people behave in a particular way (Bains, 1983; Kelley, 1972; Pittman & Pittman, 1980). More recent research has shown that, when lacking control, people engage in a search for illusory patterns or contingencies in the environment, be it on a basic perceptual level (e.g., making sense of white noise) or on the level of perceptions of causal relations in the environment: uncontrollability promotes illusory correlations in stock market information, development of superstitions, belief in paranormal abilities such as precognition, or an increased evaluation of ritual efficacy (Greenaway, Louis, & Hornsey, 2013; Legare & Souza, 2014; Whitson & Galinsky, 2008). Additionally, the use of explanatory schemas in the form of simple conspiracy theories, reducing the whole complexity of social life to the concealed and malicious impact of a certain group or institution on one's life or prosperity, seems to be largely driven by a threatened sense of control and compensatory processes that are aimed at reestablishing control perceptions (Bilewicz, Winiewski, Kofta, & Wójcik, 2013; Kossowska & Bukowski, 2015; Whitson & Galinsky, 2008).

This tendency to rely, after lack-of-control experiences, on simple cognitive structuring to bring back order, causality, and meaning to uncertain surroundings, might be considered to be a motivated and strategic way of responding. However, it might also reflect the inability of people exposed to uncontrollability to integrate new, incoming information into more-complex and flexible mental representations of reality using logical inference rules (von Hecker & Sedek, 1999). Kofta (1993) proposed that uncontrollability experiences impair the creation of mental models that would allow the individual to understand causal relations and predict future outcomes. Von Hecker and Sedek (1999) demonstrated that uncontrollability experiences do not affect identification of information that is relevant for the construction of a mental model. However, they impede the more cognitively demanding, generative process of integrating the pieces of information into a coherent mental model of sentiment relations between people. In other words, rule-based reasoning suffers from lack-of-control experiences in that the selection and implementation of a particular rule is impaired.

We propose that lack of control undermines certainty regarding the type of rules or plans that need to be used in order to achieve a particular goal and regain personal control (i.e., increases behavioral uncertainty). As a consequence, this lack of confidence results on the one hand in a broadened, less selective information-intake strategy, but on the other hand in a decreased ability to cognitively structure and integrate various, often conflicting pieces of information into a meaningful mental model that would allow the individual to understand complex causal relations in the environment. Ultimately, this process might leave the individual overloaded with information that he or she is unable to integrate in a meaningful way, leading to increased automatic search for illusory patterning and other compensatory structuring, grossly simplifying the individual's representation of reality (e.g., Legare & Souza, 2014; Whitson & Galinsky, 2008).

Uncontrollability and affect

So far, we have discussed in detail how control deprivation affects cognitive processing. However, students of loss-of-control experiences have posited from the very beginning (e.g., Seligman, 1975; see also Maier & Seligman, 1976; Miller & Seligman, 1975) that prolonged control deprivation results in a general affective deficit (arousal of a mixture of negative emotions, one of the critical symptoms of the learned helplessness syndrome) that might trigger reactive depression. This expectation has been supported by numerous findings (e.g., Hiroto & Seligman, 1975; Kofta & Sędek, 1989; Roth & Kubal, 1975; Sedek & Kofta, 1990; Tuffin, Hesketh, & Podd, 1985). However, virtually all early studies used explicit self-evaluation measures, taken after task performance, for this purpose.

In the new research to be reported (Kobyliński, Kofta, & Bukowski, 2016) we assumed that affective responses might emerge at an early stage of processing and strongly affect subsequent cognitive responses (Murphy & Zajonc, 1993; Zajonc, 1980). To better understand the role of affect in loss of control, we applied the affect-infusion model as developed by Forgas and his colleagues (e.g., Forgas, 1995, 2007; Forgas & Ciarrochi, 2000). In particular, we assumed that control deprivation experiences – experiences that are dangerous to the vital interests of the organism – are likely to produce decreased mood not only on explicit (as shown in earlier studies) but also on implicit measures. In particular, we predicted that (a) control deprivation would lead to the emergence of negative mood, and that (b) its arousal would automatically prime negative semantic content through an affect-infusion process (Bower, 1981; Forgas & Ciarrochi, 2000). This process would result in assimilation effects, i.e., increased accessibility and importance of negative information.

We also expected that the above process might modify (inter)group judgment, insofar as negative mood was linked with activated representations of a social group: negative mood, induced by an uncontrollable experience, was expected to decrease ingroup or outgroup evaluations, but only in the case when the representation of the group was activated immediately after the uncontrollability experience.

To test our predictions, the Emotional Stroop Test was used (e.g., McKenna & Sharma, 1995, 2004; Williams, Mathews, & MacLeod, 1996). In this task, the participant has to name the color of the word appearing on a computer screen as quickly as possible. Displayed words differ in their affective tone. If control deprivation automatically evokes negative mood, and the assimilation-to-affect process begins to operate, then negative mood, thus produced, should increase the accessibility of negative (but not neutral) words. Quick activation of negative words' meanings interferes with fast color naming, therefore increasing reaction times for negative words among participants pre-trained with unsolvable problems (uncontrollability condition).

We also expected that bad moods resulting from uncontrollable experiences would decrease evaluations of one's own group or of outgroups, but only when a group representation is explicitly primed, allowing the assimilation-to-affect process to operate. Therefore, in some studies, immediately after the end of control deprivation induction and application of the Emotional Stroop Test, the group representation was primed and then attitudes toward this group were measured. In three experiments, we found that control deprivation induction (exposure to a series of unsolvable problems) increased reaction times to negative (but not neutral) words in the Emotional Stroop Test, suggesting arousal of implicit negative mood, and made attitudes toward the ingroup more negative, but only when ingroup representation was primed. Moreover, in one study we found that control deprivation resulted in increased accessibility of negative stereotypical traits and decreased accessibility of positive stereotypical words of the Gypsy outgroup (the latter effect was mediated by the arousal of implicit negative mood). Interestingly enough, increased reaction times to negative words (presumably indicating arousal of negative mood) appeared only weakly related to explicit self-reports of emotions. Overall, considerable support for the hypotheses was found.

The above findings suggest that the experience of loss of control results in diffused (contentless) negative mood, which in turn – through the assimilation-to-affect process – shifts one's attitude toward a subsequent target – in this case, negatively affecting attitudes toward ingroup members and activating negative outgroup stereotypes. Our findings suggest that the role of negative affect following control deprivation should be reconsidered. Affect might emerge quite early (in one of our previous studies we found that participants reported that performing unsolvable problems was highly unpleasant already at an early phase of exposure to uncontrollability, see Sedek & Kofta, 1990). Second, affect might substantially modify cognitions about one's own group and outgroups as well, suggesting its important regulatory role in determining social judgment (particularly when dealing with positivity-negativity of social targets).

The question arises, whether the effects we found for the Emotional Stroop Test emerged due to arousal of negative mood or the impairment of cognitive processing (e.g., engaging various executive functions). Caparos and Blanchette (2014) have shown recently that trauma-exposed victims responded slower when naming the color of trauma-related words, and that there was no relationship between working-memory measures and interference on Emotional Stroop. These findings support a view of the Emotional Stroop Test as a specific measure of affective, not cognitive, disturbance. To conclude, control deprivation results in a diffused, decreased mood, exerting important influence on cognitive processes and, possibly, contributing to mental and behavioral disengagement observed after long-term exposure to uncontrollability.

3. The dynamics of control loss and restoration

So far, we have mainly examined how stable and prolonged uncontrollability experiences affect cognitive and affective functioning. However, our everyday experience with exercising control over our lives and surroundings shows that control feelings fluctuate and are a mixture of having and lacking control, rather than a stable appraisal of one's own control over the environment. We argue that the dynamics of control experiences have a crucial impact on cognitive and emotional functioning because the length, stability, and intensity of those feelings of control can in fact lead either to an impairment or to a boost of cognitive performance. As highlighted by Wortman and Brehm (1975), short experiences of lacking control can have a mobilizing effect on human motivation and behavior, whereas prolonged confrontation with uncontrollability can demobilize people and result in learned helplessness syndrome. The effort expenditure and energization processes following various experiences of lacking control are a very important aspect of reactions to control loss, but as such will not be the subject of this review (see also Brehm & Self, 1989; Gendolla & Richter, 2010; Greenaway, Philipp, & Storrs, Chapter 2, this volume; Wright, 1998). Instead, we will address a relatively underexplored domain, that is, the impact of various types of uncontrollability experiences on cognitive processes involved in coping with uncertainty and managing conflicting pieces of information.

Studies that have examined the impact of the length of uncontrollability experiences on performance, briefly addressed in the introduction, have revealed that a performance boost could be observed after one or two unsolvable tasks out of four (Mikulincer, 1994; Pittman & Pittman, 1980). However, an increase of the number of unsolvable tasks (four, six, and eight unsolvable tasks) led to deterioration of cognitive performance (Ric & Scharnitzky, 2003). These results are consistent with the cognitive exhaustion model of control deprivation, which claims that prolonged experiences of lacking control might motivate individuals to invest effort to solve the problem but at the same time might gradually decrease performance accuracy (Ric & Scharnitzky, 2003; Sedek & Kofta, 1990).

One important factor that moderates the influence of control deprivation on performance is the type of causal attribution made about the experienced failure (Abramson, Seligman, & Teasdale, 1978). Ramirez, Maldonado, and Martos (1992) showed that an immunization against learned helplessness is possible when participants are encouraged to make specific and external (vs. global and internal) attributions about the obtained negative effects. Mikulincer (1988b) showed that attributing failure to unstable causes prevented the detrimental effects of unsolvable tasks on performance. Bukowski et al. (2015) manipulated the instability of control deprivation experiences by exposing the participants to unsolvable tasks that were subsequently replaced by solvable tasks. Instability was evoked by a sudden shift from lack of control to controllable task conditions. The impact of this sequential control restoration procedure on the efficiency of attentional control was assessed (Bukowski et al., 2015). The results revealed that no attentional deficits could be observed when participants were able to restore their sense of previously deprived control in comparison to those who experienced stable control deprivation. Thus, it seems that the control restoration experience "immunized" participants against the impairment of attentional control, equalizing their performance level with the baseline group that was not exposed to any type of control-depriving experiences.

Furthermore, it was hypothesized that instable control deprivation (similarly to short experiences of lacking control) might be related to more flexible cognitive control (i.e., more efficient switching between task rules). Therefore, in a different set of studies, the impact of control restoration experiences on a task that measures the ability to switch between different levels of social categorization was tested (Bukowski et al., 2016). The results showed that participants who were exposed to a procedure in which the unsolvable problems were followed by solvable ones were more efficient in switching between different category levels (i.e., age and gender categorizations) than were participants pre-exposed only to unsolvable problems. Control restoration experiences also facilitated switching between social categorization levels related to stereotype-congruent vs. stereotype-incongruent information (Bukowski et al., 2016). In other words, control restoration experiences in fact boosted cognitive flexibility.

The findings discussed above seem consistent with research on the impact of rewards and incentives on cognitive control processes, because they illustrate that motivational incentives can enhance cognitive control (Botvinick & Braver, 2015; Padmala & Pessoa, 2011). Recent studies revealed that rewards can reduce cognitive conflict, probably via changes in dopamine levels (Padmala & Pessoa, 2011; van Steenbergen, Band, & Hommel, 2009). Incentives, modulated by the dopaminergic system, were also shown to potentiate flexible behavior, assessed within a task-switching paradigm (Aarts, van Holstein, Cools, 2011). In line with these results, Bukowski et al. (2016) provided evidence that an increased subjective sense of control restoration, which in itself has a positive and rewarding value, evoked in one task, can boost performance on a subsequent task that assesses cognitive flexibility. It seems plausible that the amount of rewarding experiences has a crucial influence on how the cognitive system deals with behavioral uncertainty. If we assume that control deprivation experiences activate behavioral uncertainty and cognitive conflict related to the filtering of relevant from irrelevant information, then small amounts of conflict might be adaptive, because they prepare the cognitive system to manage new conflicting information after previous exposure to cognitive conflict (see Botvinick, Braver, Barch, Carter, & Cohen, 2001).

In sum, research reviewed in this chapter supports the original idea of Wortman and Brehm (1975) that short exposure to lack of control enhances cognitive performance but prolonged and stable experiences of uncontrollability interfere with it. Perhaps environments that evoke a sense of instability or randomness of contingencies between goals and outcomes can paradoxically immunize the individual against the negative impact of control-loss experiences on cognition. However, growing behavioral uncertainty and its concomitant − conflict processing − can impede the ability to process the increased amount of information. This can interfere with the cognitive control that is involved in goal-driven and rule-based processing strategies.

4. A dynamic approach to control: Implications for social cognition

In this chapter, we discussed the impact of control deprivation on cognitive processing and affect. Despite recently observed, impressive developments, this research area is fragmented and suffers from lack of conceptual coherence. Still, certain theoretical approaches focus exclusively on detrimental effects of uncontrollability experience on cognition, performance, and affect, taking the learned helplessness theory perspective. People are depicted there as victims of unmanageable situations, showing cognitive impairment and disturbed affective responding. However, others take the opposite view: for them, humans confronted with control deprivation are, primarily, active agents trying to regain control via direct action or (if control restoration efforts fail) via compensatory cognitive activity.

Focusing on a particular conceptual perspective is, of course, fully justified since it allows us to place research in a clear-cut theoretical framework and generate testable hypotheses. However, in this chapter we suggest that the delineated approaches are not necessarily in conflict, and might be integrated into a coherent higher-order frame. Inspired by the seminal work of Wortman and Brehm (1975), we suggest taking a dynamical approach to control deprivation and postulate that short exposure to uncontrollability is likely to provoke various coping attempts, whereas only long-term uncontrollability experiences result in disengagement and helplessness.

Within this framework, we discussed in detail which cognitive strategies are probably preferred in the first, coping stage. Accumulating findings, gathered in laboratories including our own, suggest that early control deprivation results in effortful processing that provides an extended pool of hypotheses to solve the problem. These changes could be seen as adaptive responses of the human cognitive system to lack of control, because they enable broadening the scope of alternative actions to be considered. Ironically, however, this strategic shift increases behavioral uncertainty and makes processing of conflicting information more and more difficult. Thus, an initially adaptive shift in cognitive strategies might ultimately increase distractibility and interfere with top-down processing necessary for effective goal attainment.

Equally important, the boost of cognitive openness initially engendered by lack-of-control experiences might lead to a gradual increase of behavioral uncertainty, which is highly aversive. This type of uncertainty is also enhanced by growing problems with generation and application of mental models (flexible mental instruments enabling structuring of processing and reduction of uncertainty). The process sketched here not only impairs constructive processing but in addition generates diffused negative mood, adversely affecting problem solving and social cognition.

Ultimately, people withdraw from investing mental energy into problem-solving activity and incur depressive feelings (i.e., in the state of learned helplessness).

We believe that the approach outlined in this chapter is not only useful for bridging helplessness and coping traditions in research on control deprivation, but also has important implications for social cognition. It goes beyond the scope of this chapter to develop this idea in detail. However, let us illustrate the potential contribution of the present (phasic) perspective to political psychology. Within the area of political cognition, researchers have recently shown that, when deprived of personal control, people are more likely to identify powerful negative social agents, e.g., collective enemies (Sullivan, Landau, & Rothschild, 2010; also Sullivan & Stewart, Chapter 6, this volume), and to look for external sources of control over the world, such as a well-functioning judicial system, an efficient economy, a controlling God, or science (e.g., Kay et al., 2009; see also Rutjens & Kay, Chapter 5, this volume). These processes presumably help us to indirectly regain a sense of control or predictability. However, an overwhelming majority of the research efforts to fit personal control into the social-political context tacitly assumes that (a) there is a simple, linear relationship between rising control deprivation and subsequent changes in political cognition (e.g., identifying collective enemies, see Sullivan et al., 2010), and that (b) compensation is a modal way of responding to control deprivation (e.g., Kay et al., 2009; Sullivan et al., 2010; Whitson & Galinsky, 2008). From the present perspective, it seems that those assumptions oversimplify reality. First, people could also use more direct ways of control restoration in societal settings by engaging in active coping with lack of control and making attempts to restore a primary sense of control by identifying with agentic groups or promoting social change (Fritsche et al., 2013; Stollberg et al., Chapter 8, this volume; see also recent studies on social movements, e.g., Drury & Reicher, 2005). Also, the present approach suggests that exposure to collective lack of control, if long lasting, may result in behavioral/mental disengagement and helplessness symptoms, not compensatory strategies. Still, moderate or instable experiences of uncontrollability and uncertainty can enhance active, problem-focused, and flexible coping.

Finally, it seems important to point to some boundary conditions of the model we propose in this chapter, with regard to the notion of behavioral uncertainty. Let us make a conceptual distinction between the development of personal control in new environments and the perception of having (or not having) control in a given situation. Note that in situations of the first type, people do not know in advance whether they will be able to establish control, and are motivated to try. In this context, deprivation of control is an "emerging experience", a conclusion of unsuccessful attempts to discover an effective program of action. In the second type of situations, "we already know" that we have, or do not have, control (e.g., I am aware that I could not obtain a higher position in my organization no matter how hard I tried, because I belong to a stigmatized group). Obviously, the idea of behavioral uncertainty as an explanation of control deprivation applies exclusively to the first case, i.e., to situations when we attempt to develop control by generating new behaviors or action programs to attain personal goals, in other words, when we are "experimenting with the environment". The idea that exposure to an uncontrolla-ble situation results in growing and irreducible behavioral uncertainty makes sense only in this "developmental" or learning context. If I feel that I do not have control due to lack of abilities or a subordinated position in a power relationship, the degree of uncertainty is probably very low (I know for sure what would happen if I tried to exercise control: I would certainly fail).

5. Concluding remarks

In the present chapter, we traced the effects of prolonged exposure to lack of con-trol on cognitive and affective processes, reviewing numerous findings from our and others' laboratories. What can be concluded? First, coping and helplessness perspectives on lack-of-control effects should not be seen as competitive views of the process. They actually refer to different stages of confrontation with uncontrol-lability (coping in early stages, helplessness in the late stage). Second, and perhaps most importantly: according to our proposal, increasing impairment of information processing after exposure to uncontrollability is due to the fact that people are cognitively active, e.g., continue problem-solving attempts in an objectively uncon-trollable situation (particularly likely when important life goals are in jeopardy). Maintaining their overoptimistic expectations, they simply assume that (actually unsolvable) social and intellectual tasks are difficult but manageable, and they gener-ate a range of hypotheses of problem solutions. Thus, we propose, it is not learning of response-outcome non-contingency, but rather intense cognitive coping aimed at control restoration over an actually uncontrollable situation, that accounts for growing cognitive deficits at the level of attentional processing and generation of mental models. In this sense, our approach is consistent with the functionalist view of control deprivation and cognition, in which enhanced cognitive activity serves the goal of achieving predictability and control. Still, we highlight the importance of growing behavioral uncertainty as a process that can eventually turn cognitive mobilization and openness into exhaustion and withdrawal from action.

One may wonder whether this model, based on experimental laboratory studies, is realistic. Our answer would be affirmative. In many important life situations, peo-ple establish ambitious goals and try to achieve them despite numerous obstacles and repeated failures (intermixed with successful episodes). In real-world settings, unmanageable difficulties with goal attainment may stem from two distinct sources. One is the objective uncontrollability of a given situation (our environment might be unresponsive, e.g., when social and cultural barriers – social-role expectations and stereotypes – make it impossible for an individual to advance in an organiza-tion despite intense effort). The other factor creating uncontrollability is lack of abilities, knowledge, and competences necessary to attain a particular goal. Here, in principle, the objective situation is controllable; however, an individual does not have sufficient resources to effectively gain control. Our feeling is that both situa-tions are modeled in laboratory studies. One of the counterintuitive implications of the present analysis is that the stronger a person's motivation to regain control in actually uncontrollable settings, the higher the chance of developing deep cognitive impairment accompanied by a generalized affective deficit. Paradoxically, however, it seems that exposure to frequent, unstable, and low-intensity experiences of losing and regaining control might immunize a person against detrimental effects on affect and cognition.

Note

1 More recent studies reveal some parallels in cognitive functioning between anxious people and those who experience stable and prolonged control deprivation: in both cases attentional control is less efficient, and stimulus-driven processes override goal-driven ones (Bukowski, Asanowicz, Marzecová, & Lupiáñez, 2015; Pacheco-Unguetti, Acosta, Callejas, & Lupiáñez, 2010).

References

Aarts, E., van Holstein, M., & Cools, R. (2011). Striatal dopamine and the interface between motivation and cognition. *Frontiers in Psychology, 2*, 163.

Abramson, L.Y., Seligman, M. E. P., & Teasdale, J. D. (1978). Learned helplessness in humans: Critique and reformulation. *Journal of Abnormal Psychology, 87*, 49–74.

Bains, G. (1983). Explanations and the need for control. In M. Hewstone (Ed.), *Attribution theory: Social and functional extensions* (pp. 126–143). Oxford, UK: Blackwell.

Bandura, A. (1977). Self-efficacy: Toward a unifying theory of behavioural change. *Psychological Review, 84*, 191–215.

Bilewicz, M., Winiewski, M., Kofta, M., & Wójcik, A. (2013). Harmful ideas. The structure and consequences of anti-Semitic ideas in Poland. *Political Psychology, 34*, 821–839.

Botvinick, M., & Braver, T. (2015). Motivation and cognitive control: From behavior to neural mechanism. *Annual Review of Psychology, 66*, 83–113.

Botvinick, M. M., Braver, T. S., Barch, D. M., Carter, C. S., & Cohen, J. D. (2001). Conflict monitoring and cognitive control. *Psychological Review, 108*, 624–652.

Bower, G. H. (1981). Mood and memory. *American Psychologist, 36*, 129–148.

Brehm, J. (1966). *A theory of psychological reactance.* New York: Academic Press.

Brehm, J. W., & Self, E. A. (1989). The intensity of motivation. *Annual Review of Psychology, 40*, 109–131.

Brehm, S. S., & Brehm, J. W. (1981). *Psychological reactance: A theory of freedom and control.* San Diego: Academic Press.

Bukowski, M., Asanowicz, D., Marzecová, A., & Lupiáñez, J. (2015). Limits of control: The effects of uncontrollability experiences on the efficiency of attentional control. *Acta Psychologica, 154*, 43–53.

Bukowski, M., de Lemus, S., Marzecová, A., & Lupiáñez, J., Gocłowska, M. (2016). *Different faces of uncontrollability: Control deprivation and restoration modulate the flexibility of social categorization.* Manuscript submitted for publication.

Burger, J. M. (1992). *Desire for control: Personality, social, and clinical perspectives.* New York: Plenum.

Caparos, S., & Blanchette, I. (2014). Emotional Stroop interference in trauma-exposed individuals: A contrast between two accounts. *Consciousness and Cognition, 28*, 104–112.

DeCharms, R. (1968). *Personal causation: The internal affective determinants of behavior.* New York: Plenum.

Drury, J., & Reicher, S. (2005). Explaining enduring empowerment: A comparative study of collective action and psychological outcomes. *European Journal of Social Psychology, 35*, 35–58.

Fast, N. J., Gruenfeld, D. H., Sivanathan, N., & Galinsky, A. D. (2009). Illusory control: A generative force behind power's far-reaching effects. *Psychological Science, 20*, 502–508.

Forgas, J. P. (1995). Mood and judgment: The affect infusion model AIM. *Psychological Bulletin, 117*, 39–66.

Forgas, J. P. (2007). Affect, cognition, and social behavior: The Effects of mood on memory, social judgments, and social interaction. In M. A. Gluck, J. R. Anderson, & S. M. Kosslyn (Eds.), *A Festschrift for Gordon H. Bower* (pp. 261–279). Mahwah, NJ: Erlbaum.

Forgas, J. P., & Ciarrochi, J. (2000). Affect infusion and affect control: The interactive role of conscious and unconscious processing strategies in mood management. In Y. Rossetti & A. Revonsuo (Eds.), *Beyond dissociation: Interaction between dissociated implicit and explicit processing* (pp. 243–271). Amsterdam: John Benjamin Publishing Company.

Fritsche, I., Jonas, E., Ablasser, C., Beyer, M., Kuban, J., Manger, A. M., & Schultz, M. (2013). The power of we: Evidence for group-based control. *Journal of Experimental Social Psychology, 49*, 189–132.

Fritsche, I., Jonas, E., & Kessler, T. (2011). Collective reactions to threat: Implications for intergroup conflict and for solving societal crises. *Social Issues and Policy Review, 5*, 101–136.

Gendolla, G. H. E., & Richter, M. (2010). Effort mobilization when the self is involved: Some lessons from the cardiovascular system. *Review of General Psychology, 14*, 212–226.

Gentner, D., & Stevens, A. L. (1983). *Mental models*. Hillsdale, NJ: Erlbaum.

Gollwitzer, P. M., & Kinney, R. F. (1989). Effects of deliberative and implemental mind-sets on illusion of control. *Journal of Personality and Social Psychology, 56*, 531–542.

Greenaway, K. H., Louis, W. R., & Hornsey, M. J. (2013). Belief in precognition increases perceived control and loss of control increases belief in precognition. *Plos One, 8*(8), 1–6. DOI:10.1371/journal.pone.0071327

Hertel, P. T. (2000). The cognitive-initiative account of depression-related impairments in memory. In D. Medin (Ed.), *The psychology of learning and motivation* (Vol. 39, pp. 47–71). New York: Academic Press.

Hertel, P. T., & Hardin, T. S. (1990). Remembering with and without awareness: Evidence of deficits in initiative. *Journal of Experimental Psychology: General, 119*, 45–59.

Hertel, P. T., & Rude, S. S. (1991). Depressive deficits in memory: Focusing attention improves subsequent recall. *Journal of Experimental Psychology: General, 120*, 301–309.

Hiroto, D. S., & Seligman, M. E. P. (1975). Generality of learned helplessness in man. *Journal of Personality and Social Psychology, 31*, 311–327.

Hogg, M. A. (2000). Subjective uncertainty reduction through self-categorization: A motivational theory of social identity process. *European Review of Social Psychology, 11*, 223–255.

Johnson-Laird, P. N. (1983). *Mental models*. Cambridge, MA: Harvard University Press.

Kay, A. C., Gaucher, D., McGregor, I., & Nash, K. (2010). *Religious belief as compensatory control. Personality and Social Psychology Review, 141*, 37–48.

Kay, A. C., Whitson, J. A., Gaucher, D., & Galinsky, A. D. (2009). Compensatory control: Achieving order through the mind, our institutions, and the heavens. *Current Directions in Psychological Science, 18*, 264–268.

Kelley, H. H. (1972). Attribution in social interaction. In E. E. Jones, E. Kanouse, H. H. Kelley, R. E. Nisbett, S. Valins, & B. Weiner (Eds.), *Attribution: Perceiving the causes of behavior* (pp. 1–26). Morristown, NJ: General Learning Press.

Kobyliński, P., Kofta, M., & Bukowski, M. (2016). *Effects of control deprivation on implicit negative mood*. Manuscript in preparation.

Kofta, M. (1993). Uncertainty, mental models, and learned helplessness: An anatomy of control loss. In G. Weary, F. Gleicher, & K. Marsh (Eds.), *Control motivation and social cognition* (pp. 122–153). New York: Springer.

Kofta, M., & Sędek, G. (1989). Repeated failure: A source of helplessness, or a factor irrelevant to its emergence? *Journal of Experimental Psychology: General, 118*, 3–12.

Kofta, M., & Sedek, G. (1998). Uncontrollability as a source of cognitive exhaustion: Implications for helplessness and depression. In M. Kofta, G. Weary, & G. Sedek (Eds.), *Personal control in action: Cognitive and motivational mechanisms* (pp. 391–418). New York: Plenum Press.

Kofta, M., & Sedek, G. (1999). Uncontrollability as irreducible uncertainty. *European Journal of Social Psychology, 29*, 577–590.

Kofta, M., Weary, G., & Sedek, G. (1998). *Personal control in action: Cognitive and motivational mechanisms.* New York: Plenum Press.

Kossowska, M., & Bukowski, M. (2015). Motivated roots of conspiracies: The role of certainty and control motives in conspiracy thinking. In: M. Bilewicz, A. Cichocka, & W. Soral (Eds.), *The psychology of conspiracy* (pp. 145–161). London: Taylor & Francis Group, LLC.

Lazarus, R. S., & Folkman, S. (1984). *Stress, appraisal, and coping.* New York, NY: Springer.

Legare, C. H., & Souza, A. L. (2014). Searching for control: Priming randomness increases the evaluation of ritual efficacy. *Cognitive Science, 38*, 152–161.

Maier, S. E., & Seligman, M. E. P. (1976). Learned helplessness: Theory and evidence. *Journal of Experimental Psychology: General, 105*, 3–46.

McIntosh, D. N., Sedek, G., Fojas, S., Brzezicka-Rotkiewicz, A., & Kofta, M. (2005). Cognitive performance after pre-exposure to uncontrollability and in a depressive state: Going with a simpler plan B. In R. W. Engle, G. Sedek, U. von Hecker, & D. N. McIntosh (Eds.), *Cognitive limitations in aging and psychopathology* (pp. 219–246). Cambridge, MA: Cambridge University Press.

McKenna, F. P., & Sharma, D. (1995). Intrusive cognitions: An investigation of the emotional Stroop task. *Journal of Experimental Psychology: Learning, Memory, and Cognition, 21*, 1595–1607.

McKenna, F. P., & Sharma, D. (2004). Reversing the emotional Stroop effect reveals that it is not what it seems: The role of fast and slow components. *Journal of Experimental Psychology: Learning, Memory, and Cognition, 30*, 382–392.

Mikulincer, M. (1988). The relation between stable/unstable attribution and learned helplessness. *British Journal of Social Psychology, 27*, 221–230.

Mikulincer, M. (1994). *Human learned helplessness: A coping perspective.* New York: Plenum Press.

Mikulincer, M., Kedem, P., & Zilcha-Segal, H. (1989). Learned helplessness, reactance, and cue utilization. *Journal of Research in Personality, 23*, 235–247.

Miller, W. R., & Seligman, M. E. P. (1975). Depression and learned helplessness in man. *Journal of Abnormal Psychology, 84*, 228–238.

Minor, T. R., Jackson, R. L., & Maier, S. F. (1984). Effects of task-irrelevant cues and reinforcement delay on choice escape learning following inescapable shock: Evidence for a deficit in selective attention. *Journal of Experimental Psychology: Animal Behavior Processes, 10*, 543–556.

Miron, A. M., & Brehm, J. W (2006). Reactance theory – 40 years later. *Zeitschrift für Sozialpsychologie, 37*(1), 9–18.

Murphy, S. T., & Zajonc, R. B. (1993). Affect, cognition, and awareness: Affective priming with optimal and suboptimal stimulus exposures. *Journal of Personality and Social Psychology, 64*, 723–739.

Pacheco-Unguetti, A. P., Acosta, A., Callejas, A., & Lupiáñez, J. (2010). Attention and anxiety: Different attentional functioning under state and trait anxiety. *Psychological Science, 21*, 298–304.

Padmala, S., & Pessoa, L. (2011). Reward reduces conflict by enhancing attentional control and biasing visual cortical processing. *Journal of Cognitive Neuroscience, 23*, 3419–3432.

Petersen, S. E., & Posner, M. I. (2012). The attention system of the human brain: 20 years after. *Annual Review of Neuroscience, 35*, 73–89.

Pittman, T. S., & D'Agostino, P. R. (1989). Motivation and cognition: Control deprivation and the nature of subsequent information processing. *Journal of Experimental Social Psychology, 25*, 465–480.

Pittman, T. S., & Pittman, N. L. (1980). Deprivation of control and the attribution process. *Journal of Personality and Social Psychology, 39*, 377–389.

Posner, M. I., & Rothbart, M. K. (2007). Research on attention networks as a model for the integration of psychological science. *Annual Review of Psychology, 58*, 1–23.

Ramirez, E., Maldonado, A., & Martos, R. (1992). Attributions modulate immunization against learned helplessness in humans. *Journal of Personality and Social Psychology, 62*, 139–146.

Ric, F., & Scharnitzky, P. (2003). Effects of control deprivation on effort expenditure and accuracy performance. *European Journal of Social Psychology, 33*, 103–118.

Roth, S., & Kubal, L. (1975). The effects of noncontingent reinforcement on tasks of differing importance: Facilitation and learned helplessness effects. *Journal of Personality and Social Psychology, 32*, 680–691.

Sedek, G., & Kofta, M. (1990). When cognitive exertion does not yield cognitive gain: Toward an informational explanation of learned helplessness. *Journal of Personality and Social Psychology, 58*, 729–743.

Sedek, G., Kofta, M., & Tyszka, T. (1993). Effects of uncontrollability on subsequent decision making: Testing the cognitive exhaustion hypothesis. *Journal of Personality and Social Psychology, 65*, 1270–1281.

Sedek, G., & McIntosh, D. N. (1996). Uncontrollability and dual task processing: Results of experimental and educational studies. Unpublished manuscript.

Seligman, M. E. P. (1975). *Helplessness: On depression, development, and death.* San Francisco: Freeman.

Skinner, E. A. (1996). A guide to constructs of control. *Journal of Personality and Social Psychology, 71*, 549–570.

Sullivan, D., Landau, M. J., & Rothschild, Z. K. 2010). An existential function of enemyship: Evidence that people attribute influence to personal and political enemies to compensate for threats to control. *Journal of Personality and Social Psychology, 98*, 434–449.

Swann, W. B. Jr (2012). Self-verification theory. In P. A. M. van Lange & E. T. Higgins (Eds.), *Handbook of theories of social psychology* (pp. 23–42). Los Angeles: Sage.

Tennen, H., Drum, P. E., Gillen, R., & Stanton, A. (1982). Learned helplessness and the detection of contingency: A direct test. *Journal of Personality, 50*, 426–441.

Tuffin, K., Hesketh, B., & Podd, J. (1985). Experimentally induced learned helplessness: How far does it generalize? *Social Behavior and Personality, 13*, 55–62.

van Steenbergen, H., Band, G. P. H., & Hommel, B. (2009). Reward counteracts conflict adaptation: Evidence for a role of affect in executive control. *Psychological Science, 20*, 1473–1477.

von Hecker, U., & Sedek G. (1999). Uncontrollability, depression, and the construction of mental models. *Journal of Personality and Social Psychology, 77*, 833–850.

Weary, G., & Edwards, J. A. (1996). Causal-uncertainty beliefs and related goal structures. In R. M. Sorrentino & E. T. Higgins (Eds.), *Handbook of motivation and cognition, vol. 3: The interpersonal context* (pp. 148–181). New York: Guilford.

White, R. W. (1959). Motivation reconsidered: The concept of competence. *Psychological Review, 66*, 297–333.

Whitson, J. A., & Galinsky, A. D. (2008). Lacking control increases illusory pattern perception. *Science, 322*, 115–117.

Williams, J. M. G., Mathews, A., & MacLeod, C. (1996). The Emotional Stroop Task and psychopathology. *Psychological Bulletin, 120*, 3–24.

Wortman, C. B., & Brehm, J. W. (1975). Reponses to uncontrollable outcomes: An integration of reactance theory and the learned helplessness model. In L. Berkowitz (Ed.), *Advances in experimental social psychology* (Vol. 8, pp. 277–336). New York: Academic Press.

Wright, R. A. (1998). Ability perception and cardiovascular response to behavioral challenge. In M. Kofta, G. Weary, & G. Sedek (Eds.), *Personal control in action: Cognitive and motivational mechanisms* (pp. 197–232). New York: Plenum Press.

Zajonc, R. B. (1980). Feeling and thinking: Preferences need no inferences. *American Psychologist, 35*, 151–175.

2

THE MOTIVATION FOR CONTROL

Loss of control promotes energy, effort, and action

Katharine H. Greenaway, Michael C. Philipp,
and Katherine R. Storrs

Address correspondence to Katharine H. Greenaway, School of Psychology, McElwain building, The University of Queensland, Brisbane, QLD, 4072, Australia
Email: k.greenaway@psy.uq.edu.au

It can be unpleasant to reflect on how little control we have in our everyday lives. From losing a job, to contracting an illness, or even just sitting in the passenger seat of a car, we often lack control over our environment and outcomes. This is such a major concern for people that the theme of lack of control pervades popular culture. Newspaper and magazine articles focus on how to "stay in control" of our lives. Hundreds of self-help books are written on the assumption that being in control of our choices and actions can help to resolve many of life's problems. This motivation for control has been hypothesized to fuel people to engage in activities that bring about desired outcomes or prevent undesired outcomes (Skinner, 1996). As a result, people's drive to feel in control motivates them to act to restore perceived control when it has been diminished (Pittman & D'Agostino, 1985). In this chapter we review common reactions to instances of control deprivation and consider the psychological lengths to which people will go in order to regain perceived control.

A reader who has only a passing acquaintance with the control literature might find it odd to think of people responding with vigor and determination to an instance of control loss. The prototypical image of a control-deprived individual is that of a listless, apathetic person who has given up on trying to achieve his or her goals. This image was made popular by seminal work on learned helplessness (Seligman, 1975; see also Rydzewska, Rusanowska, Krejtz, & Sedek, Chapter 4, this volume). In a now-classic demonstration of the effects of long-term control deprivation, Seligman and Maier (1967) exposed dogs to inescapable electric shocks, before later exposing them to electric shocks that could be escaped by jumping over a low partition. Dogs that were first trained in uncontrollable circumstances eventually stopped trying to avoid the shocks, and later did not take advantage of opportunities for escape. While those deprived of control became helpless, passive, and withdrawn, dogs that were exposed to *controllable* aversive shocks did not display the same evidence of learned helplessness.

This observation fundamentally shaped the literature on control deprivation, and provided a basis for contemporary understanding of human depression (Alloy, Peterson, Abramson, & Seligman, 1984; Brown & Siegel, 1988). It is now generally accepted that long-term experiences of control deprivation ultimately sap people's energy, desire, and will to act. Over an extended period, people who feel they have little control become passive, exert minimal effort, and show reduced attentional control (e.g., Bukowski, Asanowica, Marzecova, & Lupiáñez, 2015; see also Bukowski & Kofta, Chapter 1, this volume; Lefcourt, 1976, 1980; Seligman, 1975). Considered in total, being unable to control one's outcomes appears to be a mentally draining experience that reduces people's well-being, cognitive capacity, and ability to cope with adversity (e.g., Glass & Singer, 1972; Judge, Erez, Bono, & Thoresen, 2002).

Yet, this view of the helpless and passive control-deprived individual did not go unchallenged. While a range of early research confirmed the reliability of the learned helplessness effect (Fosco & Geer, 1971; Hiroto, 1974; Hiroto & Seligman, 1975; Klein, Fencil-Morse, & Seligman, 1976; Krantz, Glass, & Snyder, 1974), other work found seemingly contradictory effects. For example, Thornton and Jacobs (1972) found that participants who were exposed to inescapable shocks in a training phase subsequently showed *improved* performance on a verbal and mathematical ability test. Similarly, Roth and Bootzin (1974) found that participants who received random (i.e., low-control) feedback on a concept-learning task showed greater evidence of action and engagement than participants who received accurate feedback. That is, control-deprived participants were more likely to stand up to attempt to fix an apparent problem with the experimental apparatus or collect the experimenter to make the appropriate adjustment; actions that have been taken in other work as evidence of heightened approach motivation (Galinsky, Gruenfeld, & Magee, 2003). In addition, Roth and Kubal (1975) found that participants with short-term exposure to control deprivation showed greater ability and persistence on a subsequent problem-solving task than participants who were not deprived of control. More recent research has shown that control deprivation causes people to process information in a more effortful and deliberate manner (Zhou, He, Lao, & Baumeister, 2012), which can improve performance on cognitive tasks (Pittman & D'Agostino, 1989).

Research therefore suggests that short-term reactions to control deprivation are quite different from the listless profile seen over the longer term in learned helplessness paradigms. Indeed, the helpless prototype is at odds with a range of research reviewed in this book suggesting that people often respond to loss of control with energy, effort, and action to restore that which has been lost. Control motivation theory (Pittman & D'Agostino, 1985) postulates that aversive feelings of low control should cause individuals to process new information in a careful manner in order to understand and rectify the loss of control. As a result, people sometimes show *improved* performance on cognitively demanding tasks following a loss of control (Pittman & D'Agostino, 1989). This suggests that people who lack control can become motivated to engage with tasks that they see as offering the opportunity to restore perceived control.

This image of enhanced vigor and effort following control deprivation fits with theoretical perspectives on methods people use to feel in control of their lives. Brehm's (1966) *reactance theory* is premised on the idea that when people's behavioral freedom is compromised—when they are deprived of control—they respond with renewed efforts to restore their independence. Other researchers have distinguished two types of psychological strategies to maintain the perception of control, termed *primary* control strategies and *secondary* control strategies (Heckhausen & Schulz, 1995; Rothbaum, Weisz, & Snyder, 1982). Primary control involves active attempts to change the world to fit one's needs and desires. Primary control strategies are generally utilized when people have actual control over the environment and are able to act in the moment to re-establish control. In contrast, secondary control involves more indirect attempts at regaining perceived control, including accepting or reinterpreting the situation or relying on sources of control that are external to the self. Therefore, while people may not be able to objectively change a situation, they can influence the way in which they think about or place value on it. Note that primary control is not always available to a person, while secondary control may always be subject to change. People can thus exert cognitive effort following a loss of control, performing "psychological gymnastics" in order to feel in control once more.

Modern literature demonstrates that people initially respond to control deprivation actively, creatively, and with cognitive effort, rather than submitting helplessly at the first sign of control loss. For example, when deprived of personal control, people cling strongly to social ingroups (Agroskin & Jonas, 2013; Fritsche, Jonas, & Fankhanel, 2008; Fritsche et al., 2013); actively disparage social outgroups (Greenaway, Louis, Hornsey, & Jones, 2014; Rothschild, Landau, Sullivan, & Keefer, 2012); strive to perceive patterns in random noise (Whitson & Galinsky, 2008); report greater endorsement of secular and spiritual authorities (Kay, Gaucher, Napier, Callan, & Laurin, 2008; Kay, Shepherd, Blatz, Chua, & Galinsky, 2010; Kay, Whitson, Gaucher, & Galinsky, 2009; Knight, Tobin, & Hornsey, 2014; Rutjens & Kay, Chapter 5, this volume; Shepherd, Kay, Landau, & Keefer, 2011); and endorse a range of palliative beliefs, from belief in scientific progress (Rutjens, van Harreveld, van der Pligt, Kreemers, & Noordewier, 2013; Rutjens, van Harreveld, & van der Plight, 2013; Rutjens, van der Plight, & van Harreveld, 2010) to paranormal abilities (Greenaway, Louis, & Hornsey, 2013) or the power of ritual behavior (Norton & Gino, 2013). These represent a large range of control strategies, but all demonstrate the determined efforts of individuals to restore the perception of control when it has been lost.

Taken together, the literature appears to show that loss of control is mobilizing in the short term and de-motivating in the long term. Indeed, researchers have theorized that control deprivation leads to exhaustion and apathy in the long term expressly *because* of a boost in effort and motivation in the short term (e.g., Sedek, Kofta, & Tyszka, 1993; Wortman & Brehm, 1975). These initial boosts in activity are relatively short-lived; although brief experiences of control deprivation improve ability and persistence on cognitive tasks, repeated experiences of control loss elicit learned helplessness (Roth & Kubal, 1975). In this chapter we review research that demonstrates evidence for this initial motivational push following control deprivation, showing that in the short term, loss of control promotes approach motivation and cognitive effort. We will outline two lines of research we have conducted that demonstrate this point.

Loss of control promotes approach motivation

Research in the threat compensation literature, of which uncontrollability forms a small part, suggests that threat stimulates motivational processes aimed at restoring psychological equilibrium. A recent taxonomy of different types of threat unified these findings into an overarching model of threat compensation (Jonas et al., 2014). According to this model, when expectations are violated people experience aversive arousal that leads to a variety of compensatory behaviors designed to regulate the experience of arousal (see above for examples in the control threat domain; Heine, Proulx, & Vohs, 2006; Proulx & Inzlicht, 2012; Proulx, Inzlicht, & Harmon-Jones, 2012). One particular compensation strategy is termed *reactive approach motivation* (McGregor, Nash, Mann, & Phills, 2010; McGregor, Nash, & Prentice, 2010), in which people become narrow in their attentional focus and driven to achieve important goals as a method of counteracting psychological threat.

This approach state is regulated by the behavioral activation system (BAS), which is activated by the prospect of attaining desired outcomes. In addition to being activated by reward, the BAS stimulates approach behavior to pursue goals and attain further rewards (Elliot, 2008; Elliot & Covington, 2001). An alternative force on human behavior is the behavioral inhibition system (BIS), which regulates conflicts between desires to approach and avoid (Gray, 1982, 1990). The BIS acts as an "alarm system" indicating conflict in the environment; it responds with arousal and vigilance to potential threats and aids avoidance of aversive stimuli (Corr, DeYoung, & McNaughton, 2013). According to the anxiety-to-approach model of threat defense (Jonas et al., 2014), psychological threat stimulates BIS avoidance-oriented processes and associated aversive arousal, which in turn activates BAS approach-oriented processes in an attempt to dampen the BIS response. This may help to explain why individuals who experience a loss of control show an initial burst of motivation following the control deprivation episode.

In a series of experiments we tested directly whether loss of control stimulated approach motivation (Greenaway et al., 2015). We manipulated control using a paradigm in which participants listened to sounds at an unpleasant volume and either had control or no control over the timing of the stimulus onset (adapted from methods by Warburton, Williams, & Cairns, 2006). This manipulation was designed to engender a mindset in participants of having or lacking control, with participants then responding to dependent measures in a second, ostensibly unrelated, task. That is, rather than focusing on people's reactions during experiences of control loss, the manipulation first evoked loss of control and then examined how this influenced responses on subsequent outcome variables of interest. We return to this methodological point later in this chapter.

In two experiments we assessed approach motivation in the form of self-reported motivation to achieve goals and the experience of "high approach" feelings (e.g., Gable & Harmon-Jones, 2008, 2011). *High approach* characterizes feelings of energy and excitement observed when people are in pursuit of a goal or reward. In contrast, *low approach* characterizes feelings of satiation and contentment observed after a goal or reward has been attained. We found that participants in the low control condition reported greater motivation to achieve their goals and greater high approach (but not low approach) feelings compared to participants in the high control condition. These findings suggest that loss of control creates an approach mindset that is characterized by determined and energetic pursuit of a goal— presumably the goal to restore perceived control.

In a second experiment we tested a mechanism of the effect by introducing a manipulation shown to mitigate the experience of arousal. We reasoned that if arousal is a process through which approach motivation is stimulated following control threat (Jonas et al., 2014), then introducing conditions that defuse feelings of arousal would eliminate the effect (Spencer, Zanna, & Fong, 2005). We therefore had participants misattribute their arousal to an external source by having them take a pill that they believed caused feelings of heightened arousal (increased heart beat, breathing, and sweating) or had no physical side effects. This manipulation has been shown to eliminate other threat-compensation effects (Kay, Moscovitch, & Laurin, 2010). In our experiment, participants in the misattribution condition did not show an effect of loss of control on high approach feelings. Consistent with the finding in our previous experiment, participants who *did not* misattribute their arousal reported more high approach feelings when in the low control compared to high control condition.

Another series of experiments tested the approach effect implicitly using a behavioral measure that acted as an indirect indicator of a neurological pattern associated with approach motivation. For this purpose we used the line bisection task, which has been conceptualized as a measure of activation asymmetry between the two frontal cerebral hemispheres (Jewell & McCourt, 2000). In the task, participants mark the perceived midpoint of a series of lines, and the distance between their judgment and the objective midpoint is measured. A tendency towards rightward errors indicates relatively greater left (vs. right) prefrontal hemisphere activity, which is indicative of approach motivation (Harmon-Jones, 2003; Nash, McGregor, & Inzlicht, 2010).

Participants completed a line bisection task immediately prior to and following the control manipulation, and rightward errors on the second task were assessed controlling for performance on the first task. We hypothesized that participants in the low control condition would show relatively more rightward errors on the second line bisection task, revealing greater approach motivation, than participants in the high control condition.

However, we did not find reliable support for this indicator of approach. While our first experiment produced a significant effect in which participants in the low control condition showed a greater shift toward rightward errors than participants in the high control condition ($p = .031$), in a second experiment this effect was only marginal ($p = .078$), and in a third experiment was a non-significant trend ($p = .738$). A meta-analysis of the results suggested that the effect size, while varying in individual experiments (Cohen's d Experiment 1 $= .61$; Experiment 2a $= .37$; Experiment 2b $= .09$), was significant when averaged across experiments ($d = .31$, $p = .027$, 95% CI $= 0.031$ to 0.591). Nevertheless, we believe the results should be interpreted with caution.

In all, the findings indicated that loss of control can stimulate approach motivation, although how approach is measured may influence the effect. This work therefore provides a motivational lens through which to view a range of compensatory control efforts observed across the literature. Rather than showing immediate signs of helplessness, individuals initially show signs of energy and determined goal pursuit following a loss of control. We theorize that control deprivation activates a goal to restore control, which both generates and is pursued via enhanced approach.

Approach motivation in this context may serve a number of purposes. One school of thought is that activation of approach processes following threat is purely palliative, in that approach serves no more specific purpose than to make people feel better (e.g., McGregor et al., 2010). However, the finding is also open to an additional interpretation, that approach here represents a goal-directed pursuit of control restoration. This interpretation is consistent with research suggesting that control deprivation activates a goal to restore control (Fritsche et al., 2008, Study 5), and theorizing that approach facilitates goal pursuit (Carver & White, 1994). This emphasis on function in complement to palliation fits with theorizing by Jonas and colleagues (2014) that anxiety aroused by threat can be dampened either through palliation (e.g., secondary control) *or* through direct attempts to resolve the threat (e.g., primary control—by acting in a way that restores control).

Loss of control promotes cognitive effort

In addition to enhancing motivation, research suggests that control deprivation promotes other, more cognitive forms of energy and action. A variety of work shows that immediate reactions to loss of control often include evidence of *increased* cognitive effort and performance (Roth & Kubal, 1975; Pittman & Pittman, 1980;

Thornton & Jacobs, 1972; Zhou et al., 2012). We measured the cognitive effects of control deprivation using the same sound-based manipulation described above (Greenaway et al., 2015) in two unpublished experiments with a measure typically used as an indicator of executive function: the spatial Stroop task.

In the spatial Stroop task, participants viewed arrows pointing up or down on a computer screen and pressed an up or down arrow on the keyboard to indicate the direction. Arrows were presented above or below a line in the centre of the screen. On congruent trials, an up arrow was presented above the centre line, and a down arrow was presented below the centre line. On incongruent trials, an up arrow was presented below the centre line, and a down arrow was presented above the centre line, thus creating perceptual conflict. The reaction time for *correct responses to incongruent trials* was the dependent measure. Faster reaction times on incongruent trials would indicate greater cognitive inhibition (and therefore greater cognitive effort), because participants are successfully able to inhibit cognitive conflict associated with arrow direction. As expected, in both experiments participants in the low control condition tended to respond faster on incongruent trials than participants in the high control condition, $p_{\text{Experiment 1}} = .020$ and $p_{\text{Experiment 2}} = .187$, indicating greater cognitive inhibition.

We also assessed the effects of lack of control on aggression – a social tendency that is indicative of approach (Hortensius, Schutter, & Harmon-Jones, 2012; Peterson, Shackman, & Harmon-Jones, 2008). In Experiment 1, aggression was measured using a word-completion task, which consisted of 35 incomplete words relating to aggressive cognitions (e.g., attack, angry). Each word could be completed in an aggressive or neutral manner (e.g., sho_t becomes shoot or short). In Experiment 2, aggression was measured behaviorally by having participants choose the sound level at which future participants would hear the control manipulation, with higher scores indicating greater aggression. Previous research shows that control deprivation can provoke aggression and motivation to punish (e.g., Warburton et al., 2006). Consistent with these findings, in both of our experiments, loss of control increased aggression, leading to significantly more aggressively completed words (Experiment 1, $p = .001$) and marginally higher sound levels (Experiment 2, $p = .065$) compared to the high control condition.

These findings can be interpreted as showing evidence for the threat compensation process outlined by Jonas et al. (2014). Insofar as enhanced Stroop performance is indicative of cognitive inhibition, this process may reflect initial activation of the BIS immediately following a loss of control. However, we propose caution in interpreting the results in this light. It is unclear whether improved Stroop performance here is associated more with BIS or with BAS. It is possible that after activating a goal to restore control (following control deprivation), individuals invested greater effort in the next cognitive task to aid this goal pursuit (as theorized by Pittman & D'Agostino, 1989). That is, enhanced Stroop performance may actually represent greater approach than inhibition in this case. This perspective fits with findings in the tradition of reactive approach motivation (McGregor et al., 2010) that approach states lead to greater cognitive focus (see also Gable, Pool, & Harmon-Jones, 2015).

This possibility is supported by inspection of performance on separate congruent and incongruent Stroop trials. Although the results reported above tend to show an effect of control deprivation on reaction times for correct responses on incongruent trials, we also found significant effects of the manipulation on *congruent* trials ($p_{\text{Experiment 1}}$ = .015 and $p_{\text{Experiment 2}}$ = .003). That is, participants appeared to be investing cognitive effort to perform with speed and accuracy on all Stroop trials, which suggests overall cognitive activation rather than evidence of cognitive inhibition specifically.

Another reason we are hesitant to claim these results as evidence of BIS activation following control deprivation concerns the timing of the procedure. The anxiety-to-approach model proposes that BIS is immediately activated following control (or other) threat, which is then regulated by activation of the BAS. Although participants performed the Stroop task soon after control manipulation, the timing of the presentation of this measure was similar to that in our approach studies described above (i.e., a few minutes after the completion of the control manipulation). Research on reactive approach motivation postulates that a delay between threat manipulations and measures of approach is necessary to observe the hypothesized processes (McGregor et al., 2010). In future, measures of inhibition and approach should be administered at multiple time points to clarify the motivational processes underlying our cognitive effects.

Temporal tensions in control research

It is clear from the reviewed findings that time is important in control threat effects. Time is implicated in the behavioral shift in control deprivation effects— from effort and action to listlessness and passivity—and in the intrapsychic "switch" from avoidance to approach processes theorized in threat compensation effects (Jonas et al., 2014). Turning to the first issue, a range of research now suggests that initial reactions to loss of control are characterized by energy, effort, and action. This perspective is supported by demonstrations of enhanced concentration, persistence, and performance following control deprivation; evidence of active attempts to compensate for loss of control; and theorizing on the functions of primary and secondary control strategies. Only after these efforts to maintain control are thwarted consistently over the long-term do individuals show evidence of learned helplessness (Roth & Kubal, 1975; Sedek et al., 1993; Wortman & Brehm, 1975).

It is still relatively unclear at what point and under what conditions the shift from active to passive behavior occurs. Research on learned helplessness suggests that *repeated and unvarying* failure is necessary for passivity to take effect – although exactly *when* passivity takes hold in our minds (and whether this fixed point differs based on individual differences) remains an open question. In contrast, weak or inconsistent deprivation of control appears to have an energizing effect. For example, Bukowski and colleagues (2015) found that six uninterrupted trials of unsolvable puzzles worsened executive attention, whereas three trials of unsolvable puzzles followed by three trials of solvable puzzles restored cognitive performance to baseline levels.

The exact timing of control manipulations is not routinely reported in papers, as presumably researchers place greater importance on the procedural, rather than temporal, aspects of control deprivation paradigms. Considering cognitive effects, we can compare our results described above with those of Bukowski and colleagues (2015). We found evidence of enhanced cognitive effort and concentration (i.e., better performance on the spatial Stroop) after a control deprivation paradigm lasting four minutes, whereas Bukowski et al. found evidence of reduced cognitive attention and processing after a control deprivation paradigm lasting 15 minutes (although these manipulations also differed in that Bukowski's participants experienced repeated failure, as opposed to our participants, who were exposed to only one uncontrollable trial). As a caveat to this point, these studies used different control manipulations and different measures of cognitive effort. Future research would benefit from varying the time of control deprivation episodes in a linear fashion and measuring performance on the same cognitive test to shed light on this issue.

Of course, control manipulations also differ across studies on dimensions other than timing. One particular dimension on which they appear to vary is on whether people are passive or active in the control deprivation episode. For example, our control deprivation manipulation involves passive experience of negative stimuli (aversive sounds). Another common control manipulation involves people actively recalling and writing about an event in which they lacked control (e.g., Fritsche et al., 2008; Rutjens et al., 2010). Traditional learned helplessness paradigms involve an even greater degree of personal engagement in which people repeatedly attempt impossible tasks (see also Bukowski et al., 2015). Future research might consider exploring whether there are different effects of these different manipulations, and whether control deprivation on certain dimensions (e.g., passive vs. active) elicits effects on specific dependent variables (e.g., approach vs. avoidance).

Turning to the second issue, the time course of intrapsychic threat compensation effects (i.e., the switch from avoidance to approach) is beginning to be of interest to researchers (e.g., Jonas et al., 2014; see page 230 for a figure representing this process). The exact temporal dynamics of the threat compensation process remain fuzzy, although the use of temporally precise neuroimaging techniques (e.g., EEG) is an exciting development in this space. Temporally sensitive measures will be important in cataloguing exactly *when* the switch from anxious inhibition to approach takes place following a loss of control. As Jonas and colleagues (2014) note, this switch may happen quite quickly. A concrete test of the hypothesized temporal sequence could involve measuring approach and avoidance – for example, using a line bisection task or EEG – while the control manipulation is ongoing (e.g., while participants are listening to uncontrollable sounds) and at several time points after its completion to determine when exactly the switch to approach-related processes occurs.

Social tensions in control research

So far we have taken an individual focus in understanding the processes and out-comes of control deprivation. Yet, an astute reader will note that several of the out-comes assessed in our own research, and in the broader control literature, are social in nature. This can create interesting tensions between personal goals and social goals. Our research demonstrates that loss of control puts people in an approach mindset that facilitates effortful goal pursuit (Greenaway et al., 2015). That is, peo-ple become focused on achieving important personal goals – often the goal of restoring perceived control – even if that comes at the expense of social goals, such as maintaining positive interpersonal or intergroup relationships.

Research has documented that personal control threats can have negative social effects (although in a way that is structured by shared social identity; Fritsche et al., 2008, 2013; see also Stollberg, Fritsche, Barth, & Jugert, Chapter 8, this volume). For example, loss of control has been shown to promote social aggression (Warbur-ton et al., 2006), prejudice (Greenaway et al., 2014), and scapegoating (Rothschild et al., 2012). These negative social practices have all been hypothesized to serve a function of increasing perceived control. Indeed, in our own unpublished research we have observed that expressing prejudice increases perceived personal control relative to expressing a personal attitude about everyday activities. This means that people may act negatively on the group level to restore a sense of personal con-trol. People who are deprived of control therefore may face a trade-off between the personal goal of restoring perceived control and the social goal of maintaining relational harmony. Exploring the processes and consequences of these tensions is an interesting direction for future research. It may be, for example, that a focus on personal goals is the process through which negative social behavior occurs (i.e., my willingness to put my personal outcomes ahead of other people's).

One possible way to assess these trade-offs would be to prime personal goals (i.e., independent orientation) vs. social goals (e.g., interdependent orientation), and assess negative social outcomes to control threat, such as aggression. A straight-forward prediction would be that the effect of control deprivation on aggression would be eliminated when interdependence is primed, because people are mindful of a goal to maintain social harmony. Relatedly, research could vary the target of aggressive actions to be an ingroup member or an outgroup member. Follow-ing control threat, one would expect to see greater aggression directed towards an outgroup target than a control (i.e., no group membership) target, but per-haps *less* aggression directed towards an ingroup target than a control target. This is because people identify more with social ingroups following personal control threat (Fritsche et al., 2008, 2013), in part because people derive a sense of per-sonal control through important group memberships (Greenaway et al., 2015). In line with self-categorization principles (Turner, Hogg, Oakes, Reicher, & Weth-erell, 1987), the effects described above should be heightened by making group (vs. personal identity) salient prior to the control manipulation (in a way that mirrors similar effects observed in mortality salience studies; Giannakakis & Fritsche, 2011).

Conclusions

In this chapter, we reviewed a range of evidence showing that individuals become initially motivated and energized by loss of personal control. It is only after an extended period of control deprivation that people present the profiles of listlessness and passivity made famous by early work on learned helplessness. Indeed, in the short-term, individuals show evidence of *increased* cognitive engagement and goal-directed effort. These effects indicate a motivated attempt to restore perceived control, which nevertheless may come at the expense of more distal goals to maintain social harmony. In all, this presents a functional picture of the human motivational system in addressing short-term goal conflicts, yet one that is sometimes curiously flawed in meeting long-term goals.

References

Agroskin, D., & Jonas, E. (2013). Controlling death by defending ingroups – mediational insights into terror management and control restoration. *Journal of Experimental Social Psychology, 49*, 1144–1158. doi:10.1016/j.jesp.2013.05.014

Alloy, L. B., Peterson, C., Abramson, L. Y., & Seligman, M. E. (1984). Attributional style and the generality of learned helplessness. *Journal of Personality and Social Psychology, 46*, 681–7.

Brehm, J. W. (1966). *A theory of psychological reactance*. New York: Academic Press.

Brown, J. D., & Siegel, J. M. (1988). Attributions for negative life events and depression: The role of perceived control. *Journal of Personality and Social Psychology, 54*, 316–322. doi:10.1037/0022-3514.54.2.316

Bukowski, M., Asanowicz, D., Marzecová, A., & Lupiáñez, J. (2015). Limits of control: The effects of uncontrollability experiences on the efficiency of attentional control. *Acta Psychologica, 154*, 43–53.

Carver, C. S., & White, T. (1994). Behavioral inhibition, behavioral activation, and affective responses to impending reward and punishment: The BIS/BAS scales. *Journal of Personality and Social Psychology, 67*, 319–333.

Corr, P. J., DeYoung, C. G., & McNaughton, N. (2013). Motivation and personality: A neuropsychological perspective. *Social and Personality Psychology Compass, 7*(3), 158–175.

Elliot, A. J. (Ed.). (2008). *Handbook of approach and avoidance motivation*. New York: Taylor & Francis.

Elliot, A. J., & Covington, M. V. (2001). Approach and avoidance motivation. *Educational Psychology Review, 13*, 73–92.

Fosco, E., & Geer, J. H. (1971). Effects of gaining control over aversive stimuli after differing amounts of no control. *Psychology Reports, 29*, 1153–1154.

Fritsche, I., Jonas, E., Ablasser, C., Beyer, M., Kuban, J., Manger, A., & Schultz, M. (2013). The power of we: Evidence for group-based control. *Journal of Experimental Social Psychology, 49*, 19–32.

Fritsche, I., Jonas, E., & Fankhanel, T. (2008). The role of control motivation in mortality salience effects on ingroup support and defense. *Journal of Personality and Social Psychology, 95*, 524–541.

Gable, P. A., & Harmon-Jones, E. (2008). Approach-motivated positive affect reduces breadth of attention. *Psychological Science, 19*, 476–482.

Gable, P. A., & Harmon-Jones, E. (2011). Attentional consequences of pregoal and postgoal positive affects. *Emotion, 11*, 1358–1367.

Gable, P. A., Poole, B. D., & Harmon-Jones, E. (2015). Anger perceptually and conceptually narrows cognitive scope. *Journal of Personality and Social Psychology, 109*(1), 163–174.

Galinsky, A. D., Gruenfeld, D. H., & Magee, J. C. (2003). From power to action. *Journal of Personality and Social Psychology, 85*, 453–466.

Giannakakis, A. E., & Fritsche, I. (2011). Social identities, group norms, and threat: On the malleability of ingroup bias. *Personality and Social Psychology Bulletin, 37*(1), 82–93.

Glass, D. C., & Singer, J. E. (1972). Behavioral aftereffects of unpredictable and uncontrollable aversive events: Although subjects were able to adapt to loud noise and other stressors in laboratory experiments, they clearly demonstrated adverse aftereffects. *American Scientist, 60*, 457–465.

Gray, J. A. (1982). *The neuropsychology of anxiety*. New York: Oxford University Press.

Gray, J. A. (1990). Brain systems that mediate both emotion and cognition. *Cognition and Emotion, 4*, 269–288.

Greenaway, K. H., Haslam, S. A., Cruwys, T., Branscombe, N. R., Ysseldyk, R., & Heldreth, C. (2015). From "we" to "me": Group identification enhances perceived personal control with consequences for health and well-being. *Journal of Personality and Social Psychology, 109*, 53–74.

Greenaway, K. H., Louis, W. R., & Hornsey, M. J. (2013). Belief in precognition increases perceived control and loss of control increases belief in precognition. *Plos One, 8*(8), 1–6. doi:10.1371/journal.pone.0071327

Greenaway, K. H., Louis, W. R., Hornsey, M. J., & Jones, J. M. (2014). Perceived control qualifies the effects of threat on prejudice. *British Journal of Social Psychology, 53*, 422–442. doi:10.1111/bjso.12049

Greenaway, K. H., Storrs, K., Philipp, M. C., Louis, W. R., Hornsey, M. J., & Vohs, K. D. (2015). Loss of control stimulates approach motivation. *Journal of Experimental Social Psychology, 56*, 235–241. doi:10.1016/j.jesp.2014.10.009

Harmon-Jones, E. (2003). Clarifying the emotive functions of asymmetrical frontal cortical activity. *Psychophysiology, 40*, 838–848.

Heckhausen, J., & Schulz, R. (1995). A life-span theory of control. *Psychological Review, 102*(2), 284.

Heine, S. J., Proulx, R., & Vohs, K. D. (2006). The meaning maintenance model: On the coherence of social motivations. *Personality and Social Psychology Review, 10*, 88–110. doi:10.1207/s15327957pspr1002_1

Hiroto, D. S. (1974). Locus of control and learned helplessness. *Journal of Experimental Psychology, 102*, 187–193.

Hiroto, D. S., & Seligman, M. E. P. (1975). Generality of learned helplessness in man. *Journal of Personality and Social Psychology, 31*, 311–327.

Hortensius, R., Schutter, D. J. L. G., & Harmon-Jones, E. (2012). When anger leads to aggression: Induction of relative left frontal cortical activity with transcranial direct current stimulation increases the anger-aggression relationship. *Social Cognitive Affective Neuroscience, 7*, 342–347.

Jewell, G., & McCourt, M. E. (2000). Pseudoneglect: A review and metaanalysis of performance factors in line bisection tasks. *Neuropsychologia, 38*, 93–110.

Jonas, E., McGregor, I., Klackl, J., Agroskin, D., Fritsche, I., Holbrook, C., Nash, K., Proulx, T., & Quirin, M. (2014). Threat and defense: From anxiety to approach. *Advances in Experimental Social Psychology, 49*, 219–286.

Judge, T. A., Erez, A., Bono, J. E., & Thoresen, C. J. (2002). Are measures of self-esteem, neuroticism, locus of control, and generalized self-efficacy indicators of a common core construct?. *Journal of Personality and Social Psychology, 83*(3), 693.

Kay, A. C., Gaucher, D., Napier, J. L., Callan, M. J., & Laurin, K. (2008). God and the Government: Testing a compensatory control mechanism for the support of external systems. *Journal of Personality and Social Psychology, 95*, 18–35.

Kay, A. C., Moscovitch, D. M., & Laurin, K. (2010). Randomness, attributions of arousal, and belief in God. *Psychological Science, 21*, 216–218.

Kay, A. C., Shepherd, S., Blatz, C. W., Chua, S. N., & Galinsky, A. D. (2010). For God (or) country: The hydraulic relation between government instability and belief in religious sources of control. *Journal of Personality and Social Psychology, 5*, 725–739.

Kay, A. C., Whitson, J., Gaucher, D., & Galinsky, A. D. (2009). Compensatory control: In the mind, in our institutions, in the heavens. *Current Directions in Psychological Science, 18*, 264–268.

Klein, D. C., Fencil-Morse, E., & Seligman, M. E. (1976). Learned helplessness, depression, and the attribution of failure. *Journal of Personality and Social Psychology, 33*(5), 508.

Knight, C. G., Tobin, S. J., & Hornsey, M. J. (2014). From fighting the system to embracing it: Control loss promotes system justification among those high in psychological reactance. *Journal of Experimental Social Psychology, 54*, 139–146.

Krantz, D. S., Glass, D. C., & Snyder, M. L. (1974). Helplessness, stress level, and the coronary-prone behavior pattern. *Journal of Experimental Social Psychology, 10*(3), 284–300.

Lefcourt, H. M. (1976). *Locus of control: Current trends in theory and research.* Hillsdale, NJ: Erlbaum.

Lefcourt, H. M. (1980). Personality and locus of control. In J. Garber & M. E. P. Seligman (Eds.), *Human helplessness: Theory and applications,* pp. 245–259. New York: Academic Press.

McGregor, I., Nash, K., Mann, N., & Phills, C. E. (2010). Anxious uncertainty and reactive approach motivation (RAM). *Journal of Personality and Social Psychology, 99*, 133–147.

McGregor, I., Nash, K., & Prentice, M. (2010). Reactive approach motivation (RAM) for religion. *Journal of Personality and Social Psychology, 99*, 148–161.

Nash, K., McGregor, I., & Inzlicht, M. (2010). Line bisection as a marker of approach motivation. *Psychophysiology, 47*, 979–983.

Norton, M., & Gino, F. (2013). Rituals alleviate grieving for loved ones, lovers, and lotteries. *Journal of Experimental Psychology: General.* Online first publication. doi:10.1037/a0031772

Peterson, C. K., Shackman, A. J., & Harmon-Jones, E. (2008). The role of asymmetrical frontal cortical activity in aggression. *Psychophysiology, 45*, 86–92.

Pittman, T. S., & D'Agostino, P. R. (1985). Motivation and attribution: The effects of control deprivation on subsequent information processing. In J. H. Harvey & G. Weary (Eds.), *Attribution: Basic issues and applications* (pp. 117–141). San Diego, CA: Academic Press.

Pittman, T. S., & D'Agostino, P. R. (1989). Motivation and cognition: Control deprivation and the nature of subsequent information processing. *Journal of Experimental Social Psychology, 25*, 465–480.

Pittman, T. S., & Pittman, N. L. (1980). Deprivation of control and the attribution process. *Journal of Personality and Social Psychology, 39*, 377–389.

Proulx, T., & Inzlicht, M. (2012). The five "A"s of meaning maintenance: Finding meaning in the theories of sense-making. *Psychological Inquiry, 23*, 317–335.

Proulx, T., Inzlicht, M., & Harmon-Jones, E. (2012). Understanding all inconsistency compensation as a palliative response to violated expectations. *Trends in Cognitive Sciences, 16*(5), 285–291.

Roth, S., & Bootzin, R. R. (1974). Effects of experimentally induced expectancies of external control: An investigation of learned helplessness. *Journal of Personality and Social Psychology, 29*(2), 253.

Roth, S., & Kubal, L. (1975). Effects of non-contingent reinforcement on tasks of differing importance: Facilitation and learned helplessness. *Journal of Personality and Social Psychology, 32*, 680–691.

Rothbaum, F., Weisz, J. R., & Snyder, S. S. (1982). Changing the world and changing the self: A two-process model of perceived control. *Journal of Personality and Social Psychology, 42*, 5–37.

Rothschild, Z. K., Landau, M. J., Sullivan, D., & Keefer, L. A. (2012). A dual-motive model of scapegoating: Displacing blame to reduce guilt or increase control. *Journal of Personality and Social Psychology, 102*(6), 1148.

Rutjens, B. T., van der Pligt, J., & van Harreveld, F. (2010). Yes we can: Belief in progress as compensatory control. *Social Psychological and Personality Science, 1*, 246–252.

Rutjens, B. T., van Harreveld, F., & van der Pligt, J. (2013). Step by step finding compensatory order in science. *Current Directions in Psychological Science, 22*(3), 250–255.

Rutjens, B. T., van Harreveld, F., van der Pligt, J., Kreemers, L. M., & Noordewier, M. K. (2013). Steps, stages, and structure: Finding compensatory order in scientific theories. *Journal of Experimental Psychology: General, 142*(2), 313.

Sedek, G., Kofta, M., & Tyszka, T. (1993). Effects of uncontrollability on subsequent decision making: Testing the cognitive exhaustion hypothesis. *Journal of Personality and Social Psychology, 65*, 1270–1281.

Seligman, M. E. P. (1975). *Helplessness: On depression, development, and death.* San Francisco: Freeman.

Seligman, M. E. P., & Maier, S. F. (1967). Failure to escape traumatic shock. *Journal of Experimental Psychology, 74*, 1–9.

Skinner, E. A. (1996). A guide to constructs of control. *Journal of Personality and Social Psychology, 71*(3), 549.

Shepherd, S., Kay, A. C., Landau, M. J., & Keefer, L. A. (2011). Evidence for the specificity of control motivations in worldview defense: Distinguishing compensatory control from uncertainty management and terror management processes. *Journal of Experimental Social Psychology, 47*(5), 949–958.

Spencer, S. J., Zanna, M. P., & Fong, G. T. (2005). Establishing a causal chain: Why experiments are often more effective than meditational analyses in examining psychological processes. *Journal of Personality and Social Psychology, 89*, 845–851.

Thornton, J. W., & Jacobs, P. D. (1972). The facilitating effects of prior inescapable/unavoidable stress on intellectual performance. *Psychonomic Science, 26*(4), 185–187.

Turner, J. C., Hogg, M. A., Oakes, P. J., Reicher, S. D., & Wetherell, M. S. (1987). *Rediscovering the social group: A self-categorization theory.* Oxford: Blackwell.

Warburton, W. A., Williams, K. D., & Cairns, D. R. (2006). When ostracism leads to aggression: The moderating effects of control deprivation. *Journal of Experimental Social Psychology, 42*, 213–220.

Whitson J. A., & Galinsky, A. D. (2008). Lacking control increases illusory pattern perception. *Science, 322*, 115–117.

Wortman, C. B., & Brehm, J. W. (1975). Reponses to uncontrollable outcomes: An integration of reactance theory and the learned helplessness model. In L. Berkowitz (Ed.), *Advances in experimental social psychology* (Vol. 8, pp. 277–336). New York: Academic Press.

Zhou, L., & He, L., Lao, J., & Baumeister, R. F. (2012). Control deprivation and styles of thinking. *Journal of Personality and Social Psychology, 102*, 450–478.

3

IRONIC EFFECTS OF NEED FOR CLOSURE ON CLOSED-MINDED PROCESSING MODE

The role of perceived control over reducing uncertainty

Małgorzata Kossowska, Marcin Bukowski, and Sindhuja Sankaran

This research was supported by a grant from the National Science Center DEC 2011/02/A/HS6/00155 awarded to the first author.

Requests for reprints should be addressed to Małgorzata Kossowska, Institute of Psychology, Ingardena 6, 30–060 Kraków, phone number: +48519516452, e-mail address: malgorzata.kossowska@uj.edu.pl

Uncertainty can be defined as the implicit and explicit feelings people experience as an outcome of being unsure about themselves, i.e., self-image, personal attitudes, aspirations, beliefs, emotions, or self-knowledge (e.g., De Cremer & Sedikides, 2005; Van den Bos, 2001).[1] Although, to some degree, uncertainty in our lives may be stimulating, too much of it could be uncomfortable. Thus, people strive to reduce feelings of uncertainty about themselves, their social world, and their place within it – they are interested to know who they are and how to behave, who others are, and how they might behave (e.g., Van den Bos, 2001). Being properly informed in this manner renders the social world and one's place within it relatively predictable (Kruglanski & Webster, 1996). It also allows one to plan effective actions, avoid harm, know whom to trust, and so forth (Roets et al., 2015). Thus, cognition under uncertainty is guided by personal motivation to reduce it rather than by relatively involuntary and automatic processes (e.g., Berger & Calabrese, 1975; Hockey, 1986; Kruglanski, 1989). Although experiencing uncertainty may sometimes be sought out (e.g., Sorrentino, Bobocel, Gitta, Olson, & Hewitt, 1988), usually people are motivated to reduce this state by adhering to personal goals, values, or cultural worldviews (for overview: Jonas et al., 2014).

Kruglanski and colleagues (Ford & Kruglanski, 1995; Kruglanski & Webster, 1996; Kruglanski et al., 2009) claimed that experienced uncertainty increases the motivation for closure. This specific motivation, i.e., need for closure, has been described as the tendency to reduce the feeling of discomfort experienced in the face of cognitive uncertainty through the rapid formulation of a hypothesis and its brief validation (Kruglanski & Webster, 1996). It is discussed particularly as an individual difference measure of chronic need for epistemic certainty (Webster & Kruglanski, 1994). People may reduce chronically or situationally induced uncertainty differently. Imagine an uncertain situation in which an individual relocates to a new country with unfamiliar cultural norms. The adaptation to this uncertain situation, or in other words, the motivation to reduce the uncertainty imposed by this situation, could result in two different kinds of behavior. On the one hand the individual might engage in effortful strategies, such as learning the local language to interact with people from the foreign country. On the other hand an individual could reduce uncertainty by effortless strategies like interacting with expatriates from his/her own cultural background, thereby adjusting to the new country with limited exposure to its cultural norms. Indeed, most of the research on need for closure theory demonstrated that people who are motivated to reduce uncertainty (i.e., high in need for closure) tend to process information in simple, effortless, or closed-minded modes (Driscoll, Hamilton, & Sorrentino, 1991; Kruglanski et al., 2009). However, there are also some findings showing that uncertainty reduction is not always pursued via effortless processing (e.g., Kossowska, Dragon, & Bukowski, 2015; Kruglanski, Peri, & Zakai, 1991). Thus, the question remains as to why motivation to reduce uncertainty may result in divergent cognitive strategies.

In this chapter we attempt to resolve this inconsistency and we propose a theoretical framework that could explain such motivational differences in reducing uncertainty. In other words, in our model, we describe when people who are chronically motivated to reduce uncertainty use closed-minded and effortless cognitive strategies and when they are more ready to apply open-minded and effortful processing. We argue that perceived control over reducing uncertainty plays a significant role in this relationship. Specifically, we predict that when people are highly motivated to reduce uncertainty (i.e., have high need for closure) and feel that they have control over the reduction of uncertainty they may use a simple and effortless processing style. This effortless processing as an easy default option allows for quick and effective closure. This prediction is in line with the results of several previous studies (see Kruglanski, 2004, for an overview). However, when people are highly motivated to reduce uncertainty and feel low control, their lack of perceived control over this goal may induce them to abandon their dominant, effortless cognitive strategies and prompt them to achieve certainty via more effortful processing. The effortful strategies allow them to regain control over reducing uncertainty and thus attain closure. Moreover, we claim that perceived control over reducing uncertainty may be treated as an individual difference measure but also as a variable that is influenced by situations in which people's expectations are disconfirmed.

We believe that the proposed framework may be especially useful in explaining the variability in people's responses to uncertain situations. It also contributes to the discussion on the role of perceived control in social cognition in general (see Landau, Kay, & Whitson, 2015) and need for closure theory specifically (Roets et al., 2015).

Individual differences in motivation to reduce uncertainty and information processing mode

Kruglanski and colleagues (Ford & Kruglanski, 1995; Kruglanski & Webster, 1996; Kruglanski et al., 2009) claimed that experienced uncertainty increases the motivation for closure. Some research has demonstrated that effortless processing strategies to reduce uncertainty are usually utilized by individuals who have a high need for closure. This induces premature closure of decision alternatives or a restricted use of relevant cues, often leading to biased judgments, stereotyping, or prejudice (Driscoll, Hamilton, & Sorrentino, 1991; Kruglanski et al., 2009). Similar epistemic behaviors are exhibited by people when encountered with situations that induce high need for closure (e.g., time pressure, mental fatigue, environmental noise, or alcohol ingestion) (see Kruglanski, 2004, for overview).

There are, however, some findings showing that closure, and thus uncertainty reduction, is not always pursued via effortless processing. Referring to the example mentioned earlier, when going abroad, a person who tends to avoid uncertainty may invest lots of effort to effectively deal with this cultural change. In contrast, a person who can handle more uncertainty (e.g., low in need for closure) just relies on her or his ability to get along with the changing environment. In other words, when people need structure but the likelihood to achieve it is poor, they may engage in more effortful means to attain structure.

For example, Kruglanski, Peri, and Zakai (1991) found that when participants had an initial guess in which they had relatively high confidence, those who were high in need for closure searched for less information than low need for closure individuals. Under these circumstances, having high confidence in their opinion allowed them to effectively satisfy their need for closure by utilizing a simple processing strategy. However, when initial confidence was low, high (vs. low) need for closure individuals searched for more information in order to form an opinion and attain desired closure. Also Houghton and Grewal (2000) found that high need for closure resulted in a less extensive information search to make consumer decisions, but only when participants had well-formed and accessible attitudes towards the product. In addition, Vermeir, Van Kenhove, and Hendrickx (2002) found that high need for closure individuals actually sought significantly more information up to the point at which their (first) opinion was crystallized, but not thereafter.

These studies demonstrate that need for closure is associated with simple and effortless style of information processing, but only when there is an initial, satisfactory basis for closure, resulting from familiarity with a subject or having sufficiently strong confidence in one's initial opinion. If high need for closure individuals lack a knowledge base on which they can rely with relative confidence, they invest more effort to sample information in their quest for clear knowledge.

We believe that these results are better understood when taking into account how much control people perceive over the uncertainty reduction process. Thus, building on previous work we propose a novel theoretical framework that may explain the circumstances under which people who seek closure behave in relatively more closed-minded or open-minded ways.

Why people motivated to reduce uncertainty sometimes become "cognitively open": The role of perceived control over reducing uncertainty

We started this chapter with the statement that people are motivated to reduce uncertainty. It is, however, also well established that people are motivated to perceive themselves as having control over their daily lives (Landau, Kay, & Whitson, 2015). As a consequence, they normally respond to events and cognitions that reduce personal control with efforts to restore or maintain perceived control (Bukowski & Kofta, Chapter 1, this volume; Fritsche et al., 2013; Langer, 1975; Sullivan, Landau, & Rotschild, 2010). Perceptions of control increase people's confidence that particular actions can provide desired outcomes and therefore are crucial for performance, self-esteem, or well-being (Skinner, 1996). A sense of control can also provide confidence in the default way people generally think and act in their environment (Fast et al., 2009; Guinote, Weick, & Cai, 2012). Thus, for people chronically motivated to reduce uncertainty, beliefs that they have control to perform a behaviour or a set of behaviours could be crucial to produce certain outcomes or achieve certain ends. This concept of perceived control could refer to having enough skills, knowledge, and other capabilities that enable individuals to initiate action, expend effort in reducing uncertainty, and persist in the face of adversity. Consequently, when people confront circumstances (e.g., disconfirmed expectations) or experience thoughts that decrease their perceived control over reducing uncertainty, they should be ready to select means that allow them to achieve the goal, even if these means are demanding. The proposed model is depicted in Figure 3.1.

Indeed, Kossowska and Bar-Tal (2013a, 2013b) demonstrated that when people high in need for closure expect to be able to satisfy their epistemic need (i.e., they feel that they have control over the uncertainty reduction), they tend to process information in a more heuristic way, use more stereotypical traits to form an impression about the target person, and use simpler decision-making strategies. However, when these people expect to fail in achieving certainty (i.e., they feel that they have low control over the uncertainty reduction), they will process information in a less schematic way, use less stereotypical characteristics in their impression formation task, and make more complex decisions. We propose that beliefs about having low control over reducing uncertainty might motivate high need for closure individuals to choose more demanding means and invest cognitive effort to reduce

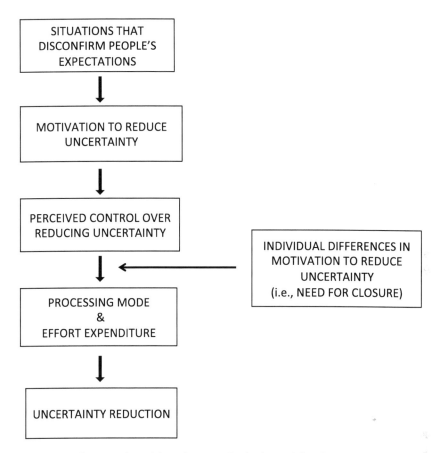

FIGURE 3.1   Theoretical model explaining why high need for closure under situations that disconfirm people's expectations leads to more effortful strategies for information processing.

uncertainty. In the studies cited above, perceived control over reducing uncertainty was treated as an individual difference measure[2] (Bar-Tal & Kossowska, 2010).

It is, however, possible that perceived control over reducing uncertainty is influenced by situational factors such as uncontrollability or ambiguity experience, threat posed to the self-image or power position, or inconsistent information about a stereotyped group. In fact, in a series of studies we found support for this claim (see Dragon, 2015; Kossowska, Dragon, & Bukowski, 2015; Kossowska, Bukowski, Guinote, Dragon, & Kruglanski, under revision). For example, some research showed that when high need for closure people were exposed to a task that led them to expect that the outcome was controllable they tended to use simple and effortless processing style manifested in better memory for schematic information, stereotyping in impression formation task, and simple decision making (Bar-Tal & Guinote, 2002; Kossowska, Dragon, & Bukowski, 2015).

However, after an informational helplessness training procedure (Sedek & Kofta, 1990) wherein a lack of control over uncertainty reduction was induced, that is, the outcome was uncontrollable, people high in need for closure processed information in a less schematic way and used less stereotypical characteristics in their impression formation task. In short, they used more effortful information-processing strategies. Moreover, in another study (Kossowska, Szwed, & Bukowski, 2015) we found that high (vs. low) need for closure people have more intense cardiovascular responses (systolic blood pressure) in an uncontrollable but not in a controllable situation. Thus, these results show that when ambiguity increases (as it does under uncontrollable conditions) people with high dispositional need for closure (compared to low NFC individuals) are motivated to reduce uncertainty, as demonstrated by the process of engagement – operationalized as cardiovascular activity. These findings are in fact in line with Wright's (1996) model of engagement-related cardiovascular reactivity.

Similar behavioral patterns were found after manipulations that lowered people's sense of power (Kossowska, Guinote, & Strojny, 2016). In these particular studies, participants were asked to report a past event in which they had power over someone or someone had power over them (Galinsky et al., 2003). Participants were then instructed to form an impression about a person from a stereotyped group. The results revealed that after inducing a feeling of powerlessness, the participants used less stereotypical information to form an impression, but only if they were high in need for closure.

In another set of studies, researchers (Kossowska, Bukowski, Guinote, Dragon, & Kruglanski, under revision) showed that when individuals high (vs. low) in need for closure formed impressions about members of stereotyped groups (Gypsies, Jews, homosexuals), they were less likely to use stereotypical traits when their self-images had been threatened. In these studies researchers focused on both incompetent and immoral behaviors as examples of self-threatening behaviors, as competence and morality are widely considered to be the defining characteristics of a person and have an important impact on cognitive and social functioning (e.g., Bliss-Moreau, Barrett, & Wright, 2008; Cosmides, 1989; Cottrell, Neuberg, & Li, 2007; Wojciszke, 2005). They argued that threat to positive self-image seems to evoke uncertainty about one's own abilities to achieve certainty (i.e. decreases feelings of control over goal attainment), which is in itself an aversive state, that especially high (vs. low) need for closure individuals strive to avoid. They additionally demonstrated that self-image threat decreases both control over reducing uncertainty and self-esteem, but it is need for closure that impacts the relationship between control over achieving closure and stereotyping. This is an important result in light of previous findings highlighting self-enhancement functions of stereotyping and prejudice for perceivers, following a threat to their self-image (Fein & Spencer, 1997). It also strengthens the argument regarding the role of perceived control over reducing uncertainty as both an outcome of the self-image threat manipulation and as a mechanism mediating between the self-image threat and stereotyping. The model verified in this study is depicted in Figure 3.2.

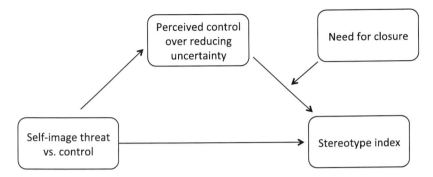

FIGURE 3.2   Moderated mediation model of the relationship between self-image threat, ability to achieve closure, need for closure and stereotyping.

Similar results pertaining to how unfreezing processes were related to lesser reliance on stereotypes were obtained by Rios et al. (2014). They showed that self-uncertainty led to the need to highlight one's distinctiveness (in the context of our research it would be supporting minorities) and increased creative generation. Another illustration of this phenomenon was demonstrated by Dragon and Kossowska (submitted), wherein the results revealed that high need for closure people easily applied heuristic rules (e.g., "if one group is warm, then the other is rather competent") that simplified intergroup perception and therefore efficiently reduced uncertainty. However, when high (vs. low) need for closure participants were provided with counter-stereotypical information about the target group (e.g., "Germans are the most likable nationality in the European Union" or "culinary school students achieved better results in intelligence test than business school students") they relied less on the simple compensatory rule ("if warm then less competent") when making impressions about the outgroup. Thus, when confronted with expectancy-inconsistent information, individuals high in need for closure evaluated the outgroup by using more data-driven processing.

We claim that all of these situations that disconfirm people's expectations increase uncertainty related to one's ability to reduce it. Thus, these situations decrease one's perceived control over pursuing the goal of attaining certainty. Hence, when experiencing low control over reducing uncertainty, high need for closure people who are especially sensitive to uncertainty may select more demanding means in order to regain certainty (see Kruglanski et al., 2012). Accordingly, in the last experiment of Kossowska et al. (under revision), less stereotyping following a self-image threat was partially mediated by feelings of low control over reducing uncertainty, which reduced stereotyping only among high, but not among low need for closure people. This means that when an important part of individuals' self-image is questioned and they are unsure how to modify this uncomfortable feeling, then they are subsequently less eager to rely on stereotypes.

Cues that allow people to increase control over reducing uncertainty

In another set of studies we additionally tested the idea that when having clear information on how to deal with a situation (i.e., having high control over reducing uncertainty), high need for closure individuals use simple cognitive strategies to satisfy their need. However, if the situation does not provide any specific cue about an optimal strategy, high need for closure people tend to invest more effort that directly leads to increased control over this goal attainment.

A study by Jaśko, Czernatowicz-Kukuczka, Kossowska, and Czarna (2015) demonstrated that when participants were presented with information that the optimal strategy to make an effective decision is simple, individuals high in need for closure examined less information and spent less time on making a decision than individuals low in need for closure. However, when the participants were informed that the optimal strategy is complex, the pattern of results was reversed: high need for closure participants searched for more information before making a decision and took longer to make the decision compared to low need for closure participants.

Two other studies (Sankaran, Czernatowicz-Kukuczka, von Hecker, & Kossowska, 2015) directly examined the idea that perceived control over reducing uncertainty is responsible for the abovementioned effects. In both studies, a causal learning paradigm (Sankaran, Greville, & von Hecker, 2015) was incorporated wherein participants had to make a judgment if an action (button press) had any effect on the outcome (lighting of a triangle on screen). Indeed, the results revealed that when an explicit rule was imposed by introducing a subjective limit (i.e., the button press was limited to 15 seconds and participants were informed that they would hear a sound every time they exceeded the limit), high and low need for closure people did not differ in their total number of button presses. This implies that high need for closure people just followed the rule as instructed and by doing so gained an immediate sense of certainty. Results from another study, however, confirmed the general idea that individuals high in need for closure tended to invest more effort in trying to reduce uncertainty in an uncertain condition by pressing the button more often than those low in need for closure. Furthermore, among high in need for closure individuals, the total number of presses mediated the relationship between uncertainty and perception of control over uncertainty reduction. In particular, high (vs. low) need for closure individuals in the condition of extreme uncertainty (i.e., when the interval for any given cause-effect pair was variable) pressed the button more often, and in consequence they felt higher perceived control over reducing uncertainty. Thus, in the face of uncertainty, it made sense for high need for closure people to invest more effort to achieve closure, thereby heightening their sense of control when they had no rule to anchor on. In general, the results show that individuals who are chronically motivated to reduce uncertainty seem to vary across conditions where they invest effort, and perceived control over uncertainty reduction plays an important role in choosing effortful or effortless means to achieve the focal goal.

All these findings thus attest to the "ironic" nature of information processing amongst need for closure individuals. It seems that high need for closure people search for the means that can serve the goal of reducing uncertainty, including both effortful and effortless strategies. In other words, when they can anchor on to an available structure, high need for closure individuals may feel more certain about the task and therefore they pursue closure via simplistic processing according to the rule. In the absence of structure, however, they experience a lack of control over uncertainty reduction and they invest more effort to feel certain.

Final remarks

In this chapter, we elaborated on the circumstances under which people motivated to reduce uncertainty either engage in more effortful and open-minded cognition or rely on simplistic processing styles, which itself uniquely contributes to need for closure theory. We also stressed the role of perceived control over the process of reducing uncertainty as an important factor that is responsible for abovementioned effects. Moreover, we demonstrated that in situations when people's expectations were disconfirmed, people felt low control over reducing uncertainty, which invariably led to more effortful strategies amongst high need for closure people. We also demonstrated that when high need for closure individuals invested more effort in resolving uncertainty, their perception of control over reducing uncertainty also increased. Thus, we also contributed to the discussion on the role of perceived control in social cognition in general. However, when control over reducing uncertainty seems impossible or the value of having control over reducing uncertainty in a particular situation is low (e.g., exerting control is related to high responsibility that someone is not willing to take) people may not be motivated to strive for control. We think that in such situations, high need for closure people might use less demanding means to achieve certainty and stop investing any additional effort in the activity at hand. Referring to the previously introduced example of how to behave in a new culture, let us assume that an individual with high need for closure is at a market trying to purchase a gift for a friend. However, this individual is under time pressure to catch a bus to a nearby town. The shopkeeper, however, does not speak the same language and is asking for an exorbitant amount for the gift that needs to be purchased. At this point, the individual is feeling uncertain as s/he is not sure how to bargain and communicate with the shopkeeper and given the time constraint believes that it is absolutely futile that s/he would gain any certainty over this situation. Thus, instead of trying to get a translator or trying to understand slowly (effortful means), s/he might either pay the expensive amount or go to another shop (less demanding means) to attain her/his goal. This assumption is in line with motivational intensity theory (Brehm & Self, 1989), which states that people are more inclined to conserve energy when task difficulty is very high and clear. We believe that people high in need for closure will show greater readiness to disengage in unprofitable energy investment than their low need for closure counterparts when it is not necessary or simply impossible. Further research is needed, however, to test this hypothesis.

In sum, we believe that our findings contribute to the general discussion on the very nature of need for closure. It is worth stressing that although originally need for closure is defined as the desire for "an answer on a given topic, any answer . . . compared to confusion and ambiguity" (Kruglanski, 1990, p. 337), a more recent conceptualization stresses that need for closure denotes an inclination to seize quickly on information that promises to bring about closure (Kruglanski & Webster, 1996). Thus it seems that theoretically for high need for closure individuals, immediate closure is desirable and any further postponement is felt to be bothersome. Our findings, however, showed that need for closure is not a tendency to seize quickly on information but to seize on information that promises effective closure and to process it as long as is needed to achieve certainty. Thus it seems that need for closure is a general motivation to reduce uncertainty, and uncertainty reduction may be achieved via various means. In general, the proposed perspective is consistent with extant research showing that humans are characterized by behavior flexibility, in line with the *active self* (a part of the self that is currently activated), which can be consistent with chronically accessible response patterns associated with dispositions or with alternatives activated in context (Wheeler, DeMarree, & Petty, 2014). It means that high need for closure people sometimes may strive for fast and simple cognition and sometimes not, depending on situational constraints. In this chapter we attempted to show that perceived control over reducing uncertainty plays a crucial role in determining the way they process information.

Notes

1 The other type of uncertainty that people often face involves having less information available than one ideally would like to have to form a social judgment in a confident manner (see, e.g., Kahneman, Slovic, & Tversky, 1982; Phelps, 1970). It is called informational uncertainty.
2 Perceived control over uncertainty reduction, originally called "ability to achieve closure", has usually been measured by a nine-item scale developed by Bar-Tal and Kossowska (2010). Sample items are "I hesitate to make important decisions, even after long deliberation" (low control) or "I make even important decisions quickly and confidently" (high control).

References

Bar-Tal, Y., & Guinote, A. (2002). Who exhibits more stereotypical thinking? The effect of need and ability to achieve cognitive structure on stereotyping. *European Journal of Personality, 16*, 313–331. doi:10.1002/per.453

Bar-Tal, Y., & Kossowska, M. (2010). Efficacy at fulfilling need for closure: The construct and its measurement. In J. P. Villanueva (Ed.), *Personality traits: Classifications, effects and changes* (pp. 47–64). New York: Nova Publishers.

Berger, C. R., & Calabrese, R. J. (1975). Some explorations in initial interaction and beyond: Toward a developmental theory of interpersonal communication. *Human Communication Research, 1*(2), 99–112. http://doi.org/10.1111/j.1468–2958.1975.tb00258.x

Bliss-Moreau, E., Barrett, L. F., & Wright, C. I. (2008). Individual differences in learning the affective value of others under minimal conditions. *Emotion, 8*, 479–493.

Brehm, J. W., & Self, E. A. (1989). The intensity of motivation. *Annual Review of Psychology, 40*, 109.

Cosmides, L. (1989). The logic of social exchange: Has natural selection shaped how humans reason? Studies with the Wason selection task. *Cognition, 31*, 187–276.

Cottrell, C. A., Neuberg, S. L., & Li, N. P. (2007). What do people desire in others? A socio-functional perspective on the importance of different valued characteristics. *Journal of Personality and Social Psychology, 92*, 208–231.

De Cremer, D., & Sedikides, C. (2005). Self-uncertainty and responsiveness to procedural justice. *Journal of Experimental Social Psychology, 41*, 157–173.

Dragon, P. (2015). *The compensation effect in perceptions of groups: The role of epistemic motivation.* Unpublished doctoral thesis supervised by Małgorzata Kossowska and Arie W. Kruglanski. Jagiellonian University, Kraków.

Dragon, P., & Kossowska, M. (submitted). *Motivational underpinnings of compensatory group perception: The ironic effect of expectancy-inconsistent information.*

Driscoll, D. M., Hamilton, D. L., & Sorrentino, R. M. (1991). Uncertainty orientation and recall of person-descriptive information. *Personality and Social Psychology Bulletin, 17*(5), 494–500. doi:10.1177/0146167291175003

Fast, N., Gruenfeld, D., Sivanathan, N., & Galinsky, A. (2009). Illusory control: A generative force behind power's far-reaching effects. *Psychological Science, 20*, 502–508. 10.1111/j.1467–9280.2009.02311.x

Fein, S., & Spencer, S. J. (1997). Prejudice as self-image maintenance: Affirming the self through derogating others. *Journal of Personality and Social Psychology, 73*, 31–44.

Ford, T. E., & Kruglanski, A. W. (1995). Effects of epistemic motivations on the use of accessible constructs in social judgment. *Personality and Social Psychology Bulletin, 21*, 950–962. doi:10.1177/0146167295219009

Fritsche, I., Jonas, E., Ablasser, C., Beyer, M., Kuban, J., Manger, A.-M., & Schultz, M. (2013). The power of we: Evidence for group-based control. *Journal of Experimental Social Psychology, 49*, 19–32. doi:10.1016/j.jesp.2012.07.014

Galinsky, A. D., Gruenfeld, D. H., & Magee, J. C. (2003). From power to action. *Journal of Personality and Social Psychology, 85*, 453–466. doi:10.1037/0022-3514.85.3.453

Guinote, A., Weick, M., & Cai, A. (2012). Does power magnify the expression of dispositions? *Psychological Science, 23*, 475–482. doi:10.1177/0956797611428472

Hockey, G. R. J. (1986). A state control theory of adaptation and individual differences in stress management. In G. R. J. Hockey, A. W. K. Gaillard, & M. G. H. Coles (Eds.), *Energetics and human information processing* (pp. 285–298). Dordrecht, The Netherlands: Kluwer Academic.

Houghton, D., & Grewal, R. (2000). Let's get an answer – any answer: Need for consumer cognitive closure. *Psychology and Marketing, 17*, 911–934. doi:10.1002/1520-6793(200011)17: 11<911::AID-MAR1>3.0.CO;2–4

Jaśko, K., Czernatowicz-Kukuczka, A., Kossowska, M., & Czarna, A. Z. (2015). Individual differences in response to uncertainty and decision making: The role of behavioral inhibition system and need for closure. *Motivation & Emotion*. doi:10.1007/s11031-015-9478-x

Jonas, E., McGregor, I., Klackl, J., Agroskin, D., Fritsche, I., Holbrook, C., . . . Quirin, M. (2014). Threat and defense: From anxiety to approach. In J. M. Olson & M. P. Zanna (Eds.), *Advances in experimental social psychology* (Vol. 49, pp. 219–286). San Diego, CA: Academic Press. 10.1016/B978–0–12–800052–6.00004–4

Kahneman, D., Slovic, P., & Tversky, A. (Eds.). (1982). *Judgment under uncertainty: Heuristics and biases.* Cambridge: Cambridge University Press.

Kossowska, M., & Bar-Tal, Y. (2013a). Need for closure and heuristic information processing: The moderating role of the ability to achieve the need for closure. *British Journal of Psychology, 104*, 457–480. doi:10.1111/bjop.12001

Kossowska, M., & Bar-Tal, Y. (2013b). Positive mood boosts the expression of a dispositional need for closure. *Cognition & Emotion, 27,* 1181–1201.

Kossowska, M., Bukowski, M., Guinote, A., Dragon, P., & Kruglanski, A. W. (under revision). *When self-image threat leads to stereotyping and when it does not: The role of motivation toward closure.*

Kossowska, M., Dragon, P., & Bukowski, M. (2015). When need for closure leads to positive attitudes towards a negatively stereotyped outgroup. *Motivation and Emotion, 39,* 88–98. doi:10.1007/s11031-014-9414-5

Kossowska, M., Guinote, A., & Strojny, P. (2016). Power boosts reliance on preferred processing styles. *Motivation and Emotions, 40,* 556–565. doi:10.1007/s11031-016-9548-8

Kossowska, M., Szwed, P., & Bukowski, M. (2015). Uncontrollability and need for closure. *Unpublished manuscript.*

Kruglanski, A. W. (1989). *Lay epistemic and human knowledge: Cognitive and motivational bases.* New York: Plenum.

Kruglanski, A. W. (1990). Lay epistemic theory in social-cognitive psychology. *Psychological Inquiry, 1*(3), 181-197.

Kruglanski, A. W. (2004). T*he psychology of closed mindedness.* New York: Psychology Press.

Kruglanski, A. W., Bélanger, J. J., Chen, X., Köpetz, C., Pierro, A., & Mannetti, L. (2012). The energetics of motivated cognition: A force-field analysis. *Psychological Review, 119,* 1–20. http://doi.org/10.1037/a0025488

Kruglanski, A. W., Dechesne, M., Orehek, E., & Pierro, A. (2009). Three decades of lay epistemics: The why, how and who of knowledge formation. *European Review of Social Psychology, 20,* 146–191. doi:10.1080/10463280902860037

Kruglanski, A. W., Peri, N., & Zakai, D. (1991). Interactive effects of need for closure and initial confidence on social information seeking. *Social Cognition, 9,* 127–148. doi:10.1521/soco.1991.9.2.127

Kruglanski, A. W., & Webster, D. M. (1996). Motivated closing of the mind: "Seizing" and "freezing". *Psychological Review, 103,* 263–283. doi:10.1037/0033-295X.103.2.263

Landau, M. J., Kay, A. C., & Whitson, J. A. (2015). Compensatory control and the appeal of a structured world. *Psychological Bulletin, 141,* 694–722. doi:10.1037/a0038703

Langer, E. J. (1975). Illusion of control. *Journal of Personality and Social Psychology, 32,* 311–328. http://dx.doi.org/10.1037/0022–3514.32.2.311

Phelps, E. S. (1970). *Microeconomic foundations of employment and inflation theory.* New York: Norton.

Rios, K., Markman, K. D., Schroeder, J. R., & Dyczewski, E. (2014). A (creative) portrait of the uncertain individual: Self-uncertainty and individualism enhance creative generation. *Personality and Social Psychology Bulletin, 4,* 1–13. doi:10.1177/0146167214535640

Roets, A., Kruglanski, A., Kossowska, M., Pierro, A., & Hong, Y. (2015). The motivated gatekeeper of our minds: New directions in need for closure theory and research. *Advances in Experimental Social Psychology, 52,* 221–283.

Sankaran, S., Czernatowicz-Kukuczka, A., Von Hecker, U., & Kossowska, M. (2015). *When do they push the right buttons? The role of control motivation and effort investment in need for closure.* Manuscript in preparation.

Sankaran, S., Greville, W., & Von Hecker, U. (2015). *Examining perceived controllability amongst 'chokers' and 'non-chokers': Evidence towards a learned helplessness model.* Manuscript in preparation.

Sedek, G., & Kofta, M. (1990). When cognitive exertion does not yield cognitive gain: Toward an informational explanation of learned helplessness. *Journal of Personality and Social Psychology, 58,* 729–743. doi:10.1037/0022-3514.58.4.729

Skinner, E. A. (1996). A guide to constructs of control. *Journal of Personality and Social Psychology, 71*, 549–570.

Sorrentino, R. M., Bobocel, D. R., Gitta, M. Z., Olson, J. M., & Hewitt, E. C. (1988). Uncertainty orientation and persuasion: Individual differences in the effects of personal relevance on social judgments. *Journal of Personality and Social Psychology, 55*, 357–371.

Sullivan, D., Landau, M. J., & Rothschild, Z. K. (2010). An existential function of enemyship: Evidence that people attribute influence to personal and political enemies to compensate for threats to control. *Journal of Personality and Social Psychology, 98*, 434–449. http://dx.doi.org/10.1037/a0017457

Van den Bos, K. (2001). Uncertainty management: The influence of uncertainty salience on reactions to perceived procedural fairness. *Journal of Personality and Social Psychology, 80*, 931–941.

Vermeir, I., Van Kenhove, P., & Hendrickx, H. (2002). The influence of need for closure on consumer choice behaviour. *Journal of Economic Psychology, 23*, 703–727. doi:10.1016/s0167-4870(02)00135-6

Webster, D. M., & Kruglanski, A. W. (1994). Individual differences in need for cognitive closure. *Journal of Personality and Social Psychology, 67*, 1049–1062.

Wheeler, S. C., DeMarree, K. G., Petty, R. E. (2014). Understanding prime-to-behavior effects: Insights from the active-self account. *Social Cognition, 32*, 109–123.

Wojciszke, B. (2005). Morality and competence in person and self-perception. *European Review of Social Psychology, 16*, 155–188.

Wright, R. A. (1996). Brehm's theory of motivation as a model of effort and cardiovascular response. In P. M. Gollwitzer, J. A. Bargh, P. M. Gollwitzer, & J. A. Bargh (Eds.), *The psychology of action: Linking cognition and motivation to behavior* (pp. 424–453). New York, NY: Guilford Press.

4

UNCONTROLLABILITY IN THE CLASSROOM

The intellectual helplessness perspective

Klara Rydzewska, Marzena Rusanowska, Izabela Krejtz, and Grzegorz Sedek

Corresponding Author: Grzegorz Sedek
SWPS University of Social Sciences and Humanities, Interdisciplinary Center for
Applied Cognitive Studies (ICACS)
ul. Chodakowska 19/31, 03–815 Warsaw, Poland
E-mail: gsedek@swps.edu.pl
Phone: +48 22 5179876

The concept of intellectual helplessness

The fact that a lot of times students try to solve math tasks without understanding the problem is often recognized by educational researchers. The classical example (cited by Schoenefeld, 1988) comes from the third National Assessment of Educational Progress, which used a random national sample of 45,000 13-year-old students. Among many other tasks, students were given the following problem: "An army bus holds 36 soldiers. If 1128 soldiers are being bussed to their training site, how many buses are needed?" Only 23% gave the correct answer "32"; however, 29% of the students wrote that the number of buses needed is "31 remainder 12." Obviously, "31 reminder 12" is the result of dividing 1128 by 36, but such a *precise answer* is completely absurd in the real-world situation. In the educational literature such examples of absurd or mindless answers to task problems in different educational subjects are typically seen as the lack of a skill in transforming abstract knowledge into real-world situations. However, in this chapter we will try to demonstrate that they might be better conceptualized as the symptoms of intellectual helplessness among students.

The chapter focuses on the role of lack of control experience in early educational settings. The main aim of this chapter is to clearly demonstrate that chronic experience of uncontrollability might be context-embedded (e.g., intellectual helplessness in math is uncorrelated with intellectual helplessness in the Polish language domain). First, starting from the cognitive exhaustion model of learned helplessness (e.g., Kofta & Sedek, 1998; Sedek & Kofta, 1990), we analyze the roots and manifestations of the phenomenon of intellectual helplessness in the classroom. We hope to show how the abstract ideas of the psychology of personal control might help to better understand psychological phenomena in real-life settings. Second, we reveal social settings that might be important real-life determinants of the loss-of-control experience in the classroom: the faulty teaching style. Third, we demonstrate that even chronic loss-of-control experience does not necessarily make people completely passive, but motivates them to engage in compensatory behavior. For example, intellectually helpless students frequently switch to "survival strategies" which only simulate understanding of the lesson content. Finally, we present findings suggesting that intellectual helplessness is a significant predictor of early school achievement even when intellectual capabilities and working memory are controlled for.

Cognitive exhaustion model

Cognitive exhaustion model has been developed as the cognitive model of experienced uncontrollability and subclinical depression. This approach (Kofta & Sedek, 1998; Sedek & Kofta, 1990; Sedek, Kofta, & Tyszka, 1993; von Hecker & Sedek, 1999) assumes that people are likely to engage in systematic mental activity when dealing with problem-solving situations. They attempt to understand the requirements of a task, notice and pay attention to diagnostic pieces of information, detect regularities or inconsistencies, and so forth. In controllable situations, these mental activities stimulate people to engage in more generative modes of thinking, like the construction of integrative memory representations such as mental models or elaborating complex cognitive strategies with a hierarchy of sub goals. However, in uncontrollable surroundings, such activity is futile because it cannot lead to real progress in problem solving. Therefore, although an individual might generate preliminary hypotheses, they would eventually not be able to differentiate between good and poor solutions. As it has been empirically demonstrated, the engagement in task resolution under induced uncontrollability leads to a heightened uncertainty, which cannot be reduced (Kofta & Sedek, 1999).

It is hypothesized that prolonged cognitive effort without cognitive gain results in an altered psychological state, which we term "cognitive exhaustion", characterized by a generalized impairment of constructive mental processing (Kofta & Sedek, 1998; Sedek & Kofta, 1990; von Hecker & Sedek, 1999). Therefore, after uncontrollable pre-exposure, the ability to generate new ideas and hypotheses is diminished. In terms of general adaptive functions, cognitive exhaustion states seem especially disruptive to more complex problem solving tasks requiring non-routine, flexible steps of processing in either achievement or interpersonal domains. The primarily cognitive nature of this phenomenon is supported by the data showing that these deficits emerge in conditions which minimize the likelihood of effort withdrawal as an ego-protective maneuver, i.e., in the absence of social performance feedback, as well as in situations when negative mood is statistically controlled for (Kofta & Sedek, 1989; Sedek & Kofta, 1990). In another study, after uncontrollability treatment, participants tended to avoid effortful information-gathering strategies prior to decision making, which is indicative of cognitive exhaustion (Sedek, Kofta, & Tyszka, 1993).

In a number of studies over the last decades, we have used a laboratory paradigm, which, as we argue later, is analogous to a crucial aspect of depressive style of rumination, in order to investigate cognitive deficits associated with cognitive effort without cognitive gain (Sedek & Kofta, 1990; Sedek et al., 1993; von Hecker & Sedek, 1999). This Informational Helplessness Training (IHT) paradigm differs from behavioral learned helplessness approaches to depression in such a way that it does not require ineffective behavior for the deficits to appear. It is important to note that during IHT, participants from both control and uncontrollable groups do not respond overtly, and consequently there is no evaluative feedback concerning their responses. The essence of this procedure is, in the helpless condition, an exposure to inconsistent task information that does not enable formulation of or support for any reasonable task solution, even when a considerable amount of cognitive effort is invested in solving the task. As we discuss below, some persistent mental activities among depressed individuals, such as ruminations or counterfactual thinking, might be conceptualized as self-generated forms of informational helplessness training.

In our sets of experiments (Sedek & Kofta, 1990; von Hecker & Sedek, 1999) we supported the hypothesis that after pre-exposure to informational uncontrollability, performance in more complex tasks (such as complex avoidance learning or building mental models of social cliques) is grossly impaired, while performance on simpler tasks remains intact. In our recent reviews (Sedek, Brzezicka, & von Hecker, 2010; von Hecker, McIntosh, & Sedek, 2015; von Hecker, Sedek, & Brzezicka, 2013) we presented the research evidence that is in line with the cognitive exhaustion model, namely the unique cognitive limitation in subclinical depression consists of the impairment of mental model construction.

The model of intellectual helplessness and preliminary findings with Intellectual Helplessness Scale

The preliminary model of intellectual helplessness (Sedek, 1995; Sedek & Kofta, 1992) applied the cognitive exhaustion view of uncontrollability to the acquisition of school knowledge. Accordingly, it assumes that the repeated inabilities to understand new material in class despite prolonged mental effort are critical situations. As in laboratory experiments prolonged effort with no progress leads to deterioration of solving cognitively demanding tasks, such repeated situations during class learning block active problem thinking (e.g., involving comparison, reasoning, or building consistent knowledge schemas). Eventually knowledge schemas in that particular domain may become disorganized and it becomes nearly impossible for students to learn with comprehension. Importantly, we assume that when the critical situations (i.e., inability to understand new concepts despite intense effort) are repeated many times during the same lessons (e.g., during chemistry classes), transitory states of intellectual helplessness might stabilize and cues specific for a given domain (e.g., chemistry formulas) may acquire the potency for triggering this state without prior helplessness training. Consistently, we indicate that the states of intellectual helplessness may be content-specific (e.g., students may be helpless in math but masterly in native language or vice versa) and mostly caused by faulty instruction – which arises from the lack of skills among some teachers in promotion of understanding during learning new and difficult topics.

In our previous chapter (Sedek & McIntosh, 1998), we described the construction of scale measuring intellectual helplessness with regard to various school subjects (math, physics, Polish language). Students rated on a 5-point Likert type scale to what extent they experience intellectual helplessness symptoms during, for example, math class. The scale consists of 20 statements about feelings and thoughts that accompany math classes, e.g., *I find I don't understand what I'm writing in my notes; It almost takes a physical effort to keep my mind on the lesson; I feel empty-headed; I feel helpless; It feels like it is all Greek to me* (for the full version of the scale, see Sedek & McIntosh, 1998). The scale proved to be highly internally consistent, with the Cronbach's Alpha coefficients calculated across different samples having very high values between .92 and .95. As predicted, there were no significant correlations between symptoms of intellectual helplessness on math and Polish language lessons as measured by IHS.

Additionally, we constructed several questionnaires assessing teachers' behavior during learning in classes; the tool which was used for asking students directly about the extent to which a teacher promoted understanding of the topics during lessons was the most important among them. This Promotion of Understanding Scale was filled out by students of given teachers and described these teachers' behaviors that are conducive to learning a new material with comprehension during classes. The creation of the described scale was inspired directly by the intellectual helplessness model, which argues that the intellectual helplessness to a given school subject might be caused by inappropriate teaching skills during introduction of new material in class. Hence, a group of students evaluated whether their teachers make sure that they get a good grasp of the new concepts introduced in class, encourage them to ask questions and signal their doubts, and whether or not teachers carefully analyze the reasons underlying the incorrect answers, etc.

Mediational structural equation analyses showed (Sedek & McIntosh, 1998) that for both math and Polish language the level of the evaluated teacher's skill in promotion of understanding influenced directly and positively the school achievement (latent measure defined by grades and specific tests), as well as indirectly and negatively influenced the school achievement via mediation by intellectual helplessness (as measured by IHS at the beginning of the school year). Aggregated correlations (with the classes as units of analyses) clearly showed the strong and negative correlations between the mean level of intellectual helplessness in given classes and the mean level of skill in promotion of understanding among teachers in those classes as rated by pupils.

In the rest of this chapter we will present new data findings (re-analyses of previous research or just currently conducted studies) that shed more light on the phenomenon of intellectual helplessness. First, we will verify whether intellectual helplessness induced in laboratory settings relates to the phenomenon observed in real-life classroom settings. Second, we will present pupils' strategies that help them survive classes during which they experience lack of control. Finally, we will report findings demonstrating that intellectual helplessness is independent from intellectual capabilities and that it is a strong predictor of school achievement.

The relationship between laboratory learned helplessness and Intellectual Helplessness Scale: The role of cognitive effort without cognitive gain

The lack of information gain in result of exposition to incoherent, mutually contradictory data (informational helplessness training) in laboratory experiments leads to a changed psychological state, referred to as the cognitive exhaustion state. The question is whether or not the Intellectual Helplessness Scale used in the classroom setting has something to do with the learned helplessness phenomena in the laboratory research. It can be hypothesized that the scale measures just the aversion or the anxiety of a pupil toward a given school subject. If the Intellectual Helplessness Scale is an accurate measure of cognitive exhaustion during lessons of some particular school subject, then it should be strongly connected with the frequency of intellectual helplessness episodes experienced during given classes in primary school.

In order to explore some such important experiences in primary school, pupils were asked several questions regarding the last two grades of primary school. Firstly, they were asked about the grades from three school subjects (mathematics, physics, and Polish language) at the end of the seventh and eighth grades. Moreover, they were asked about experiences during lessons, including the episodes of intellectual helplessness in classroom ("Did it happen to you that regardless of a lot of effort and a number of trials you could not understand something in mathematics [physics, polish language] class?") and periods of cognitive demobilization in classroom ("Did you have periods of feeling down as you were not able to deal with the school subject, had an aversion to learning, and got bad grades?"). In case of positive answers to the above questions, pupils were asked about the frequency of these experiences. The first question constitutes the operationalization of the key psychological mechanism postulated by the informational helplessness model. In line with this model, the lack of information gain during helplessness training leads to a cognitive exhaustion syndrome. On the other hand, the second question consists of a concise cognitive demobilization description resulting from the previous syndrome. The above questions not only test the extent of generalization of primary school experiences to high school experiences, but also allow for testing the theoretical accuracy of the Intellectual Helplessness Scale in classroom settings.

Additionally, we were interested in analyzing teaching styles of primary school teachers. In line with the informational model, teachers who are not able to convey a subject in a clear way and to spark interest in the subject are likely to evoke intellectual helplessness syndrome among pupils. The opinions regarding primary school teachers were of a retrospective nature, therefore four simple questions were asked in order to diagnose their teaching styles (pupils answered on a six-point Likert scale ranging from "certainly no" to "certainly yes"):

1. Did (the mathematics, physics, Polish teacher) transmit knowledge in a clear and systematic way?
2. Did the teacher try to interest pupils with the subject and to stimulate their curiosity?
3. Did the teacher encourage discussion and asking questions in class?
4. Did the teacher check whether a pupil understood what he or she was learning?

The answers to this short scale were very coherent: Cronbach's alpha equaled to .92 for mathematics, .91 for physics, and .93 for Polish language.

A number of analyses were conducted in order to test expectations regarding the role of primary school experiences for forecasting intellectual helplessness at the beginning of high school education. The results of intellectual helplessness for a given school subject were predicted in the following steps: grades in the eighth grade, teaching style, number of intellectual helplessness episodes, and cognitive demobilization periods. If the intellectual helplessness model is valid, then the eighth-grade grades and teaching style should be weak predictors of intellectual helplessness. On the other hand, early helplessness training (and accompanying cognitive demobilization syndrome) should affect occurrence of intellectual helplessness the most.

Table 4.1 presents aggregated results of hierarchical regression analyses for mathematics (reanalyses of findings of longitudinal study, Sedek, Krejtz, & Szymaszek, 2010/2011), however, the findings for physics and Polish language were very similar.

As Table 4.1 shows, helplessness training in primary school is the strongest predictor of intellectual helplessness at the beginning of high school. What is more, grades at the end of the eighth grade were a significant predictor of intellectual helplessness. Moreover, teaching style in primary school was an important predictor

TABLE 4.1 Hierarchical regression analyses: The results of the Intellectual Helplessness Scale (IHS) predicted by experiences connected with primary school for mathematics.

Step	Variable	R^2	R^2 change	β
1.	Grades – eighth grade	.08	.08	−.17**
2.	Teacher in primary school	.11	.03	−.11*
3.	Helplessness training	.27	.16	.32***
	Cognitive demobilization			.16**

Note: *p < .05; **p < .01; ***p < .001

of intellectual helplessness; however, its impact was relatively weaker than the impact of helplessness experiences in the classroom.

Survival strategies of helpless pupils

A few studies (Sedek et al., 2010/2011) have considered the way high school pupils attempt to cope with a situation which potentially leads to the occurrence of intellectual helplessness symptoms. For instance, adapting strategies that help them pass a class in which they do not understand the key elements at all. This topic is of special interest for the general goal of this edited volume, as it is dedicated to the mechanisms of coping with uncontrollability. In case of pupils who deal effectively with a given school subject, active strategies could be expected to be used: asking questions in the classroom, learning material on one's own, asking fellow pupils or parents for help. However, passive or even survival strategies of dealing with school situations are also used. The most popular of such strategies are avoiding eye contact with a teacher (hopefully he or she will not ask me a question) and acquiescing when new material is introduced which simulates understanding of a lesson content. During testing situations, such passive strategies may include reliance on cheat sheets and hints from colleagues, logorrhea based on a quick linkage to a well-known issue and talking about everything that is somehow related to it. Sometimes pupils use even more inventive passive strategies, such as faking fainting or excusing themselves for not being prepared due to serious life problems.

In order to evoke active or passive strategies employed by pupils during lessons, they were confronted with two different classroom situations – introducing new material or being called on to answer questions during class. In the first situation pupils were given the following issue:

"You sit in the classroom. The mathematics (Polish language) lesson is taking place. The teacher is introducing new material. You try very hard to understand it, but you do not understand any of it or only a very small part of the new subject. Please try to imagine yourself in the above situation. Please describe in detail what you do in such situation. Write down possibly the most accurate description of your behaviors and thoughts".

In the second situation of being called to answer questions, pupils were confronted with the following:

"You are in the following situation. A mathematics (Polish) teacher called on you to answer questions. You are well aware of the fact that you are not able to answer the teacher's question in a satisfactory manner because you do not know the material well and do not understand much of it. You care about a passing grade because the assessment of your answer will largely affect your overall grade for the mathematics (Polish) class. Close your eyes for a little while and imagine the above situation. Now describe what exactly you do in that situation. Please write down in details your behaviors and thoughts".

Gathered answers were classified as active strategies (e.g., asking a teacher to explain the issue again, asking colleagues or family members for help in understanding the issue, learning from a textbook by oneself) or passive strategies (acquiescence, looking into a teacher's eyes, pretending to take notes, avoiding the gist of a question, talking about everything that is known on a given issue).

According to the first study, the number and variability of employed strategies during a given class subject depends on the intellectual helplessness (measured by the Intellectual Helplessness Scale) in that school subject and on intrinsic motivation. The higher the intellectual helplessness for the Polish language lessons, the more passive strategies were used during both acquiring and recalling the material. On the contrary, pupils with the low level of helplessness in Polish employed a number of active strategies in order to gain understanding on unclear issues. Moreover, strong negative correlations between the level of intellectual helplessness and intrinsic motivation to acquire knowledge in both mathematics and Polish were found. In case of mathematics, the level of intrinsic motivation played the main role in determining a strategy for dealing with that school subject. The higher the level of intrinsic motivation, the more active strategies applied when introducing new material by a teacher and less passive strategies when recalling material.

The next study attempted to better understand the relationship between a faulty teaching style in the classroom (low scores of a given teacher on the Promotion of Understanding Scale), intellectual helplessness, and using passive or active strategies for dealing with difficult situations during Polish or mathematics lessons. A series of path analyses proved the mediating role of intellectual helplessness in the relationships between faulty teaching styles and employing survival (passive) or active strategies. It turns out that faulty teaching style promotes intellectual helplessness, which in turn leads to a number of passive strategies to deal with Polish and mathematics classes. In addition, the opposite model was found in regard to active strategies, but only in mathematics: faulty teaching style led to the intellectual helplessness, which blocked (negative correlation) using active strategies (e.g., asking questions).

To summarize, school pupils (and probably university students as well) develop a number of strategies for dealing with situations when nothing is understood during lessons or when answering questions regarding unclear issues. A lack of skill in promotion of understanding among teachers of a given school subject most probably leads to the intellectual helplessness among pupils, intrinsic motivation (pleasure of learning a given subject) disappears, and pupils (instead of trying to understand the material) focus on developing survival strategies which help them pass classes despite the lack of understanding the subject.

The role of intellectual helplessness as predictor of school achievement when considering the role of working memory functions and fluid intelligence

The aim of this section is to provide convincing empirical support for the claim that intellectual helplessness remains a significant predictor explaining differences in learning outcomes, even after we control for well-established cognitive factors which influence school achievement, i.e., fluid intelligence and working memory, along with an affective factor, math anxiety.

Fluid intelligence, working memory functions, and math anxiety as predictors of school achievement

Fluid intelligence (Spearman, 1914) as the fundamental ability to reason is on the first place among the key factors explaining the differences in learning and performing complex cognitive tasks (e.g., Deary, Strand, Smith, & Fernandes, 2007; Gray & Thompson, 2004; Jaeggi et al., 2010; Rohde & Thompson, 2007; te Nijenhuis, van Vianen, & van der Flier, 2007). Moreover, fluid intelligence is related to another factor that has been successfully introduced to educational psychology, namely working memory.

Working memory is the ability to maintain a small amount of information in highly accessible form and management that can be used in execution of demanding cognitive tasks (e.g., Cowan, 2014; Kane, Hambrick, & Conway, 2005; Oberauer, Wilhelm, Schulze, & Süß, 2005). Oberauer et al. (2005) proposed that working memory can be differentiated according to cognitive functions. On the functional facet, they distinguish three categories that together cover most of the functions attributed to working memory in the literature. The first category is simultaneous storage and processing, which is commonly used as the definition of working memory as a whole (e.g., Daneman & Carpenter, 1980; Kyllonen & Christal, 1990; Salthouse, 1991). The authors defined processing as the transformation of information or the derivation of new information, in contrast to cognitive activities that maintain the information as given. On the other hand, storage was defined as the retention of briefly presented new information over a period of time in which the information is no longer present. The second category of functions was labeled as the supervision processes. Supervision refers to the monitoring of ongoing cognitive processes and actions, the selective activation of relevant representations and procedures, and the suppression of irrelevant, distracting ones, most prominently featuring in Baddeley's notion of the central executive (Baddeley, 1986). The third category proposed by Oberauer and collaborators (2005) is the coordination of information elements into structures. The cognitive system constructs new relations, thereby establishing a mental structure that forms an essential basis for the required response.

Capacity and functions of working memory are strongly associated with the effectiveness of learning. Therefore, working memory is associated with mental processes of text comprehension and reading (e.g., Baddeley, 1986; Daneman & Carpenter, 1980; Perfetti, 1985), speech production (e.g., Peña & Tirre, 1992; Woltz, 1988), and arithmetic problem solving (Geary & Widaman, 1992). What is more, working memory capacity is negatively associated with math anxiety (Ashcraft & Kirk, 2001).

The math-anxiety literature across the past years attests to pervasive, long-term, damaging consequences of math anxiety (Hembree, 1990). There is accumulating empirical evidence that the performance of anxious individuals is more impaired by distracting stimuli than is that of non-anxious individuals (e.g., Ashcraft & Kirk, 2001; Hopko, Ashcraft, Gute, Ruggiero, & Lewis, 1998). For example, Ashcraft and Kirk (2001) showed that math anxiety disrupts working memory processing when a cognitive task involves arithmetic or math-related processes.

However, our longitudinal study (Sedek & McIntosh, 1998) demonstrated that although intellectual helplessness is strongly and positively correlated with the level of math anxiety, only intellectual helplessness was a significant predictor of subsequent school achievement for both math and Polish language. However, current research enables us to consider whether it still holds true when other important cognitive factors, such as fluid intelligence and working memory functions, are taken into account.

Linear structural modelling of the relation between predictors of school success

Our general prediction (Sedek et al., 2010/2011) is that intellectual helplessness remains a significant predictor of school achievement after controlling for the influence of fluid intelligence, math anxiety, and working memory. To test this prediction, we took two steps to construct an overall model of relations between these factors. In the first model, we tested the impact of two affective predictors – math anxiety and intellectual helplessness on mastery in math, including intellectual abilities in the model. In the second model, a mediating role of working memory was verified.

Children (10–12 years old) reported their intellectual helplessness and anxiety experienced during math classes; moreover, their fluid intelligence and working memory were assessed. Working memory was operationalized using two tasks corresponding to working memory functions: *storage and processing* (pattern transformation task, Oberauer, Süß, Schulze, Wilhelm, & Wittmann, 2000), and *supervision* (switching task, Oberauer et al., 2000). The level of academic achievement was the main dependent variable defined by math grades from the first and second school term. The relationships between predictors and mathematical achievement were tested in the structural equation modeling.[1]

In the first model, intellectual helplessness, math anxiety, and intellectual abilities served as predictors of achievement in mathematics (see Figure 4.1).

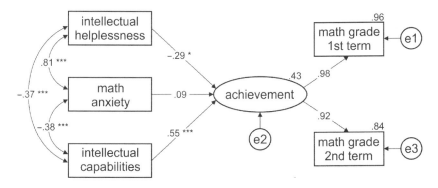

FIGURE 4.1   Model testing intellectual helplessness, intellectual capabilities, and math anxiety as predictors of math achievement.

As expected, intelligence had a substantial and positive influence on math achievement (β = .55). Intellectual helplessness and math anxiety were highly correlated with each other, suggesting that they are similar constructs; however, intellectual helplessness negatively predicted mathematical performance (β = −.29), ruling out math anxiety from the predictors significantly influencing school performance. Overall, the predictors accounted for 43% of the variance in math grades. In the second step, we verified whether the significant impact of intellectual helplessness and intelligence on school achievement is direct or rather mediated by cognitive capacities, represented by two working-memory functions. The latent construct of working memory was then entered into the first revised model in which mediated paths were added (see Figure 4.2).

This model fit the data well, and the three predictors accounted for 57% of the variance in math performance. Even with working memory in the model, intellectual helplessness was still negatively related to math performance (β = −.20). Working memory partially mediated the relationship between intelligence and school achievement on school performance (without mediator: β = .54, and with the mediator: β = .30).

To sum up, in this section we confronted the predictive value of intellectual helplessness with coronary factors determining school achievements. Intelligence directly and indirectly, through the mediation of working memory, influenced math grades. Most importantly, intellectual helplessness had a detrimental impact on math performance, even after controlling for other factors, especially math anxiety. Moreover, intellectual helplessness and math anxiety are constructs closely related

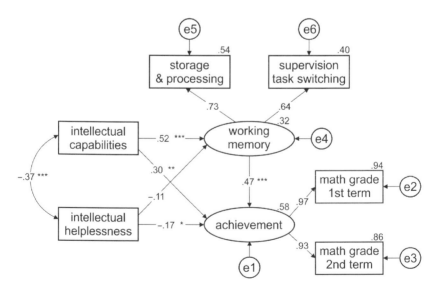

FIGURE 4.2 Model testing the mediating role of working memory functions on relations between IH, intelligence, and school achievement.

to each other. When both were entered into the model, intellectual helplessness was a better predictor of math grades than of math anxiety.

The lack of competence of teachers as the source of class intellectual helplessness

As has been already described earlier in this chapter, faulty teaching style of teachers contributes to the intellectual helplessness of students, which in turn blocks using active strategies for dealing with school situations. Therefore, one could say that since defective style of teaching underpins the intellectual helplessness experienced by pupils, then simply eliminating such faulty teaching style by a teacher in question should be a natural step. However, the real problem is not the incompetence of the teachers by itself (as it could be potentially corrected if one was aware of it), but rather the lack of recognizing the fact that they are incompetent. As Dunning, Johnson, Ehrlinger, and Kruger (2003) point out, people fail to recognize their own incompetence in knowledge and expertise, which is true in various intellectual and social domains. People tend to overestimate their expertise when lacking knowledge or abilities and believe that they are doing fine even when exactly the opposite holds true. Therefore, people who perform poorly are not only deprived of coping successfully with given issues, but also lack the expertise necessary to notice that their performance is poor. The source of such ignorance is the fact that oftentimes the very same skills that are needed to solve given tasks are also necessary for assessing one's own performance. Moreover, perceptions of performance are based partly on notions regarding one's own skills and these do not always overlap with reality, which leads to impaired judgments of one's own performance.

Ehrlinger, Johnson, Banner, Dunning, and Kruger (2008) conducted five studies that demonstrated poor performers being overly optimistic about their performance in a variety of settings, including real-life settings: assessing one's own performance on a challenging exam right after completing it (with participation of college students); assessing one's own performance on a debate tournament by college students; estimating one's performance regarding firearms safety completed by gun owners; assessing performance on Logical Reasoning Ability test by college students with the use of either monetary or social incentives. In all these cases, poorly performing individuals lacked the insight into their own incompetence, even in real-life settings and in the presence of incentives, to be accurate in regard to their own performance.

On a similar note, Sedek and associates (2010/2011) raised a question of how teachers and students assess the competences of teachers in transferring knowledge clearly and how it is connected to the feelings of intellectual helplessness among students. In the study students were asked to evaluate teachers' teaching styles while teachers were asked for self-evaluation. The Promotion of Understanding Scale was used for the assessment. Additionally, students evaluated their own level of intellectual helplessness related to each of the school subjects. The assessments of teachers' performance were aggregated and analyzed separately for each of the classes. All together, there were 14 assessments of teachers and 14 results describing the levels of helplessness in each of the classes for different school subjects.

Another factor considered in the study was the discrepancy between the teachers' self-assessments and the assessments of the teachers given by their students. The results showed that the intellectual helplessness of students correlated positively with the discrepancy between teachers' self-evaluations and students' evaluations of teachers. In other words, discrepancy between teachers' and students' evaluations of how clearly teachers explained the material increased together with the levels of intellectual helplessness among students (see Figure 4.3). An additional and possibly worrying result was that in each case teachers assessed their clarity of teaching higher than their students did, which showed that teachers regularly overestimated their teaching skills.

Summing it up, results show that when teachers are self-confident about their teaching but their students disagree, the intellectual helplessness among students is higher than in classes where students assess the clarity of teaching in a similar way as teachers assess themselves. In other words, highly incompetent teachers are also the ones who are least aware of their poor teaching style and produce highest levels of intellectual helplessness.

These results are compatible with the research by Ehrlinger and Dunning (2003). Students were asked to evaluate their own performance during the exam. The subjective assessments of their own performance differed significantly from the

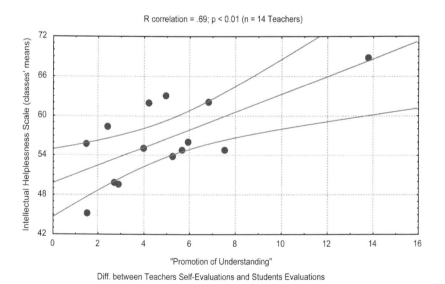

FIGURE 4.3 The regression line of relationship between promotion of understanding (differences between self-evaluations of teachers and mean evaluations of their pupils) and classes' means of intellectual helplessness. Bullet points represent the aggregated measures for a given teacher (difference) and level of intellectual helplessness in a given class.

objective results of the test. The most interesting result was that the weakest students displayed the highest discrepancy between the subjective and objective evaluation of the test results. On the other hand, the best students evaluated their performance as worse than it objectively was.

The above-presented studies show that people are consequently overconfident of their own work and performance, which may lead to more grave consequences; for example, it can stimulate feelings of helplessness in others or feelings of injustice when evaluating one's own work.

Interestingly, classical works of Dweck and associates on the sources of sex differences in helplessness among schoolchildren also indicated the role of teachers in developing inappropriate attributional styles after experiencing failure. Negative teacher evaluations of girls' performance were almost exclusively limited to lack of ability, while only about a half of boys' failures were attributed to intellectual aspects. What is more, teachers were more likely to evaluate boys' compared to girls' poor performance in terms of lack of motivation. Therefore, girls attributed their failures more to intellectual inadequacies than to lack of motivation and displayed learned helplessness in failure situations to a larger degree than boys did (Dweck, Davidson, Nelson, & Enna, 1978). Moreover, as noted by Diener and Dweck (1978, 1980), helpless children had the tendency to underestimate the number of their own successes and overestimate the number of failures. They also did not anticipate successes in the future and did not perceive them as demonstration of ability, but rather focused on the sources of failure.

Recent data (Yeager & Dweck, 2012) suggests that students who are taught that intellectual abilities can be developed, rather than that they are fixed, are more likely to display a higher level of school achievement, which again clearly points to the crucial role of teacher and teaching style.

Summary and future research questions

The main goal of this chapter was to present the history and new findings concerning intellectual helplessness in educational settings, which may be exemplified as the uncontrollability in the classroom. The idea of intellectual helplessness was derived from the more general cognitive exhaustion model of uncontrollability and depression formulated by Kofta and Sedek. The important step in operationalization of this construct was construction of the domain specific questionnaire IHS (Intellectual Helplessness Scale). In this chapter we showed several new empirical findings concerning the role of intellectual helplessness in school learning.

At the beginning we demonstrated that intellectual helplessness in high school (in the domain of mathematics) was grossly predicted by the episodes of helplessness training in primary school and experiences of cognitive demobilization, thereby proving close links between cognitive deficits caused by helplessness training in the lab and subject-specific intellectual helplessness during school learning.

Next we showed that high school students developed a rich battery of "survival strategies" for coping with situations of helplessness during school lessons. The interesting and to our knowledge completely unexplored research question is whether the early experience of acute uncontrollability during some school subjects and subsequent coping in the form of survival strategies during classes (like mindless talking and guessing, expressing completely random associations, etc.) might be an antecedent of further, eager acceptance of magical or conspiracy thinking in adulthood. Let's notice here that in order to give a knowledgeable and correct answer to questions concerning some specific topics in math, chemistry, or biology, well-established and specific knowledge structures are necessary. However, the survival strategy of "just expressing any associations you have with this topic" is universal and might be applied as a coping strategy against uncontrollability in any school subject. In similar vein, giving a knowledgeable and correct answer to specific topics regarding difficulties concerning for instance financial markets, global economy, poverty, or unemployment, demands deep and specialist knowledge specific to a given domain. The conspiracy thinking, for example, in the form of "conspiracy plot of Jews against our nation" is universal and might be applied convincingly to any of the above-mentioned issues.

In the next section we presented that when additional cognitive (functions of working memory, fluid intelligence – Raven Scale) and emotional (math anxiety) mechanisms were taken into account and partialled out, the intellectual helplessness was still a reliable and significant predictor of educational achievement. Interestingly, in the world's biggest educational evaluation program assessing student educational achievement – PISA 2012 Program for International Student Assessment (Organization for Economic Cooperation and Development, 2014) – math anxiety was defined not only by the four typical items concerning emotional and tension aspects, such as "I get very tense when I have to do mathematical homework" or "I worry that I will get poor grades in mathematics", but also by the item *"I feel helpless when doing mathematics problems"*, which directly resembles item from our Intellectual Helplessness Scale. According to the presented research, helplessness in the classroom is a distinctive (although correlated) phenomenon from math anxiety. Moreover, intellectual helplessness is a better predictor of achievement than math anxiety, and it would be very interesting to make appropriate re-analyses of publicly available PISA data files and reports.

Finally, the last section has the most social implications of all. At the beginning of the work with the intellectual helplessness construct, it was demonstrated that the role of teaching style, especially lack of skill in promotion of understanding, is the fundamental antecedent for the development of intellectual helplessness symptoms among students. Our research showed clearly that regarding incompetent teachers who lack elementary skills in promoting understanding during class learning: (a) they are completely unaware that they are incompetent; (b) the higher the disparity between evaluation of teachers and evaluation of their students as concern the clarity of teaching, the higher the level of intellectual helplessness among their students. We demonstrated it as the exemplification of a more general and quite well-confirmed social phenomenon that people who are unskilled in a given profession or knowledge domain are completely unaware of this fact.

Ehrlinger et al. (2008), at the beginning of their recent paper summarizing findings on the topic, cited Bertrand Russell: "One of the painful things of our time is that those who feel certainty are stupid, and those with any imagination and understanding are filled with doubt and indecision". When we tried to make more general and social implications for our findings, we have been struck with how much Russell's observation is still valid nowadays, especially in the domain of social life and politics. Let us notice that the crucial mechanism that is responsible for the development of intellectual helplessness according to our theoretical model, namely the long lasting cognitive effort which does not yield cognitive gain, may not only occur when students try to understand novel and difficult material during school lessons but may be also prevalent when citizens try to understand complex economical and political problems. Hence, we address the new and potentially fruitful research questions of whether the populist solutions offered by politicians and social movement leaders (often lacking self-insight of their own incompetence) might be closely related to the intellectual helplessness in the domain of economy and global politics among their supporters.

Funding

This work was supported by the National Science Centre, Poland, under Grant 2015/17/B/HS6/04185, awarded to Grzegorz Sedek.

Note

1 Both models were evaluated by the value of the chi-square, the normed fit index (Bentler & Bonett, 1980), and the root mean squared error of approximation (Browne & Cudeck, 1993).

References

Ashcraft, M. H., & Kirk, E. P. (2001). The relationships among working memory, math anxiety, and performance. *Journal of Experimental Psychology: General, 130*, 224–237.

Baddeley, A. D. (1986). *Working memory*. Oxford: Oxford University Press.

Bentler, P. M., & Bonett, D. G. (1980). Significance tests and goodness-of-fit in the analysis of covariance structures. *Psychological Bulletin, 88*, 588–606.

Browne, M. W., & Cudeck, R. (1993). Alternative ways of assessing model fit. In K. A. Bollen, & J. S. Long (Eds.), *Testing structural equation models* (pp. 136–162). Beverly Hills, CA: Sage.

Cowan, N. (2014). Working memory underpins cognitive development, learning, and education. *Educational Psychology Review, 26*(2), 197–223.

Daneman, M., & Carpenter, P. A. (1980). Individual differences in working memory and reading. *Journal of Verbal Learning and Verbal Behavior, 19*, 450–466.

Deary, I. J., Strand, S., Smith, P., & Fernandes, C. (2007). Intelligence and educational achievement. *Intelligence, 35*(1), 13–21.

Diener, C. I., & Dweck, C. S. (1978). An analysis of learned helplessness: Continuous changes in performance, strategy, and achievement cognitions following failure. *Journal of Personality and Social Psychology, 36*, 451–462.

Diener, C. I., & Dweck, C. S. (1980). An analysis of learned helplessness: II. The processing of success. *Journal of Personality and Social Psychology, 39*, 940–952.

Dunning, D., Johnson, K., Ehrlinger, J., & Kruger, J. (2003). Why people fail to recognize their own incompetence. *Current Directions in Psychological Science, 12*(3), 83–87.

Dweck, C. S., Davidson, W., Nelson, S., & Enna, B. (1978). Sex differences in learned helplessness: II. The contingencies of evaluative feedback in the classroom and III. An experimental analysis. *Developmental Psychology, 14*(3), 268–276.

Ehrlinger, J., & Dunning, J. (2003). How chronic self-views influence (and potentially mislead) estimates of performance. *Journal of Personality and Social Psychology, 84*(1), 5–17.

Ehrlinger, J., Johnson, K., Banner, M., Dunning, D., & Kruger, J. (2008). Why the unskilled are unaware: Further explorations of (absent) self-insight among the incompetent. *Organizational Behavior and Human Decision Processes, 105*, 98–121.

Geary, D. C., & Widaman, K. F. (1992). Numerical cognition: On the convergence of componential and psychometric models. *Intelligence, 16*, 47–80.

Gray, J. R., & Thompson, P. M. (2004). Neurobiology of intelligence: science and ethics. *Nature Reviews. Neuroscience, 5*(6), 471–482.

Hembree, R. (1990). The nature, effects, and relief of mathematics anxiety. *Journal for Research in Mathematics Education, 21*, 33–46.

Hopko, D. R., Ashcraft, M. H., Gute, J., Ruggiero, K. J., & Lewis, C. (1998). Mathematics anxiety and working memory: Support for the existence of a deficient inhibition mechanism. *Journal of Anxiety Disorders, 12*, 343–355.

Jaeggi, S. M., Studer-Luethi, B., Buschkuehl, M., Su, Y.-F., Jonides, J., & Perrig, W. J. (2010). The relationship between n-back performance and matrix reasoning – implications for training and transfer. *Intelligence, 38*(6), 625–635.

Kane, M., Hambrick, D., & Conway, A. (2005). Working memory capacity and fluid intelligence are strongly related constructs: Comment on Ackerman, Beier, and Boyle (2005). *Psychological Bulletin, 131*(1), 66–71.

Kofta, M., & Sedek, G. (1989). Repeated failure: A source of helplessness, or a factor irrelevant to its emergence? *Journal of Experimental Psychology: General, 118*, 3–12.

Kofta, M., & Sedek, G. (1998). Uncontrollability as a source of cognitive exhaustion: Implications for helplessness and depression. In M. Kofta, G. Weary, & G. Sedek (Eds.), *Personal control in action: Cognitive and motivational mechanisms* (pp. 391–418). New York: Plenum Press.

Kofta, M., & Sedek, G. (1999). Uncontrollability as irreducible uncertainty. *European Journal of Social Psychology, 29*, 577–590.

Kyllonen, P. C., & Christal, R. E. (1990). Reasoning ability is (little more than) working-memory capacity? *Intelligence, 14*, 389–433.

Oberauer, K., Süß, H. M., Schulze, R., Wilhelm, O., & Wittmann, W. W. (2000). Working memory capacity facets of a cognitive ability construct. *Personality and Individual Differences, 29*, 1017–1045.

Oberauer, K., Wilhelm, O., Schulze, R., & Süß, H. M. (2005). Working Memory and Intelligence: Their correlation and their relation: Comment on Ackerman, Beier and Boyle (2005). *Psychological Bulletin, 131*, 61–65.

Organization for Economic Cooperation and Development (OECD). (2014). *PISA 2012 technical report*. Paris: Author.

Peña, M. C., & Tirre, W. C. (1992). Cognitive factors involved in the initial stage of programming skill acquisition. *Learning and Individual Differences, 4*(4), 311–334.

Perfetti, C. A. (1985). *Reading ability*. New York: Oxford University Press.

Rohde, T. E., & Thompson, L. A. (2007). Predicting academic achievement with cognitive ability. *Intelligence, 35*, 83–92.

Salthouse, T. A. (1991). Mediation of adult age differences in cognition by reductions in working memory and speed of processing. *Psychological Science, 2*, 179–183.

Schoenfeld, A. H. (1988). When good teaching leads to bad results: The disasters of "well taught" mathematics courses. *Educational Psychologist, 23*(2), 145.

Sedek, G. (1995). *Bezradność intelektualna w szkole.* [Intellectual helplessness at school.] Warszawa: IP PAN.

Sedek, G., Brzezicka, A., & von Hecker, U. (2010). The unique cognitive limitation in subclinical depression: The impairment of mental model construction. In A. Gruszka, G. Matthews, & B. Szymura (Eds.), *Handbook of individual differences in cognition: Attention, memory, and executive control* (pp. 335–352). New York, NY: Springer Science + Business Media.

Sedek, G., & Kofta, M. (1990). When cognitive exertion does not yield cognitive gain: Toward an informational explanation of learned helplessness. *Journal of Personality and Social Psychology, 58*, 729–743.

Sedek, G., & Kofta, M. (1992). Cognitive helplessness in the classroom: A preliminary report. Unpublished manuscript. University of Warsaw, Department of Psychology.

Sedek, G., Kofta, M., & Tyszka, T. (1993). Effects of uncontrollability on subsequent decision making: Testing the cognitive exhaustion hypothesis. *Journal of Personality and Social Psychology, 65*, 1270–1281.

Sedek, G., Krejtz, I., & Szymaszek, A. (2010/2011). *Intellectual helplessness and school learning.* Series of papers presented during REMICS (Research Methods in Cognitive Studies). Intensive Erasmus Programme, Zakopane, Poland.

Sedek, G., & McIntosh, D. N. (1998). Intellectual helplessness: Domain specificity, teaching styles, and school achievement. In M. Kofta, G. Weary, & G. Sedek (Eds.), *Personal control in action: Cognitive and motivational mechanisms* (pp. 391–418). New York: Plenum Press.

Spearman, C. (1914). The theory of two factors. *Psychological Review, 21*, 101–115.

te Nijenhuis, J., van Vianen, A. E. M., & van der Flier, H. (2007). Score gains on g-loaded tests: No g. *Intelligence, 35*, 283–300.

von Hecker, U., McIntosh, D. N., & Sedek, G. (2015). Mental model construction, not just memory, is a central component of cognitive change in psychotherapy. *Behavioral and Brain Sciences, 38*, e28.

von Hecker, U., & Sedek, G. (1999). Uncontrollability, depression, and the construction of mental models. *Journal of Personality and Social Psychology, 77*, 833–850.

von Hecker, U., Sedek, G., & Brzezicka, A. (2013). Impairments in mental model construction and benefits of defocused attention: Distinctive facets of subclinical depression. *European Psychologist, 18*(1), 35–46.

Woltz, D. J. (1988). An investigation of the role of working memory in procedural skill acquisition. *Journal of Experimental Psychology: General, 117*, 319–331.

Yeager, D. S., & Dweck, C. S. (2012). Mindsets that promote resilience: When students believe that personal characteristics can be developed. *Educational Psychologist, 47*(4), 302–314.

PART 2

Socially grounded responses to perceived lack of control

From compensation to active coping

5

COMPENSATORY CONTROL THEORY AND THE PSYCHOLOGICAL IMPORTANCE OF PERCEIVING ORDER

Bastiaan T. Rutjens and Aaron C. Kay

The writing of this chapter was supported by an AXA Research Fund grant awarded to Bastiaan T. Rutjens.
Contact: bastiaan.rutjens@gmail.com

Control can be defined as the individual's perceived impact on events and the ability to bring the environment in line with individual wishes and motives. Experiencing a sense of control over life's outcomes and one's physical and social environment is considered a basic human need with far-reaching consequences for psychological as well as physical well-being. As a result, lacking desired levels of control has been found to be generally experienced as aversive (e.g., Heckhausen & Schulz, 1995; Langer & Rodin, 1976; Maier & Seligman, 1976; Moulding & Kyrios, 2006; Sedek & Kofta, 1990; Skinner, 1996; Thompson & Spacapan, 1991). Given that perceived control is such an important motivation for adaptive and healthy functioning, an obvious question arises: how do people cope with inevitably fluctuating levels of personal control in their daily lives? Indeed, in the last five years or so we have seen a rapid increase in the amount of research aimed at documenting and explaining the various ways in which people respond to instances of lowered personal control. In this chapter, we review Compensatory Control Theory (CCT; Kay et al., 2008), which was developed to help answer this question, as well as research that is directly or indirectly inspired by its central tenets.

The origins of CCT

CCT was formulated to help provide an answer to the following question: Assuming that the need for control is pivotal, how do people maintain a belief in control when they face all of the events in their daily lives that challenge it? It is obvious that it is oftentimes not possible to maintain perceptions of control, either because of external causes (e.g., social developments such as financial crises or terrorist threats) or because of personal causes (e.g., personal situations or events such as getting fired over poor performance or a relationship breakup). Moreover, although control is an important motivation, instances do occur in which people would rather leave responsibility to others (e.g., to the pilot when airborne, to the surgeon when deciding on the viability of an operation; see also Burger, 1989). This brings us to the question of how people cope with situations in which the fundamental motive to perceive personal control is threatened. What do people do when they encounter situations in which personal control is either *threatened* or *undesired*?

A seminal paper by Rothbaum et al. (1982), which forms one of the pillars that CCT builds on, posits a dual-process model of perceived control. That model outlined four *secondary control* strategies people may employ when they lack *primary* (or personal) control. While primary control refers to the person's ability to bring the environment in line with the self, secondary control can be defined as an attempt to bring the self in line with the environment. Two of the secondary control strategies that have been most influential are illusory control and vicarious control. Illusory control (Langer, 1975) refers to the tendency to attribute chance to skill or ability; an example is the erroneous belief that a powerful throw of the dice leads to a higher roll (Plous, 1993). Another example is that people are more reluctant to exchange lottery tickets that they purchased themselves, because they somehow feel that the act of choosing one's own ticket influences lottery outcomes (Langer, 1975; Thompson, 2004). Indeed, many manifestations of superstitious behavior and magical thinking – which are often sparked by situations of low control and uncertainty – are driven by illusions of control (Malinowski, 1979; Matute, 1994; Matute et al., 2010; Vyse, 1997). Vicarious control, on the other hand, refers to aligning oneself with a powerful other agent, such as a powerful ingroup, a political party, or a controlling deity. An example of vicarious control constitutes praying to God in order to obtain or prevent a certain outcome (Rothbaum et al., 1982). Below we briefly touch upon how we may view the concepts of illusory and vicarious control through the lens of CCT and explain how CCT differs from the aforementioned dual-process approach to control.

Regarding dual-process models of control, there are different views on the extent to which primary control is to be preferred over secondary control (Heckhausen & Schulz, 1995), and some theorists even argue that secondary control cannot be equated with control in the first place (but should rather be seen as a form of *accommodation* to the uncontrollable context; Skinner, 1996). CCT, however, argues that primary (i.e., personal) and compensatory control are *functionally equivalent* and therefore substitutable. Thus, although the concept of compensatory control might at first glance seem closely related to the concept of vicarious control, they are different models that offer different predictions: Vicarious control refers to the acknowledgment that there is a powerful external agent (e.g., God, a political party, a powerful ingroup) with which one can align the self in order to (a) share in their power and (b) make certain that particular goals are met that the individual by itself cannot accomplish (Fritsche, Jonas, & Fankhänel, 2008), and/or (c) appeal to the higher power to act on the self's behalf, for example via prayer. Compensatory control on the other hand refers to merely endorsing faith in a powerful other and thus affirming the belief that "things are under control" rather than random (see Kay et al., 2008, p. 32). Sometimes, these two predictions are difficult to distinguish from another. For example, consistent with both models, several lines of research have shown that a threat to personal control leads to the endorsement of such external systems, both secular and religious, that are capable of controlling the social world. This may result in, for example, a tendency to bolster a strong government or defend the legitimacy of the social system (i.e., system justification; Jost, Glaser, Kruglanski, & Sulloway, 2003) and an enhanced belief in a controlling deity (Kay et al., 2008, 2010). Though it might be tricky in cases such as these to determine whether an instance of increased religious or political faith following a control threat is indicative of compensatory control processes, secondary control processes, or some combination of both, the empirical distinction between these processes will be made more clear in subsequent sections, especially those addressing "non-agentic" sources of compensatory control.

Religion provides an especially potent source of compensatory control, since belief in God's control is relatively infallible and non-falsifiable. Unfalsifiable beliefs are particularly well-suited to satiate psychological needs related to existential concerns and motivations (Friesen, Campbell, & Kay, 2015). Another reason that religion is a powerful source of compensatory control is that God is seen by many believers as omnipotent and therefore as capable of controlling everything; that is, there is literally no event that a true believer could not attribute to God's will, as opposed to randomness or chance. Indeed, long before CCT was introduced, Spilka et al. (1985) and Rothbaum et al. (1982) argued that an important psychological function of religious belief is that it effectuates the need for control. However, it is important to distinguish this early idea of God as a source of vicarious control (which is more sensitive to the valence of a certain event; what use is God *as a source of control* when something bad happens to us?) from the notion posited by CCT that God is in control regardless of what happens, which facilitates perceptions of the world as a place that is orderly and under control. Though this latter belief cannot, like vicarious control, offer the individual an indirect means (e.g., prayer and appeals) by which they can exert control over the environment, it is still presumed to be control-restoring. A world rife with order and structure, rather than randomness and chaos, affords predictability and the basic set of epistemic beliefs – e.g., contingencies between actions and outcomes – needed to afford efficacious action (Landau, Whitson, & Kay, 2015). Supporting this notion of the functional basis of perceiving structure in the world, recent work has shown that belief in a controlling God can both help and hinder the detection of structure, depending on whether God's intervention follows a systematic logic or is unpredictable (Kay, Landau, & Khenfer, & Keefer, under review). In one illustrative study, for example, it was observed that amongst those who view God's control as characterized by predictable and understandable rules, higher belief in God was associated with increased efficacy and self-regulatory confidence, but amongst those who view God's control as "mysterious", the reverse relationship was found: higher belief in God was associated with decreased efficacy and self-regulatory confidence.

In short, CCT posits that a key motive is to perceive the world in which one lives as orderly; that is, a structured, predictable, and sensible place in which things do not just happen haphazardly. Compensatory control, such as the endorsement of external religious and sociopolitical systems, does therefore not necessarily need to encompass an attempt to bolster agency by (indirectly or vicariously) regaining personal control through external systems that one can either appeal to or align with. While not disputing this does indeed happen, CCT instead emphasizes the utility of external agents of control in re-affirming epistemic beliefs in the non-randomness of the world, which beliefs in personal control can then be built upon (more on this in a later section).

Order as a basic motive

As described in the above paragraphs, CCT crucially diverges from previous theories on control motivation by emphasizing order as a basic motivation that can underlie direct and indirect attempts to obtain control. Maintaining a belief in order and non-randomness in the environment can be achieved either through exerting personal control or through the endorsement of external systems of control (i.e., compensatory control), such as God or government. CCT proposes that personal control and compensatory control function in a hydraulic fashion as different routes to order.[1] Thus, if one of these perceptions is threatened, increasing faith in the other can be an effective means of coping, and vice versa (see also Kay et al., 2010).

The notion that perceiving order and structure in the world is a powerful human motivation is common in the history of psychology (Kay, Landau, & Sullivan, 2015). People want to believe that the world and their social environments are orderly, predictable, and make sense (Janoff-Bulman, 1992; Krantz, 1998; Kruglanski & Webster, 1996; Landau et al., 2004; Lerner, 1980; Pittman, 1998). The naturally occurring tendency to impose structure on and derive patterns from the things that surround us has been argued to stem from the evolutionary error-management motives to protect oneself from making what is often referred to as type II errors (e.g., overlooking a pattern, resulting in being devoured by a sabretooth tiger; Foster & Kokko, 2009; see also Haselton & Buss, 2000). It has even been suggested that this innate preference for order over disorder extends beyond humans and is found in animals such as chickens (Chiandetti & Vallortigara, 2011).

Initially, CCT provided two types of evidence for the notion that perceptions of control can sometimes be a means to an end (order). The first is by focusing on the aforementioned substitutability of different sources of personal and external control. Not only do fluctuations in personal control alter the belief in and defense of external sources of control (e.g., God, government) and vice versa, but affirming (threatening) one source of external control (e.g., God) subsequently impacts the motivated belief in and defense of other sources of external control (e.g., government). This observation helps us understand the impact of fluctuations in the perceived strength of governmental systems. For example, one study looked at the impact of elections in Malaysia and found that the elections (which constitute a temporal threat to governmental stability) had an effect on belief in God among the Malaysian population. Indeed, belief in God increased as a result of the destabilizing effects of the election, and – pivotally – was restored to baseline after the elections (when governmental stability was restored; Kay et al., 2010, Study 3).

Other evidence for the notion that order is the central motive constituted an experiment in which, rather than threatening or affirming a particular source of control, order perceptions were directly lowered by means of a randomness prime (Kay, Moscovitch, & Laurin, 2010). Employing the scrambled sentences method (Srull & Wyer, 1979) in order to supraliminally prime randomness, it was found that belief in a controlling God was enhanced as a result of such a direct threat to order perceptions. In a similar vein, Meijers and Rutjens (2014) have shown that the same randomness primes increased the motivation to exert personal control. Related to these findings, Whitson and Galinsky (2008) focused on order perceptions as outcome variables. They offer a number of demonstrations of the effect of control threats on preferences for order and structure, including illusory pattern perception, conspiratorial thinking, and personal need for structure. In a related vein, work by Cutright (2011) has shown that control threat leads to preference for consumer products that offer structure (for example through clearly bounded logos or design).

More recently, Rutjens and colleagues (2010, 2013) followed up on the Whitson and Galinsky (2008) findings that compensatory control processes can unfold without any external source of control that is capable of acting on the individual's behalf (see also Cutright, 2011). Based on the central tenet of CCT that control is a means to establish perceptions of order, the reasoning in this line of work was as follows: If order is basic, then affirmations of order that do not involve external agents of control should suffice as compensation for threats to control and order. In a first test of this idea, Rutjens, van der Pligt, and van Harreveld (2010) gauged the effects of control threat on the endorsement of different views on the origins of life, particularly evolutionary theory and intelligent design. It was hypothesized that a threat to personal control would result in an increased preference for a view that stresses belief in an external source of control (a controlling deity), but only when the alternative view did not provide a notion of an orderly world. This is exactly what was found: control threat enhanced preferences for intelligent design (an external agent controls outcomes) only when the alternative option was evolutionary theory framed in terms of unpredictable and unstructured processes. However, when evolutionary theory was framed in terms of an orderly and structured process (Conway-Morris, 2005), this effect disappeared. Thus, an increased preference for views that provide an orderly perspective on the origins of life was observed, regardless of whether or not a tangible agent (in this case, God) was involved in the process.

A second test of this idea was conducted a few years later in a line of research focusing on scientific theory preferences (Rutjens, van Harreveld, van der Pligt, Kreemers, & Noordewier, 2013). Certain scientific theories might be better equipped to impose order on the world than others. Stage theories are a good example, since these describe certain phenomena or processes as occurring in a predictable series of discontinuous steps, and as such offer a more orderly and predictable account of human and societal development. By contrast, non-stage theories such as continuum theories generally describe similar phenomena or processes in terms of gradual transitions without clear disruptions or discernable steps. An initial study showed that people rate different stage theories as more ordered and predictable (while less credible) than their continuum counterparts. In the subsequent series of studies, participants were asked to indicate their preference for stage versus continuum theories across a number of domains (moral development, grief, Alzheimer's disease). It was found that a threat to personal control enhanced preference for stage theories, and that a motivated search for order underlies these preference shifts. More specifically, in one study it was observed that illusory pattern perception (see Whitson & Galinsky, 2008) mediated the effects of control threat on stage theory preference. Here, we see how people compensate for a temporary reduction in personal control by seeking order in the environment without any reference to external agency.

A third and related test of the idea that maintaining perceptions of an orderly world is primary pertains to work on preferences for hierarchy in organizations (Friesen, Kay, Eibach, & Galinsky, 2014). Compared to equality, hierarchy is seen as providing more organizational order and guidance. Similar to the previously described findings on the ordered nature of stage theories, an initial study revealed that people view hierarchy as more ordered and less chaotic (though less fair) than equality. Subsequently, it was found across several studies that threats to personal control triggered an increase in perceptions of hierarchy in social situations as well as an increase in preferences for hierarchy in workplace contexts. Hierarchies were shown to be appealing specifically because they provide order. The effects were moderated by need for structure and also reversed if a manipulation was included that described hierarchy as actually inserting randomness and disorder into the system. What's more, these effects were obtained independent of whether people assumed they would be at the top or bottom of the hierarchy. The latter finding tells us that people may sometimes seek out order at a certain cost; despite remaining at the bottom of the hierarchy (and despite viewing hierarchy as less fair than equality), those low in personal control still prefer to exist in a structured environment, even if it affords them little power and status. A similar cost was observed in the research on stage theory preference described before, where people whose control was threatened preferred the orderly view on disease progression, despite this view being more pessimistic than its less orderly counterpart (and despite rating stage theories as less credible than continuum theories). Other examples, whereby embracing order comes at a cost, include demonstrations that threats to personal control increase affirmation of negatively valenced order, such as increased conspiracy theory endorsement (Whitson & Galinsky, 2008) and increased belief in the existence of powerful, nefarious enemies and malevolent forces (Rotschild, Landau, Sullivan, & Keefer, 2012; Sullivan, Landau, & Rotschild, 2010). Though none of these promise positive outcomes, they all offer means of explaining (negative) events as non-random, and thereby can serve as effective means of compensatory control.

What the above lines of research show is that people seem to be relatively flexible in finding compensation for threats to control and order. While CCT initially focused on compensatory efforts characterized by (external) agency ("compensatory control"), subsequent research has broadened the scope of compensatory options by focusing more on order-providing theories and worldviews that do not involve agency. Interestingly, these non-agentic compensatory options entail a search for interpretations of the environment that provide order, yet these do not need to be related to the context in which control is reduced. In these cases, a process which has been labelled "nonspecific structure affirmation" takes place (Landau, Whitson, & Kay, 2015). This notion allows for a set of theoretical predictions that further address the notion that, indeed, order can be seen as the primary motive underlying compensatory control effects. First, as mentioned above, when control is threatened, people will be motivated to seek out interpretations of the environment that are unrelated to the context in which they perceive a lack of control. Second, such interpretations can be independent of agency beliefs. Third, such interpretations may arise at the cost of other motivations related to well-being (in the broadest sense) and might otherwise be considered aversive. We have described some of the evidence for these predictions in the current paragraph, reviewing work on illusory pattern perception, on preferences for bounded consumer products, scientific stage theories, and hierarchies, as well as on beliefs related to conspiracies and enemies. As a result, CCT has evolved into a broader motivational theory aimed at understanding the interchangeable ways in which people protect their epistemic understandings of the world as orderly and predictable, and the ways in which this can facilitate (and sometimes hinder) motivation (Landau et al., 2015). We explore this latter issue in more detail in the next section.

The boons and banes of perceiving order

Recently, there has not only been an increase in work on compensatory order (or "nonspecific structure affirmation"; Landau et al., 2015) as an outcome variable, but also an intensification of research gauging the effects of exposing individuals to orderly versus disorderly stimuli and environments. If CCT processes are truly adaptive, then the outcome of imbuing the world with order should be functional and facilitative of personal agency. An orderly environment is more easily navigable than a disorderly one, mainly because contingencies between action and outcome are more easily perceived. In other words, when the environment consists of a range of predictabilities, people can quite easily determine what the effects of a certain action will be and as such predict the (probability of the) consequences of that particular action (see Landau et al., 2015). It is much harder to predict these probabilities when the environment is disorderly. Thus, perceiving order facilitates commitment to a functional course of action (Harmon-Jones, Amodio, & Harmon-Jones, 2009) and leads to (long-term) goal pursuit and goal-directed action.

Building on this notion, a recent line of work focused on the functional value of perceiving order in the world (Kay et al., 2014). In these studies, the effects of order (or *structure*) affirmations on goal pursuit were assessed. Employing different ways to manipulate order perceptions, for example by utilizing an essay describing nature in terms of orderly (versus neutral or random) processes, it was consistently found that exposure to order increased goal-directed motivation in domains unrelated to the manipulations. More specifically, affirming order increased the motivation to plan and pursue personally important long-term goals (e.g., related to careers or relationships). These findings make sense when considering the aforementioned notion that an orderly, structured world is also an easily navigable one in which contingencies between actions and outcomes can be expected and observed. Conversely, long-term goal planning might seem futile in a haphazard world in which such action-outcome contingencies are not quite as clear. A recent study provided the most direct evidence to date for this notion, by showing that an affirmation of science as a source of order and predictability not only increases perceptions of the world as orderly, but also heightened perceptions of personal control. Moreover, the effect of affirmed belief in science on personal control was fully mediated by the increased orderly world perceptions (Rutjens, unpublished study, 2015).

Although perceiving order thus has obvious psychological advantages, there may also be instances when order affirmations backfire or demotivate people to exert personal action, especially when these order affirmations involve a belief in specific systems solving something for us (Meijers & Rutjens, 2014; see also Shepherd & Kay, 2012). Meijers and Rutjens (2014) explored this idea within the context of environmental behavior and belief in scientific progress. What they found was that exposing participants to a text which strongly affirmed the potency of science to advance and come up with potential solutions to pressing problems such as climate change actually decreased the motivation to engage in personal action. Crucially, affirming scientific progress was shown to increase order perceptions, which in turn affected personal motivation. Similarly, directly priming order (versus randomness) decreased personal motivation to the same extent. These results suggest that perceiving the world as orderly and under control decreases the motivation to engage in personal action. The motivation to perceive order is met, and so the need to draw (exaggerated) perceptions of personal control from one's actions in the environment is reduced. Note that this finding converges with the study mentioned above where it was found that a similar affirmation of science heightened perceptions of order as well as personal control. When personal control perceptions are heightened (through perceptions of order) there is no motivational pressure[2] to *further enhance* (or exaggerate) perceptions of personal control through action. Similar findings have been reported by Laurin, Kay, and Fitzsimons (2012), who found that reminding people of a controlling God decreased their willingness to expend effort to pursue long-term goals, and by Laurin, Shariff, Henrich, and Kay (2012), who showed that those who believe in intervening and controlling deities rely less on earthly punishment.

The above research findings suggest that perceiving the world as sufficiently orderly can both help and hinder the motivation to engage in personal action. One variable that might determine the direction of the effects on personal action pertains to the extent to which people feel their own actions can exert any effects at all. An orderly world that is governed entirely – or even predetermined – by an intervening God might reduce people's faith in their own actions sorting any impact at all (Kay et al., 2014). Likewise, a reduced sense of urgency that might be triggered by the notion that things are already taken care of might reduce people's motivation to expend any effort (Meijers & Rutjens, 2014). Related to this, people might sometimes wish to "outsource" responsibility to an external agent of system (e.g., in the case of punishing transgressors, see Laurin, Shariff, Kay, & Henrich, 2012), perhaps to conserve effort or because they feel they are not up to the task (see also the examples discussed by Burger, 1989, e.g., the pilot flying an airplane rather than oneself). Finally, a recent paper (Kay et al., under review) provides evidence for an important moderator that helps understand when belief in a controlling God facilitates or impairs the motivation to engage in personal action: predictability. That is, when relying on an external agent to control outcomes, the extent to which the agent's interventions are presumed to follow predictable and systematic rules determines whether people feel efficacious enough to engage in personal action. An agent that controls outcomes in ways we cannot fathom ("God works in mysterious ways") decreases personal action, while an agent that follows systematic rules facilitates order and as a consequence strengthens people's perceptions of personal control. It is a good possibility that one of the reasons that participants in the Meijers and Rutjens (2014) studies, described a little earlier, were less inclined to engage in personal action after reading about science's potential to solve environmental problems was that they did not feel they understood exactly *how* science would help combat these problems. In other words, they might have felt that science too works in mysterious ways.

In sum, whether affirming order perceptions helps or hinders the expenditure of desired actions and behaviors likely depends on a host of potential moderators: perceptions of external agency and particularly the predictable nature of those external agents' actions, the perceived impact of one's own actions, and the willingness (and perceived capability) to engage in (a particular) personal action.

Related work and future directions

In the previous paragraph we described a number of recent strands of research investigating the boons and banes of perceiving order. Sometimes perceiving order facilitates motivated action and sometimes it does not. Taking that research one step further, different programs of research that are relevant but not directly related to

CCT reveal the potentially more detrimental or undesired consequences of perceiving order. We will briefly discuss two.

First, recent work has shown that perceptions of external control (i.e., God) in the form of reminding people of God increases risk taking (Chan, Tong, & Tan, 2014; Kupor, Laurin, & Levav, 2015). In a similar vein, enhanced perceptions of personal control also drive risk taking (Kouchaki, Oveis, & Gino, 2014). In all these cases, people feel safe and secure, confident, and protected enough to take "a leap of faith" (Chan et al., 2014), and so they consequentially engage in risky behaviors more often. It is likely that an important moderator here is whether people believe that the external source of control is benign and cares about their well-being. Put differently, merely believing that an external agent (e.g., God, government) provides order is not sufficient to increase risk; in an orderly and just world the individual might still be punished for taking risks. Rather, people must either believe that they themselves can control outcomes and thus feel less vulnerable (i.e., God provides them with personal control; Chan et al., 2014) or that an external agent controls outcomes (i.e., God cares about them and provides protection; Kupor et al., 2015).

Second, a recent paper discusses an intriguing experiment in which it is shown that a radically predictable and structured situation can even trigger the tendency to engage in self-inflicted pain stimulation. More specifically, participants in this study were asked to sit in a room by themselves with nothing to do. Strikingly, 67% of the male and 25% of the female participants voluntarily exposed themselves to negative stimuli (i.e., administered electric shocks to themselves; Wilson et al., 2014). Sitting alone with nothing to do was apparently aversive enough that it drove a substantial number of participants to self-administer electric shocks. This finding can be linked to the literature on boredom, which generally tends to define boredom as an aversive affective state characterized by a lack of challenge and oftentimes by a lack of meaning (e.g., Bench & Lench, 2013; Van Tilburg & Igou, 2012). Arguably, boredom can be labelled as a monotonous state, characterized by a lack of simulation and relatively high levels of order and predictability. Indeed, a recent perspective argues how highly predictable states (e.g., certain instances of routine and boredom) reflect an "order overdose" (Rutjens, van Harreveld, & Cunningham, in preparation). Here, several experiments show that manipulations aimed to induce such a state of order overdose (e.g., boredom, undesirable routine) lead to a preference for unpredictability and, consequentially, to increased risk taking. Thus, if we view boredom and highly predictable routine as experiences characterized by overly high levels of perceived order, we can interpret the findings described above as at least partially reflecting the motivational consequences of order perceptions.

The research reviewed in the second part of this chapter prompts us to believe that there are many exciting future directions for research on compensatory control and the importance of perceiving order in our natural and social environments. We are gradually starting to uncover how, when, and why perceptions of external control and perceptions of order and structure impact personal action as well as motivation more generally (e.g., Fennis & Wiebenga, 2015; Kay et al., under review; Landau et al., 2015; Meijers & Rutjens, 2014; Rutjens et al., in preparation).

Although the current chapter covered a number of important moderators of these effects, we think that there are several fruitful avenues for future research to further our understanding of compensatory control and order motivation processes and its impact on cognition, motivation, and behavior. One obvious example is to further uncover the situational and individual factors that determine when compensatory control and order perceptions facilitate versus hamper personal action. Second, an important lacuna in the literature relates to the *functional value* of the vast array of compensatory beliefs and behaviors that have been documented so far (Landau et al., 2015; Rutjens, van Harreveld, & van der Pligt, 2013). Again depending on situational and personal factors, some compensatory strategies might be functionally superior to others (e.g., see Helzer & Jayawickreme, 2015). And, finally, future research could zoom in more on the properties of "socially constructive" versus less constructive (and often more defensive) reactions to threats to order and control. For example, while endorsing conspiracies or enemies seem functionally equivalent to, say, belief in scientific progress, they obviously have drastically different consequences for other aspects of social cognition and motivation. Understanding why and when people bolster either of these types of compensatory beliefs, while also taking into account its effects on personal action and the functional value of these beliefs, will help to further elucidate compensatory processes related to control and order motivation.

Notes

1 The notion that exerting control is one way to perceive order is also present in the work of Pittman (1998), who argued that control provides people with the idea that their direct environment (and the world as such) is predictable, structured, and coherent (see also Kay, Landau, & Sullivan, 2014; Krantz, 1998).
2 Although, of course, *other* motivations unrelated to maintaining order (e.g., desiring to contribute to health or a green environment) might still play an important role in determining personal action.

References

Bench, S. W., & Lench, H. C. (2013). On the function of boredom. *Behavioral Sciences, 3*(3), 459–472.

Burger, J. M. (1989). Negative reactions to increases in perceived personal control. *Journal of Personality and Social Psychology, 56*, 246–256.

Chan, K. Q., Tong, E. M. W., & Tan, Y. L. (2014). Taking a leap of faith: Reminders of God lead to greater risk taking. *Social Psychological and Personality Science, 5*, 901–909.

Chiandetti, C., & Vallortigara, G. (2011). Chicks like consonant music. *Psychological Science, 22*, 1270–1273.

Conway-Morris, S. (2005). *Life's solution: Inevitable humans in a lonely universe.* Cambridge: Cambridge University Press.

Cutright, K. M. (2012). The beauty of boundaries: When and why we seek structure in consumption. *Journal of Consumer Research, 38*(5), 775-790.

Fennis, B. M., & Wiebenga, J. H. (2015). Disordered environments prompt mere goal pursuit. *Journal of Environmental Psychology, 43*, 226–237.

Foster, K. R., & Kokko, H. (2009). The evolution of superstitious and superstition-like behaviour. *Proceedings of the Royal Society B, 276*, 31–37.

Friesen, J. P., Campbell, T. H., & Kay, A. C. (2015). The psychological advantage of unfalsifiability: The appeal of untestable religious and political ideologies. *Journal of Personality and Social Psychology, 108*(3), 515.

Friesen, J. P., Kay, A. C., Eibach, R. P., & Galinsky, A. D. (2014). Seeking structure in social organization: Compensatory control and the psychological advantages of hierarchy. *Journal of Personality and Social Psychology, 106*(4), 590.

Fritsche, I., Jonas, E., & Fankhänel, T. (2008). The role of control motivation in mortality salience effects on ingroup support and defense. *Journal of Personality and Social Psychology, 95*, 524–541.

Harmon-Jones, E., Amodio, D. M., & Harmon-Jones, C. (2009). Action-based model of dissonance: A review, integration, and expansion of conceptions of cognitive conflict. *Advances in Experimental Social Psychology, 41*, 119–166.

Haselton, M. G., & Buss, D. M. (2000). Error management theory: A new perspective on biases in cross-sex mind reading. *Journal of Personality and Social Psychology, 78*(1), 81.

Heckhausen, J., & Schulz, R. (1995). A life-span theory of control. *Psychological Review, 102*, 284–304.

Helzer, E. G., & Jayawickreme, E. (2015). Control and the "good life": Primary and secondary control as distinct indicators of well-being. *Social Psychological and Personality Science, 6*, 653–660.

Janoff-Bulman, R. (1992). *Shattered assumptions: Towards a new psychology of trauma.* New York: Free Press.

Jost, J. T., Glaser, J., Kruglanski, A. W., & Sulloway, F. J. (2003). Political conservatism as motivated social cognition. *Psychological Bulletin, 129*, 339–375.

Kay, A. C., Gaucher, D., Napier, J. L., Callan, M. J., & Laurin, K. (2008). God and the government: Testing a compensatory control mechanism for the support of external systems. *Journal of Personality and Social Psychology, 95*, 18–35.

Kay, A. C., Landau, M. J., Khenfer, J., & Keefer, L. A. (under review). On the self-regulatory consequences of supernatural belief: When and why does belief in a controlling god strengthen goal commitment?

Kay, A. C., Landau, M. J., & Sullivan, D. L. (2014). *Agency and control. APA handbook of personality and social psychology: Attitudes and social cognition.* Washington, DC: American Psychological Association.

Kay, A. C., Laurin, K., Fitzsimons, G. M., & Landau, M. J. (2014). A functional basis for structure-seeking: Exposure to structure promotes willingness to engage in motivated action. *Journal of Experimental Psychology: General, 143*(2), 486.

Kay, A. C., Moscovitch, D. A., & Laurin, K. (2010). Randomness, attributions of arousal, and belief in God. *Psychological Science, 21*, 216–218.

Kay, A. C., Shepherd, S., Blatz, C. W., Chua, S. N., & Galinsky, A. D. (2010). For God (or) country: The hydraulic relation between government instability and belief in religious sources of control. *Journal of Personality and Social Psychology, 99*(5), 725–739.

Kouchaki, M., Oveis, C., & Gino, F. (2014). Guilt enhances the sense of control and drives risky judgments. *Journal of Experimental Psychology: General, 143*(6), 2103.

Krantz, D. L. (1998). Taming chance: Social science and everyday narratives. *Psychological Inquiry, 9*, 87–94.

Kruglanski, A. W., & Webster, D. M. (1996). Motivated closing of the mind: "seizing" and "freezing." *Psychological Review, 103*, 263–283.

Kupor, D. M., Laurin, K., & Levav, J. (2015). Anticipating divine protection? Reminders of god can increase nonmoral risk taking. *Psychological Science, 26*(4), 374–384.

Landau, M. J., Johns, M., Greenberg, J., Pyszczynski, T., Martens, A., Goldenberg, J. L., & Solomon, S. (2004). A function of form: Terror management and structuring the social world. *Journal of Personality and Social Psychology, 87*, 190–210.

Landau, M. J., Kay, A. C., & Whitson, J. A. (2015). Compensatory control and the appeal of a structured world. *Psychological Bulletin, 141*, 694–722.

Langer, E. J. (1975). The illusion of control. *Journal of Personality and Social Psychology, 32*, 311–328.

Langer, E. J., & Rodin, J. (1976). The effects of choice and enhanced personal responsibility for the aged: A field experiment in an institutional setting. *Journal of Personality and Social Psychology, 34*, 191–198.

Laurin, K., Kay, A. C., & Fitzsimons, G. M. (2012). Divergent effects of activating thoughts of god on self-regulation. *Journal of Personality and Social Psychology, 102*, 4–21.

Laurin, K., Shariff, A. F., Henrich, J., & Kay, A. C. (2012). Outsourcing punishment to God: beliefs in divine control reduce earthly punishment. *Proceedings of the Royal Society of London B: Biological Sciences, 279*, 3272–3281.

Lerner, M. J. (1980). *The belief in a just world: A fundamental delusion.* New York: Plenum.

Maier, S. F., & Seligman, M. E. P. (1976). Learned helplessness: Theory and evidence. *Journal of Experimental Psychology: General, 195*, 3–46.

Malinowski, B. (1979). The role of magic and religion. In W. A. Lessa & E. Z. Vogt (Eds.), *Reader in comparative religion: An anthropological approach.* New York: Harper and Row, 1972.

Matute, H. (1994). Learned helplessness and superstitious behavior as opposite effects of uncontrollable reinforcement. *Learning and Motivation, 25*, 216–232.

Matute, H., Yarritu, I., & Vadillo, M. A. (2010). Illusions of causality at the heart of pseudoscience. *British Journal of Psychology, 102*, 392–405.

Meijers, M. H. C., & Rutjens, B. T. (2014). Affirming belief in scientific progress reduces environmentally friendly behaviour. *European Journal of Social Psychology, 44*, 487–495.

Moulding, R., & Kyrios, M. (2006). Anxiety disorders and control related beliefs: The exemplar of Obsessive Compulsive Disorder (OCD). *Clinical Psychology Review, 26*, 573–583.

Pittman, T. S. (1998). Motivation. In D. T. Gilbert, S. T. Fiske, & G. Lindzey (Eds.), *The handbook of social psychology* (Vol. 1, 4th ed., pp. 549–590). New York: MacGraw-Hill.

Plous, S. (1993). *The psychology of judgment and decision making.* New York: McGraw-Hill.

Rothbaum, F., Weisz, J. R., & Snyder, S. S. (1982). Changing the world and changing the self: A two-process model of perceived control. *Journal of Personality and Social Psychology, 42*, 5–37.

Rothschild, Z. K., Landau, M. J., Sullivan, D., & Keefer, L. A. (2012). A dual-motive model of scapegoating: Displacing blame to reduce guilt or increase control. *Journal of Personality and Social Psychology, 102*(6), 1148.

Rutjens, B. T. (2015). Unpublished dataset, University of Amsterdam, the Netherlands.

Rutjens, B. T., van der Pligt, J., & van Harreveld, F. (2010). Deus or Darwin: Randomness and belief in theories about the origin of life. *Journal of Experimental Social Psychology, 46*, 1078–1080.

Rutjens, B. T., van Harreveld, F., & Cunningham, W. A balance perspective on threat compensation. *In preparation.*

Rutjens, B. T., van Harreveld, F., & van der Pligt, J. (2013). Step by step: Finding compensatory order in science. *Current Directions in Psychological Science, 22*, 250–255.

Rutjens, B. T., van Harreveld, F., van der Pligt, J., Kreemers, L. M., & Noordewier, M. K. (2013). Steps, stages, and structure: Finding compensatory order in scientific theories. *Journal of Experimental Psychology: General, 142*, 313–318.

Sedek, G., & Kofta, M. (1990). When cognitive exertion does not yield cognitive gain: Toward an informational explanation of learned helplessness. *Journal of Personality and Social Psychology, 58*(4), 729.

Shepherd, S., & Kay, A. C. (2012). On the perpetuation of ignorance: System dependence, system justification, and the motivated avoidance of sociopolitical information. *Journal of Personality and Social Psychology, 102*(2), 264.

Skinner, E. A. (1996). A guide to constructs of control. *Journal of Personality and Social Psychology, 71*, 549–570.

Spilka, B., Shaver, P., & Kirkpatrick, L. A. (1985). A general attribution theory for the psychology of religion. *Journal for the Scientific Study of Religion, 24*, 1–20.

Srull, T. K., & Wyer, R. S. (1979). The role of category accessibility in the interpretation of information about persons: Some determinants and implications. *Journal of Personality and Social Psychology, 37*(10), 1660–1672.

Sullivan, D., Landau, M. J., & Rothschild, Z. K. (2010). An existential function of enemyship: Evidence that people attribute influence to personal and political enemies to compensate for threats to control. *Journal of Personality and Social Psychology, 98*(3), 434.

Thompson, S. C. (2004). Illusions of control. In R. Pohl (Ed.), Cognitive illusions (pp. 113-126). New York: Taylor & Francis.

Thompson, S. C., & Spacapan, S. (1991). Perceptions of control in vulnerable populations. *Journal of Social Issues, 47*, 1–22.

van Tilburg, W. A., & Igou, E. R. (2012). On boredom: Lack of challenge and meaning as distinct boredom experiences. *Motivation and Emotion, 36*(2), 181–194.

Vyse, S. A. (1997). *Believing in magic: The psychology of superstition.* New York: Oxford University Press.

Whitson, J. A., & Galinsky, A. D. (2008). Lacking control increases illusory pattern perception. *Science, 322*, 115–117.

Wilson, T. D., Reinhard, D. A., Westgate, E. C., Gilbert, D. T., Ellerbeck, N., Hahn, C., . . . Shaked, A. (2014). Just think: The challenges of the disengaged mind. *Science, 345*(6192), 75–77.

6

PERCEIVED UNCONTROLLABILITY AS A COPING RESOURCE

The control-serving function of enemies and uncertainty

Daniel Sullivan and Sheridan A. Stewart

Contact: swolf22@email.arizona.edu

As we write this chapter, the departmental office of one of the authors is closed due to an apparent threat made toward a staff member. As the author walks in to begin work each day, he passes a locked door and a hanging sign indicating that the Psychology Main Office is closed until further notice. He knows almost nothing about why this rather radical change has occurred. He has only a vague notion based on a mass email that the well-being of someone in the building has been threatened.

What is perhaps most remarkable about this state of affairs is how little the author is alarmed by it, and how little it does to alter his daily routine. Imagine that the psychology department was a village in Medieval Europe, and a person had publicly announced their intention to use witchcraft against a local magistrate. The village would be thrown into an uproar. Overcome with fear, people would talk incessantly of the looming threat. They would likely band together to track down the supposed witch. Instead, the author is somewhat concerned about the well-being of the staff member, and somewhat (a little less) concerned about his own. But he knows almost nothing about the nature of the threat, whom it is directed against and why, and what the authorities are doing to stop it. Rather than experiencing paralysis from this lack of knowledge, the author simply ignores the issue, assuming it is being competently handled by the authorities and will soon be resolved. He is primarily concerned that he is temporarily unable to store his lunch in the office refrigerator.

The dissonance of perceived control and uncontrollability in contemporary culture

Consider what this preceding example tells us about the experience of control and uncontrollability in contemporary postindustrial culture. It speaks volumes about the "banality of threat." Death threats, bomb threats, actual instances of public shootings and terrorist attacks – these things are so familiar that they do not demand the psychological attention that they might have had at an earlier time in history. And yet they are there, in the news and on the streets, potentially contributing to perceived uncontrollability and anxiety among members of postindustrial societies.

At the same time, this example shows that at least the middle- and upper-class citizens in these societies – concerned as they may be with perceived insecurity in their world – do not *behave* as if they are particularly concerned. For the most part, they go to work and go on vacation, drive cars and fly in airplanes, and even walk the streets at night as if they were completely safe. Indeed, studies show that U.S. citizens are comparatively biased to believe that risks are far more likely to befall other people than themselves (Klein & Helweg-Larsen, 2002).

It appears that materially secure members of postindustrial societies are in a perennial state of potential cognitive dissonance. They hold two seemingly contradictory cognitions: (1) the perception, fueled by the media and daily events in their own and close others' lives, that the world is a chaotic, uncertain, and often violent place; and (2) the embodied experience of relative safety and comfort. One common way in which dissonance is resolved is through attitude modification (Festinger, 1957). In many unfortunate cases, people are forced to modify these attitudes through the terrible experience of trauma – being the victim of a death threat, of rape, of a school shooting. Such experiences typically cause survivors to modify Cognition 2, such that they no longer believe the world to be a secure place (Janoff-Bulman, 1992). But what about those who are fortunate enough not to experience trauma?

We propose that most secure people in postindustrial cultures resolve this dissonance in another way, namely by adding the cognition that although the world is a violent and uncertain place, *they personally* are in control and safe. However, while perspectives from just world theory (Lerner, 1980), attribution theory and social cognition (Taylor & Brown, 1988), and compensatory control theory (Kay, Gaucher, Napier, Callan, & Laurin, 2008; see also Rutjens & Kay, Chapter 5, this volume) have made this observation many times in different guises, we propose here to explore the generally overlooked existential implications and cultural foundations of this contradictory attitude toward control.

We will do so from the recently specified perspective of *cultural-existential psychology* (Sullivan, 2016), which brings together experimental existential psychology and cultural psychology. Practitioners of experimental existential psychology use modern experimental methods to test classic existentialist and psychodynamic ideas about human motivation (Greenberg, Koole, & Pyszczynski, 2004). For example, hundreds of psychological studies carried out in dozens of countries have shown that reminding people temporarily of their own death increases their investment in cultural beliefs or markers of their personal value (Greenberg, Solomon, & Arndt, 2008). The highly important research in this area has suffered from a limitation – it tends to focus on cultural universals and to underappreciate the great diversity that exists in the ways people cope with death, guilt, and anxiety. The cultural-existential approach overcomes this limitation by connecting existential research to cultural psychology (Kitayama & Cohen, 2007), which examines variation in motivational processes as a function of the cultural worlds humans construct.

In bringing together these two research fields, cultural-existential psychology posits three fundamental principles (Sullivan, 2016) relevant to the current discussion of perceived control and uncontrollability in contemporary culture. The first is that humans are unique animals by virtue of their capacity for symbolic consciousness, a notion rooted in evolutionary perspectives (e.g., Deacon, 1998; Langer, 1988). This implies that perceptions relevant to personal control do not arise solely from rational deliberative or even irrational social cognitive processes, nor are they merely the result of social, political, or media factors. Such factors are important, but a full account of these perceptions requires an understanding of the existential and motivational role they play in the individual's phenomenological experience.

The second principle of cultural-existential psychology is that culture is both a defense against and a source of the problems of theodicy and nihilism. In other words, cultural systems provide "threat orientations" – they predispose us to experience certain kinds of events as threatening, while also simultaneously providing characteristic means of interpreting and defending against those threats. In this chapter we are focused on the unique threat orientation of individualist culture in postindustrial society, which revolves around notions of control and uncontrollability.

Finally, the third principle of cultural-existential psychology is that multiple, interdisciplinary methods are required to fully understand how the individual's experience of threat and suffering is shaped by culture. Beyond experiments and surveys, the framework contends that qualitative studies are necessary to more fully understand how members of different cultural groups invoke local interpretations to make sense of threats to order.

We begin our cultural-existential analysis of control perception in postindustrial societies with an examination of the existential strategies individuals in such settings use to balance control and uncontrollability. We then shift to considerations of the cultural underpinnings of these strategies, reviewing relevant empirical literature throughout. We conclude by bringing together this cultural-existential perspective with extant qualitative research on contentious politics and further psychological research on moral attitudes in order to illustrate how, in the postindustrial U.S. context, a modern threat orientation has framed responses to the 2008 financial crisis and intergroup relations among university students.

Defensive dynamics in control perceptions: Denial and projection

We have observed that secure members of individualist societies tend to have dissonant perceptions of control – they see reported risks all around them, but experience their own lives as relatively stable. We would like to explore the possibility that this dissonance may arise partly as a result of existentially motivated defense mechanisms.

Smelser (1987) built upon psychoanalytic perspectives to outline the primary psychological defenses that individuals employ to cope with threats in their environment. Under circumstances of intractable perceived uncertainty and threat to the self, Smelser proposed, individuals often respond either with *denial* – convincing themselves that they are not actually at risk – or with *projection* – attaching the feelings of anxiety they are experiencing to some source external to the self. Based on recent research in social psychology, we propose that individuals in postindustrial societies routinely cope with anxiety using *both* of these strategies.

On the one hand, just world research demonstrates how people often react with denial to perceived threats to certainty and control. In one pertinent study, Xie, Liu, and Gan (2011) demonstrated that, in the wake of the disastrous Wenchuan Earthquake of 2008, participants who had a stronger belief in a just world felt less uncertainty surrounding the impact of natural disasters, which in turn led to a more optimistic orientation toward the future. Goode and Keefer (2015) similarly found that when perceptions of a meritocratic society were threatened, individuals reported increased control and more optimism about their economic futures. Quite simply, people routinely deny information suggesting the world's complexity, reducing it to simplistic explanations and optimistic formulae. From a cultural-existential perspective, it is important to recognize that this denial is not simply an automatic process; rather, it is a motivated defense mechanism. Indeed, in his original presentation of just world theory, Lerner (1980) suggests that people deny the possibility that bad things can happen to good, undeserving people as a cognitive means of buttressing personal agency. By denying that the world is an unjust place, people retain the belief that good outcomes will follow if they exert agency and pursue normative aims. Similarly, U.S. participants exposed to a video of a devastating tornado (compared to controls) defensively bolster their belief that the world is a just place, and this compensatory increase is associated in turn with heightened perceived personal control (Sullivan, 2016).

On the other hand, people in postindustrial societies do not always deny the reality of uncontrollability through just world beliefs and similar tactics. Indeed, such individuals often acknowledge a variety of risks to which they believe they are susceptible. However, people do not evaluate all risks in equivalent terms, but rely on heuristics which elevate the accessibility of particular threats (Johnson & Tversky, 1983). Again, from a cultural-existential perspective, we propose that these heuristics are more than mere examples of cognitively biased information processing – they have motivational and functional significance for the individual.

Here we come to the defensive mechanism of projection, broadly understood as the focalization of internally registered anxiety on some external source. In a line of research and theorizing we have been carrying out with our colleagues in recent years (Sullivan, Landau, Rothschild, & Keefer, 2014; Sullivan & Palitsky, 2015), we have gathered diverse evidence that people cope with anxious uncontrollability by identifying particular sources of risk in their environment, often personal or political enemies. For instance, in a field study conducted on the eve of the 2008 U.S. Presidential Election, we (Sullivan, Landau, & Rothschild, 2010) asked some participants to complete a questionnaire strategically designed to include questions threatening personal control (for example, asking how much control they have over natural disasters). Other participants filled out an innocuous version. We found that participants who completed the threatening questionnaire were subsequently more likely to endorse conspiracy theories that the candidate they opposed was secretly stealing the election.

People feeling anxiety about uncontrollability scan their environment for a more concrete source to which they can attach those feelings. Even if a conspirator is invisible and powerful, the fact that he is *known* to be the focal source of one's downfall provides greater assurance than seeing hazards as diffuse and indifferent (Becker, 1969). In this way, the identification of a particular source of uncontrollability actually acts as a coping resource to restore controllability.

If this is true, then two hypotheses follow: (1) the increased tendency to attribute malevolent influence to conspirators and enemy figures after threat should be mediated by diminished perceptions of control, and (2) exposure to an enemy or conspiracy theory after a control threat should actually *increase*, rather than decrease, people's perceptions of control. We (Rothschild, Landau, Sullivan, & Keefer, 2012) tested (1) by confronting some participants with a portrayal of uncontrollable hazards resulting from environmental destruction (while others read a portrayal that did not threaten control). We then measured participants' perceptions that society can control environmental hazards, before giving them the opportunity to blame a specific target (oil companies) for the problem of environmental destruction. We found that feelings of reduced control after exposure to the threat mediated a corresponding increase in attributions of blame to oil companies. In short, participants cope with perceived uncontrollability by projecting their anxiety onto specific scapegoat targets.

But do such acts of projection actually maintain perceived control? This is what we (Sullivan et al., 2010) found in a study in which some U.S. citizens were first reminded of random threats in their environment, while others were given a neutral comparison induction. After this manipulation some participants read a portrayal of the terrorist group Al Qaeda as an active threat to U.S. security, while others read a portrayal framing the group as harmless. Counterintuitively, when we measured participants' perceived personal control at the end of the study, it was those participants who had initially received a control threat and then read about Al Qaeda as a dangerous enemy who showed the *highest* level of control. A mediation analysis suggested that this effect occurred because those participants who contemplated Al Qaeda as an enemy were less likely to see risk as randomly distributed throughout their environment.

Primary and secondary control in projection

The question may be posed as to whether the identification of enemy figures actually enhances feelings of personal control, or whether these findings are only documenting temporarily elevated *perceptions* of control or order. The classic distinction made by Rothbaum, Weisz, and Snyder (1982) between primary control – the agent's ability to actively manipulate their environment – and secondary control – the agent's capacity to passively adapt to their environment – is significant in this connection. Does the reduction of perceived risk through projection onto enemy targets give agents the feeling that they actually have the ability to influence their environment, or does it simply give them a reassuring sense of "interpretive control" in relation to that environment (Rothbaum et al., 1982)?

While we acknowledge the theoretical importance of this distinction, we also believe it is frequently exaggerated in analyses of control motivation. In short – as we will address further in the next section – whether one is asserting primary or secondary control in a given instance is often a matter of perspective and scope. Consider Pyszczynski et al.'s (1990) application of the cybernetic self-regulation and action identification theories to the experience of symbolic threat and defense. From this perspective, each act of asserting primary control – say, walking to work in the morning despite inclement weather – is, when considered at a more abstract level, also an act of secondary control – say, affirming that one is a dedicated employee of an organization that provides stability and meaning in a chaotic economy. When considering this hierarchy in reverse, it becomes clear that the opposite is also generally true – every act of secondary control seeking does, in some sense, set the stage for future instances of primary control assertion (e.g., believing that the U.S. government has the power to protect against terrorist attacks gives one the license to travel by air to a desired destination). Indeed, there are a host of threats in human experience – death being the ultimate example – which cannot possibly ever be fully managed in the strict sense of primary, agentic control. And yet, if individuals did not find ways to manage these threats through a variety of secondary control mechanisms, they would be rendered psychologically helpless, crippled with anxiety and incapable of asserting basic agency in their daily lives (Pyszczynski et al., 1990).

Thus individual acts – both of perception and behavior – tend to establish both primary and secondary control in a way that is typically underacknowledged. Evidence supporting this contention comes from recent studies suggesting that establishing secondary control helps to re-establish primary control and agentic motivation. This has been shown to happen in a domain-fluid way, meaning that perceiving any kind of structure in one context increases the individual's willingness to engage in goal-directed activity in a different context (Kay, Laurin, Fitzsimons, & Landau, 2014). More germane to the present research, this process also occurs in the context of the projection of anxiety onto enemy figures.

Interestingly, recent data highlight the importance of emotion in this process. By focusing on a specific source of uncontrollability (e.g., an enemy), the individual gains a cognitive foothold for translating the aversive emotion of anxiety into the more approach-oriented emotion of anger. Because anger is typically a control-restorative emotion (Lerner & Keltner, 2001), this paves the way for taking action in one's environment. This is consistent with a broader emerging consensus in the literature that defensive responses to control threat often follow an avoidance-approach motivational sequence (Greenaway, Philipps, & Storrs, Chapter 2, present volume; Jonas et al., 2014; Stroessner, Scholer, Marx, & Weisz, 2015). For instance, in a daily diary study, researchers (Kim, Ford, Mauss, & Tamir, 2014) found that better-adapted individuals intentionally amplified their anger when engaging in confrontational exchanges. In another study, we (Motro & Sullivan, 2015) asked a large sample of working U.S. citizens to contemplate threats to control which they experience at their workplace. We then asked some participants to describe a personal enemy at their job whom they thought might be responsible for those uncertainties, but importantly we varied whether participants were also asked to describe the emotion of anger they feel in connection with this person or not. Results demonstrated that only those participants given the opportunity to express anger at their enemy co-worker subsequently showed bolstered levels of personal control. An additional study confirmed that contemplating an enemy responsible for negative uncertainties in one's life increases motivation and work performance (Motro & Sullivan, 2015).

Summarizing the foregoing, there is mounting evidence that when individuals experience global threats to control, they first establish secondary control by scrutinizing their environment for focal enemy figures who can be viably scapegoated. Having projected anxiety onto this central target, individuals are then free to assert primary control and take action, either against the enemy or in an unrelated domain. Thus, the literature shows that individuals alternate between Smelser's (1987) strategies of denial and projection when confronted with aversive uncontrollability. While this tactical shifting provides the individual with multiple motivational avenues for coping, it also ultimately reinforces the dissonant experience identified at the outset of this chapter. If the person combines denials of the reality of risk with magnified perceptions of the threat stemming from certain sources, they will indeed have the contradictory experience of believing themselves to be simultaneously safe and imperiled.

There are several assumptions built into the preceding discussion of the existential significance of denial and projection which, on a cultural-existential psychological view, warrant deeper scrutiny. To unpack these assumptions we will consider how the specific circumstances of postindustrial individualist culture provide the foundation for the use of enemies and uncertainty as a paradoxical coping resource.

The relationship of contemporary individualism to perceived control

One of the strengths of the present volume is the attention paid in several chapters to the effect of social structural factors (e.g., SES) on experiences of control and uncontrollability. In this connection we will draw on the ideas of Max Horkheimer (1947). Specifically, Horkheimer developed a series of hypotheses regarding the relationships between postindustrial capitalist social structure, individualist culture, and perceptions of control. We will use these hypotheses to organize the scattered social psychological literature on these topics.

To begin, Horkheimer (1947) proposed that contemporary individualism is "a culture of self-preservation for its own sake" (p. 94). In particular, he saw individualism as both a product of and a contributor to economic and ideological trends of materialism, consumerism, and social Darwinism. Indeed, cross-cultural studies (Clarke & Micken, 2002) support the notion that individualism is correlationally associated with materialist values. Furthermore, experimental primes of materialist and consumerist tendencies reduce the desire for deep social involvement and increase both competitive and self-enhancing tendencies, all indicators of an individualist orientation (Bauer, Wilkie, Kim, & Bodenhausen, 2012). In general, relative to other forms of cultural orientation, unchecked individualism encourages prioritization of financial goals, consumerist leisure activities, and a view of society as a competitive, Hobbesian marketplace (see also Sullivan, Stewart, & Diefendorf, 2015).

An important aspect of the association between materialism and individualism as discussed by Horkheimer (1947) is the tendency for contemporary individualist societies to be dominated by "invisible" forms of social control (Bernstein, 1990; Sullivan, 2016). What this means is the alleged freedom to pursue personal goals in an individualist society, often with relatively little consideration for others, can only occur against an institutional and technological backdrop of complex control mechanisms. Secure members of postindustrial society perceive things to be "under control" much of the time because they routinely rely on infrastructures (roads, buildings), devices (cars, cell phones, elevators), and institutionalized systems (the value of the Euro, the responsiveness of the police) which they understand almost nothing about. These are all sources of social order which form an "invisible," taken-for-granted backdrop against which the person perceives herself to be asserting her freedom. In reality, what has occurred in postindustrial society – compared to agricultural or hunter-gatherer societies – is that many of the daily decisions apparently made by the individual have in fact been largely outsourced to the environment. Consider the case of driving a car – here it would seem obvious that we, the drivers, are in control. Yet Horkheimer (1947) offers a different view:

> It is as if the innumerable laws, regulations, and directions with which we must comply were driving the car, not we. There are speed limits, warnings to drive slowly, to stop, to stay within certain lanes, and even diagrams showing the shape of the curve ahead. We must keep our eyes on the road and be ready at each instant to react with the right motion. Our spontaneity has been replaced by a frame of mind which compels us to discard every emotion or idea that might impair our alertness to the impersonal demands assailing us.
>
> (p. 98)

Postindustrial society affords high psychological autonomy – the sense that one is free to express one's personal identity – but low action autonomy – the ability to survive primarily on the basis of one's own repertoire of skills (Keller, 2012). Purchasing power has in many ways been substituted for practical knowledge and ability.

On the one hand, individuals gain a heightened (if illusory) sense of personal control through their increased ability to rely on experts, technologies, and institutions that remove personal responsibility for navigating the world. On the other hand, Horkheimer (1947) suggested, when one's life functions according to a strictly regulated routine – the mechanics of which one has little knowledge of – then disruptions in that routine exacerbate the dissonance described throughout this chapter. This is the basis of Horkheimer's (1947) assertion that, contrary to the accepted wisdom in the literature, secure individuals in postindustrial societies actually experience fairly high levels of perceived uncontrollability and anxiety.

This claim may seem quite strange because its veracity rests largely on how we conceptualize uncontrollability and anxiety. Certainly, disenfranchised individuals from lower social class backgrounds experience a very real lack of personal control in their lives and are more frequently subjected to stressful events (e.g., Kraus, Piff, & Keltner, 2009). However, the very experience of material insecurity often prompts individuals from such backgrounds to develop or endorse communal coping methods (Piff, Stancato, Martinez, Kraus, & Keltner, 2012) and religious meaning systems (Norris & Inglehart, 2012), which mitigates the psychological threat of uncontrollability (see also Sullivan, 2016). By contrast, those in more privileged social positions take the controllability of their lives for granted, and so have only their own underdeveloped resources and abilities to rely on when threats arise. Furthermore, it should be noted that, as a result of growing income inequality in the United States and other postindustrial societies (Duménil & Lévy, 2011), increasingly large numbers of people are entering into situations of relative deprivation, leading to heightened competitive anxiety and distrust of government and institutions (Delhey & Dragolov, 2014; Oishi, Kesebir, & Diener, 2011). Thus, Horkheimer's (1947) analysis offers the perhaps surprising prediction that, at least under some circumstances, greater individualism and materialism will be associated with more perceived (if not actual) uncontrollability and anxiety.

Indeed, despite the fact that they experience objectively fewer stressors, people from more materialist backgrounds show a heightened affective forecasting bias when imagining the experience of loss (Hartnett & Skowronski, 2008). More materially secure individuals experience anxiety about the possible loss of their security. Additionally, there is evidence that immersion in individualist culture increases anxiety. In Taiwan, less collectivist participants reported higher levels of the social Darwinist attitudes Horkheimer associated with modern individualism, as well as higher levels of status anxiety (Chiou & Pan, 2008). Further, people from more individualistic religious backgrounds report higher levels of future-oriented anxiety compared to those from a more collectivist religious group (Sullivan, 2016).

What are the consequences of this uncertain existence in a culture of self-preservation? Horkheimer (1947) proposes that the consequences are a heightened dependency on exactly those psychological defense mechanisms discussed in the preceding section, namely denial and projection. Where denial is concerned, Horkheimer suggests that contemporary individualists respond to their increased dependency on external economic and institutional forces by denying that very dependency, insisting instead on their autonomy and personal responsibility for their material successes. The literature supports this contention: endorsement of individualist values is associated both with consumerist attitudes and belief in the Protestant Work Ethic (Lee, Pant, & Ali, 2010), namely the conviction that people achieve rewards through hard work and self-control.

Where the mechanism of projection is concerned, there is growing evidence that individualist culture promotes defensive identification of sources of anxiety and uncontrollability in the environment, as we have suggested. This projective tendency manifests in a number of ways. For instance, individualists are more likely to demonstrate self-serving biases (Twenge, Zhang, & Im, 2004): they routinely shift blame for potential personal failures onto a perceived hostile and uncertain world.

Another line of evidence comes from studies on the psychology of power. Although it is rarely acknowledged in the literature, the vast majority of recently documented effects of primed or dispositionally felt power – such as decreased conformity and strengthened commitment to personal goals (Guinote, 2015) – are essentially the same list of tendencies that is displayed by cultural individualists (Cross, Hardin, & Gercek-Swing, 2011). Once we acknowledge the intrinsic connection between individualism and perceived power, a host of findings bring into focus another way in which individualism encourages defensive projection. It has been established that individuals in situations of high power tend to rely on stereotypic and objectified perceptions of others (Fiske & Morling, 1996; Gruenfeld, Inesi, Magee, & Galinsky, 2008). Again, this is not merely a social cognitive tendency associated with the situation of being in power; objectification may also be interpreted as one manifestation of the individualist proclivity toward projection. Individualists cope with personal anxiety by dehumanizing others or seeing them in terms of their instrumental value, which increases perceived control by making others seem easier to manage and dominate (Keefer, Landau, Sullivan, & Rothschild, 2014; Landau, Sullivan, Keefer, Rothschild, & Osman, 2012).

Finally, there is some direct evidence that individualist beliefs undergird the tactical use of enemyship as a source of perceived control. For example, correlational research (Christopher et al., 2008) shows that endorsement of the Protestant Work Ethic is associated with belief in a just world (denial of risk) as well as social dominance orientation and right-wing authoritarianism (projection of anxiety onto vilified outgroup enemies). In addition, in a study of the relationship between economic uncertainty and political attitudes among East Germans, Hagan, Rippl, Boehnke, and Merkens (1999) found hierarchic self-interest (an indicator of competitive individualism) to be predictive of right-wing extremism and negative attitudes toward immigrants and foreigners.

In summary, Horkheimer (1947) proposed that a culture of competitive individualism, afforded by a postindustrial capitalist social structure, would encourage the tendencies toward denial and projection discussed in the preceding section.

Although the evidence is often indirect and scattered among disparate literatures, this broad hypothesis has already received considerable support. Future research should of course investigate the relationship between individualism, tendencies toward denial and projection, and control perceptions in a more systematic fashion. As it stands, this cultural-existential psychological analysis provides a compelling explanation for what might otherwise be the puzzling phenomenon of dissonant perceptions of control and uncontrollability in contemporary culture.

Naturally, people in individualist cultures do not always employ projection onto enemies as their primary defense against threats to control. This analysis can be sophisticated by recognizing that projection does not always take the form of focalization of threat onto a scapegoat, but often instead takes the form of "transference" of power to idealized leaders and institutions (Becker, 1973; Smelser, 1999). Indeed, there is a great deal of evidence documenting that, in modern, individualist settings, people often respond to control threat by bolstering benevolent sources of protection and secondary control – investing greater perceived power in and allegiance to entities such as God, the government, or powerful social groups (Kay, Gaucher, Napier, Callan, & Laurin, 2008; Stollberg, Fritsche, & Bäcker, 2015). Given that projection in the face of control threat can take the form either of scapegoating enemies, or transferring power to benevolent leaders and ingroups, under what circumstances will people in individualist cultures engage in one form of defense versus the other?

Addressing this issue, Sullivan and Palitsky (2015) recently proposed a "capabilities/motivation" account of belief in conspiracy theories and enemyship. The essence of this account is that enemyship projection results from an interaction between individual-level motivation to restore threatened control and culture-level "capabilities" that predispose the individual toward this specific defense mechanism. In short, threatened individuals will only be likely to restore perceived control via enemyship processes if the surrounding cultural circumstances and norms support this form of defense. Experimental (Sullivan et al., 2010) and sociological evidence (for review, see Sullivan et al., 2014) converges to show that enemyship is more likely to be used as a defense mechanism under general conditions of *system disorder* – i.e., when individuals do not perceive that governmental and economic institutions can be trusted to provide protection. In postindustrial, individualist cultures, system disorder is most likely to take the form of systemic economic failure leading to high levels of income inequality. When many individuals in a society do not feel that their jobs are secure or that their incomes are sufficient to fulfill their desires, while simultaneously believing that a small cadre of elites are hoarding society's wealth, those individuals become particularly susceptible to beliefs that personal enemies are responsible for their relative deprivation (Motro & Sullivan, 2015; Sullivan et al., 2014).

To conclude our chapter, we consider some cases of U.S. citizens turning to enemyship beliefs as a result of the experience of system disorder under conditions of income inequality, economic failure, and changing patterns of intergroup relations. In so doing, we draw on the third principle of cultural-existential psychology, namely the necessity of mixed methods to understand the interaction between culture and the experience of threat. We will review a few crucial qualitative studies that shed important light on the phenomenology of control and uncontrollability in contemporary individualist culture, as seen through the experience of political mobilization in the wake of the 2008 financial crisis and increasing diversity in higher education.

Moral panic in the modern world: The tea party, microaggressions, and immunitas

One way of understanding the sometimes paradoxical threat orientation of contemporary individualism in postindustrial society is through Roberto Esposito's (2013) concept of *immunitas*. This is a worldview built around the cultural logic of immunization, which instructs the individual to protect herself from any potential threats or unwanted obligations. This logic is reflected in the emphasis placed in contemporary democracies on individual rights, privacy, and the pursuit of personal goals. Psychologically, *immunitas* manifests as a desire to maintain high personal control and self-esteem. Interestingly, as in the case of biological immunity, the psychological immunity of the individual's perceived control is achieved only at the cost of integrating some small element of the disease into the self – in other words, perceiving uncontrollability in small, manageable doses, such as objectified enemies.

One might object that this orientation of *immunitas* is a cultural universal and not specific to contemporary society. To demonstrate the existence of meaningful cultural variation in these phenomena we will consider a typically modern incarnation of what might seem an age-old process. Our starting example contrasted a closed office and inconvenienced author with a medieval reaction to the threat of witchcraft. The medieval reaction could be described as a moral panic – a collective experience of disproportionate concern for an exaggerated threat (Goode & Ben-Yehuda, 1994). While such panics might seem a thing of the past, here we will consider qualitative research on a *contemporary* moral panic, namely, the emergence of the Tea Party in the United States. We propose that contemporary moral panics have unique qualities of *immunitas* – they combine the identification of enemies with an emphasis on personal agency, against a backdrop of invisible social control.

We have suggested that individuals in contemporary postindustrial societies inhabit a world structured by impersonal forces, permitting the perception of great personal control. Sometimes, however, these forces are thrown out of balance and that stability is shattered. Ross and Squires (2011) interviewed homeowners who were adversely affected by the subprime mortgage crisis, finding that individuals at risk of losing their homes were impacted in far-reaching ways. The authors report that informants saw their homes as sources of security, stability, and continuity, and that losing them removed any certainty about day-to-day life (p. 152). The individuals had placed their trust in the financial industry, the economy, and the institution of homeownership, but they had ultimately fallen prey to predatory lending. Informants described shame, embarrassment, depression, anxiety, and other negative effects on their well-being. The authors report that although the pervasive experience of the threat of foreclosure "reflects a range of institutional processes and risks that are largely unseen by prospective borrowers" (Ross & Squires, 2011, p. 155), the modern cultural context leads the individual to feel responsible. The denial of uncontrollability inherent to daily life in the modern world can thus trap individuals into powerlessness when their own agency fails them and their invisibly controlled world founders.

Scholarship on social movements suggests that such threats to perceptions of order, to systems of meaning, or to the routine patterns of daily life and subsistence can serve as potent stimuli for political mobilization (Fligstein & McAdam, 2012; McAdam, 2004; Snow et al., 1998). Unsurprisingly, then, financial troubles, political turmoil, and racial tension fomented by a bad economy, bailouts, and the election of Barack Obama as President of the United States motivated many to project their anxiety onto various social ills, individuals, or groups around them, endowing them with exaggerated influence over events. The Tea Party arose in this context from various directions – as Skocpol and Williamson (2012) put it, "Grassroots activists, roving billionaire advocates, and right-wing media purveyors" (p. 13) – with President Obama as a lightning rod for many due to his ethnic and national heritage, his political views, and his education.

The trajectory of the Tea Party can be represented in a few historic sequences which suggest its fit with an *immunitas* threat orientation. First, prior to the Great Recession, personal control was maintained by denial of uncontrollability and reliance on impersonal forces. Many members of the Tea Party had long-held beliefs about limited government and public spending (Skocpol & Williamson, 2012), which are in turn rooted in ideas about deservingness associated with belief in a just world and the Protestant Work Ethic.

However, in a second historical moment, strategies of denial failed in the face of economic crisis, leading to projection of the resulting anxiety onto targets such as the president and the federal government. Barack Obama has played the role of a "folk devil" within the movement (Cunningham, 2012). Projecting diffuse anxiety about the machinations of the economy onto the Obama administration and the Affordable Care Act allowed many Tea Party members to re-establish some sense of control.

This renewed sense of agency – strengthened, in keeping with the logic of *immunitas*, by the identification of enemy figures – can be observed in the third, most recent phase of the movement, which has brought about a return to the strategy of denial of uncontrollability. The Tea Party has become increasingly institutionalized, leading to a streamlining of its message and goals to better fit the legitimate channels of political action in the United States. Prior (2014) suggests that movement organizations and leaders became invested in a process of "quality control": efforts to keep adherents focused on core issues (for example, constitutionally limited government). Although individuals were passionate about other issues, such as immigration or religion, those issues were bracketed off during meetings and events in order to prevent divisive positions from diluting or obscuring the message, fragmenting the group, or feeding into media narratives about racism or other offensive beliefs. Prior (2014) highlights the struggle of Tea Party organizers to contain disruptive actions, prevent the carrying of racist or overly personal signs, and keep adherents energized about political action through legitimate channels.

In short, the Tea Party demonstrates a thoroughly modern dynamic of *immunitas*: initial threats to control were projected onto clear enemies, and this strategy was quickly amended by reinvigorated denial of uncontrollability through an emphasis on political agency. Just as in the case of biological immunization, the identification of a threat to personal control enhanced the perceived control of Tea Party members, producing a strengthened immune response. Skocpol and Williamson (2012) quote a participant who captures this dynamic:

> We always voted, but being busy people, we just didn't keep as involved as maybe we should have. And now we're to the point where we're really worried about our country. I feel like we came out of retirement. We do Tea Party stuff to take the country back to where we think it should be.
>
> (p. 46)

The Tea Party arose as moral panic similar to a medieval witch-hunt, but through the modern dynamics of *immunitas* it emerged as a powerful electoral force.

These dynamics are not the unique province of the political right. Consider, at the opposite end of the political spectrum, what Campbell and Manning (2014, p. 715) label an instance of a "culture of victimhood," a diffuse "movement" associated with college campuses in the developed world. These authors contend that decreased stratification and increased diversity have actually fostered *greater* concern about intergroup conflict on college campuses through heightened sensitivity to remaining inequalities. Stephens et al. (2012) find that increasing numbers of first-generation students hail from cultural backgrounds that do not match the university environment, generating feelings of isolation and uncertainty which can increase perceptions of threat from dissimilar groups (Bobo & Hutchings, 1996) and encourage in-group bias (Stollberg et al., 2015). The notion of competitive victimhood (Noor, Shnabel, Halabi, & Nadler, 2012; Sullivan, Landau, Branscombe, & Rothschild, 2012) posits that victim status can be wielded to increase moral standing relative to dominant collective actors (see also Jeffries et al., 2012). From this perspective, one way in which students from minority-group backgrounds may attempt to establish agency is by – paradoxically – elevating their perceived victim status.

According to Campbell and Manning (2014), these processes have facilitated the publicizing of incidents of *microaggressions* (for a review of relevant research, see Wong et al., 2014) and their transformation into an issue demanding collective action. In contrast to a culture of honor (where minor offenses are met with direct aggression) and a culture of dignity (where such offenses are ignored, and serious threats necessitate help from third parties), the resultant culture of victimhood entails heightened sensitivity to offensive speech or symbols combined with a reliance on third parties to resolve conflict. Campbell and Manning (2014) further note that minor grievances become more powerful sources of victimhood and more effective tools for forming coalitions when the grievances are pooled together and reframed as systemic injustice. In this way, activists involved in this movement construct a powerful enemy – a racist or otherwise unjust system – with which various oppressed minority groups and their allies struggle. This form of projection involves discursively relinquishing control to an enemy by claiming victimhood, yet simultaneously bolsters control and felt agency in the immediate environment (i.e., the university campus). Such control is achieved through demands made on formal, administrative institutions on campus. This process, which has already resulted in policy changes and the resignations of top officials at several universities, exemplifies an *immunitas* threat orientation: internalizing a threat by identifying as its victim immunizes and elevates the group, reestablishing control.

Schwartz (2016) analyzes this use of victimhood to gain control in connection with a series of racially charged events at Oberlin College in 2013. Throughout February 2013, the campus witnessed the dissemination of racist, homophobic, and anti-Semitic messages, and in early March a student reported seeing a lone figure in Ku Klux Klan attire in the middle of the night. These events resulted in canceled classes and a "Day of Solidarity." Dissatisfied with the administration's handling of the matter, student protesters interrupted a live, televised interview with the university president with chants and an angry tirade culminating in a sexist insult. When called upon to apologize for misrepresenting the university, one of the protesters – the senior class president – instead wrote in support of the disruption in the college newspaper, using victimhood to justify the incident:

> Students who are not directly targeted by recent events cannot judge nor invalidate the actions of students who are continually marginalized and oppressed, institutionally and interpersonally; instead, we all must listen to the experiences of students of color and queer students and must commit ourselves to allyship when asked to. . . . [W]e all must engage in allyship; allyship means to be committed to actions, accountability, and self-reflection that aim to dismantle structural injustices and daily microaggressions.
>
> (Hogan, 2013, quoted in Schwartz, 2016)

Although the offensive messages were discovered to be a hoax perpetrated by two students – one a left-leaning activist – and the robed figure was determined by campus security to have likely been a female student wrapped in a blanket, Schwartz (2016) argues that through a process of projection, this moral panic created its own reality that these revelations could not have stopped. Like the Tea Party activists, Oberlin students – galvanized by a moral panic – went on to demand far-reaching changes in the campus climate through institutional mechanisms, including, for example, mandatory training regarding privilege and oppression for both students and faculty.

In conclusion, we propose that a cultural-existential perspective is vital for understanding the paradoxical dynamics of perceived control and uncontrollability, and the interplay of denial and projection, in contemporary postindustrial culture. Contentious political movements and other forms of collective action can exert real influence on our societies to the extent that their leaders understand the schizophrenic commingling of agency and powerlessness, safety and threat in the worldviews of modern individualists. It is the duty of psychologists to cast light on these existential dynamics, and link them to the unseen workings and potent problems of our culture, in order to offer guidance in the wake of real threats like the Great Recession.

References

Bauer, M. A., Wilkie, J. E. B., Kim, J. K., & Bodenhausen, G. V. (2012). Cuing consumerism: Situational materialism undermines personal and social well-being. *Psychological Science, 23*, 517–523.

Becker, E. (1969). *Angel in armor.* New York: The Free Press.

Becker, E. (1973). *The denial of death.* New York: The Free Press.

Bernstein, B. (1990). *Class, codes and control: The structuring of pedagogic discourse v. 4.* New York: Routledge.

Bobo, L., & Hutchings, V. L. (1996). Perceptions of racial group competition: Extending Blumer's theory of group position to a multiracial social context. *American Sociological Review, 61*, 951–972.

Campbell, B., & Manning, J. (2014). Microaggression and moral cultures. *Comparative Sociology, 13*(6), 692–726.

Chiou, J., & Pan, L. (2008). The impact of social Darwinism perception, status anxiety, perceived trust of people, and cultural orientation on consumer ethical beliefs. *Journal of Business Ethics, 78*, 487–502.

Christopher, A. N., Zabel, K. L., Jones, J. R., & Marek, P. (2008). Protestant ethic ideology: Its multifaceted relations with just world beliefs, social dominance orientation, and right-wing authoritarianism. *Personality and Individual Differences, 45*, 473–477.

Clarke, I., & Micken, K. S. (2002). An exploratory cross-cultural analysis of the values of materialism. *Journal of International Materialism, 14*, 65–89.

Cross, S. E., Hardin, E. E., & Gercek-Swing, B. (2011). The what, how, why, and where of self-construal. *Personality and Social Psychology Review, 15*, 142–179.

Cunningham, J. L. (2012). *Obama as folk devil: A frame analysis of race, nationalism, and moral panic in the era of Obama.* (Unpublished master's thesis.) Sacramento: California State University.

Deacon, T. W. (1998). *The symbolic species: The co-evolution of language and the brain.* New York: W. W. Norton & Company.

Delhey, J., & Dragolov, G. (2014). Why inequality makes Europeans less happy: The role of distrust, status anxiety, and perceived conflict. *European Sociological Review, 30*, 151–162.

Duménil, G., & Lévy, D. (2011). *The crisis of neoliberalism.* Cambridge, MA: Harvard University Press.

Esposito, R. (2013). *Terms of the political: Community, immunity, biopolitics.* Trans. R. N. Welch. New York: Fordham University Press.

Festinger, L. (1957). *A theory of cognitive dissonance.* Stanford: Stanford University Press.

Fiske, S. T., & Morling, B. (1996). Stereotyping as a function of personal control motives and capacity constraints: The odd couple of power and anxiety. In R. M. Sorrentino & E. T. Higgins (Eds.), *Handbook of motivation and cognition* (Vol. 3, pp. 322–346). New York: Guilford Press.

Fligstein, N., & McAdam, D. (2012). *A theory of fields.* New York: Oxford University Press.

Goode, C., & Keefer, L. A. (2015). Grabbing your bootstraps: Threats to economic order boost beliefs in personal control. *Current Psychology.* Advance Online Publication. doi:http://dx.doi.org.ezproxy1.library.arizona.edu/10.1007/s12144-015-9376-0

Goode, E., & Ben-Yehuda, N. (1994). Moral panics: Culture, politics, and social construction. *Annual Review of Sociology, 20,* 149–171.

Greenberg, J., Koole, S. L., & Pyszczynski, T. (2004). *Handbook of experimental existential Psychology.* New York: The Guilford Press.

Greenberg, J., Solomon, S., & Arndt, J. (2008). A basic but uniquely human motivation: Terror management. In J. Shah (Ed.), *Handbook of motivation science* (pp. 114-134). New York: Guilford Press.

Gruenfeld, D. H., Inesi, M. E., Magee, J. C., & Galinsky, A. D. (2008). Power and the objectification of social targets. *Journal of Personality and Social Psychology, 95,* 111–127.

Guinote, A. (2015). Social cognition of power. In M. Mikulincer & P. R. Shaver (Eds.), *APA handbook of personality and social psychology* (Vol. 1, pp. 547–569). Washington, DC: APA Press.

Hagan, J., Rippl, S., Boehnke, K., & Merkens, H. (1999). Interest in evil: Hierarchic self-interest and right-wing extremism among East and West German youth. *Social Science Research, 28,* 162–183.

Hartnett, J., & Skowronski, J. J. (2008). Cash, money, woes: The match between a person's level of materialism and the materialistic (or non-materialistic) character of events alters affective forecasts. *North American Journal of Psychology, 10,* 647–644.

Hogan, A. D. (2013). Apology for the divisive nature of responses, not for protesting Kislov. *The Oberlin Review.* Retrieved from http://oberlinreview.org/1939/opinions/apology-for-divisive-nature-of-responses-not-for-protesting-krislov/

Horkheimer, M. (1947). *The eclipse of reason.* New York: Oxford University Press.

Janoff-Bulman, R. (1992). *Shattered assumptions: Towards a new psychology of trauma.* New York: Free Press.

Jeffries, C. H., Hornsey, M. J., Sutton, R. M., Douglas, K. M., & Bain, P. G. (2012). The David and Goliath principle: Cultural, ideological, and attitudinal underpinnings of the normative protection of low-status groups from criticism. *Personality and Social Psychology Bulletin, 38*(8), 1053–1065.

Johnson, E. J., & Tversky, A. (1983). Affect, generalization, and the perception of risk. *Journal of Personality and Social Psychology, 45,* 20–31.

Jonas, E., McGregor, I., Klackl, J., Agroskin, D., Fritsche, I., & Holbrook, C., . . . Quirin, M. (2014). Threat and defense: From anxiety to approach. *Advances in Experimental Psychology, 49,* 219–286.

Kay, A. C., Gaucher, D., Napier, J. L., Callan, M. J., & Laurin, K. (2008). God and the government: Testing a compensatory control mechanism for the support of external systems. *Journal of Personality and Social Psychology, 95,* 18–35.

Kay, A. C., Laurin, K., Fitzismons, G. M., & Landau, M. J. (2014). A functional basis for structure-seeking: Exposure to structure promotes willingness to engage in motivated action. *Journal of Experimental Psychology: General, 143,* 486–491.

Keefer, L. A., Landau, M. J., Sullivan, D., & Rothschild, Z. K. (2014). The object of affection: Subjectivity uncertainty increases objectification in close relationships. *Social Cognition, 32,* 484–504.

Keller, H. (2012). Autonomy and relatedness revisited: Cultural manifestations of universal human needs. *Child Development Perspectives, 6,* 12–18.

Kim, M. Y., Ford, B. Q., Mauss, I., & Tamir, M. (2014). Knowing when to seek anger: Psychological health and context-sensitive emotional preferences. *Cognition and Emotion, 29,* 1126–1136.

Kitayama, S., & Cohen, D. (2007). *Handbook of cultural psychology*. New York: Guilford Press.

Klein, C. T. F., & Helweg-Larsen, M. (2002). Perceived control and the optimistic bias: A meta-analytic review. *Psychology and Health, 17*, 437–446.

Kraus, M. W., Piff, P. K., & Keltner, D. (2009). Social class, sense of control, and social explanation. *Journal of Personality and Social Psychology, 97*, 992–1004.

Landau, M. J., Sullivan, D., Keefer, L. A., Rothschild, Z. K., & Osman, M. (2012). Subjectivity uncertainty theory of objectification: Compensating for uncertainty about how to positively relate to others by downplaying their subjective attributes. *Journal of Experimental Social Psychology, 48*, 1234–1246.

Langer, S. K. (1988). *Mind: An essay on human feeling* (abridged version). Baltimore: Johns Hopkins University Press.

Lee, M., Pant, A., & Ali, A. (2010). Does the individualist consume more? The interplay of ethics and beliefs that governs consumerism across cultures. *Journal of Business Ethics, 93*, 567–581.

Lerner, J. S., & Keltner, D. (2001). Fear, anger, and risk. *Journal of Personality and Social Psychology, 81*, 146–159.

Lerner, M. (1980). *The belief in a just world: A fundamental delusion*. New York: Plenum Press.

McAdam, D. (2004). Revisiting the U.S. civil rights movement: Toward a more synthetic understanding of the origins of contention. In J. Goodwin & J. M. Jasper (Eds.), *Rethinking social movements: Structure, meaning, and emotion* (pp. 201–232). Lanham, MD: Rowman & Littlefield Publishers, Inc.

Motro, D., & Sullivan, D. (2015). *Integrating negative emotion and work motivation: An existential approach*. Manuscript in preparation. Tucson: University of Arizona.

Noor, M., Shnabel, N., Halabi, S., & Nadler, A. (2012). When suffering begets suffering: The psychology of competitive victimhood between adversarial groups in violent conflicts. *Personality and Social Psychology Review, 16*(4), 351–374.

Norris, P., & Inglehart, R. (2012). *Sacred and secular: Religion and politics worldwide*. Cambridge: Cambridge University Press.

Oishi, S., Kesebir, S., & Diener, E. (2011). Income inequality and happiness. *Psychological Science, 22*, 1095–1100.

Piff, P. K., Stancato, D. M., Martinez, A. G., Kraus, M. W., & Keltner, D. (2012). Class, chaos, and the construction of community. *Journal of Personality and Social Psychology, 103*, 949–962.

Prior, F. B. (2014). Quality controlled: An ethnographic account of Tea Party messaging and action. *Sociological Forum, 29*(2), 301–317.

Pyszczynski, T., Greenberg, J., Solomon, S., & Hamilton, J. (1990). A terror management analysis of self-awareness and anxiety: The hierarchy of terror. *Anxiety Research, 2*, 177–195.

Ross, L. M., & Squires, G. D. (2011). The personal costs of subprime lending and the foreclosure crisis: A matter of trust, insecurity, and institutional deception. *Social Science Quarterly, 92*(1), 140–163.

Rothbaum, F., Weisz, J. R., & Snyder, S. S. (1982). Changing the world and changing the self: A two-process model of perceived control. *Journal of Personality and Social Psychology, 42*, 5–37.

Rothschild, Z. K., Landau, M. J., Sullivan, D., & Keefer, L. A. (2012). A dual-motive model of scapegoating: Displacing blame to reduce guilt or increase control. *Journal of Personality and Social Psychology, 102*, 1148–1163.

Schwartz, H. S. (2016). *Political correctness and the destruction of social order: Chronicling the rise of the pristine self*. New York: Palgrave Macmillan.

Skocpol, T., & Williamson, V. (2012). *The Tea Party and the remaking of Republican conservatism*. Oxford University Press.

Smelser, N. J. (1987). Depth psychology and the social order. In J. C. Alexander, B. Giesen, R. Münch, & N. J. Smelser (Eds.), *The micro-macro link* (pp. 267–286). Berkeley: University of California Press.

Smelser, N. J. (1999). *The social edges of psychoanalysis.* Berkeley: University of California Press.

Snow, D. A., Cress, D. M., Downey, L., & Jones, A. W. (1998). Disrupting the "quotidian": Reconceptualizing the relationship between breakdown and the emergence of collective action. *Mobilization: An International Journal, 3*(1), 1–22.

Stephens, N. M., Fryberg, S. A., Markus, H. R., Johnson, C. S., & Covarrubias, R. (2012). Unseen disadvantage: How American universities' focus on independence undermines the academic performance of first-generation college students. *Journal of Personality and Social Psychology, 102*(6), 1178.

Stollberg, J., Fritsche, I., & Bäcker, A. (2015). Striving for group agency: Threat to personal control increases the attractiveness of agentic groups. *Frontiers in Psychology, 6*, 649.

Stroessner, S. J., Scholer, A. A., Marx, D. M., & Weisz, B. M. (2015). When threat matters: Self-regulation, threat salience, and stereotyping. *Journal of Experimental Social Psychology, 59*, 77–89.

Sullivan, D. (2016). *Cultural-existential psychology: The role of culture in suffering and threat.* Cambridge: Cambridge University Press.

Sullivan, D., Landau, M. J., Branscombe, N. R., & Rothschild, Z. K. (2012). Competitive victimhood as a response to accusations of ingroup harm doing. *Journal of Personality and Social Psychology, 102*(4), 778.

Sullivan, D., Landau, M. J., & Rothschild, Z. K. (2010). An existential function of enemyship: Evidence that people attribute influence to personal and political enemies to compensate for threats to control. *Journal of Personality and Social Psychology, 98*, 434–449.

Sullivan, D., Landau, M. J., Rothschild, Z. K., & Keefer, L. A. (2014). Searching for the root of all evil: An existential-sociological perspective on political enemyship and scapegoating. In J. van Prooijen & P. A. M. van Lange (Eds.), *Power, politics, and paranoia: Why people are suspicious about their leaders* (pp. 292–311). Cambridge: Cambridge University Press.

Sullivan, D., & Palitsky, R. (2015). A cultural-existential account of variation in conspiracy beliefs. Paper presented at the Conspiracy Theories Conference. Miami: University of Miami.

Sullivan, D., Stewart S. A., & Diefendorf, J. (2015). Simmel's time-space theory: Implications for experience of modernization and place. *Journal of Environmental Psychology, 41*, 45–57.

Taylor, S. E., & Brown, J. D. (1988). Illusion and well-being: A social psychological perspective on mental health. *Psychological Bulletin, 103*, 193–210.

Twenge, J. M., Zhang, L., & Im, C. (2004). It's beyond my control: A cross-temporal meta-analysis of increasing externality of control, 1960–2002. *Personality and Social Psychology Review, 8*, 308–319.

Wong, G., Derthick, A. O., David, E. J. R., Saw, A., & Okazaki, S. (2014). The *what*, the *why*, and the *how*: A review of racial microaggressions research in psychology. *Race and Social Problems, 6*(2), 181–200.

Xie, X., Liu, H., & Gan, Y. (2011). Belief in a just world when encountering the 5/12 Wenchuan Earthquake. *Environment and Behavior, 43*, 566–586.

7

GIVING IN AND GIVING UP

Accommodation and fatalistic withdrawal as alternatives to primary control restoration

Joseph Hayes, Mike Prentice, and Ian McGregor

Author Note

Correspondence concerning this article should be addressed to Joseph Hayes, Acadia University, Department of Psychology, Horton Hall, 18 University Avenue, Wolfville, NS, B4P 2R6, Canada, Email: jhayes@acadiau.ca

The motivational impetus to maintain control over events in our lives is very strong (see e.g., Burger, 1992; Kay, Gaucher, Napier, Callan, & Laurin, 2008; Kelly, 1955; Rothbaum, Weisz, & Snyder, 1982). Indeed, without a sense of control, people would be unable to engage in goal-directed activity (Bandura, 1997; Kelly, 1955; Landau, Kay, & Whitson, 2015). There are times in life, however, when our ability to control important outcomes is stretched to the breaking point. In such times, we can feel overwhelmed with anxiety and uncertain about how to proceed. Although one way to overcome these anxious feelings is to flex one's muscles, redouble one's efforts, and strive harder to retain a sense of control over the situation, another way to resolve the issue is to loosen one's grip, accept that one does not have control, and give in to the overpowering nature of the situation. Whereas the former option entails struggling to bring the environment in line with the needs and desires of the self, the latter option involves bringing the self into line with the demands of the environment. According to Rothbaum et al. (1982), the first strategy represents efforts to retain primary control whereas the second strategy represents engagement in secondary control.

In this chapter, we combine insights from Rothbaum et al.'s (1982) classic dual-process model, with recent theoretical advances in threat compensation literature (Hayes, Ward, & McGregor, 2016; Jonas et al., 2014). We maintain that secondary control processes represent avoidance-oriented resolutions to motivational conflicts aroused by threats that challenge primary control. By contrast, approach-oriented resolutions to such conflicts entail persisting in primary control efforts or finding an alternative domain in which to engage primary control.

Although much research from the reactive approach motivation (RAM) model (McGregor, Nash, Mann, & Phills, 2010) has focused on these approach-oriented efforts to retain primary control, comparatively little research has focused explicitly on avoidance-oriented efforts to employ secondary control. After a brief exposition of these classic and contemporary perspectives on control and threat, we review evidence showcasing two specific secondary control processes: accommodation and withdrawal. We show that these processes are most likely to occur when approach-oriented efforts to retain primary control appear overly difficult or impossible due to situational or dispositional limitations. The central purpose of this chapter is to show that accommodation and withdrawal are effective means of resolving motivational conflict, and therefore provide relief from anxiety. However, these secondary control strategies can sometimes be suboptimal, because the same motivational processes can produce vulnerabilities when they are over-extensive, and can thereby pose additional problems for adaptive functioning and psychological well-being.

Primary and secondary control

In their classic two-process model of control, Rothbaum et al. (1982) distinguish between primary and secondary means of control. Primary control is the prototypical way in which people tend to think about control striving. Behavior falling under this category is active, goal-oriented, and involves operating on the environment in a way that elicits desired outcomes. Rothbaum et al. (1982), however, maintain that control striving can also include behaviors that may not be immediately recognizable as efforts to engage control. These researchers argue that behavior such as passivity, withdrawal, and submissiveness, which are normally thought to represent a lack of control, are in fact instances of secondary control. In essence, whereas primary control refers to the ability to bring the environment in line with the needs and desires of the self, secondary control refers to the ability to adapt to the environment and bring the self into line with current demands. From this perspective, both processes represent control striving, but whereas one process involves controlling or modifying the environment, the other involves controlling or modifying the self.

According to Rothbaum et al. (1982), these distinct modes of control are analogous to the processes of assimilation and accommodation outlined by Piaget (1977). In Piagetian terms, assimilation entails using existing beliefs and knowledge structures to make sense of incoming stimuli. This process is often attempted even when stimuli do not perfectly conform to the knowledge structures. In other words, much like primary control, assimilative processes sometimes involve conceptually molding or manipulating information to fit with existing beliefs. By contrast, accommodation involves molding one's beliefs to correspond as accurately as possible with perceived reality. According to Piaget, assimilation is the default mode of processing, and accommodation is undertaken only when existing knowledge structures are consistently at odds with one's experience of reality. The same is true for secondary control processes. Rothbaum et al. (1982) maintain that primary control is the default control process, and it is only when primary control proves to be ineffective due to repeated instances of failure that secondary control processes are employed.

Rothbaum et al. (1982) outline several examples of secondary control, such as downgrading expectations of personal success (i.e., predictive control) and submissively associating the self with powerful others (i.e., vicarious control). A common element in all of these processes is the avoidance of negative outcomes that could result from attempts to persist in the use of primary control. For example, Rothbaum et al. (1982) state that downgrading expectations functions to avoid the pain of disappointment associated with personal failure. Similarly, submissively aligning oneself with others can allow the self to share in others' successes, but shield the self from the sting of failure (cf., Cialdini et al., 1976). Accordingly, we maintain that secondary control strategies represent avoidance-oriented resolutions to the motivational conflict aroused by threats to primary control.

Approach vs. avoidance following threat

Recent perspectives in threat compensation literature have emphasized the implications that threatening events have for ongoing goal activity (e.g., Hayes et al., 2016; Jonas et al., 2014; McGregor et al., 2010). According to these perspectives, situational threats arouse a discrepancy between ambient goal-approach motivation and threat-avoidance motivation. For example, experiencing failure on an important anatomy test may pose a problem for one's goal of becoming a medical doctor. Under these circumstances, the individual is torn between the desire to continue directing activity toward achieving goal-success, and the nagging realization that this goal may never be accomplished and should therefore be abandoned. At a basic motivational level, this situation represents a conflict between the motivation to continue the approach-oriented activity that entails persisting in the threatened goal, and the motivation to withdraw from the threatened goal in order to avoid the frustration and disappointment associated with never achieving success. Given that one cannot simultaneously persist and withdraw from a threatened goal, one outcome will have to win out over the other.

According to Gray and McNaughton (2000; see also McNaughton & Corr, 2004), this sort of motivational conflict is regulated by a neural subsystem termed the behavioral inhibition system (BIS). The BIS functions to resolve the situation by promoting processes that side with either approach-oriented persistence or avoidance-oriented withdrawal. This task is accomplished by initially inhibiting ongoing goal-activity and arousing a state of anxious vigilance that serves to identify additional threats and risks involved in persistence (see Jonas et al., 2014 for a recent review of evidence). This vigilant state is also believed to aid in identification of alternative routes to goal completion that are not mired by risk and threat. If such an alternative can be identified, approach-motivation increases, goal-directed activity resumes, and anxiety is abated. In some cases, the individual may even switch to alternative goals that may be unrelated, or only distally related to one another (e.g., failure on an exam may trigger increased social affiliation as an alternate means of attaining self-esteem; see Pyszczynski & Greenberg, 1992). Either way, the motivational conflict is resolved by increasing approach-motivation, which deactivates the BIS (McGregor et al., 2010). However, if no alternative route to goal completion can be found, or all potential routes appear too risky or unlikely to succeed, the BIS will side with avoidance-motivation and trigger an impulse to withdraw from the conflicted goal (cf., Carver & Scheier, 1998). To be clear, rather than representing a continuation of BIS-process involving vigilant arousal and preoccupation with threat, we maintain that avoidance-oriented withdrawal represents a resolution to the motivational conflict, and thereby deactivates the BIS. Thus, although extant goal regulation frameworks for understanding threat and defense tend to prioritize approach-oriented resolutions (e.g., Jonas et al., 2014), we see avoidance-oriented withdrawal as the neglected other half of potential resolutions to motivational conflict aroused by threat. From this perspective, the basic function of the BIS is to restore motivational clarity in the interest of promoting a single behavioral output: approach-oriented persistence or avoidance-oriented withdrawal. Once the operations of the BIS have produced a clear favorite, the BIS relaxes (having served its function) and anxious vigilance is replaced by goal persistence or goal withdrawal.

Combining insights: Secondary control as avoidance-oriented resolution to threat

Within the context of control motivation, we maintain that avoidance-oriented withdrawal represents the motivational underpinnings of secondary control. To clarify, events that challenge the ability to successfully engage primary control arouse a motivational conflict between whether to persist in primary control efforts, or to succumb to the situation, withdraw from primary control, and thereby engage secondary control processes. Although people may often attempt to retain primary control in these cases, situational or dispositional factors that limit the perceived efficacy of these attempts will tip the balance in favor of secondary control. In the subsections that follow, we review evidence for this proposition.

Withdrawing from primary control

The core of our theoretical position is that secondary control processes represent a withdrawal from efforts to retain primary control. Evidence for this position can be found in research by Arndt and Solomon (2003), who examined the effects of mortality salience (MS) on the desire for personal control (i.e., a type of primary control). To elaborate, thoughts related to death are potent reminders of one's inability to control environmental outcomes (Agroskin & Jonas, 2013; Fritsche, Jonas, & Frankhanel, 2008). Despite our efforts to preserve ongoing life, we all recognize that these efforts will ultimately fail. Death is also a constant source of motivational conflict for ongoing goal activity (McGregor, Prentice, & Nash, 2013a). Indeed, death represents the terminal point of all our temporal goals. Nevertheless, people strive to both prevent death at all costs, and to make something of themselves while they are alive (Becker, 1973; Solomon, Greenberg, & Pyszczynski, 1991). Thus, for the present purposes, death represents a potent threat to one's ability to successfully engage primary control, which often invigorates primary control efforts as a way of reducing anxiety (e.g., Arndt & Solomon, 2003; McGregor, Gailliot, Vasquez, & Nash, 2007; Peters, Greenberg, Williams, & Schneider, 2005).

According to our goal-regulation premises, the ability to engage primary control in response to death-thoughts is contingent upon dispositional and situational factors that facilitate approach-oriented persistence in primary control activity. One dispositional factor that appears to hinder such persistence is emotional lability, or neuroticism. Dispositional neuroticism has been linked to sensitivities in the operations of the BIS (Corr, DeYoung, & McNaughton, 2013) and is strongly associated with a tendency toward withdrawal, especially in response to threat (DeYoung, 2010; DeYoung, Quilty, & Peterson, 2007). Thus, people who are high in neuroticism should be less likely to resolve motivational conflict with approach-oriented persistence, and should therefore be most likely to withdraw primary control efforts in response to MS. In support of this reasoning, Arndt and Solomon (2003) found that people high in neuroticism responded to MS by reducing their self-reported desire for personal control (Burger & Cooper, 1979). By contrast, those low in neuroticism responded to MS with increased desire for control. In other words, participants whose dispositional makeup was conducive to approach-oriented resolutions to threat (i.e., low neuroticism) sought to reaffirm their primary control after MS, whereas those whose disposition posed a hindrance to approach-oriented resolutions chose to abandon primary control.

In addition to dispositional factors, situational factors are equally important in determining whether approach-avoidance conflict will be resolved via persistence or withdrawal. One important situational factor that will favor persistence is a clear indication of *how* to persist in goal activity. In other words, when primary control is challenged by threat, approach-oriented persistence rests upon a coherent set of rules regarding which actions will be met with rewards, as well as an orderly and well-structured system of knowledge about how the world works (Landau et al., 2004, 2015). In other words, primary control requires having a worldview in place that provides an understanding of how to influence environmental outcomes. Moreover, in order to fully benefit from the worldview's ability to support primary control in this way, people must have faith in its validity. Accordingly, people who lack this faith or feel momentarily detached from the control-supporting structure of the worldview should find it more difficult to engage primary control, and should therefore be more likely to withdraw the desire to exert such control in response to MS. Consistent with this reasoning, Arndt and Solomon (2003) showed that when faith in the primary control-supporting structure of the worldview was hampered by reading an essay that challenged its validity, participants who otherwise favored persistence (i.e., those with low neuroticism) instead responded to MS by withdrawing from personal control.

Overall, these studies show that a potent threat to primary control (i.e., thoughts of death) will lead people to abandon personal forms of primary control when situational factors (worldview threat) or dispositional factors (high neuroticism) limit the ability to confidently mount efforts to retain primary control.

Secondary control vs. switching between sources of primary control

Despite evidence from Arndt and Solomon (2003) that people will sometimes withdraw from personal forms of primary control, it is important to note that relinquishing personal control does not necessarily imply the abandonment of primary control in favor of secondary control. A large and growing body of research in support of compensatory control theory (Rutjens & Kay, Chapter 5, this volume) and the group-based control model (Stollberg, Fritsche, Barth, & Jugert, Chapter 8, this volume) shows that when personal control appears limited, people will sometimes respond by affirming social institutions (e.g., governments) or other powerful external sources of control (e.g., God, groups). Although compensatory control effects are often referred to as secondary control (e.g., Kay et al., 2008; Landau et al., 2015), we maintain that these effects only represent secondary control to the extent that they involve withdrawing from primary control (i.e., reducing efforts to bring the environment in line with personal desires, and instead bringing the self in line with the environment). More often than not, both compensatory and group-based control reflect switching between different sources of primary control, rather than secondary control per se. For example, abandoning personal control over a life-threatening illness while simultaneously affirming an all-powerful and benevolent God who will ensure that one overcomes the illness and thus survives, does not represent secondary control in the way that we are referring to it because the person continues to persist in the goal of overcoming the illness (i.e., changing the world). Similarly, group-based control allows people to feel empowered by their group-membership (Fritsche et al., 2008, 2013). When a person feels as though he has the backing of his group, he can confidently persist in primary control efforts, despite situational risks or constraints (see also Navarrete, 2005). Moreover, groups are often the only means of effectively manipulating the environment, and affirming social ingroups has been shown to be a powerful lever of approach-motivation (Agroskin et al., 2013; Jonas et al., 2014). Thus, these compensatory and group-based efforts often reflect approach-oriented resolutions to motivational conflict rather than the avoidance-oriented resolutions that are the basis of secondary control.

According to Rothbaum et al. (1982), the key ingredient in secondary control is an effort to "change the self so as to fit more effectively with the environment [that] overshadows a tendency to change the environment so that it fits the self's needs" (p. 11; see also Morling & Evered, 2006 for evidence in favor of a fit-focused definition of secondary control). In our view, secondary control entails processes that *overshadow* primary control because the very nature of these processes involves a withdrawal from primary control. From this perspective, defensive compensation to threatened control only reflects secondary control to the extent that it entails withdrawing from efforts to manipulate the event that poses a threat to primary control. Nonspecific structuring effects (e.g., pattern recognition, conspiracy theories, enemyship) could potentially fall into this category (see Landau et al., 2015 for a review). For instance, Sullivan, Landau, and Rothschild (2010) found that threats to primary control led participants to attribute more power and influence to a personal enemy. Moreover, consistent with our perspective that secondary control is most likely when dispositional or situational factors limit the perceived efficacy of persistence in primary control, this effect was only observed among participants who were dispositionally low in perceived control. From a compensatory control perspective, nonspecific structuring is aimed primarily at understanding seemingly unpredictable negative events rather than at trying to outright control them (Landau et al., 2015). In our view, the shift from trying to *control* to merely trying to *understand* reflects a withdrawal from primary control and engagement in secondary control. In other words, the individual concedes that attempting to control the unpredictable event is not viable, and in order to avoid repeated surprise encounters with such events, instead seeks to understand or make meaning of them in order to better accept them or even anticipate them in the future. Notably, attempts to make meaning of seemingly unpredictable events need not have any basis in reality for them to be considered secondary control. The mere attempt to understand an unpredictable event by changing the way in which one thinks about it suffices (i.e., changing the self rather than changing the world). Thus, conspiracy theories and other explanations that often appear outlandish or illusory nevertheless represent secondary control. Of course, it remains possible that attributions related to conspiracy theories or powerful enemies lay the groundwork for primary control efforts (e.g., identifying enemies or conspirators in the interest of eradicating them). However, the key point that we wish to convey here is that abandoning one source of control (e.g., personal control) in favor of another source (e.g., God, government) does not reflect secondary control unless it involves withdrawing from ongoing primary control efforts to manipulate the environment. Quite often, compensatory control reflects switching between different sources of primary control, and thus entails efforts to retain ongoing primary control.

Accommodating the self

Recent research by Hayes et al. (2015) provides a clearer example of secondary control that involves withdrawing from primary control. According to Rothbaum et al. (1982), secondary control is akin to accommodative efforts to adapt to the environment by bringing the self in line with situational demands. The prototypical instance of accommodation involves changing one's beliefs and knowledge-structures to accord with novel events that cannot be easily assimilated (Piaget, 1977). By contrast, compensatory efforts to retain primary control in response to information that is inconsistent with extant beliefs would involve increasing one's conviction in these beliefs (McGregor, Zanna, Holmes, & Spencer, 2001) and forcing one's belief-system upon reality (Lord, Ross, & Lepper, 1979). These efforts ultimately preserve the threatened beliefs, even though they may not accurately capture the true state of affairs.

Evidence from persuasion and threat compensation literatures shows that biased assimilation can be aided by derogation of the source of the information (e.g., Greenberg et al., 1990; Hovland, Janis, & Kelley, 1953; Saucier, Webster, Hoffman, & Strain, 2014). If the source of counter-attitudinal information is deemed non-credible, then it can be easily and confidently dismissed. Hayes et al. (2015), however, show that threats to primary control will lead people to accommodate their beliefs instead of derogating the source of belief-inconsistent information, but only among people who lack the dispositional makeup to confidently persist in primary control. In other words, the secondary control process of belief-accommodation is only undertaken when the ability to defend (and thereby retain) the beliefs appears unlikely to be successful.

In this research, Hayes et al. (2015) sampled among atheist participants who reported a strong belief in an evolutionary account of the origins of life. These participants were exposed to a cogent argument against an evolutionary account of origins. In essence, they read an article in favor of creation by intelligent design that highlighted the fact that evolution cannot explain how self-replicating organisms arose in the first place, and therefore cannot account for life's origins. After reading the article, participants were asked to rate the extent to which they believed in evolutionary theory's ability to account for the origins of life, as well as to indicate their attitudes toward the author of the essay. Participants exposed to MS prior to reading the article showed two distinct patterns of response: one corresponding to effortful retention of primary control, the other representing the abandonment of such efforts and engagement in secondary control. Which strategy was favored was a function of participants' level of trait self-esteem.

Prior research shows that self-esteem is a strong indicator of approach- vs. avoidance-oriented responses to threat (e.g., Baumeister, Tice, & Hutton, 1989; Cavallo, Holmes, Fitzsimmons, Murray, & Wood, 2012; Landau & Greenberg, 2006; McGregor et al., 2007). Although people with high self-esteem tend to increase approach-oriented efforts characteristic of primary control, people with low self-esteem tend to reduce approach-motivation and thus renounce primary control in favor of secondary control. Consistent with this research, Hayes et al. (2015) found that participants with high self-esteem reduced their willingness to accommodate their belief in an evolutionary account of origins following MS. Instead, these participants chose to derogate the author of the worldview-threatening article. This pattern reflects attempts to exert primary control by rigidly defending pre-existing beliefs and insisting that the author of the article must be wrong. By contrast, participants with low self-esteem opted for a secondary control strategy under these circumstances, which involved accommodating their beliefs to accord with the evidence presented in the article. These participants were significantly more likely to agree that evolutionary theory cannot explain the origins of life. And as a result, they were significantly less derogatory toward the author of the article.

Hayes et al. (2015) observed parallel findings among participants who held beliefs on the opposite side of the creation-evolution debate, which suggests that this phenomenon is not specific to secular atheists. More specifically, another study sampled among participants who possessed a strong belief in creationism and disbelief in evolution, and exposed them to an article reporting scientific evidence in support of macro-evolutionary processes. Once again, when mortality was salient, participants with high self-esteem fought to retain primary control by resisting accommodation and derogating the source of the article. Participants with low self-esteem who were primed with death, by contrast, responded by increasing their agreement with the idea that naturalistic processes must have caused species to evolve over time. Thus, these participants increased their willingness to modify pre-existing beliefs in accordance with the evidence. We maintain that this represents a secondary control process that entails withdrawing from primary control and accommodating the self. Consistent with our reasoning, this process was most pronounced when primary control was threatened, and only among participants who lacked the confidence (i.e., self-esteem) to defend primary control.

On the benefits and risks of engaging secondary control processes

Thus far, the focus of this chapter has been to show that the motivational conflict aroused by threats to primary control can promote approach-oriented efforts to persist in primary control or avoidance-oriented withdrawal from primary control and engagement of secondary control that involves accommodating the self. In this section, we highlight the benefits and risks of engaging secondary control processes.

Although the main purpose of engaging secondary control is to shield the self from the potentially negative consequences of engaging primary control (i.e., avoidance of personal failure), we maintain that an additional benefit of employing secondary control strategies is the relief from anxiety that accompanies the resolution of approach-avoidance conflict. Much like approach-oriented responses to threat that ultimately function to mute BIS-activation (Jonas et al., 2014; McGregor, Prentice, & Nash, 2013b), avoidance-oriented responses (which include engagement of secondary control) are equally capable of deactivating the BIS. According to McNaughton and Corr (2004), when the BIS-process has produced a clear favorite between conflicting approach and avoidance motivation, the BIS will relax regardless of which motivational tendency is ultimately favored. Once the BIS-process is terminated, the state of anxious vigilance that is characteristic of BIS-activation is abated. Thus, an important benefit of engaging secondary control processes that entail siding with motivational avoidance is the relief from anxiety that accompanies these processes.

However, despite this relief from anxiety, secondary control strategies also come with substantial risks. First, although belief-accommodation should offer defense against threat, and should therefore deactivate the BIS, going too far and accommodating core aspects of one's belief-system may jeopardize one's ability to maintain a structured and coherent view of reality. In other words, accommodating too much can ultimately compromise the functioning of the worldview, and given that a well-structured belief system is necessary for reducing anxieties regarding uncontrollability (Landau et al., 2004; Landau et al., 2015), this can render the process ineffective. Moreover, when threats to primary control produce a withdrawal process that is over-extensive, it can instill a sense of complete helplessness and thereby lead to depression.

Accommodating peripheral vs. core worldview beliefs

Hayes et al. (2015) found evidence for the risks associated with accommodating too much of the belief system by differentiating between core and peripheral aspects of the worldview (Kelly, 1955). Recall that in these studies, participants had pre-existing beliefs about God and evolutionary theory and were exposed to information that contradicted these beliefs. For the most part, the accommodation effects in these studies were limited to beliefs regarding evolution, while beliefs about God remained highly resistant to change. We reasoned that this pattern suggests that beliefs regarding God represented core aspects of our participants' worldview, whereas beliefs regarding evolution were relatively peripheral to the overall organization of the belief system. Thus, in this case, changing only peripheral beliefs regarding evolutionary theory to accord with the evidence, while simultaneously clinging to core beliefs about God, allowed participants to defuse the threat without compromising the core structure of the worldview. Consistent with this perspective, relative differences in the extent to which participants accommodated these core vs. peripheral worldview beliefs provided evidence for both the benefits and the risks inherent in accommodation.

In one study, Hayes et al. (2015) assessed vigilant attention to threat-related stimuli – a cardinal feature of BIS-activation – after participants were given an opportunity to accommodate their beliefs. Given that the source of threat was mortality salience, we administered a measure of death-thought accessibility (DTA). This measure involves completing a series of word fragments with the first word that comes to mind. Embedded in the task are several fragments that can be completed using a death-related word (e.g., DE_ _ = dead), thereby providing an indication of the extent to which threat-related thoughts are accessible to conscious awareness. Research on terror management theory has shown that people are most defensive when DTA is high, and having an opportunity to engage effective defenses subsequently reduces DTA (see Hayes, Schimel, Arndt, & Faucher, 2010 for a review). Thus, DTA appears to represent a basic aspect of BIS aroused by MS. In support of the idea that accommodation is effective in reducing BIS-vigilance toward threat-related stimuli, participants who evinced the most accommodation also completed the fewest number of word fragments in a death-related manner. In other words, accommodation was negatively correlated with DTA. However, this pattern was only observed when considering peripheral belief-change. In fact, the opposite pattern emerged when considering core beliefs. Although the extent of core belief-change was very low, those who changed these beliefs showed somewhat higher levels of DTA. In another study, the same overall pattern was observed on fluid defensiveness in a domain unrelated to the threat. Specifically, whereas peripheral belief-change resulted in lower punishment attributions for a worldview violator, core belief-change led to higher punishment. Given that fluid defensiveness is believed to stem from BIS-processes associated with anxiety (Jonas et al., 2014; Proulx, Inzlicht, & Harmon-Jones, 2012), reduced fluid defense suggests that the BIS process has been terminated, whereas increased defense suggests the BIS is still activated. These results are consistent with the idea that accommodation can be an effective means of deactivating the BIS, but accommodating too much of one's worldview can render this process ineffective. Thus, the secondary control process of accommodation is an important means of reducing threat and adapting to environmental constraints, but it can be ineffective when the process is widespread.

Fatalistic withdrawal

The adaptive problems inherent in the overextension of the avoidance-oriented processes that underlie secondary control are also apparent in widespread withdrawal. Although the engagement of secondary control involves withdrawal from primary control, sometimes the withdrawal process can be all-inclusive, which poses additional problems for optimal functioning and psychological well-being.

Perhaps one of the most important ways in which people exercise primary control is through their continued efforts to sustain ongoing life. In other words, people are almost constantly doing things that maximize the likelihood that they will continue living from one moment to the next. Mundane activities, such as going to work or even just preparing food, represent ongoing primary control activity aimed at securing continued life (cf., Pyszczynski, Greenberg, Solomon, & Hamilton, 1990). Thus, although the awareness of inevitable death reminds us of our powerlessness, at the most basic level, death is in conflict with the desire for life (Greenberg, Pyszczynski, & Solomon, 1986). The awareness of death therefore arouses a motivational conflict between whether to continue in one's efforts to live (primary control), or accept that death is inevitable and withdraw the desire for continued life (secondary control). Given what is at stake, this conflict is usually resolved via approach-oriented means that involve affirming life and persisting in life-sustaining primary control efforts despite the inevitability of death (see Greenberg, 2012 for a recent review of evidence). However, the secondary control process, which entails letting go of efforts to preserve life, is always available as an option to resolve the motivational conflict when the struggle to retain primary control becomes too much to bear.

This reasoning was recently tested in a series of studies assessing the impact of death-thoughts on the desire for continued life (Hayes et al., 2016). We reasoned that people who experience difficulty obtaining the rewards that life has to offer should be particularly likely to withdraw from life-affirming efforts when reminded of the inevitability of death. More specifically, in these studies we assessed participants' overall life satisfaction (Diener, Emmons, Larsen, & Griffin, 1985), and furthermore manipulated their ability to engage approach-motivation following MS. Accordingly, after the usual delay period during which approach-oriented efforts are typically observed following MS (see Jonas et al., 2014; Pyszczynski et al., 1999), participants were asked to recall a time in which they tried hard to achieve a goal that was important to them. Whereas some participants were asked to recall a goal that ultimately led to success, others were asked to recall a goal that failed despite their efforts. In other words, for participants in the failure condition, primary control efforts to affirm life by striving toward life-sustaining goals were impeded by salient thoughts of a time in which these efforts failed. Thereafter, withdrawal from the goal for continued life was assessed by asking participants how old they hoped to be when they die. Consistent with hypotheses, participants with low life satisfaction whose primary control efforts were blocked by failure responded to MS by significantly reducing the age at which they reported wanting to die. Thus, these participants showed signs of withdrawal from life itself.

Subsequent studies confirmed the idea that withdrawal from life constitutes widespread withdrawal from all (or nearly all) goal-directed activity. The goal to continue living is perhaps the most superordinate goal in the goal-hierarchy (Carver & Scheier, 1998; Pyszczynski et al., 1990). Thus, when a person gives up on this goal, they simultaneously give up on all of the goals that furnish their life. In support of this idea, Hayes et al. (2016) found that participants with low life satisfaction who contemplated failure responded to MS with general reductions on various indicators of goal-approach motivation. Specifically, these participants showed reduced willingness to delay gratification for instrumental ends, reduced orientation toward the future, reduced drive and responsiveness to rewards (i.e., behavioral activation system sensitivity; Carver & White, 1994), and increased levels of pessimism and fatalism. Overall, the conditions that lead to withdrawal from life also produced a fatalistic withdrawal from all motivational pursuits. In essence, these participants showed signs of beginning to give up on everything.

Importantly, the evidence also showed that fatalistic withdrawal effectively deactivated the BIS. Indeed, participants who abandoned the desire for life in the face of death evinced significantly lower levels of anxious uncertainty. Anxiety and uncertainty are key features of the BIS-state, and once a motivational conflict is resolved – even via avoidance-oriented withdrawal from life – the BIS has served its function and is therefore deactivated. However, despite the relief from anxiety offered by fatalistic withdrawal, this state was associated with increased levels of depression. These results are consistent with the idea that submitting to uncontrollability and withdrawing from efforts to engage primary control can lead to generalized feelings of helplessness and can ultimately produce clinical depression (Abramson, Metalsky, & Allow, 1989; Seligman, 1975). Thus, when the avoidance-oriented resolution to motivational conflict that underlies secondary control processes leads to widespread withdrawal, the detriment to psychological well-being may vastly outweigh the benefits of reduced anxiety.

Taken together, these studies show that the secondary control processes of accommodation and withdrawal following threats to primary control are effective at muting the BIS and thereby relieving anxiety. However, these processes can also pose additional problems for optimal functioning and psychological well-being when they are over-extensive. Although accommodation that entails changing only relatively peripheral worldview beliefs appears to be adaptive, accommodating too much of one's worldview can compromise the anxiety-buffering function of a clear and coherent conception of reality. Similarly, although goal-withdrawal can often reduce the anxiety associated with the struggle to maintain primary control under conditions of threat, withdrawing from goals that occupy superordinate positions in the goal-hierarchy can lead to a collapse in the goal-system and result in generalized decrements in the ability to mount any approach-motivation at all. Thus, secondary control processes are most effective when they are fairly conservative and do not impinge upon too much of one's core beliefs and goals.

Summary and conclusion

In this chapter, we have argued that secondary control processes can be conceptualized as avoidance-oriented resolutions to the motivational conflict aroused by threats to primary control. More specifically, events that lead us to question our ability to successfully control outcomes, such as thoughts of impending death, arouse a motivational conflict between whether to persist in efforts to control the situation or withdraw from such efforts in order to avoid failure. Whereas the former option represents an approach-oriented resolution to the conflict, the latter option represents an avoidance-oriented resolution. These approach–avoidance conflicts are characterized by anxiety, uncertainty, and a vigilant search for ways out of the conflict. Thus, people are highly motivated to obtain a resolution as quickly as possible (McNaughton & Corr, 2004). When the situation appears entirely uncontrollable (for either situational or dispositional reasons), people will tend to choose the avoidance-oriented resolution. In the case of control motivation, this resolution involves withdrawing from primary control activities aimed at changing the environment and instead engaging secondary control aimed at changing the self.

In support of these ideas, we reviewed research showing that threats to primary control will lead people to abandon the desire for primary control, accommodate their beliefs, and withdraw from important high-level goals. These secondary control strategies are only observed when situational or dispositional factors limit the perceived likelihood that primary control efforts will be successful. Consistent with the idea that secondary control represents an effective resolution to the motivational conflict aroused by threat, this research also shows that exercising these strategies reduces anxiety, vigilant preoccupation with threat-related stimuli, and fluid defensiveness in an alternative domain. However, when these processes are too extensive, they become ineffective and can even lead to psychological problems such as depression.

The delicate balance between engaging secondary control but not overdoing it by withdrawing from too much of one's core beliefs and goals underscores a key feature of adaptive control striving. The classic perspectives that we built upon in this chapter also emphasized the importance of achieving this balance. Piaget (1977) argued that optimal cognitive development entails an equilibration of assimilative and accommodative processes. That is, accommodative efforts are only effective to the extent that they facilitate subsequent assimilation of the novel information that posed a threat to the belief system in the first place. Indeed, accommodation is often required for people to accept negative life events, and grow from adverse experience (Tedeschi & Calhoun, 2004). Thus, effective accommodation should reduce future instances of threat, whereas maladaptive accommodation will leave the belief-system in a state of disarray, leading to further difficulties with assimilation and thus more instances of threat. Similarly, Rothbaum et al. (1982) argued that a balance of primary and secondary control is necessary to efficaciously navigate the world. In other words, secondary control processes are most effective when they enable disengagement of primary control that will never be successful (cf., Brandstädter & Renner, 1990; Heckhausen, Wrosch, & Schultz, 2010; Pyszczynski & Greenberg, 1992). There are certain events in life that simply cannot be controlled, and doggedly persisting in efforts to control them will only lead to a prolonged, futile, anxiety-ridden struggle. In such cases, the ability to give up and withdraw one's efforts is a crucial step in successfully adapting to the situation. In essence, secondary control is most adaptive when it facilitates letting go and moving on, but least adaptive when it leads to letting go of everything and thereby impedes the ability to move on.

The research reviewed in this chapter adds substantial support for these perspectives. Plus, this research also suggests that the same basic need for balance between complimentary control processes extends to the way in which we manage approach-avoidance conflicts generally. Although both approach and avoidance resolutions to such conflicts can offer relatively immediate relief from anxiety, the most adaptive compensation in response to threat involves approaching and persisting when such activity is viable, but avoiding and withdrawing when it is not. Thus, avoidance is often both appropriate and adaptive, but only to the extent that it does not compromise subsequent approach. To put it succinctly, adaptively coping with threat often requires us to give in, but the same process will be maladaptive if it leads us to completely give up.

References

Abramson, L.Y., Metalsky, G. I., & Allow, L. B. (1989). Hopelessness depression: A theory-based subtype of depression. *Psychological Review, 96*, 358–372. doi:10.1037/0033-295X.96.2.358

Agroskin, D., & Jonas, E. (2013). Controlling death by defending ingroups – Mediational insights into terror management and control restoration. *Journal of Experimental Social Psychology, 49*, 1144–1158. doi:10.1016/j.jesp.2013.05.014

Arndt, J., & Solomon, S. (2003). The control of death and the death of control: The effects of mortality salience, neuroticism, and worldview threat on the desire for control. *Journal of Research in Personality, 37*, 1–22. doi:10.1016/S0092-6566(02)00530-5

Bandura, A. (1997). Self-efficacy: Toward a unifying theory of behavioral change. *Psychological Review, 84*, 191–215. doi:10.1037/0033-295X.84.2.191

Baumeister, R. F., Tice, D. M., & Hutton, D. G. (1989). Self-presentational motivations and personality differences in self-esteem. *Journal of Personality, 57*, 547–579. doi:10.1111/j.1467-6494.1989.tb02384.x

Becker, E. (1973). *The denial of death*. New York: Free Press.

Brandstädter, J., & Renner, G. (1990). Tenacious goal pursuit and flexible goal adjustment: Explication and age-related analysis of assimilative and accommodative strategies of coping. *Psychology and Aging, 5*, 58–67.

Burger, J. M. (1992). *Desire for control: Personality, social, and clinical perspectives*. New York, NY: Plenum Press.

Burger, J. M., & Cooper, H. M. (1979). The desirability of control. *Motivation and Emotion, 3*, 381–393. doi:10.1007/BF00994052

Carver, C. S., & Scheier, M. F. (1998). *On the self-regulation of behavior*. New York: Cambridge University Press.

Carver, C. S., & White, T. L. (1994). Behavioral inhibition, behavioral activation, and affective responses to impending reward and punishment: The BIS/BAS scales. *Journal of Personality and Social Psychology, 67*, 319–333. doi:10.1037/0022-3514.67.2.319

Cavallo, J., V., Holmes, J. G., Fitzsimmons, G. M., Murray, S. L., & Wood, J. V. (2012, June 4). Managing motivational conflict: How self-esteem and executive resources influence self-regulatory responses to risk. *Journal of Personality and Social Psychology*. Advance online publication. doi:10.1037/a0028821

Cialdini, R. B., Borden, R. J., Thorne, A., Walker, M. R., Freeman, S., & Sloan, L. R. (1976). Basking in reflected glory: Three (football) field studies. *Journal of Personality and Social Psychology, 34*, 366–375. doi:10.1037/0022-3514.34.3.366

Corr, P. J., DeYoung, C. G., & McNaughton, N. (2013). Motivation and personality: A neuropsychological perspective. *Social and Personality Psychology Compass, 7*, 158–175. doi:10.1111/spc3.12016

DeYoung, C. G. (2010). Personality neuroscience and the biology of traits. *Social and Personality Psychology Compass, 4*, 1165–1180. doi:10.1111/j.1751-9004.2010.00327.x

DeYoung, C. G., Quilty, L. C., & Peterson, J. B. (2007). Between facets and domains: 10 aspects of the Big Five. *Journal of Personality and Social Psychology, 93*, 880–896. doi:10.1037/0022-3514.93.5.880

Diener, E., Emmons, R. A., Larsen, R. J., & Griffin, S. (1985). The satisfaction with life scale. *Journal of Personality Assessment, 49*, 71–75. doi:10.1207/s15327752jpa4901_13

Fritsche, I., Jonas, E., Ablasser, C., Beyer, M., Kuban, J., Manger, A., & Schultz, M. (2013). The power of we: Evidence for group-based control. *Journal of Experimental Social Psychology, 49*, 19–32. doi:10.1016/j.jesp.2012.07.014

Fritsche, I., Jonas, E., & Frankhanel, T. (2008). The role of control motivation in mortality salience effects on ingroup support and defense. *Journal of Personality and Social Psychology, 95*, 524–541. doi:10.1037/a0012666

Gray, J. A., & McNaughton, N. (2000). *The neuropsychology of anxiety: An enquiry into the functions of the septo-hippocampal system* (2nd ed.). Oxford: Oxford University Press.

Greenberg, J. (2012). Terror management theory: From genesis to revelations. In P. R. Shaver & M. Mikulincer (Eds.), *Meaning, mortality, and choice: The social psychology of existential concerns* (pp. 17–35). Washington, DC: American Psychological Association. doi:10.1037/13748-001

Greenberg, J., Pyszczynski, T., & Solomon, S. (1986). The causes and consequences of a need for self-esteem: A terror management theory. In R. F. Baumeister (Ed.), *Public self and private self* (pp. 189–212). New York: Springer-Verlag. doi:10.1007/978-1-4613-9564-5_10

Greenberg, J., Pyszczynski, T., Solomon, S., Rosenblatt, A., Veeder, M., Kirkland, S., & Lyon, D. (1990). Evidence for terror management theory II: The effects of mortality salience on reactions to those who threaten or bolster the cultural worldview. *Journal of Personality and Social Psychology, 58*, 308–318. doi:10.1037/0022-3514.58.2.308

Hayes, J., Schimel, J., Arndt, J., & Faucher, E. H. (2010). A theoretical and empirical review of the death-thought accessibility concept in terror management research. *Psychological Bulletin, 136*, 699–739. doi:10.1037/a0020524

Hayes, J., Schimel, J., Williams, T. J., Howard, A. L., Webber, D., & Faucher, E. H. (2015). Worldview accommodation: Selectively modifying committed beliefs provides defense against worldview threat. *Self and Identity, 14*, 521–548. doi:10.1080/15298868.2015.1036919

Hayes, J., Ward, C., & McGregor, I. (2016). Why bother? Death, failure, and fatalistic withdrawal from life. *Personality and Social Psychology, 110*, 96–115. doi:10.1037/pspp0000039

Heckhausen, J., Wrosch, C., & Schulz, R. (2010). A motivational theory of life-span development. *Psychological Review, 117*, 32–60. doi:10.1037/a0017668

Hovland, C. I., Janis, I. L., & Kelley, H. H. (1953). *Communication and persuasion*. New Haven, CT: Yale University Press.

Jonas, E., McGregor, I., Klackl, J., Agroskin, D., Fritsche, I., Holbrook, C., Nash, K., Proulx, T., & Quirin, M. (2014). Threat and defense: From anxiety to approach. In J. M. Olson & M. P. Zanna (Eds.), *Advances in experimental social psychology* (Vol. 49, pp. 219–286). Burlington: Academic Press. doi:10.1016/b978-0-12-800052-6.00004-4

Kay, A. C., Gaucher, D., Napier, J. L., Callan, M. J., & Laurin, K. (2008). God and the government: Testing a compensatory control mechanism for the support of external systems. *Journal of Personality and Social Psychology, 95*, 18–35. doi:10.1037/0022-3514.95.1.18

Kelly, G. A. (1955). T*he psychology of personal constructs*. New York: Norton.

Landau, M. J., & Greenberg, J. (2006). Play it safe or go for gold? A terror management perspective on self-enhancement and self-protection motivates in risky decision making. *Personality and Social Psychology Bulletin, 32*, 1633–1645. doi:10.1177/0146167206292017

Landau, M. J., Johns, M., Greenberg, J., Pyszczynski, T., Martens, A., Goldenberg, J. L., & Solomon, S. (2004). A function of form: Terror management and structuring the social world. *Journal of Personality and Social Psychology, 87*, 190–210. doi:10.1037/0022-3514.87.2.190

Landau, M. J., Kay, A. C., & Whitson, J. A. (2015). Compensatory control and the appeal of a structured world. *Psychological Bulletin, 141*, 694–722. doi:10.1037/a0038703

Lord, C. G., Ross, L., & Lepper, M. R. (1979). Biased assimilation and attitude polarization: The effects of prior theories on subsequently considered evidence. *Journal of Personality and Social Psychology, 37*, 2098–2109. doi:10.1037/0022-3514.37.11.2098

McGregor, I., Gailliot, M. T., Vasquez, N. A., & Nash, K. A. (2007). Ideological and personality zeal reactions to threat among people with high self-esteem: Motivated promotion focus. *Personality and Social Psychology Bulletin, 33*, 1587–1599. doi:10.1177/0146167207306280

McGregor, I., Nash, K., & Mann, N., & Phills, C. E. (2010). Anxious uncertainty and reactive approach motivation (RAM). *Journal of Personality and Social Psychology, 99*, 133–147. doi:10.1037/a0019701

McGregor, I., Prentice, M., & Nash, K. (2013a). Anxious uncertainty and reactive approach motivation (RAM) for religious, idealistic, and lifestyle extremes. *Journal of Social Issues, 69*, 537–563. doi:10.1111/josi.12028

McGregor, I., Prentice, M., & Nash, K. (2013b). Approaching relief: Compensatory ideals relieve threat-induced anxiety by promoting approach-motivated states. *Social Cognition, 30*, 689–714. doi:10.1521/soco.2012.30.6.689

McGregor, I., Zanna, M. P., Holmes, J. G., & Spencer, S. J. (2001). Compensatory conviction in the face of personal uncertainty: Going to extremes and being oneself. *Journal of Personality and Social Psychology, 80*, 472–488. doi:10.1037//0022-3514.80.3.472

McNaughton, N., & Corr, P. J. (2004). A two-dimensional neuropsychology of defense: Fear/anxiety and defensive distance. *Neuroscience and Biobehavioral Reviews, 28*, 285–305. doi:10.1016/j.neubiorev.2004.03.005

Morling, B., & Evered, S. (2006). Secondary control reviewed and defined. *Psychological Bulletin, 132*, 269–296. doi:10.1037/0033-2909.132.2.269

Navarrete, C. D. (2005). Death concerns and other adaptive challenges: The effects of coalition-relevant challenges on worldview defense in the US and Costa Rica. *Group Processes & Intergroup Relations, 8*, 411–427. doi:10.1177/1368430205056468

Peters, H. J., Greenberg, J., Williams, J. M., & Schneider, N. R. (2005). Applying terror management theory to performance: Can reminding individuals of their mortality increase strength output? *Journal of Sport & Exercise Psychology, 27*, 111–116.

Piaget, J. (1977). *The development of thought: Equilibration of cognitive structures.* New York: The Viking Press.

Proulx, T., Inzlicht, M., & Harmon-Jones, E. (2012). Understanding all inconsistency compensation as a palliative response to violated expectations. *Trends in Cognitive Sciences, 16*, 285–291. doi:10.1016/j.tics.2012.04.002

Pyszczynski, T., & Greenberg, J. (1992). *Hanging on and letting go: Understanding the onset, progression, and remission of depression.* New York, NY: Springer-Verlag.

Pyszczynski, T., Greenberg, J., & Solomon, S. (1999). A dual-process model of defense against conscious and unconscious death-related thoughts: An extension of terror management theory. *Psychological Review, 106*, 835–845. doi:10.1037/0033-295X.106.4.835

Pyszczynski, T., Greenberg, J., Solomon, S., & Hamilton, J. (1990). A terror management analysis of self-awareness and anxiety: The hierarchy of terror. *Anxiety Research, 2*, 177–195. doi:10.1080/08917779008249335

Rothbaum, F., Weisz, J. R., & Snyder, S. S. (1982). Changing the world and changing the self: A two-process model of perceived control. *Journal of Personality and Social Psychology, 42*, 5–37.

Saucier, D. A., Webster, R. J., Hoffman, B. H., & Strain, M. L. (2014). Social vigilantism and reported use of strategies to resist persuasion. *Personality and Individual Differences, 70*, 120–125. doi:10.1016/j.paid.2014.06.031

Seligman, M. E. P. (1975). *Helplessness: On depression, development, and death.* San Francisco: Freeman.

Solomon, S., Greenberg, J., & Pyszczynski, T. (1991). A terror management theory of social behavior: The psychological functions of self-esteem and cultural worldviews. In M. Zanna (Ed.), *Advances in experimental social psychology* (Vol. 24, pp. 93–159). Orlando, FL: Academic Press.

Sullivan, D., Landau, M. J., & Rothschild, Z. K. (2010). An existential function of enemyship: Evidence that people attribute influence to personal and political enemies to compensate for threats to control. *Journal of Personality and Social Psychology, 98*, 434–449. doi:10.1037/a0017457

Tedeschi, R. G., & Calhoun, L. G. (2004). Posttraumatic growth: Conceptual foundations and empirical evidence. *Psychological Inquiry, 15*, 1–18. doi:10.1207/s15327965pli1501_01

8

EXTENDING CONTROL PERCEPTIONS TO THE SOCIAL SELF

Ingroups serve the restoration of control

Janine Stollberg, Immo Fritsche, Markus Barth, and Philipp Jugert

Contact: janine.stollberg@uni-leipzig.de

Author's note

The contribution by Immo Fritsche and Janine Stollberg was partially funded by the German Research Foundation (DFG; FR 2067 3-1).

Introduction

Humans are motivated to maintain a sense of control. Throughout their lives, people face various important situations they cannot control. They walk the road of life unwaveringly until something makes them stumble or sink into soggy ground, pulling the rug from under their feet. When their sense of general control is shaken, they might feel as if the ground had vanished, while at the same time, they will try to regain a foothold on firm ground. Economic crises and instable conditions of employment, severe diseases of loved ones, and sudden breakups of important relationships represent examples of ground-shaking experiences that can diminish confidence in control over one's own life. Even just anticipating such events is sufficient to threaten perceived control, leading to the fundamental feeling that one can no longer master any situation or event. To alleviate the negative impact of low personal control and to reestablish a sense of personal influence, people can use different strategies to get out of the quicksand of control loss and to get back on firm ground again. Apart from merely idiosyncratic personal strategies, like putting more effort into personal professional goals after an uncontrollable partnership breakup, people can also use social strategies, like defending their own national values or supporting a collective movement, that involve the social environment to regain perceived control. In this chapter, we focus exclusively on social reactions to control threat that people use to maintain or restore a sense of control, specifically when personal control seems futile.

We present a group-based control approach to understand the social reactions to personal control loss, thereby adding a social identity perspective to established concepts of control. We propose that people can experience control on both a personal and a social level of their self. When people have lost control as individuals, they may still be able to restore a sense of control as group members. Thus, group membership can provide that firm ground people need to feel their self is in control. We start the chapter with a conceptual overview of different control strategies that assume the self as the controlling agent (primary control) or that assume that the source of control lies somewhere outside the self (secondary control). We explain how a social identity perspective could extend our understanding of primary control strategies, hereby adding the social self as another controlling agent (extended primary control). After introducing the model of group-based control and its implications for socially defensive reactions to personal control threat, we review empirical evidence for the group-based control mechanism (Fritsche, Jonas, & Fankhänel, 2008; Fritsche et al., 2013; Stollberg, Fritsche, & Bäcker, 2015). Then, we discuss how a group-based process can account for attempts of control restoration following control threat, and how it is related to the secondary control process of external structure seeking, postulated by the compensatory control model (Kay, Gaucher, Napier, Callan, & Laurin, 2008; Kay, Whitson, Gaucher, & Galinsky, 2009). Finally, we propose an integrative approach of control restoration that integrates both group-based control and compensatory control processes. Based on this model we discuss how these processes could be distinguished and empirically tested.

Control through the social self: Extended primary control

Personal control is a central human need and people are motivated to maintain a sense of control (Fiske, 2003; Pittman & Zeigler, 2007; White, 1959). People who experience personal control perceive themselves as efficacious agents that are capable to exert influence on important aspects of their environment (White, 1959). This feeling is often referred to as agency, efficacy, or mastery and focuses on the agentic and goal-directed component of control (Skinner, 1996, 2007). As Skinner (1996) noted in her influential review article, most definitions of control cover some relation between agents, means, and ends. That is, personal control occurs when the controlling self is affecting end states via goal-directed action. In other words, the decisive criterion for perceptions of personal control is the potential to perceive the self as agentic (cf. Preston & Wegner, 2005).

Can control only be regained by perceiving the self as agentic? Social psychological research on this question has identified other control processes as well. One of the most influential approaches, the two-process model by Rothbaum, Weisz, and Snyder (1982), distinguishes between primary and secondary control processes. As primary control processes involve the self as the most powerful agent that has the ability to change the environment, primary control is equivalent to control through the agentic self. When attempts of primary control fail, people engage in secondary control (Rothbaum et al., 1982; Skinner, 1996, 2007). Secondary control reflects the accommodation of the self to the environment with upholding a sense of order and structure as well as accepting and supporting control by external agents outside the self as possible strategies. Rothbaum and colleagues (1982) assert that although strategies of secondary control may appear as if people were giving up the pursuit of control, these strategies in fact allow people to uphold a sense of control through accommodation of the self (e.g., pulling oneself together when a predicted but personally uncontrollable event occurs; Frey & Jonas, 2002).

Social defensiveness as a response to personal control threat

In the present chapter, we focus on the various social responses people show to maintain or restore a global sense of control. Social responses to threat are nested in the social environment of the individual and can be distinguished from personal responses independent of the social environment (Jonas et al., 2014). A lack of personal control increases responses that can be labeled socially defensive (Fritsche et al., 2008, 2013; Greenaway, Louis, Hornsey, & Jones, 2014). People express more ingroup favoritism, defend values and norms that are approved by important national and cultural groups they belong to (Fritsche et al., 2008, 2013; Stollberg, Fritsche, & Jonas, 2015) and increase negative attitudes against outgroups (Agroskin & Jonas, 2013; Fritsche et al., 2013). For instance, people who were just reminded of the possibility of becoming a victim of a terrorist act showed more prejudice against immigrants than people who were made to perceive some degree of control over becoming a victim of terrorism (Greenaway et al., 2014). The defense of social belief systems that are held by a specific group or the broader society (e.g., belief in science or general progress) is another social response to perceived control threat (Fritsche, Koranyi, Beyer, Jonas, & Fleischmann, 2009; Kay et al., 2008, 2009; Kay, Gaucher, McGregor, & Nash, 2010; Rutjens, van der Pligt, & van Harreveld, 2010; Rutjens, van Harreveld, & van der Pligt, 2010; see also Greenaway, Philipp, & Storrs, Chapter 2, this volume), as well as the endorsement of conspiracy theories (Whitson & Galinsky, 2008). Perceived low control also accounted for an increase in blaming personal enemies for harmful actions (Rothschild, Sullivan, Landau, & Keefer, 2012), as a means to cope with personal control loss.

In sum, these findings show converging evidence that threat to personal control motivates different kinds of socially defensive reactions. They all have in common that they are unspecific responses that are not related to the domain where the control threat is perceived. However, as we will discuss in this chapter, these responses differ with regard to their assumed underlying motivational process and can be interpreted as representing either primary or secondary control.

Extended primary control

Rothbaum and colleagues (1982) propose the concept of vicarious control to explain socially defensive responses to control loss. Most often vicarious control has been discussed as a strategy of secondary control, describing passive submission of the self under the power of external agents, by showing submissiveness and conformity with systems and groups. At the same time, and less often cited, Rothbaum et al. also considered *primary* forms of vicarious control that reflect the instrumental behavior of people to actively imitate or manipulate significant others or groups to regain personal influence over the situation. On the basis of this two-process model, however, most authors have yet interpreted support of groups and group-based systems as a secondary control strategy, because they have seen groups as external agents that are not a part of the self (Kay et al., 2008, 2009; Rothschild et al., 2012; Rutjens, van Harreveld, & van der Pligt, 2010; Rutjens, van der Pligt, & van Harreveld, 2010; Sullivan, Landau, & Rothschild, 2010). In contrast, research based on social identity theory (Tajfel & Turner, 1979) and self-categorization theory (Turner et al., 1987) has shown that definitions of the self are not restricted to perceptions of who "I am" in contrast to other persons, but extend to perceptions of who "we are" in contrast to other groups. Depending on individual preferences and salient situational group-membership (Hogg & Turner, 1987), people identify with certain groups (ingroups) and with others they do not (outgroups). Instead, outgroups often serve as comparison standard against which people contrast the ingroup self. However, the two-process model of control strategies (Rothbaum et al., 1982) does not distinguish between self-defining ingroups that constitute an important part of one's identity and outgroups that are not part of one's identity. We argue that this very distinction between ingroups and outgroups is an important key to re-conceptualize groups as a source of *extended primary control*. Therefore, applying a self-categorization perspective to primary and secondary control strategies helps to clarify whether group-related responses can be linked to primary or secondary mechanisms of control restoration.

When people categorize themselves as members of groups, these groups become part of their social identity and prototypical attributes and actions of the ingroup become attributes and actions of the self ("self-stereotyping"; Turner et al., 1987). Thus, when group-membership is salient to people, they do not perceive their ingroup to be independent of their self, but think of themselves as "we" instead of "I". Accordingly, acting and thinking as an ingroup member, is acting and thinking in terms of the self – the social level of the self. If people define themselves as ingroup members and act on behalf of their ingroup to emphasize perceptions of control, they should perceive their social self as an active agent who exerts control over the environment. We classify this process as primary control, not secondary control. This means, primary control cannot only be understood in terms of "I am in control", but equally as "We are in control", because both subjects refer to the self as a powerful agent. Pursuing control through the social self is currently not considered in the two-process model, but can be integrated as strategy of *extended primary control.* To summarize, exerting control through either the personal or the social self, represent both processes of primary control.

As a consequence, increased support of groups in response to control threat can either be a strategy of extended primary control or a strategy of secondary control. Whether the support of groups and their norms or system represents a primary or a secondary control mechanism depends on the group's self-relevance – on whether they are in- or outgroups. When people cling to a salient self-defining ingroup to strengthen the perception of the self as controlling agent, they engage in extended primary control, whereas the support of others considered as outgroups and the submission to their control strengthens the perception of external forces as controlling agents, and is therefore an expression of secondary control. In the next section, we introduce a model of group-based control that assumes extended primary control as a restoring mechanism people use to cope with low personal control.

Extended primary control: The model of group-based control

Responses of extended primary control have been described as group-based control. The model of group-based control (Fritsche et al., 2011, 2013) assumes a social identity process underlying socially defensive reactions to control threat. Specifically, the model suggests that the social self provides a firm ground for agency perceptions to which people can retreat when control is threatened fundamentally on the level of the personal self. Accordingly, people engage in thinking and acting as an ingroup member to maintain the perception that the self is still the controlling agent. This allows for specific predictions that can be derived from the model to test a group-based control mechanism: Most basically, threat to control should increase (a) ethnocentric thinking, such as ingroup favoritism, (b) conformity with ingroup norms and pro-ingroup action intentions, and (c) the attractiveness of agentic compared to non-agentic possible ingroups. The latter effects should be most pronounced (d) when people highly identify with the group in focus or (e) when collective agency of an important ingroup seems threatened. The latter hypothesis matches the notion that people defend those ingroup properties that are subjectively relevant in a situation (Correll & Park, 2005).

Testing the model of group-based control

The specific assumptions that follow from a group-based control perspective have received empirical support. To test the effects of a deprived sense of personal control, researchers used a salience manipulation to remind people of a past situation or aspects of their life over which they had or have no control, which they compared with a salience manipulation of high personal control. As primary control can be maintained on the personal and on the social level of the self, lack of personal control should lead people to switch to the social part of their self. General evidence for group-based responses following threat to personal control has been provided by a host of studies showing increased ethnocentric tendencies, such as ingroup bias and ingroup support (Fritsche et al., 2008, 2013) following reminders of low control over important aspects of one's own life, such as unemployment, relationship loss or death. A study by Fritsche et al. (2013, Study 2) on ingroup bias in the judgment of football nations revealed that these effects were most pronounced among highly identified group members. This speaks for a group-based control explanation of the control threat effects on ethnocentrism.

In line with the second assumption, acting in terms of ingroup norms and collective goals may allow people to experience collective control through their individual actions. Thus, threat to control should increase conformity with ingroup norms and pro-ingroup action intentions. Findings that show increased conformity with ingroup norms supporting change for control-deprived people support this prediction (Stollberg, Fritsche, & Jonas, 2015). Students, who perceived personal control to be low, supported bogus innovation projects that were directed to change the current lecture system only when their ingroup of German students was supportive, too. Innovation projects that were supported by outgroups or that were not supported by any group norm, were not affected by control threat (Stollberg, Fritsche, & Jonas, 2015). As norm conformity was specific for ingroup norms and not a general tendency to become more susceptible to social influence, thinking and acting on behalf of an ingroup seems to represent a control restorative strategy that reestablishes a sense of agency on the social level of the self. As the potential to restore a sense of self-agency is an inherent feature that characterizes ingroups, but not outgroups, group-based control is only possible through conformity to ingroup but not to outgroup norms. Of interest, the finding that threatened control increases the support of innovation norms further bolsters an explanation in terms of extended primary control. This is because a secondary control account may have predicted that people become more conservative and rigid to reduce uncertainty and affirm the existing structure (Kay et al., 2009). Instead, threatened people supported group norms of change, supposedly because pursuing change demonstrates agency much more clearly than rigidly preserving the status quo.

This directly leads to the third hypotheses derived from the group-based control model: The specific role of perceived ingroup agency for driving the effects of control threat on ingroup support. To restore a sense of primary control, control-deprived people should prefer agentic to non-agentic possible ingroups, when both are salient to them. In line with this assumption, we have recently shown that the perception of a group as agentic was a crucial factor for group attractiveness and ingroup identification following control threat (Stollberg, Fritsche, & Bäcker, 2015). People identified more strongly with agentic task groups, but not with less agentic intimacy groups or social categories following control threat. The proposed underlying mechanism of experiencing extended primary control through the social self was further supported by the mediating role of group identification. People who lacked control on a personal level increased their identification with task groups, which in turn enhanced their perceptions of the group as an efficacious agent (Stollberg, Fritsche, & Bäcker, 2015). Moreover, in studies by

Greenaway et al. (2015) group identification increased personal control perceptions that were threatened previously, indicating a control restorative function of group membership. Thus, ingroup support and defense that increases for people with low personal control perceptions speaks for a motivated, socially defensive response that is specific for attempts to restore primary control.

The specific role of group agency for group-based control shows additionally that some groups are better suited to restore a sense of collective agency than others. Low personal control attracts people to agentic ingroups, that is, to groups that share a common goal, which they pursue voluntarily in an active, coordinated manner to achieve a certain outcome. It is the perceived potential of an ingroup to act as collective agent, and therefore extended primary control that makes these groups attractive to people with a deprived sense of control. Other features, such as similarity among group members that increase the perceived structure of a group, and therefore secondary control, do not moderate the attractiveness of groups for people who try to restore a sense of control on a collective level (Stollberg, Fritsche, & Bäcker, 2015). Thus, although ingroups may provide structure *and* agency for their members, only ingroup agency, but not ingroup similarity (i.e. structure), leads to group-based control effects. This supports our conceptual distinctions between extended primary control, where the self maintains a sense of agency on the group level, and secondary control, where the self adapts to a given (group) structure thereby ceding primary control.

In sum, it can be concluded that being part of a powerful and agentic ingroup extends the basis, on which the self can experience control. The social self can thus be conceptualized as another source of primary control. Accordingly, extended primary control always refers to the perception of the self as an agent. Consequently, control through external agents, such as outgroups, cannot restore a sense of primary control, unless a common ingroup is possible via recategorization on a higher level. Together, these findings further support our assumption that membership in agentic groups restores a sense of the self as a controlling agent, and that primary control exerted through the social self represents a control restorative strategy that is conceptually independent from secondary control processes. However, the interplay of extended primary and secondary control processes for socially defensive reactions to control threat is not fully understood, yet. Although some of our findings indicate that the revealed effects of threatened personal control can be explained in terms of extended primary control but not secondary control, this does not preclude that some of our effects had been fueled by secondary control processes as well. For instance, expressing ingroup bias may confirm previous expectations and thus bolster order, structure, and personal certainty (e.g., Kruglanski, Pierro, Mannetti, & DeGrada, 2006). In addition, other socially defensive reactions to personal control threat have been interpreted as secondary control attempts as well (Kay et al., 2008, 2009; Rothschild et al., 2010; Sullivan et al., 2010). Support of external agents following control threat has been postulated as a strategy of secondary control that represents a need to perceive the world as a non-random and structured place by the compensatory control model (Kay et al., 2008, 2009, 2010; see also

Rutjens & Kay, Chapter 5, this volume). In the next section, we will review the compensatory control approach, and show how a compensatory control process can be differentiated conceptually from a group-based control process.

Distinguishing extended primary and secondary control processes

Predicting secondary control: The compensatory control model

The compensatory control model proposes that responses to threatened control are not restricted to a restored sense. On the contrary, perceptions of an agentic self are not considered necessary for coping with a lack of personal control. Structure and causality that could be provided by any external system are proposed to be equally sufficient for satisfying a need for control (Landau, Kay, & Whitson, 2015). Therefore, increased support for governments, as well as support of ideological belief systems, such as religion (Kay et al., 2008, 2009, 2010) or scientific worldviews (Rutjens, van Harreveld, & van der Pligt, 2010), have been counted among social reactions to personal control threat that represent a compensatory control mechanism. According to the compensatory control model, such reactions are motivated by the fundamental need to perceive the world as an orderly non-random place (Kay et al., 2008, 2010). Thus, the endorsement of structure provided by external agents following personal control threat represents a control strategy in which the self is not involved. In line with Rothbaum et al.'s (1982) two-process model of control we will argue that compensatory control is a secondary control strategy, whereas group-based control resembles primary control.

Similarities and differences between group-based and compensatory control

Both the model of group-based control and the compensatory control model predict control threat to motivate similar socially defensive reactions to regain perceptions of control. However, they assume different underlying motivational processes and different social targets of control restorative attempts. While the group-based control model postulates an extended primary control mechanism, representing a need to perceive the self as being in control, the compensatory control approach postulates a secondary control mechanism, representing a need to perceive that things are under control by any powerful agent. By implication, group-based control assumes responses on the level of the social self (i.e. the ingroup), such as ethnocentrism or action intentions in line with collective norms and goals. In contrast, compensatory control can be attained by the support of systems and social agents external to the self, such as economic systems, God (Kay et al., 2008), or even personal enemies (Sullivan et al., 2010). From the perspective of group-based control, however, relinquishing control to powerful collective agents that are *not* part of the self, such as outgroups, is not an option to restore (primary) control. As a result, the group-based control model and the model of compensatory control predict different responses to control threat.

The model of group-based control predicts that only ingroups should be supported following control threat, whereas compensatory control predicts the support of any group or agent providing structure to the individual. While ingroups as well as outgroups can provide structure and order to the control-deprived individual, only ingroups represent people's self and can thus restore a perception of the self as agentic. Although outgroups could also be perceived as effective agents that act in line with individual's self-interests (i.e. benevolent outgroups), they will not restore perceptions of the (social) self as agentic. For instance, receiving help from an outgroup may even imply a threat to control through the self (Nadler & Halabi, 2006).

Distinguishing processes of group-based and compensatory control seems warranted not only for theoretical clarity but also for predicting what kinds of groups or social agents will be supported under different conditions of threat. Personal as well as societal crises may differ with regard to whether people's sense of personal control or their sense of structure and order is at stake. For instance, living under a bureaucratic dictatorship will provide most citizens with a sense of structure and order but will at the same time threaten their personal control. This should increase the identification with and support of agentic ingroups as this is a way to restore primary control. However, in contrast, a state of social anomy might lead people to support any order-conferring group available, not restricted to social ingroups but also powerful outgroups or autocratic parties, such as radical militias in failed states. Some initial research on distinguishing between the effects of threatened control vs. uncertainty has been provided by Shepherd, Kay, Landau, and Keefer (2011). This distinction is important, because it has different implications for the groups people tend to support when experiencing a lack of personal control. In the next section, we review findings on different socially defensive reactions to personal control threat and discuss whether group-based and compensatory control processes can be clearly distinguished in these studies. We also take a look at boundary conditions that determine which of the two processes will be most likely to occur.

Primary or secondary control mechanism? Support of god and government as extended control through the social self

Given the different predictions of extended primary and compensatory control, it should be possible to distinguish group-based and compensatory control responses empirically. However, most previous control threat research is not sufficiently specific regarding what type of motivational process and what type of social response is involved in the investigated effects.

Research on compensatory control strategies has shown that people increase their belief in a controlling God and defend their government, when their sense of personal control is threatened (Kay et al., 2008). These findings are interpreted by the authors as a secondary compensation mechanism to maintain a certain level of predictability and structure by increasing one's perceptions of external agency.

However, it is not clear whether these findings represent a secondary control mechanism: Are God and the national government agents, who are external to the self? On the one hand, they might be perceived as a mighty force one can passively submit in order to regain the perception that a powerful entity is in control over one's life. On the other hand, however, people identify as national citizens, and religious beliefs are part of their (religious) identity. Both, the national government and a controlling God might be agentic representatives of an ingroup. Thus, it is possible to interpret the defense of God and the government following control threat as a defense of agentic leaders of an ingroup (i.e. religion or nation), and therefore as group-based control. This alternative explanation would also be in line with the finding that benevolence moderated the effects of control threat on government defense (Kay et al., 2008). Participants, who experienced a lack of personal control, defended their government, only if they perceived it as benevolent, that is, as a government that acts in line with the interests and goals of its citizens. While recently, benevolence has been interpreted as the factor that distinguishes external agency from structure maintenance as compensatory control strategies (Landau et al., 2015), we propose that benevolence might as well be seen as a proxy for shared ingroup membership. As ingroups mostly act in accordance with values and goals shared by their members, they are benevolent agents that act in line with their own goals and self-interests.

Further support for this group-based explanation could be obtained from findings showing that people do not defend any social belief systems to the same extent (Rutjens, van Harreveld, & van der Pligt, 2010). In other words, people do not support any worldview; they only support those views that are already part of their identity (i.e., the worldview that is represented by their ingroup). For instance, non-religious people with low control perceptions showed increased support of a belief in progress, but did not increase their belief in a controlling God (Rutjens, van Harreveld, & van der Pligt, 2010). This indicates that worldviews are not interchangeable for people to compensate for lowered feelings of personal control. Control threatened people appear to support ingroup but not outgroup norms, which could be understood as joining in collective goal pursuit (e.g., for societal progress). Moreover, increasing one's belief in progress might also be indicative of a striving of the social self for agency, as belief in progress can provide people with a sense of predictability of the future, because the use of progressive knowledge permits for controlling the environment (Rutjens, van Harreveld, & van der Pligt, 2010), and thus strengthens the perceived agency of their group. To summarize, defending social belief systems or national systems in response to control threat may reestablish a sense of structure, but it may also provide a sense of group-based control through the social self, because belief systems and national systems might constitute an important part of one's identity. Obviously, these studies are not suitable to gain unequivocal evidence for compensatory control processes to occur independent of group-based control.

In addition, findings showing increased support of hierarchies, independent of power and status perceptions, following control threat (Friesen, Kay, Eibach, &

Galinsky, 2014) could also be interpreted as both: secondary control compensation through preference of structure or extended primary control through group-based agency. Hierarchical groups were perceived as more stable and predictable, but also as more efficient and well coordinated (Friesen et al., 2014). Moreover, clear hierarchies at one's workplace are positively associated with occupational self-efficacy, and therefore control (Friesen et al., 2014). Thus, hierarchical ingroups provide their members with a certain kind of structure that is at the same time associated with ingroup agency. Within-group hierarchies facilitate group goal pursuit in an active and coordinated manner, which in turn enhances perceptions of collective agency.

In a similar vein, perceptions of collective agency might have contributed to findings on increased support of mighty enemies following personal control threat (Sullivan et al., 2010). Sullivan et al. (2010) showed that the salience of a powerful or weak enemy (Al Qaeda) whose activities are clearly understood and tracked by the ingroup (U.S. intelligence) bolstered feelings of a previously threatened sense of personal control. Whereas the salience of an ambiguous enemy, whose activities and strengths are poorly understood by the ingroup, who could hardly fight against it, did not buffer personal control threat. While the authors interpret these findings as evidence for a secondary control mechanism that increased control perceptions through salience of a structured and orderly system, represented by a clear and unambiguous enemy, a group-based control explanation seems also plausible. The manipulation of enemy salience also contained information about the agency of the ingroup: First, a weak enemy does not pose a threat to the ingroup's agency as the group is in full control. Second, a powerful enemy is challenging, but the ingroup knows his or her capabilities very well and is able to anticipate his or her next steps, and could therefore be perceived as the controlling agent. Whereas in the unambiguous enemy condition, the ingroup does not know what to do against it; thus, the group cannot act effectively and is not in control of the situation. Therefore, the effects of threatened control may have been buffered by attributing negative events to unambiguous outgroup enemies, because this provides a sense of group-based control.

In another study, Rothschild et al. (2012) showed that a viable scapegoat (international oil companies) that was presented to people following a threat to control through climate change increased people's perceptions of personal control, whereas a non-viable scapegoat (the Amish) did not. Again, secondary control processes of structure enhancement and extended primary, group-based control might have worked in parallel. The salience of an oil company that could be blamed for climate change threat makes the world more predictable and reliable (secondary control), but it may also activate group norms and set collective goals that initiate collective action and thus give rise to a sense of collective agency. Similarly, research showing increased obedience to authority following control threat (Fennis & Aarts, 2012) might also be interpreted as obedience to salient ingroup norms and ingroup leadership.

To summarize, previous findings on reactions to control threat allow no easy distinction between effects based on secondary control strategies and effects based on extended primary control. For many of the discussed results, both interpretations are viable, as they can be explained by secondary control compensation through external structure enhancement, as well as by the pursuit of group-based agency when primary control is at stake. How both processes contribute to social defensiveness following personal control threat and under which circumstances one of both processes becomes more probable is still an open empirical question.

Secondary control strategies following control threat: Enhancement of perceived structure

We have reviewed evidence that clearly supports a group-based control mechanism to underlie reactions to control threat existing independent of possible parallel effects of compensatory control. After reporting findings that could be driven by both, external structure enhancement and group membership, we will now turn to results that indicate a general cognitive tendency to search for structure following control threat. When personal agency is low and could not be restored, people engaged in secondary control and showed enhanced perceptions of unspecific structure (Whitson & Galinsky, 2008). That means, they subjectively perceived more contingencies on a perceptual and on a cognitive level. Threat to personal control increased contingency perceptions and led people to perceive subjectively more structure than objectively exists: Control-deprived people showed more illusory correlations, increased beliefs in conspiracy and superstitions, saw more perceptual patterns in random pictures, and reported a higher need for structure (Whitson & Galinsky, 2008; see also Agroskin & Jonas, 2013).

Although these findings nicely demonstrate a general cognitive tendency of structure seeking in control-deprived people, it is an open question, whether structure enhancement is sufficient for control compensation, or whether it is an initial step to regain a sense of agency (i.e. through group membership) when this is possible. Mediational evidence supports the notion that personal need for structure mediates the effect of control threat on socially defensive reactions, such as ingroup bias, at least for people with low self-esteem (Agroskin & Jonas, 2013). Structure and causality seem to be inherent features of agency, as without them self-outcome-contingency is not possible (Preston & Wegner, 2005). They increase perceptions of predictability, an antecedent of personal control (Skinner, 1996). However, while a specific structure provided by an ingroup should increase perceptions of group agency and control through the self, structure provided by an outgroup could even impair group agency and lower personal control. Research on structure salience and goal engagement support this view. People who did not believe that their own actions would lead to certain outcomes (i.e. lacking contingency beliefs) were more prone to engage in goal engagement when structure principles were made salient to them (Kay, Laurin, Fitzsimons, & Landau, 2014). However, the salience of a higher power controlling one's fate, which probably imposed a lower level of self-outcome contingencies and therefore a structure that impaired personal agency, decreased people's engagement in active goal pursuit (Laurin, Kay, & Moscovitch, 2008). Together, these findings suggest that people seek out a structure and contingency that helps to regain a sense of agency through the self and thus primary control.

Ingroups can provide both structure and agency to its members. However, when agency – and therefore primary control – is not available at any personal or social level of the self, any kind of structure might be preferred to chaos and unpredictability. The investigation of the interplay of these two motivational processes has important implications for the prediction of how control-deprived people might behave, especially when confronted with an ingroup that aims at destabilizing the environment and external forces that stabilize the environment but decrease people's own agency. In the next section, we conclude the chapter with a two-process model that integrates the group-based control model and the compensatory control model, and we report initial evidence for the predictions that are derived from this new approach.

An integrative two-process model of control restoration

According to the group-based control approach, agentic ingroups are preferred to agentic outgroups, as they have the potential to reestablish a sense of the self as a controlling agent (Fritsche et al., 2013; Stollberg, Fritsche, & Bäcker, 2015; Stollberg, Fritsche, & Jonas, 2015). In addition to this process of extended primary control through the social self, secondary control through enhancement of and belief in external structure represents another compensation process, when perceptions of control are at stake.

However, it is an empirical question, how these two processes are intertwined, and whether a primacy of primary or secondary control exists. We have argued in the above sections that support of benevolent systems as response to threatened personal control (Kay et al., 2009) might be reinterpreted as support of ingroup systems. We further argued that support of hierarchies might represent both a secondary compensation strategy of external structure seeking (Friesen et al., 2014) and a primary control strategy to restore a sense of personal agency, as hierarchies facilitate goal pursuit and therefore perceptions of collective agency. To test how extended primary control of the social self and external structure-seeking contribute to socially defensive reactions to control threat, both processes, agency restoration and self-unrelated structure enhancement, have to be distinguished empirically. This distinction is important, because it has different implications for the groups people tend to support when experiencing a lack of personal control. Different motivations following threat (structure and agency) might lead to different strategies of control restoration (extended primary vs. secondary control) and result in different social reactions.

Building on the model by Rothbaum et al. (1982) distinguishing between primary and secondary control, we propose an extended two-process-model of control restoration (see Figure 8.1). It predicts that people with a deprived sense of

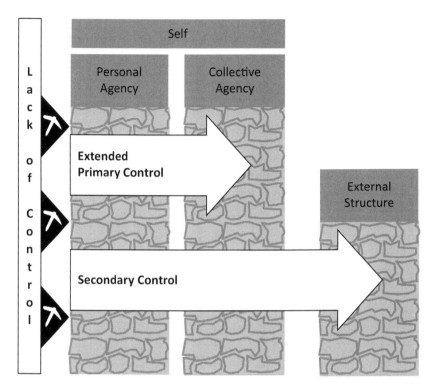

FIGURE 8.1   Integrative two-process model of control restoration. The model assumes
that people with a lack of personal control prefer extended primary control to secondary control strategies. Extended primary control restores a
sense of the self being in control through perceptions of collective agency,
whereas secondary control restores a sense of things being under control
through perceptions of external structure.

personal control initially look for extended primary control through the social self,
and only switch to secondary strategies of external structure enhancement, when
personal agency could not be restored through self-categorization and acting as a
group member. When control is threatened on the personal level of the self, people
initially attempt to regain control on the social level of the self through ingroup
identification and support. However, if there is no ingroup available that could
restore perceptions of control, people might engage in external structure seeking
to assure themselves that there is at least any kind of control in the world. In other
words, we propose a hierarchy of control strategies: In the first instance people
strive for self-agency (i.e., primary or extended primary control), unless neither
personal control nor group-based control is perceived. If the latter should be the
case, attempts of secondary control come into play to provide a sense of structure. This assumption leads to empirically testable hypotheses.

First, people with a lack of control should prefer "systems" that provide agency
and therefore efficacious goal attainment to systems that are orderly but impair

personal or collective agency. While ingroups represent such internal agents that have an inherent structure that enhances agency through the self, outgroups are agents who are external to the self, also providing contingency and non-random-ness, but impeding personal agency. Assuming the primacy of collective agency to external structure enhancement, people should support ingroup systems, but not outgroup systems following control threat, when both are perceived as potent agents that could help to resolve an uncontrollable situation at the same time. First evidence for these predictions could be obtained from initial studies from our lab. These studies show that participants who experienced low control due to the consequences of the economic crisis in Europe evaluated actions of their ingroup to stabilize the financial market more positively compared to actions of China, which was depicted as a benevolent outgroup that served the ingroup's interests. Although participants were presented simultaneously with two powerful agents that both aimed to stabilize the economic situation, lack of personal control led people to support their ingroup and not the outgroup (Lell, 2013). These results support the notion of the two-process model that people are primarily motivated to maintain or restore a sense of control through the social self, as they prefer ingroup to outgroup help. The preference of ingroup agency to outgroup structure gains further support from another study showing that control-deprived people favor an ingroup belief system that allows for personal agency. When people were reminded of low personal control over their lives, students evaluated an internal God (i.e., someone who can be influenced by prayers) more favorably than an external God (i.e., someone who acts unforeseeably on his own). In sum, these initial results are encouraging first support of our prediction that restoring personal agency through ingroup support is different from structure enhancement through outgroup support, and they affirm the primacy of primary control (agency restora-tion) to secondary control (external structure seeking), when both are salient to control-deprived people.

However, the two-process model also predicts that, if an agentic ingroup is not available, control-deprived people might also seek out for outgroup agency, because any structure is at least better than chaos. Future research should more rigorously disentangle, striving for self-agency and striving for external structure enhance-ment, and should directly test whether different motivations lead to different social reactions.

Conclusion

In this chapter, we reviewed different social responses to threatened control that we think reflect people's efforts to cope with threatened personal control. We concep-tually distinguished attempts to restore a sense of the self as the controlling agent (primary control) from compensatory reactions of maintaining a sense of structure without regaining a sense of agency (secondary control). By introducing a social identity perspective, we proposed the possibility of extended primary control. This reflects efforts of maintaining or restoring control on the social level of the self.

When perceptions of control are shaken on the personal level, people may switch to their social level of the self to be on a firm ground again. We provided empirical evidence that group-based control can account for socially defensive reactions following control threat. In a next step, we reviewed the empirical findings on control threat and social defensiveness and argued that in many cases, both extended primary control as well as secondary control could represent the underlying process of social responses to control threat, a reasoning that has not been directly tested yet. We then proposed a two-process model that predicts a two-step approach of control restoration strategies. First, it postulates a primacy of primary control and thus, it predicts that ingroups are preferred to outgroups when both are salient resources for control restoration, because only ingroups can provide a sense of agency through the self. Second, seeking for external structure following control threat should be enhanced, when primary control is available neither through the person nor through group membership, because it serves as an antecedent of control perceptions as it reestablishes a sense of causality and predictability.

People use various strategies to get out of the quicksand of control loss. Adding a social identity perspective suggests an extension of the self to the social level that allows people to stand on firm ground when they fear the ground dropping out from beneath their feet. Extended primary control restoration could explain why people with low feelings of control cease to support an existing political system or a social order and start to support progressive movements. Even if the system provides external structure and therefore secondary control, it does not provide disidentified people with a sense of agency, whereas social movements that demonstrate collective agency through conspicuous activities and that allow for stronger ingroup identification might become attractive, as they could reestablish a sense of agency. In consequence, lack of control could motivate social change and progress, but at the same time it bears the risk to give rise to equally agentic but unprogressive movements.

References

Agroskin, D., & Jonas, E. (2013). Controlling death by defending ingroups – Mediational insights into terror management and control restoration. *Journal of Experimental Social Psychology, 49*, 1144–1158. doi:10.1016/j.jesp.2013.05.014

Correll, J., & Park, B. (2005). A model of the ingroup as a social resource. *Personality and Social Psychology Review, 9*, 341–359. doi:10.1207/s15327957pspr0904_4

Fennis, B. M., & Aarts, H. (2012). Revisiting the agentic shift: Weakening personal control increases susceptibility to social influence. *European Journal of Social Psychology, 42*, 824–831. doi:10.1002/ejsp.1887

Fiske, S. T. (Ed.). (2003). *Five core social motives, plus or minus five.* Vol. 9. Mahwah, NJ: Lawrence Erlbaum Associates Inc.

Frey, D., & Jonas, E. (2002). Die Theorie der kognizierten Kontrolle [The theory of perceived control]. In D. Frey & M. Irle (Eds.), *Theorien der Sozialpsychologie. Band 3: Motivations-, Selbst- und Informationsverarbeitungstheorien* [Theories in social psychology, Vol 3: Theories of motivation, self and information processing] (pp. 13–50). Bern: Huber.

Friesen, J. P., Kay, A. C., Eibach, R. P., & Galinsky, A. D. (2014). Seeking structure in social organization: Compensatory control and the psychological advantages of hierarchy. *Journal of Personality and Social Psychology, 106*, 590–609. doi:10.1037/a0035620

Fritsche, I., Jonas, E., Ablasser, C., Beyer, M., Kuban, J., Manger, A. M., & Schultz, M. (2013). The power of we: Evidence for group-based control. *Journal of Experimental Social Psychology, 49,* 19–32. doi:10.1016/j.jesp.2012.07.014

Fritsche, I., Jonas, E., & Fankhänel, T. (2008). The role of control motivation in mortality salience effects on ingroup support and defense. *Journal of Personality and Social Psychology, 95,* 524–541. doi:10.1037/a0012666

Fritsche, I., Jonas, E., & Kessler, T. (2011). Collective reactions to threat: Implications for intergroup conflict and for solving societal crises. *Social Issues and Policy Review, 5,* 101–136.

Fritsche, I., Koranyi, N., Beyer, C., Jonas, E., & Fleischmann, B. (2009). Enemies welcome: Personal threat and reactions to outgroup doves and hawks. *International Review of Social Psychology, 22*(3/4), 157–179.

Greenaway, K. H., Haslam, S. A., Cruwys, T., Branscombe, N. R., Ysseldyk, R., & Heldreth, C. (2015). From "we" to "me": Group identification enhances perceived personal control with consequences for health and well-being. *Journal of Personality and Social Psychology, 109,* 53–74.

Greenaway, K. H., Louis, W. R., Hornsey, M. J., & Jones, J. M. (2014). Perceived control qualifies the effects of threat on prejudice. *British Journal of Social Psychology, 53,* 422–442. doi:10.1111/bjso.12049

Hogg, M. A., & Turner, J. C. (1987). Intergroup behaviour, self-stereotyping and the salience of social categories. *British Journal of Social Psychology, 26*(4), 325–340.

Jonas, E., McGregor, I., Klackl, J., Agroskin, D., Fritsche, I., Holbrook, C., Nash, K., Proulx, T., & Quirin, M. (2014). Threat and defense: From anxiety to approach. In J. M. Olson & M. P. Zanna (Eds.), *Advances in experimental social psychology* (Vol. 49, pp. 219–286). San Diego, CA: Academic Press.

Kay, A. C., Gaucher, D., McGregor, I., & Nash, K. (2010). Religious belief as compensatory control. *Personality and Social Psychology Review, 14,* 37–48. doi:10.1177/1088868309353750

Kay, A. C., Gaucher, D., Napier, J. L., Callan, M. J., & Laurin, K. (2008). God and the government: Testing a compensatory control mechanism for the support of external systems. *Journal of Personality and Social Psychology, 95,* 18–35.

Kay, A. C., Laurin, K., Fitzsimons, G. M., & Landau, M. J. (2014). A functional basis for structure-seeking: Exposure to structure promotes willingness to engage in motivated action. *Journal of Experimental Psychology, 143,* 486–491.

Kay, A. C., Whitson, J. A., Gaucher, D., & Galinsky, A. D. (2009). Compensatory control: Achieving order through the mind, our institutions, and the heavens. *Current Directions in Psychological Science, 18,* 264–268.

Kruglanski, A. W., Pierro, A., Mannetti, L., & De Grada, E. (2006). Groups as epistemic providers: Need for closure and the unfolding of group-centrism. *Psychological Review, 113,* 84–100. doi:10.1037/0033-295X.113.1.84

Landau, M. J., Kay, A. C., & Whitson, J. A. (2015). Compensatory control and the appeal of a structured world. *Psychological Bulletin, 141,* 694–722. doi:10.1037/a0038703

Laurin, K., Kay, A. C., & Moscovitch, D. A. (2008). On the belief in God: Towards an understanding of the emotional substrates of compensatory control. *Journal of Experimental Social Psychology, 44,* 1559–1562.

Lell, C. (2013). Desirability of control oder personal need for structure: Individuelle Unterschiede in der Wiederherstellung bedrohter persönlicher Kontrolle [Desirability of control or personal need for structure: Individual differences in control restoration following threat to personal control] (Unpublished master's thesis). University of Leipzig, Leipzig, Germany.

Nadler, A., & Halabi, S. (2006). Intergroup helping as status relations: Effects of status stability, identification, and type of help on receptivity to high-status group's help. *Journal of Personality and Social Psychology, 91,* 97–110. doi:10.1037/0022-3514.91.1.97

Pittman, T. S., & Zeigler, K. R. (2007). Basic human needs. In A. W. Kruglanski & E. T. Higgins (Eds.), *Social psychology: Handbook of basic principles* (2nd ed., pp. 473–489). New York: Guilford Press.

Preston, J., & Wegner, D. M. (2005). Ideal agency: On perceiving the self as an origin of action. In A. Tesser, J. Wood, & D. Stapel (Eds.), *On building, defending, and regulating the self* (pp. 103–125). Philadelphia, PA: Psychology Press.

Rothbaum, F., Weisz, J. R., & Snyder, S. S. (1982). Changing the world and changing the self: A two-process model of perceived control. *Journal of Personality and Social Psychology, 42*, 5–37. doi:10.1037/0022-3514.42.1.5

Rothschild, Z. K., Landau, M. J., Sullivan, D., & Keefer, L. A. (2012). A dual-motive model of scapegoating: Displacing blame to reduce guilt or increase control. *Journal of Personality and Social Psychology, 102*, 1148.

Rutjens, B. T., Van Der Pligt, J., & Van Harreveld, F. (2010). Deus or Darwin: Randomness and belief in theories about the origin of life. *Journal of Experimental Social Psychology, 46*(6), 1078–1080. doi:10.1016/j.jesp.2010.07.009

Rutjens, B. T., van Harreveld, F., & van der Pligt, J. (2010). Yes we can: Belief in progress as compensatory control. *Social Psychological and Personality Science, 1*(3), 246–252. doi:10.1177/1948550610361782

Shepherd, S., Kay, A. C., Landau, M. J., & Keefer, L. A. (2011). Evidence for the specificity of control motivations in worldview defense: Distinguishing compensatory control from uncertainty management and terror management processes. *Journal of Experimental Social Psychology, 47*(5), 949–958. doi:0.1016/j.jesp.2011.03.026

Skinner, E. A. (1996). A guide to constructs of control. *Journal of Personality and Social Psychology, 71*, 549–570. doi:10.1037/0022-3514.71.3.549

Skinner, E. A. (2007). Secondary control critiqued: Is it secondary? Is it control? Comment on Morling and Evered (2006). *Psychological Bulletin, 133*, 911–916. doi:10.1037/0033-2909.133.6.911

Stollberg, J., Fritsche, I., & Bäcker, A. (2015). Striving for group agency: Threat to personal control increases the attractiveness of agentic groups. *Frontiers in Psychology, 6*, 649.

Stollberg, J., Fritsche, I., & Jonas, E. (2015). *Threat to personal control strengthens the expression of the social self: Conformity to ingroup change norms as a group-based response.* Unpublished Manuscript.

Sullivan, D., Landau, M. J., & Rothschild, Z. K. (2010). An existential function of enemyship: Evidence that people attribute influence to personal and political enemies to compensate for threats to control. *Journal of Personality and Social Psychology, 98*, 434–449. doi:10.1037/a0017457

Tajfel, H., & Turner, J. C. (1979). An integrative theory of intergroup conflict. In W. G. Austin & S. Worchel (Eds.), *The social psychology of intergroup relations* (pp. 33–47). Monterey, CA: Brooks/Cole.

Turner, J. C., Hogg, M. A., Oakes, P. J., Reicher, S. D., & Wetherell, M. S. (1987). *Rediscovering the social group: A self-categorization theory.* Cambridge, MA: Basil Blackwell.

White, R. W. (1959). Motivation reconsidered: The concept of competence. *Psychological Review, 66*, 297–333. doi:10.1037/h0040934

Whitson, J. A., & Galinsky, A. D. (2008). Lacking control increases illusory pattern perception. *Science, 322*(5898), 115–117. doi:10.1126/science.1159845

9

COPING WITH IDENTITY THREATS TO GROUP AGENCY AS WELL AS GROUP VALUE

Explicit and implicit routes to resistance

Soledad de Lemus, Russell Spears, Jolien van Breen, and Maïka Telga

Author's note

This work was supported by the Spanish Ministerio de Economía y Competitividad (grant No.: PSI2013–45678-P) and by the University of Groningen Endowed Faculty chair of Russell Spears.
Contact: slemus@ugr.es

Social resistance is defined as a group's opposition to economic, political, and social circumstances that perpetuate social disadvantage, or status differences within society. Social identity researchers (SIT; Tajfel & Turner, 1979), amongst others, have theorized about the psychological processes underlying social resistance (Reicher, 2004; Spears, Jetten, & Doosje, 2001). Social identity is that part of an individual's identity derived from their membership of groups, be they chosen, such as sports-team supporters, or acquired, such as gender or ethnicity. SIT outlines various social resistance strategies, ranging from the indirect to the more direct, in response to threats to social identity (Tajfel & Turner, 1979). However, SIT typically conceptualizes identity threat in terms of threats to group value. In this chapter we argue that to conceptualize threat primarily in relation to group *value* or identity content is limiting, especially as the responses to such threats involve a range of different *actions* (Tajfel & Turner, 1979). Missing from this analysis is that identity threat also typically implies threats to the agency of the group, and thus its ability to engage in action (hence, "social resistance"), be this direct or indirect. In this chapter, in keeping with the central theme of this volume we therefore conceptualize such threats as threats to agency as well as group value and present preliminary evidence of reactions to identity threats both at the explicit (e.g., collective action) and implicit level (e.g., automatic ingroup bias). Finally, we describe some effects of identity threat on cognitive control and approach motivation. We discuss the implications of this conceptualization of identity threat as threats to agency *and* value for social identity theory as well as for the literature related to agency and control.

Beyond group value: What's threatening for social identity?

Threats to social identity are often taken to mean threats to the value of the group, defined as the content of identity in terms of traits, values, stereotypes, etc., or in terms of status in comparison to other groups (e.g., Branscombe, Ellemers, Spears, & Doosje, 1999; Ellemers, Spears, & Doosje, 2002; Ouwerkerk & Ellemers, 2002). Such identity threat undermines the value of the group's identity, by suggesting that some aspects of the group identity (e.g., its attributes or stereotypes) are negative or inferior, or indeed that the low status of the group compared to relevant other groups implies inferiority. This type of identity threat may be resisted by group members through a variety of strategies, which we call social resistance (Tajfel & Turner, 1979). Although classic SIT proposes that only the social competition strategy directly pursues social change (e.g., via collective actions), other strategies such as individual mobility or social creativity also try to deal with threats to group value (Tajfel & Turner, 1979).

Beyond threatening group value, identity threats also pose a threat to group agency, for instance by group stereotypes that assume lower competence (Abele & Wojciszke, 2007; Fiske, Cuddy, Glick, & Xu, 2002). Likewise, the low power (and to some extent low status) associated with disadvantaged groups is likely to be *perceived* as a threat to group agency. Indeed, one common definition of power is in terms of control over outcomes (Sidanius & Pratto, 2001). In the present chapter we use the term *agency* more generally as a synonym for efficacy or control (and because we use control in a more specific sense later).

The current chapter develops the idea that the social identity perspective on social resistance can be broadened to incorporate concepts related to group agency more explicitly than hitherto. We argue that (perceptions of/desire for) group agency is an aspect of any social identity, so that a group identity has value, relating to specific content such as morals or ideology, but also agency, the power to act out or defend the desired content. We propose that these two aspects of identity are closely related. Group agency gives a group the opportunity to act out identity content (Haslam & Reicher, 2007; Klein, Spears, & Reicher, 2007), while at the same time, identity content may justify the assertion of such agency and provide the motivation and means to agency, for instance by reference to in-group morality (Brambilla, Sacchi, Rusconi, Cherubini, & Yzerbyt, 2012; Leach, Ellemers, & Barreto, 2007). In the context of identity *threat*, effects on agency and value may amplify one another. For instance, when identity threat comes from a powerful out-group over whom the in-group has little or no control (or who in fact have control over the in-group), the in-group is likely to experience a stronger sense of identity threat (Stephan, Ybarra, & Rios Morrison, 2009). Hence, groups that have low power or agency are likely to experience identity threat more strongly and may be more motivated to resist such threat.

As mentioned previously, identity threat may stem from the content of a stereotype. The content of identity might incorporate different dimensions (i.e., warmth-competence, agency-communion, morality, etc.) that are differentially related to status and power of the group more broadly (c.f. Ridgeway, 2001). More specifically, different dimensions of identity might increase the perceived *value* of the group on the warmth or morality dimensions while leading to less control (i.e., in terms of less competence or *agency*) over its own outcomes, or vice versa (Kervyn, Yzerbyt, & Judd, 2011). This notion is supported by evidence from the stereotype content model (Fiske et al., 2002), showing that dimensions linked to higher agency, such as competence, often imply more negative evaluations of certain groups. The envious stereotype (e.g., prejudice against Jews, bankers, etc.) fits this profile. So although in some cases the high competence/low warmth stereotype may emphasize the agency of some stigmatized groups, the prejudice and discrimination directed towards such groups can more generally be viewed as threatening their group value. In short, even when a group has a degree of agency (e.g., by *virtue* of its status or stereotypes) this does not necessarily preclude threats to its identity through prejudice and discrimination, sometimes based on these very stereotypes. In sum, although the value and agency of group identity amplify one another, these aspects can also have complementary relations.

In some cases, then, the conceptualization of identity threat as value threat does not fully account for the meaning of disadvantage. For instance, in the case of gender relations, the classic Allportian notion of prejudice as "an *antipathy*" towards the outgroup (Allport, 1979, p. 9) is insufficient (Glick & Fiske, 1996). Research on benevolent sexism has shown, for example, that the predominantly positive value attributed to women as a group (e.g., warm, friendly, sensitive) may still imply a significant threat to women's identity and negatively influence their performance (e.g., Dardenne, Dumont, & Bollier, 2007) and their decisions (Moya, Glick, Exposito, de Lemus, & Hart, 2007). That is, threat to the positive value of the group cannot fully explain the detrimental effects of benevolent sexism. Threat to agency may play a role here. Despite its indulging tone, benevolent sexism imposes prescriptive roles on women (e.g., Prentice & Carranza, 2002) limiting women's freedom and control over their lives, especially outside of the domestic sphere. Although warmth is positive it clearly does not afford as much agency as competence does. Hence, at least in some cases, threats to identity are not directly related to threats to group value but to threats to agency.

The suggestion that an in-group has low agency creates identity threat, because individuals are motivated to have control over their own outcomes (*control motivation*; Fritsche, Jonas, & Kessler, 2011; Pittman & Zeigler, 2007). In fact, control motivation is one of the basic human motivations (Alloy & Abramson, 1982; Fiske, 2003). At a group level, control motivation should translate to a desire for the group to have an impact on the outcomes associated with group membership (Fritsche et al., 2013) or that the group is agentic and can achieve its goals (Van Zomeren, Leach, & Spears, 2010; Van Zomeren, Spears, Fischer, & Leach, 2004). Evidence for the link between control motivation and group identity is that a threat to control might be counteracted by strengthening group identity as described by Stollberg, Fritsche, Barth, & Jugert (Chapter 8, this volume). That is, lack of agency can lead to increased identification with an in-group as a way of restoring it (Fritsche et al., 2013).

In short, as well as a threat to (group) value, stereotypes could be viewed as a threat to group agency. In this sense, as we have argued elsewhere (Spears et al., 2001), group identity is not just about "being" (the attributes or stereotypes of how your group *is*) but also about "becoming" (having the agency needed to realize new goals and indeed contents to identity: what your group *could be*). This being said, it is not always clear or obvious when a particular form of social identity threat, and the resistance it evokes, is about defending and asserting group value or about defending and asserting agency, and how these can be distinguished. We argue that content and agency are closely related, and thus, that identity content must be taken into account when considering control motivation, and vice versa. Although in the studies presented below we do not clearly differentiate between these two components of identity threat (value, agency), we present preliminary evidence of how such threats to identity trigger both implicit and explicit forms of resistance. Further research is needed to test our theoretical model as we will discuss in the final section of this chapter.

The meaning of group-based control: Actual vs. perceived control

One problem for disadvantaged groups is that, precisely because of their low power or agency (and acute or chronic threats to this), achieving actual agency will not always be easy or even possible. Social power is associated with *actual* control, that is, control over the distribution of resources between groups (Guinote, 2007; Sidanius & Pratto, 2001). At a group level, this means that high status groups (often majority groups) have control over the outcomes of low status groups, for instance through their representation in government, their roles in social institutions, or through their wealth or social capital. For disadvantaged groups, this means that their perception of control is threatened by the fact that they have low social power and thus low actual control (Guinote, Brown, & Fiske, 2006).

However, in such circumstances groups can always retain a sense of subjective or *perceived* control (Skinner, 1996). In fact, perceived control is considered a more proximal and thus powerful predictor of functioning than actual control (Averill, 1973; Burger, McWard, & LaTorre, 1989). Moreover, one could argue that perceived control might still constitute a form of actual control if only defined as control over the group's psychological outcomes rather than over material outcomes (Gramsci, 1971; Leach & Livingstone, 2015). There are clear links here to secondary or coping appraisals and response- or emotion-focused coping strategies in the stress and coping literature (Lazarus, 1991; Lazarus & Folkman, 1984).

Unlike actual control, we argue that perceived psychological control can still be substantial amongst disadvantaged groups because psychological control is more subjective (Skinner, 1996). For example members of disadvantaged groups may not have the practical control to prevent discrimination on the job market but nevertheless they may have the psychological control to decide to not become downcast by it. Likewise, members of minority/low status groups can derive considerable positive identity from membership in stigmatised groups (Leach & Livingstone, 2015). Thus, low status groups have various means to maintain perceived psychological control. Nevertheless, low status groups are more often negatively stereotyped than high-status groups, so their perceived control is more often under threat than that of high status group members.

Although disadvantaged groups may experience chronic threats to control, the inherent agency of groups ("together we are strong") also points to the *collective* coping resources to restore a sense of control, inter alia through group identification. This may occur in large, socially powerful groups too, but may be especially evident in smaller and less powerful groups. Indeed, research suggests that group identification is often stronger with minority than majority groups (Simon, 1992). Recent work confirms that threats to control lead to preferences for membership in small groups that are perceived as highly agentic (Stollberg, Fritsche, & Bäcker, 2015). What seems to matter is that the identity provided by the group membership is agentic. For some majorities and powerful groups the agency lies in their dominant position in the social structure (e.g., Sidanius & Pratto, 2001). For disadvantaged groups the agency is concentrated through the common fate of shared threat (Doosje, Ellemers, & Spears, 1995; Ellemers, Spears, & Doosje, 1997, 2002; Spears, Doosje, & Ellemers, 1997) and demonstrated through collective action, activism, and other forms of social resistance aimed at rendering subjective control more real.

Resistance to identity threat: From individual reactance to group resistance

Whereas we use the term *social resistance* to refer to responses to threats to social identity in general (Tajfel & Turner, 1979), responses to specific threats to control have been considered in the literature under the rubric of (psychological) *reactance* (Brehm & Brehm, 1981), although this has traditionally been studied in the context of threats to *personal* freedom (but see Graupmann, Jonas, Meier, Hawelka, & Aichhorn, 2012; Jonas et al., 2009). We propose that threats to agency at the group level can result in a specific form of reactance: group resistance. The concept of group resistance builds on reactance theory, but extends its scope, as we conceptualize threats to social identity as threats to agency as well as value (content), a distinction that to our knowledge has not been considered at the interpersonal level.

Psychological reactance has been defined as "the motivational state that is hypothesized to occur when a freedom is eliminated or threatened with elimination" (Brehm & Brehm, 1981, p. 37). Identity threats that threaten personal freedom elicit psychological reactance, which we argue might be an important underlying mechanism of social resistance at the group level. In line with Worchel (2004), we propose that psychological reactance can be extended to "group reactance" when a relevant social identity is salient. In a situation threatening to their social identity, people may consider the interests of their group. This may be because group interests overlap with personal interests, but also because the group identity is an important part of the self (i.e., high identifiers). In sum, we propose that reactance to threats to individual freedom (i.e., control) can be broadened to include threats to group identity (implying both threat to value and agency).

Group-based actions aimed at the restoration of agency could be considered as more effective than individual action because of the collective efficacy ascribed to the group (Brewer, Hong, & Li, 2004). Group-based control restoration theory proposes that defining the self and acting in terms of a homogeneous and agentic group identity can serve to restore a generalized perception of personal control. Thus, threats to the control motive (i.e. restrictions of freedoms) can lead to stronger group identification, in-group support, and defense (Fritsche et al., 2011, 2013). In turn, stronger in-group identification is related to greater importance of the group to the self, and greater concern to protect in-group interests (e.g., Ellemers et al., 2002). Therefore, higher identification should lead to greater motivation to contest identity threat, leading to group resistance. In the following sections we first review evidence of explicit resistance to identity threat to then focus on our own work on implicit resistance.

Explicit resistance to identity threat

Collective action is one example of a resistance strategy in which agency plays an important part. Collective actions are aimed at "improving the conditions of the entire group" (Wright, Taylor, & Moghaddam, 1990) and group efficacy has proven to be an important determinant in predicting collective action (Mummendey, Kessler, Klink, & Mielke, 1999; van Zomeren, Spears, & Leach, 2008). The group efficacy concept originated from resource mobilization theory, which implies that people will attempt to challenge inequality only when they believe they have the power to do so effectively (McCarthy & Zald, 1977). However, this road to social change is not easily taken by group members as the power and group efficacy of low status and disadvantaged groups is often rather low (Tajfel & Turner, 1979).

Regardless of whether the intended goal of achieving actual control (i.e., social change) is achieved, resistance actions themselves can increase perceived group control or agency. Research has shown that collective action increases positive group identity, even when the objective is not reached (Drury & Reicher, 2005; van Zomeren, Leach, & Spears, 2012), suggesting that even unsuccessful collective action may serve an identity purpose, increasing in-group members' perceptions of agency, and consolidating group identity (Klein, Spears, & Reicher, 2007; Saab, Tausch, Spears, & Cheung, 2015).

Importantly though, perceived control can be restored through more indirect strategies that can be performed at the individual level even though they respond to a group-level concern (cf. de Lemus & Stroebe, 2015; Ellemers et al., 2002). For instance, task persistence, in-group bias or out-group derogation, may serve to counteract the threat, reaffirm positive in-group identity or reject the threatening out-group, and so restore a sense of agency at the group level.

Implicit resistance to identity threat

Even if *explicit* resistance to identity threat is sometimes difficult to exert, this does not mean that resistance to the threat will be lacking, especially if the targets of the threat are motivated to recognize it and to react against it. In such cases people may turn to more implicit forms of resistance. In this section we discuss findings from our own research showing that such resistance processes may operate at the implicit psychological level.

Those who are motivated to resist a socially threatening situation are able to do so in an automatic manner (de Lemus et al., 2013). Although the context in which the out-group is dominant facilitates the activation of in-group stereotypes (de Lemus, Moya, Lupiáñez, & Bukowski, 2014), de Lemus et al. found that Spanish women reverse automatic stereotype associations in response to an extensive exposure to traditional gender roles (de Lemus et al., 2013). That is, in baseline conditions (de Lemus et al., 2014), women who saw men and women equally represented in an office context, which is traditionally associated with male competence, were more likely to activate gender stereotypes of male competence and female warmth than those who saw men and women equally represented in a kitchen context. However, after being extensively exposed to pictures of women in a kitchen context, and men in an office context, women implicitly associated their in-group with more competence traits in both contexts (de Lemus et al., 2013). That is, after exposure to stereotypic gender roles, women implicitly associate the in-group with more *counter*-stereotypical attributes. Further, this effect was predicted by participants' own attitudes towards affirmative policies targeted at compensating the gender-role imbalance in society.

In another recent study we examined Polish men's and women's reactions to being extensively exposed to pictures of women in a cleaning context, and men in a manager office context (traditional stereotypes) vs. the reverse distribution of roles (de Lemus, Bukowski, Spears, & Telga, 2015, Study 1). Our findings show that men activate acceptance when primed with gender stereotypes, whereas women do not. Although no direct evidence of resistance activation for women was found, the fact that they do not comply with the male acceptance pattern suggests some opposition to the traditional distribution of roles primed.

Another way in which stereotyped groups might show reactance to the threat is by activating group-favouring evaluations (i.e., in-group bias) to strengthen the value of the group. Again, if this strategy is deployed at a very early stage of processing, this would suggest its automatic nature. In a set of three studies de Lemus et al. (2016) found activation of in-group bias after stereotypical exposure in women (i.e., being extensively exposed to pictures of women in a kitchen context, and men in an office context). Thus in a subsequent categorization task women responded faster to positive traits when primed with pictures depicting women (vs. men) in a context of social roles. The opposite pattern, namely faster categorization of negative traits, was facilitated by male primes. Moreover, this implicit in-group bias was positively related to negative emotions, and to persistence in a stereotypically threatening task (solving a bogus spatial intelligence test) in the threatened condition (stereotypical exposure). In sum, threats to identity may be resisted through implicit strategies.

Threats to identity may also be manifested in very subtle or even implicit ways (Swim, Aikin, Hall, & Hunter, 1995), and the literature shows that the subtler the threat, the more difficult it is to resist it. For instance, Kray and colleagues (Kray, Reb, Galinsky, & Thompson, 2004; Kray, Thompson, & Galinsky, 2001) found in a negotiation context that when stereotypes were activated explicitly, women manifested reactance to the stereotype by negotiating more aggressively and successfully than men if they had more or comparable power to their male counterparts, but when stereotypes were activated implicitly, women confirmed the gender stereotypes. This is consistent with the idea that when a threat is difficult to avoid (or not even noticed) or the restriction is perceived as absolute, this may attenuate reactance, and lead to acceptance of the situation (Laurin, Kay, & Fitzsimons, 2012b).

Could such implicit responses occur even when the threat itself is implicit, and thus occurs outside of awareness? There is evidence that under some circumstances, participants can become aware of cues of implicit identity threat (Kaiser, Vick, & Major, 2006). Our most recent research suggests that the ability to detect implicit threat cues allows for *resistance* against implicit identity threat, even when participants are not consciously aware of the threat (van Breen, de Lemus, Spears, & Kuppens, 2016b; van Breen, Spears, Kuppens, & de Lemus, 2016a). In a line of studies focusing on national stereotypes, we exposed Spanish participants to implicit associations that linked stereotypical in-group attributes of low competence with words relating to the current economic crisis. Participants showed implicit resistance when they were exposed to such associations that implied that the economic crisis was *due to* in-group incompetence. That is, participants associated the in-group with more *positive* targets compared to an out-group (i.e., Germans) (van Breen et al., 2016b). Note that it was necessary for the stereotypes to be linked to the economic crisis, providing the strongest threat to group value and agency, in order to trigger implicit resistance.

In sum, identity threats stemming from stereotypical associations activated either explicitly or implicitly lead to fast and efficient responses by the threatened group members that presumably could help them to reassert a sense of perceived agency.

Resistance depends on the content of identity

When describing identity threat earlier we noted that content and agency are closely related. This issue is also relevant when considering *resistance* to identity threat. This is reflected in studies of gender identity showing that not everyone is equally threatened by stereotypes of women (Brown & Pinel, 2003; Schmader, 2002). Whereas those who identify with feminism might perceive stereotypes as limiting women's power, those with more traditional gender identities might not be threatened by stereotypes. Indeed, van Breen et al. (2016a) found that only those who identify highly with feminists but not with women resist implicit gender stereotypes. Dutch female participants were exposed to implicit associations of men and women with (counter-) stereotypical activities (e.g., shopping, watching sports). Those who identified highly with feminists, but not with women, whom we refer to as "pure feminists", responded to these implicit stereotypes with implicit in-group bias. That is, after having been exposed to implicit in-group stereotypes, they responded with implicit in-group bias.

Additionally, after exposure to implicit stereotypes, pure feminists increased their persistence in a male-stereotypical competence domain (maths). Those who are highly identified with feminists *and* women do not show similar resistance tendencies. Therefore, it is not only about endorsing a politicized identity (i.e. feminists, Simon & Klandermans, 2001) that leads to these effects, but the specific combination of high politicized identification and low group identification. Part of the explanation for the difference between these subgroups may lie in the fact that high women's identification (high group identification) is associated with perceived femininity of the self, and self-stereotyping (Spears, Doosje, & Ellemers, 1997; van Breen, Spears, Kuppens, & de Lemus, 2016c). Thus, because high/high identifiers have internalized certain components of gender stereotypes, it makes it more difficult to resist when these components are devalued (stereotype exposure). Pure feminists instead view stereotypical gender representations more critically and (therefore) they play less of a role in how they see themselves, making it easier to resist these associations.

Taken together, these studies suggest that those who identify highly with feminists but not women are motivated to resist stereotype exposure. These women may find stereotypes threatening both to the value of their gender identity and to their sense of control. In terms of value threat, feminist identifiers may find that stereotypes of women are inaccurate and present an image of the in-group that they disagree with, threatening the value of their group identity.

In addition, pure feminists may resist implicit stereotypes because they threaten their perceived agency. Feminists perceive stereotypes of women as limiting social power and opportunities of women as a group, and preventing them from realising their potential. This threat to the in-group's agency may also motivate feminist identifiers to resist implicit stereotype exposure, both through implicit in-group bias and persistence in male-typical domains. Feminist identity is designed to be agentic, as feminists unite behind salient political goals of change; they are not just an opinion-based group but rather a "purpose-based group" (McGarty, Bliuc, Thomas, & Bongiorno, 2009). This may make the control aspect of social identity threat all the more important for feminists, motivating their response to counteract it. At the process level, why there are differences between feminists and other women in their responses to stereotypes and prejudice is still an open question.

People may differ in implicit resistance because they differ in their motivation and *ability* to exert cognitive control over responses (Dasgupta, 2009; Payne, 2005). Feminists who are more threatened by stereotypes (pure feminists) are likely to be more motivated and more able (because of repeated exposure) to show implicit resistance. We will develop this argument further in the next section.

Interestingly, in a different set of studies de Lemus et al. (2015; Study 1) have found that feminist identifiers persist more in a different male-stereotypical competence domain (bogus spatial intelligence test) after explicit *counter*-stereotypical exposure, whereas traditional women justify the system more in this same condition. Moreover, only non-sexist women exposed to traditional roles showed higher support for collective action in a context of blatant intergroup threat (Study 2). In other words, what disarms the stereotype threat for feminist women (i.e., exposure to counter-stereotypes) constitutes a threat to group values for traditional women.

Summing up, we argue that reactions to identity threats depend on the content of that identity so that the specific form resistance takes may depend on the (internalized) group norms being threatened.

Identity threat affects cognitive control and approach motivation

Explaining the relation between group agency and underlying processes such as motivation or cognitive control goes beyond the scope of this chapter, and it has been addressed more directly by other colleagues in this volume (cf., Bukowski & Kofta, Chapter 1, this volume; Greenaway, Philipp, & Storrs, Chapter 2, this volume). However, it is important to consider that *identity threats* as conceptualized in this chapter (i.e., as threats to agency as well as to value) are likely to have an impact on basic cognitive and motivational processes such as cognitive control or approach motivation. This is important because such mechanisms might be involved in (part of) the resistance process just as they have been shown to be a determinant of (overcoming) stereotype threat on performance (c.f. Schmader & Beilock, 2012).

Cognitive control is defined as "the function that allows us to successfully pursue our goals, by flexibly adapting our behavior to the environment, enhancing actions towards our goals and/or preventing actions towards unwanted outcomes" (Torres-Quesada, Milliken, Lupiáñez, & Funes, 2014). There is a conceptual link to the concept of control (and threat to it) that we have been considering at the more social level, in terms of group agency. In other words, if group agency is about the group being able to act out or defend the identity content (Haslam & Reicher, 2007; Klein et al., 2007), cognitive control is a basic cognitive tool implied in a large variety of domains that allows us to face or deal with interfering or conflicting information.

Dasgupta (2009) has proposed that social identity threat may affect implicit stereotyping by modulating cognitive control. However it is not clear in what way this might occur as much of the existing evidence is only correlational (but see Ito et al., 2015). For instance, Payne (2005) found that individuals who exhibited better cognitive control on a task unrelated to social groups also showed more controlled processing resulting in less bias towards African Americans on other race-based speed tasks (i.e., the shooter paradigm).

In an attempt to clarify the role of cognitive control in the activation of implicit stereotyping and responses to it (i.e., implicit resistance), Telga, de Lemus, and Lupiáñez (2016) explored the impact of identity threat in a cognitive control paradigm that allowed us to examine the evidence of cognitive control across two unrelated conflicts. In this study, the classical flanker task (Eriksen & Eriksen, 1974) was adapted to combine two types of trials triggering different conflicts: a cognitive conflict based on the overlap between the relevant and irrelevant stimuli of the task (i.e., letters) and a social conflict based on gender stereotypes (Kleiman, Hassin, & Trope, 2014). In the cognitive conflict, participants were asked to identify a central letter target flanked by identical (i.e., consistent condition) or different (i.e., inconsistent condition) letters. In the social conflict, the targets were either masculine or feminine names, and the distractors were adjectives that had been shown to be stereotypically feminine (e.g., weak) or masculine (e.g., strong). The combination of these four conditions resulted in consistent (i.e., feminine name flanked by stereotypically feminine adjectives and masculine name flanked by stereotypically masculine adjectives) and inconsistent (i.e., feminine name flanked by stereotypically masculine adjective and masculine name flanked by stereotypically feminine adjective) trials.

In line with previous research, slower RTs in categorizing the target were expected for inconsistent trials in both cognitive and social conditions, reflecting cognitive control implementation (Kleiman et al., 2014). Indeed, inconsistent trials contain features that may trigger control allocation and thus slower RTs since they interfere with the participants' task. In the cognitive condition, "noise" letters (distractors, different from the target) may hinder the selection of the target letter whereas in the social condition, the counter-stereotypical association between names and adjectives may provide participants with conflicting information. In a first study, this hypothesis was confirmed at baseline levels when no threat was activated. In a second study, before performing the cognitive and social flanker task, participants were either exposed to a gender-identity threatening scenario questioning women's competence by referring to increasing male representation within psychology or to a non-gender threatening scenario referring to increasing international students' representation in psychology studies (this second condition could imply a threat to national, but not gender, identity). Results showed that interference (i.e., faster RTs for consistent vs. inconsistent trials) disappeared in the social flanker task in both conditions. Therefore, when no threat is present, participants perform the task in agreement with gender stereotypes by being faster in categorizing targets presented in consistent (vs. inconsistent) stereotype contexts (Study 1). However, when an identity threat is active (regardless of whether it is specific for gender), participants seem to ignore or overcome the gender stereotypes interference since they show no difference in RT between consistent and inconsistent social flanker trials. In other words, when compared to the first study, the data from Study 2 suggest that under identity threat, the counter-stereotypical associations women-strength and men-weakness are no longer perceived as inconsistent. Interestingly, this happens independently of whether or not the identity threat is related to gender stereotypes (Study 2).

However, only the group under gender identity threat generalized these increased control abilities to the cognitive conflict, by showing a lower percentage of errors and no difference in accuracy between congruent and incongruent cognitive trials (Study 2). Thus, identity threat may have increased participants' motivation to resist gender stereotypes by implementing more cognitive control in the social flanker task. Moreover, this improvement in cognitive control abilities may transfer to an unrelated cognitive conflict. Interestingly, the group under gender identity threat also showed a greater motivation to become involved in collective actions to defend women's rights, echoing at the explicit level the control motivation observed in the flanker task. This suggests that cognitive control and implicit social responses are closely related. Although the ability to exert cognitive control seems to play an important role in social implicit responses (c.f. Dasgupta, 2009; Payne, 2005), social contexts such as identity threat can in turn modulate cognitive control by inducing a highly relevant motivation for restoring perceived agency. Overall, these results support the idea that identity threats influence cognitive control, potentially increasing it, which in turn might help to restore a sense of *perceived control* and accomplish the goal of resisting the threat.

Similarly, there is evidence that implicit identity threat inspires avoidance motivation. Approach/avoidance motivation is a basic psychological tendency regarding a desire to either approach or avoid a target. Approach and avoidance motivations can be used as an indicator of pre-conscious appraisals of stimuli, as approach or avoidance tendencies are evident before a stimulus can be consciously evaluated (e.g., Phaf, Mohr, Rotteveel, & Wicherts, 2014; Wentura, Rothermund, & Bak, 2000). It has been shown (Blascovich, 2013; Shechner et al., 2012) that the experience of threat is associated with avoidance tendencies. As such, avoidance (compared to approach) tendencies can serve as a proxy for threat that participants experience at a preconscious level. In an approach-avoidance task (De Houwer, Crombez, Baeyens, & Hermans, 2001) participants moved a small stick-woman towards or away from threatening and neutral targets. We found that, after exposure to implicit stereotypes, avoidance of threat words was faster amongst those with higher feminist identification (van Breen et al., 2016a). That is, those whom we expected, on a theoretical basis, to be most threatened by stereotypes showed this through increased avoidance motivation.

Overall the empirical evidence presented in this section suggests that the ability to exert cognitive control can be increased with the appropriate motivation (cf. Telga et al., 2016), and such motivation might arise from identity threatening conditions especially for those who are most concerned about the status of the in-group in a general intergroup context (cf. van Breen et al., 2016a).

Conclusions

In this chapter we argue that identity threat can lead to both explicit and implicit forms of resistance. Such identity threats are related both to *content* and to actual and/or perceived *agency*. That is, identity threat typically questions the value of the group, as traditionally assumed by SIT (Tajfel & Turner, 1979), but often also implies limits to the group's capacity to achieve its goals, namely agency. Therefore, we conceptualize resistance as an agentic behaviour aimed at regaining control over a threatened identity and reasserting its positive value. Value and agency are not mutually exclusive alternatives but are clearly closely related. The value of the group gives an indication of how the group is doing whereas agency also implicates the means for achieving a better group position or value (in terms of status or in-group stereotypes). Agency can clearly operate as a means to value, whereas the group value indicates whether change is desired (which it usually is for disadvantaged groups). In this sense value and agency are respectively closely related to the identity and instrumental functions associated with intergroup behavior (Klein et al., 2007; Scheepers, Spears, Doosje, & Manstead, 2006).

At the individual or interpersonal level, threats to control or agency elicit motivation to restore it as proposed by reactance theory (Brehm & Brehm, 1981). We expand this argument to the intergroup realm, suggesting that individuals can also react to group-based threats, by trying to perform actions that help them to restore their sense of group agency. This is consistent with Fritsche et al.'s group-based control model (2013) which shows that threatened personal control can be restored by bolstering social identity (cf. Stollberg et al., Chapter 8, this volume).

In the studies reviewed in this chapter we do not examine these two aspects (agency and value) separately. However, we provide support for our hypothesis that a threat to group agency is important to trigger some form of resistance response, at least in two ways. First, the manipulations of threat that we use are mainly based on exposure to social roles or stereotypical activities, including roles and activities that were similar in terms of value (e.g., the stimuli used in van Breen et al., 2016a, were pretested and equivalent in terms of valence), but clearly restrict group agency by limiting their behaviours to those implied by traditional social roles.

Second, the finding that implicit resistance to implicit threats depends on feminist identity suggests that participants' reaction was triggered also by a threat to their group agency (rather than value). Feminist identity is above all an agentic one, as it has a clear goal of achieving social change (not least because as we have shown, feminists can disagree on issues of content, such as femininity, showing that content alone is not the crucial determinant for resistance). Therefore, threat to control might be especially salient for people who endorse feminism. Moreover, an important part of feminist ideology focuses on the social power of women (or rather the lack thereof); thus, some feminists at least (pure feminists) may be particularly threatened by exposure to stereotypes, as they typically depict women in low power social positions. Nevertheless, in future studies, we should try to experimentally manipulate agency vs. value-based threat in order to examine if these two aspects equally activate resistance-related strategies, or whether both are necessary to trigger resistance at a more implicit level. This would be consistent with our findings in the study about national identity threat previously described, where only the combination of Spanish stereotypes with economic crisis triggered implicit resistance (van Breen et al., 2016b).

As in interpersonal domains (c.f. Laurin, Kay, & Fitzsimons, 2012a), the strategy of group-based resistance might only be used when there is a perceived chance of success in restoring control, at least at the explicit level (Kray et al., 2001, 2004). For instance, in the case of intergroup relations, collective action might be more likely when there is a perception of social support suggesting that the action might be effective (Van Zomeren, Postmes, & Spears, 2008). However, everyday situations give rise to identity threats that give few or no options for direct confrontation. For instance, everyday exposure to social role distributions might be a threatening experience for women's identity as they (we) are constantly reminded of their (our) inferior status and possibilities. It is quite improbable that each of these episodes is confronted by individuals explicitly. Does it mean, however, that the targets of such threats do not experience a feeling of control loss or diminished value? This is most unlikely, and probably such experiences trigger some form of reactance even if it is not observable at the explicit level. We argue that it is indeed possible to demonstrate forms of resistance or group-based reactance that occur at a very basic level and in an efficient (fast) manner.

Across several studies and lines of research we provided evidence of resistance at the implicit level in the form of stereotype reversal (de Lemus et al. 2013), ingroup bias, and persistence (de Lemus et al. 2016; van Breen et al. 2016a; van Breen et al. 2016b). Indeed the research by van Breen et al. (2016a) shows evidence for such resistance among women who have become chronically sensitive to such threats, even when the threat itself is not consciously perceived. Such implicit forms of resistance might be a proof of *perceived* psychological control if not *actual* control, suggesting that members of disadvantaged groups might actively engage in forms of psychological resistance in their everyday life much more readily than has traditionally been assumed in the social psychological literature (c.f. Leach & Livingstone, 2015). Hence, even when there is a reality constraint for group disadvantage, group members may still reassert their perceived group agency through implicit strategies. Moreover, such implicit forms of resistance might influence core, basic psychological mechanisms such as cognitive control and approach motivation that are fundamental in understanding psychological well-being and functioning.

Finally, as much as we consider control motives important to understand reactions to identity threat, we argue that *content* is needed in order to explain *how and when* control is threatened and whether it will lead to resistance. What triggers reactance-motivation is the feeling that a freedom has been threatened, but *what* is considered as a threatened freedom depends on the group values, norms, and common goals. Similarly, what is considered as a threat for more traditional women (e.g., to endorse counter-stereotypical roles) might not be perceived as such by more egalitarian pro-feminist individuals, who in turn, feel threatened by gender stereotypes and react against them, even implicitly.

References

Abele, A. E., & Wojciszke, B. (2007). Agency and communion from the perspective of self versus others. *Journal of Personality and Social Psychology, 93*(5), 751–763. doi:10.1037/0022-3514.93.5.751

Alloy, L. B., & Abramson, L. Y. (1982). Learned helplessness, depression, and the illusion of control. *Journal of Personality and Social Psychology, 42*(6), 1114–1126. doi:10.1037//0022-3514.42.6.1114

Allport, G. W. (1979). *The nature of prejudice*. Reading, MA: Addison-Wesley.

Averill, J. R. (1973). Personal control over aversive stimuli and its relationship to stress. *Psychological Bulletin, 80*(4), 286–303. doi:10.1037/h0034845

Blascovich, J. (2013). Challenge and threat. In A. J. Elliot (Ed.), *Handbook of approach and avoidance motivation* (pp. 431–446). Abingdon: Routledge. doi:10.4324/9780203888148.ch25

Brambilla, M., Sacchi, S., Rusconi, P., Cherubini, P., & Yzerbyt, V. Y. (2012). You want to give a good impression? Be honest! Moral traits dominate group impression formation. *British Journal of Social Psychology, 51*(1), 149–166. doi:10.1111/j.2044-8309.2010.02011

Branscombe, N. R., Ellemers, N., Spears, R., & Doosje, B. (1999). The context and content of social identity threat. In N. Ellemers, R. Spears, & B. Doosje (Eds.), *Social identity: Context, commitment, content* (pp. 35–58). Oxford, England: Blackwell Science.

Brehm, S., & Brehm, J. W. (1981). *Psychological reactance: A theory of freedom and control*. New York: Academic Press.

Brewer, M. B., Hong, Y.-Y., & Li, Q. (2004). Dynamic entitativity: Perceiving groups as actors. In V. Yzerbyt, C. M. Judd, & O. Corneille (Eds.), *The psychology of group perception: Perceived variability, entitativity, and essentialism* (pp. 25–38). New York, NY, US: Psychology Press.

Brown, R. P., & Pinel, E. C. (2003). Stigma on my mind: Individual differences in the experience of stereotype threat. *Journal of Experimental Social Psychology, 39*(6), 626–633. doi:10.1016/S0022-1031(03)00039-8

Burger, J. M., McWard, J., & LaTorre, D. (1989). Boundaries of self-control: Relinquishing control over aversive events. *Journal of Social and Clinical Psychology, 8*(2), 209–221. doi:10.1521/jscp.1989.8.2.209

Dardenne, B., Dumont, M., & Bollier, T. (2007). Insidious dangers of benevolent sexism: Consequences for women's performance. *Journal of Personality and Social Psychology, 93*(5), 764–779. doi:10.1037/0022-3514.93.5.764

Dasgupta, N. (2009). Mechanisms underlying the malleability of implicit prejudice and stereotypes. In T. D. Nelson (Ed.), *Handbook of prejudice, stereotyping, and discrimination* (pp. 267–284). Abingdon: Routledge.

De Houwer, J., Crombez, G., Baeyens, F., & Hermans, D. (2001). On the generality of the affective Simon effect. *Cognition & Emotion, 15*(2), 189–206. doi:10.1080/02699930125883

de Lemus, S., Bukowski, M., Spears, R., & Telga, M. (2015). Reactance to (or acceptance of) stereotypes: Implicit and explicit responses to group identity threat. *Zeitschrift für Psychologie, 223*(4), 236–246. doi:10.1027/2151-2604/a000225

de Lemus, S., Moya, M., Lupiáñez, J., & Bukowski, M. (2014). Men in the office, women in the kitchen? Contextual dependency of gender stereotype activation in Spanish women. *Sex Roles, 70*(11–12), 468–478. doi:10.1007/s11199-013-0328-6

de Lemus, S., Spears, R., Bukowski, M., Moya, M., & Lupiáñez, J. (2013). Reversing implicit gender stereotype activation as a function of exposure to traditional gender roles. *Social Psychology, 44*(2), 109–116. doi:10.1027/1864-9335/a000140

de Lemus, S., Spears, R., Lupiañez, J., Moya, M., & Bukowski, M. (2016). Implicit resistance to sexist role relations by women: The effects of stereotype exposure on in-group bias. *Manuscript in Preparation*.

de Lemus, S., & Stroebe, K. (2015). Achieving Social Change: A Matter of All for One?: Achieving Social Change. *Journal of Social Issues, 71*(3), 441–452.

Doosje, B., Ellemers, N., & Spears, R. (1995). Perceived intragroup variability as a function of status and identification. *Journal of Experimental Social Psychology, 31*, 410–436. doi:10.1006/jesp.1995.1018

Drury, J., & Reicher, S. (2005). Explaining enduring empowerment: A comparative study of collective action and psychological outcomes. *European Journal of Social Psychology, 35*(1), 35–58. doi:10.1002/ejsp.231

Ellemers, N., Spears, R., & Doosje, B. (1997). Sticking together or falling apart: Ingroup identification as a psychological determinant of group commitment versus individual mobility. *Journal of Personality and Social Psychology, 72*, 617–626. doi:10.1037/0022-3514.72.3.617

Ellemers, N., Spears, R., & Doosje, B. (2002). Self and social identity★. *Annual Review of Psychology, 53*(1), 161–186. doi:10.1146/annurev.psych.53.100901.135228

Eriksen, B. A., & Eriksen, C. W. (1974). Effects of noise letters upon the identification of a target letter in a nonsearch task. *Perception & Psychophysics, 16*(1), 143–149. doi:10.3758/BF03203267

Fiske, S. T. (2003). Five core social motives, plus or minus five. In S. J. Spencer, S. Fein, M. P. Zanna, & J. M. Olson (Eds.), *Motivated social perception: The Ontario symposium* (Vol. 9, pp. 233–246). Mahwah, NJ: Lawrence Erlbaum Associates Publishers.

Fiske, S. T., Cuddy, A. J., Glick, P., & Xu, J. (2002). A model of (often mixed) stereotype content: Competence and warmth respectively follow from perceived status and competition. *Journal of Personality and Social Psychology, 82*(6), 878–902. doi:10.1037/0022-3514.82.6.878

Fritsche, I., Jonas, E., Ablasser, C., Beyer, M., Kuban, J., Manger, A., & Schultz, M. (2013). The power of we: Evidence for group-based control. *Journal of Experimental Social Psychology, 49*(1), 19–32. doi:10.1016/j.jesp.2012.07.014

Fritsche, I., Jonas, E., & Kessler, T. (2011). Collective reactions to threat: Implications for intergroup conflict and for solving societal crises. *Social Issues and Policy Review, 5*(1), 101–136. doi:10.1111/j.1751-2409.2011.01027.x

Glick, P., & Fiske, S. T. (1996). The ambivalent sexism inventory: Differentiating hostile and benevolent sexism. *Journal of Personality and Social Psychology, 70*(3), 491–512. doi:10.1037/0022-3514.70.3.491

Gramsci, A. (1971). *Selections from the prison notebooks*. New York: International Publishers.

Graupmann, V., Jonas, E., Meier, E., Hawelka, S., & Aichhorn, M. (2012), Reactance, the self, and its group: When threats to freedom come from the ingroup versus the outgroup. *European Journal of Social Psychology, 42*, 164–173. doi:10.1002/ejsp.857

Guinote, A. (2007). Power and goal pursuit. *Personality & Social Psychology Bulletin, 33*(8), 1076–1087. doi:0146167207301011

Guinote, A., Brown, M., & Fiske, S. T. (2006). Minority status decreases sense of control and increases interpretive processing. *Social Cognition, 24*(2), 169–186. doi:10.1521/soco.2006.24.2.169

Haslam, S. A., & Reicher, S. D. (2007). Social identity and the dynamics of organizational life: Insights from the BBC prison study. In C. Bartel, S. Blader, & A. Wrzesniewski (Eds.), *Identity and the modern organization* (pp. 135–166). New York: Erlbaum.

Ito, T. A., Friedman, N. P., Bartholow, B. D., Correll, J., Loersch, C., Altamirano, L. J., & Miyake, A. (2015). Toward a comprehensive understanding of executive cognitive function in implicit racial bias. *Journal of Personality and Social Psychology, 108*(2), 187–218. doi:10.1037/a0038557

Jonas, E., Graupmann, V., Niesta-Kayser, D., Zanna, M. P., Traut-Mattausch, E., & Frey, D. (2009). Culture, self-construal and the emergence of reactance: Is there a "universal" freedom? *Journal of Experimental Social Psychology, 45*, 1068–1080. doi:10.1016/j.jesp.2009.06.005

Kaiser, C. R., Vick, S. B., & Major, B. (2006). Prejudice expectations moderate preconscious attention to cues that are threatening to social identity. *Psychological Science, 17*(4), 332–338. doi:10.1111/j.1467-9280.2006.01707.x

Kervyn, N., Yzerbyt, V.Y., & Judd, C. M. (2011). When compensation guides inferences: Indirect and implicit measures of the compensation effect. *European Journal of Social Psychology, 41*(2), 144–150. doi:10.1002/ejsp.748

Kleiman, T., Hassin, R. R., & Trope, Y. (2014). The control-freak mind: Stereotypical biases are eliminated following conflict-activated cognitive control. *Journal of Experimental Psychology: General, 143*(2), 498–503. doi:10.1037/a0033047

Klein, O., Spears, R., & Reicher, S. (2007). Social identity performance: Extending the strategic side of SIDE. *Personality and Social Psychology Review: An Official Journal of the Society for Personality and Social Psychology, Inc, 11*(1), 28–45. doi:10.1177/1088868306294588

Kray, L. J., Reb, J., Galinsky, A. D., & Thompson, L. (2004). Stereotype reactance at the bargaining table: The effect of stereotype activation and power on claiming and creating value. *Personality and Social Psychology Bulletin, 30*(4), 399–411. doi:10.1177/0146167203261884

Kray, L. J., Thompson, L., & Galinsky, A. (2001). Battle of the sexes: Gender stereotype confirmation and reactance in negotiations. *Journal of Personality and Social Psychology, 80*(6), 942–958. doi:10.1037/0022-3514.80.6.942

Laurin, K., Kay, A. C., & Fitzsimons, G. M. (2012a). Divergent effects of activating thoughts of god on self-regulation. *Journal of Personality and Social Psychology, 102*(1), 4–21. doi:10.1037/a0025971

Laurin, K., Kay, A. C., & Fitzsimons, G. J. (2012b). Reactance versus rationalization: Divergent responses to policies that constrain freedom. *Psychological Science, 23*(2), 205–209. doi:10.1177/0956797611429468

Lazarus, R. S. (1991). *Emotion and adaptation.* New York: Oxford University Press.

Lazarus, R. S., & Folkman, S. F. (1984). *Stress, appraisal, and coping.* New York: Springer.

Leach, C. W., Ellemers, N., & Barreto, M. (2007). Group virtue: The importance of morality (vs. competence and sociability) in the positive evaluation of in-groups. *Journal of Personality and Social Psychology, 93*(2), 234–249. doi:10.1037/0022-3514.93.2.234

Leach, C. W., & Livingstone, A. G. (2015). Contesting the meaning of inter-group disadvantage: Towards a psychology of resistance. *Journal of Social Issues, 71*(3), 614–632. doi:10.1111/josi.12131

McCarthy, J. D., & Zald, M. N. (1977). Resource mobilization and social movements: A partial theory. *American Journal of Sociology, 82*(6), 1212–1241. doi:10.1086/226464

McGarty, C., Bliuc, A., Thomas, E. F., & Bongiorno, R. (2009). Collective action as the material expression of opinion-based group membership. *Journal of Social Issues, 65*(4), 839–857. doi:10.1111/j.1540-4560.2009.01627

Moya, M., Glick, P., Exposito, F., de Lemus, S., & Hart, J. (2007). It's for your own good: Benevolent sexism and women's reactions to protectively justified restrictions. *Personality & Social Psychology Bulletin, 33*(10), 1421–1434. doi:0146167207304790

Mummendey, A., Kessler, T., Klink, A., & Mielke, R. (1999). Strategies to cope with negative social identity: Predictions by social identity theory and relative deprivation theory. *Journal of Personality and Social Psychology, 76*(2), 229–245. doi:10.1037/0022-3514.76.2.229

Ouwerkerk, J. W., & Ellemers, N. (2002). The benefits of being disadvantaged: Performance-related circumstances and consequences of intergroup comparisons. *European Journal of Social Psychology, 32*(1), 73–91. doi:10.1002/ejsp.62

Payne, B. K. (2005). Conceptualizing control in social cognition: How executive functioning modulates the expression of automatic stereotyping. *Journal of Personality and Social Psychology, 89*(4), 488–503. doi:10.1037/0022-3514.89.4.488

Phaf, R. H., Mohr, S. E., Rotteveel, M., & Wicherts, J. M. (2014). Approach, avoidance, and affect: A meta-analysis of approach-avoidance tendencies in manual reaction time tasks. *Frontiers in Psychology, 5*, 378. doi:10.3389/fpsyg.2014.00378

Pittman, T. S., & Zeigler, K. R. (2007). Basic human needs. In A. W. Kruglanski & E. T. Higgins (Eds.), *Social psychology: Handbook of basic principles* (pp. 473–489). New York: Guilford Press.

Prentice, D. A., & Carranza, E. (2002). What women and men should be, shouldn't be, are allowed to be, and don't have to be: The contents of prescriptive gender stereotypes. *Psychology of Women Quarterly, 26*(4), 269–228. doi:10.1111/1471-6402.t01-1-00066

Reicher, S. (2004). The context of social identity: Domination, resistance, and change. *Political Psychology, 25*(6), 921–945. doi:10.1111/j.1467-9221.2004.00403

Ridgeway, C. L. (2001). Gender, status, and leadership. *Journal of Social Issues, 57*(4), 637–655. doi:10.1111/0022-4537.00233

Saab, R., Tausch, N., Spears, R., & Cheung, W.-Y. (2015). Acting in solidarity: Testing an extended dual pathway model of collective action by bystander group members. *British Journal of Social Psychology. 54*, 539–560.

Scheepers, D., Spears, R., Doosje, B., & Manstead, A. S. (2006). Diversity in in-group bias: Structural factors, situational features, and social functions. *Journal of Personality and Social Psychology, 90*(6), 944–960. doi:10.1037/0022-3514.90.6.944

Schmader, T. (2002). Gender identification moderates stereotype threat effects on women's math performance. *Journal of Experimental Social Psychology, 38*(2), 194–201. doi:10.1006/jesp.2001.1500

Schmader, T., & Beilock, S. (2012). An integration of the processes that underlie stereotype threat. In M. Inzlicht & T. Schmader (Eds.), *Stereotype threat: Theory, process, and application* (pp. 35–50). New York: Oxford University Press.

Shechner, T., Britton, J. C., Pérez-Edgar, K., Bar-Haim, Y., Ernst, M., Fox, N. A., . . . Pine, D. S. (2012). Attention biases, anxiety, and development: Toward or away from threats or rewards? *Depression and Anxiety, 29*(4), 282–294. doi:10.1002/da.20914

Sidanius, J., & Pratto, F. (2001). *Social dominance: An intergroup theory of social hierarchy and oppression*. New York: Cambridge University Press.

Simon, B. (1992). The perception of ingroup and outgroup homogeneity: Reintroducing the intergroup context. *European Review of Social Psychology, 3*(1), 1–30. doi:10.1080/14792779243000005

Simon, B., & Klandermans, B. (2001). Politicized collective identity: A social psychological analysis. *American Psychologist, 56*(4), 319–331. doi:10.1037/0003-066X.56.4.319

Skinner, F. A. (1996). A guide to constructs of control. *Journal of Personality and Social Psychology, 71*(3), 549–570. doi:10.1037/0022-3514.71.3.549

Spears, R., Doosje, B., & Ellemers, N. (1997). Self-stereotyping in the face of threats to group status and distinctiveness: The role of group identification. *Personality and Social Psychology Bulletin, 23*(5), 538–553. doi:10.1177/0146167297235009

Spears, R., Jetten, J., & Doosje, B. (2001). The (il)legitimacy of ingroup bias: From social reality to social resistance. In J. T. Jost & B. Major (Eds.), *The psychology of legitimacy: Emerging perspectives on ideology, justice, and intergroup relations*, (pp. 332–362). New York: Cambridge University Press.

Stephan, W., Ybarra, O., & Rios Morrison, K. (2009). Intergroup threat theory. In T. D. Nelson (Ed.), *Handbook of prejudice, stereotyping, and discrimination* (pp. 43–59). Mahwah, NJ: Lawrence Erlbaum Associates.

Stollberg, J., Fritsche, I., & Bäcker, A. (2015). Striving for group agency: Threat to personal control increases the attractiveness of agentic groups. *Frontiers in Psychology, 6*, 649. doi:10.3389/fpsyg.2015.00649

Swim, J. K., Aikin, K. J., Hall, W. S., & Hunter, B. A. (1995). Sexism and racism: Old-fashioned and modern prejudices. *Journal of Personality and Social Psychology, 68*(2), 199–214. doi:10.1037/0022-3514.68.2.199

Tajfel, H., & Turner, J. C. (1979). An integrative theory of intergroup conflict. In W. G. Austin & S. Worchel (Eds.), *The social psychology of intergroup relations* (pp. 33–47). Monterey, CA: Brooks-Cole.

Telga, M., de Lemus, S., & Lupiáñez, J. (2016). Cognitive control in the social world: Influence of identity threat on social and cognitive conflicts. *Manuscript in preparation.*

Torres-Quesada, M., Milliken, B., Lupiáñez, J., & Funes, M. J. (2014). Proportion congruent effects in the absence of sequential congruent effects. *Psychological: International Journal of Methodology and Experimental Psychology, 35*(1), 101–115.

van Breen, J. A., de Lemus, S., Spears, R., & Kuppens, T. (2016b). Resistance to implicit identity threat: Stereotypes and disadvantage. *Manuscript in preparation.*

van Breen, J. A., Spears, R., Kuppens, T., & de Lemus, S. (2016a). Implicit resistance to implicit gender identity threat: Who, why, how? *Manuscript in preparation.*

van Breen, J. A., Spears, R., Kuppens, T., & de Lemus, S. (2016c). Distinguishing dimensions of gender identity: The two gender identity factor model. *Manuscript in preparation.*

van Zomeren, M., Leach, C. W., & Spears, R. (2010). Does group efficacy increase group identification? Resolving their paradoxical relationship. *Journal of Experimental Social Psychology, 46*(6), 1055–1060. doi:10.1016/j.jesp.2010.05.006

van Zomeren, M., Leach, C. W., & Spears, R. (2012). Protesters as "passionate economists": A dynamic dual pathway model of approach coping with collective disadvantage. *Personality and Social Psychology Review : An Official Journal of the Society for Personality and Social Psychology, Inc, 16*(2), 180–199. doi:10.1177/1088868311430835

van Zomeren, M., Postmes, T., & Spears, R. (2008). Toward an integrative social identity model of collective action: A quantitative research synthesis of three socio-psychological perspectives. *Psychological Bulletin, 134*(4), 504–535. doi:10.1037/0033-2909

van Zomeren, M., Spears, R., Fischer, A. H., & Leach, C. W. (2004). Put your money where your mouth is! Explaining collective action tendencies through group-based anger and group efficacy. *Journal of Personality and Social Psychology, 87*(5), 649–664. doi:10.1037/0022-3514.87.5.649

van Zomeren, M., Spears, R., & Leach, C. W. (2008). Exploring psychological mechanisms of collective action: Does relevance of group identity influence how people cope with collective disadvantage? *British Journal of Social Psychology, 47*(2), 353–372. doi:10.1348/014466607X231091

Wentura, D., Rothermund, K., & Bak, P. (2000). Automatic vigilance: The attention-grabbing power of approach-and avoidance-related social information. *Journal of Personality and Social Psychology, 78*(6), 1024–1037.

Worchel, S. (2004). The diamond in the stone: Exploring the place of free behavior in studies of human rights and culture. In R. A. Wright, J. Greenberg, & S. S. Brehm (Eds.), *Motivational analyses of social behavior. Building on Jack Brehm's contributions to psychology* (pp. 107–128). Mahwah, NJ: Erlbaum.

Wright, S. C., Taylor, D. M., & Moghaddam, F. M. (1990). Responding to membership in a disadvantaged group: From acceptance to collective protest. *Journal of Personality and Social Psychology, 58*(6), 994–1003. doi:10.1037/0022-3514.58.6.994

PART 3

Uncontrollability, powerlessness, and intergroup cognition

10

THINKING UP AND TALKING UP

Restoring control through mindreading

Susan T. Fiske, Daniel L. Ames, Jillian K. Swencionis, and Cydney H. Dupree*

*AUTHORS ARE LISTED BY PhD SENIORITY.

Contact: sfiske@princeton.edu

Suppose you are fundraising for a good cause, and you know somebody with a lot of money, who might or might not be sympathetic. As you approach this interaction, you are likely to think hard about this other person's motives, predisposition, history, and mood. All these attempts at mindreading are efforts to seek prediction, and perhaps avenues for influence and control, in service of your worthy goals. Outcome dependency is the key feature of this relationship in this context. People function in hierarchies, among other types of relationships. Status and power differences appear between rich and poor, famous and obscure, boss and subordinate, parent and child, majority and minority. Our program of research investigates some social cognitive dynamics that cut across these specific instances to what we hope are more general principles of responses to uncontrollability from occupying lower social ranks.

To preview: status and power create outcome dependency in subordinates, who lack control over prestige and resources. As reviewed next, prior research showed that outcome dependency motivates attempts at mindreading: people attend upward, make individuating dispositional inferences, and form individuating impressions, using unexpected information, in the hope of restoring control or at least prediction. More recent work, also to be reviewed, shows that these types of social cognition under outcome dependency appear in neural signatures of mindreading. Turning from interpersonal perception – thinking upward – to interpersonal interaction – talking upward – current work shows some interpersonal strategies subordinates use when interacting up the hierarchy to convey unexpected information, contradicting stereotypes of them as warm but incompetent.

Background: What it means to be subordinate

Social psychology generally, and social cognition specifically, have not typically addressed subordination as much as (for example) sociologists have. Their term, *stratification*, usefully describes the larger context of ranking people vertically by their social categories (Fiske, 2010). Stratification creates unequal access to scarce resources. The hopeful fundraiser and the prospective donor represent different strata. For present purposes, stratification combines status and power, which are often otherwise conceptually important to separate: *Status* entails social respect, importance, and prestige at upper levels of the hierarchy; hierarchies usually have societal endorsement, and ultimately status is conferred by others. *Power* controls socially valued resources, regardless of resource type (e.g., money, food, promotions) and power's basis (e.g., information, punishment; French & Raven, 1959). High power and high status, in practice, are often correlated.

Subordination sits lower within the hierarchy, correlated with less status and power. It relates to oppression and stigma, which have received attention in social psychology, under the topics of stigmatized impression management (Goffman, 1963; Jones et al., 1984), stigma's attributional ambiguity for negative outcomes (Crocker & Major, 1989), stereotype threat (Steele & Aronson, 1995), and system justification by subordinates (Jost & Banaji, 1994). Each of these analyses touches on uncontrollability, respectively: managing a spoiled impression, explaining ambiguous negative feedback, performing under pressure of negative expectations, coping with system instability. However, controllability is our central explanatory focus here.

To summarize a mammoth literature (in species that include primates and human society; Fiske, 2010), all hierarchical positions confer advantages and disadvantages, raising challenges to individual control over outcomes. Specifically, group-based status carries immediate benefits, opening doors and providing access. In the long term, status may generate risky, lifelong ambivalence across the strata created by gender, age, race, or class. (For example, in each case, the higher status group reaps advantages, but also responsibility, guilt, and threat.) Interpersonal power also has mixed effects, with debates over whether it corrupts, liberates, or constrains (respectively, Fiske, 1993; Guinote, 2007; Keltner, Gruenfeld, & Anderson, 2003). Certainly, power orients the powerful to their own higher-level goals, for better or worse (Fiske & Berdahl, 2007).

Subordination too has its pros and cons. As the literature below indicates, subordination both encourages short-term vigilance and carries long-term risks. Beginning with vigilance, depending on others motivates subordinates' immediate goal to be accurate, to afford prediction and maybe control. As the next section indicates, interpersonal outcome dependency makes subordinates attend, individuate, and often be accurate about those who control resources. Possible benefits include being more accurate and detail oriented (Guinote, 2007), but perhaps at the cost of losing the big picture.

Subordination has other immediate costs (see Fiske, 2010, for references). Subordinates disproportionately suffer (and try to avoid) their higher-strata tormenters' hassling, harassing, and aggressing. They must cope with reputational threat, and they may understandably envy those with more power and status. In the long term, these disadvantages can create stigma and attributional ambiguity, self-verification as inferior, and even disidentification with their group. Although it is less obvious, subordinates also can enjoy deniability (less responsibility), higher moral credibility, conflict avoidance, knowledge gained through vigilance, and the potential power of subordinates as a collective.

Seen from this broad-brush perspective, subordination is a mixed bag. The next sections explore the interpersonal social cognitive processes that result from outcome dependency, as people think upward, as well as the interpersonal dynamics they engage, as people talk upward.

Outcome dependency, uncontrollability, and vigilance: Social cognitive processes of thinking upward

People are fundamentally interdependent, so we routinely need each other in order to survive and thrive. Social cognition operates in the service of understanding others, particularly what they are going to do next, as that impacts our own actions. To coordinate, we must mind-read. A series of studies from our lab over the decades shows that outcome dependency motivates individuating social cognitive processes directed upward, in the service of prediction and perhaps control; recent data show the neural substrates of these processes.

The research program examines control deprivation in the form of outcome dependency, someone else having at least partial control over what happens to another. When people are not completely autonomous, they seek information about those who help determine their fates. We do not ask participants directly whether they feel less control, but instead we observe control-seeking behavior in regard to learning about the other person: attention to the most diagnostic information, interpretations about stable features of the other person (disposition) that presumably will predict future behavior, and other evidence of trying to read the other person's intentions. Some studies also separate people or experimental conditions by whether they expect or allow control, given outcome dependency.

Our first foray was informed by the hypothesis that default processes allow lazy social cognizers to rely on information that fits their expectations and stereotypes, neglecting inconsistencies. However, when motivated by outcome dependency, people work harder, trying to individuate the other, using more diagnostic information that goes beyond their initial, superficial expectations (Erber & Fiske, 1984). We predicted that they would selectively attend to inconsistency, to make sense of it. And we predicted that they would draw dispositional inferences from inconsistency because inferring a stable, coherent predisposition implies potential predictability, influence strategies, and possible control over the person who controls resources. Our experimental methods bring home these processes.

Student participants arrived for a study of how people collaborate in pairs; in the lab were a table with two chairs and a set of colorful, engaging windup toys.

Participants' job was to design educational games for children, first brainstorming ideas alone and then talking to their partner, who happened to be an education major. Half the time, they could win a prize for their solo ideas, in comparison to other non-education majors. Half the time, they could win the prize for their joint solution with their partner, making them outcome dependent. Crossed with outcome dependency, the partner (our confederate) wrote that she either expected to do well or not so well at this task, setting up a positive or negative expectancy. The partner also provided postcards with her peers' decidedly mixed comments about her teaching, creating expectancy-consistent and expectancy-inconsistent information.

After she left the room, the participant read the postcards, while the experimenter surreptitiously timed attention to cards written in blue or black ink (signaling positive and negative, hence consistent or inconsistent information, depending on expectancy). In what seems now a quaint technique, the experimenter had a stopwatch in each pocket of his jacket, but he was blind to expectancy and hence to which ink color signaled consistency in that particular session.

When participants were outcome independent – when they could win the prize alone – they attended equally to consistent and inconsistent information, but under outcome dependency, their attention to inconsistent teaching evaluations increased significantly. A second study replicated these effects of outcome dependency on attention to the most diagnostic, least redundant information, that is, expectancy-inconsistent cues.

What's more, in the second study, half the participants thought aloud into a tape recorder as they flipped through the cards. Judges blind to condition then coded dispositional statements (specific traits; e.g., "My first impression is that she would be a conscientious person.") and several other kinds less relevant here. Dispositional comments increased significantly under outcome dependency. And these comments correlated .61 with attention in that condition (other comments did not). These studies thus suggest that outcome dependency – and perhaps its attendant uncontrollability – increases attention to and dispositional inferences about the most diagnostic (unexpected) information. Outcome dependency makes people vigilant, perhaps to increase control.

Nevertheless, these studies leave several questions unanswered. First, the outcome-dependency manipulation confounded the partners' correlated outcomes (winning the prize together) with their potentially positive cooperation. Second, the results do not really demonstrate that control is the mechanism at work. Subsequent studies addressed these issues.

People are interdependent when they compete as well as when they cooperate. Negative interdependence should have similar effects on social cognition (Ruscher & Fiske, 1990): People need to know what the other person will do, in order to determine their own actions. Competition is negative interdependence, but it is still outcome dependency, just without the positivity. If diminished control is key, then, like cooperators, competitors should attend to unexpected information, infer dispositions from it, and perhaps end up with more idiosyncratic impressions because of their variable strategies for reconciling the inconsistencies into a coherent overall impression.

Using much the same procedure, except for placing the participant and confederate in competitive outcome dependency (or not), a new experiment showed that inconsistency received both increased attention and dispositional inferences under outcome dependency. Impressions were also reliably more varied, as predicted. However, these effects held only for participants who reported they had some confidence in their ability to do the task; those who felt utterly incompetent did not make the cognitive effort to use the diagnostic information. This then implicated the mechanism of control; participants who felt unable to do the task did not bother attempting to increase predictability and control. A second study, which made all participants sufficiently confident, replicated the earlier study and showed that the inconsistency effect on attention and dispositional inferences held only for task-relevant (i.e., diagnostic) information.

Again, this fits the interpretation of these processes (attention and dispositional inferences) as efforts to enhance control. A more direct investigation of the role of control manipulated participants' accuracy goals in a similar paradigm and found conceptually similar results (Neuberg & Fiske, 1987).

So far, the research all had examined symmetrical interdependence, but in the interest of understanding stratification other studies examined whether asymmetrical outcome dependency likewise focuses attention and dispositional inference on inconsistency. The earlier results with symmetrical (cooperative) interdependence could be due to concern for the partner's outcomes, rather than trying to control their own outcomes. One study closely followed the previous paradigm's independent and interdependent conditions but included asymmetrical outcome dependency as well (Stevens & Fiske, 2000, Study 1). In both dependency conditions, participants attended more to inconsistency than did independent participants; consistent information showed no differences as a function of interdependence.

A new paradigm (Dépret & Fiske, 1999) further tested asymmetrical dependency: Participants signed up for "how to study with noisy housemates," and learned that their job would be to attempt a task requiring concentration, while others tried to distract them. The distractors would have either low power, with limited means for disruption, or high power, with unlimited means for disruption and the ability to make the participant restart the task. In the interpersonal condition (most relevant here), participants learned about one of the distractors, either an art major or a math major, presenting a profile of mixed expectancy-consistent and expectancy-inconsistent traits. Attention was measured by tape-recording and later timing the sound of turning the pages. Dispositional inferences were measured by participants listing additional personality traits to describe the individual distractor. As predicted, distractor power increased both attention to inconsistent information and dispositional inferences.

Another condition, the intergroup condition, also crossed power and consistency, but was designed to show that these effects do not occur when participants have no hope of control. The interpersonal condition, just described, entailed an aggregate of distractors from a variety of majors. Therefore, we predicted that participants would expect to be able to predict and possibly control their own outcomes in the face of an aggregate of individuals by learning about them. In the intergroup condition, the participant (always a psychology major) faced a uniform monolith of distractors, either all math majors or all art majors. We predicted that, faced with a powerful, unified outgroup, they would not expect any potential control, so they would give up. Indeed, in this intergroup condition, neither the attentional nor dispositional inference results emerged.

In still other circumstances, social cognizers also might expect uncontrollability. All the interdependence operationalizations so far involve outcome dependency for task performance. We hypothesized that outcome dependency for more global evaluations of the self would test the limits of people's expected control, so two separate papers respectively examined evaluative dependency and romantic dependency, cases in which we expected people to experience even more uncontrollability.

The evaluative dependency research (Steven & Fiske, 2000) explicitly compared asymmetrical task outcomes (Study 1) and evaluative outcomes (Study 2) in the same paradigm. Evaluative outcomes were manipulated by eligibility for a prize, based not on working with a partner, but on the partner's evaluation of their performance at the wind-up toy, creative games task. Instead of focusing on inconsistency, as in task outcome dependency, evaluatively outcome-dependent participants attended selectively to negative information about their evaluator, which negative information they then discounted in their think-aloud protocols. This pattern of wishful thinking contrasts with the reliable task-dependency focus on dispositional inferences; wishful thinking contrasts as well with Study 1's findings, which showed that task dependency *reduced* discounting, making the task-outcome-dependent perceivers potentially more accurate. Under evaluative-outcome dependency, however, discounting appeared in statements that denied negative information about their evaluator's competence.

This verbal discounting carried over to their evaluations of the person's probable competence: evaluation-dependency made people inflate judgments of the incompetent evaluator to equivalence with the competent-expectancy evaluator. Nondependent participants in contrast recognized the difference between competent and incompetent evaluators. Thus, evaluative dependency produced wishful thinking (attention to negativity, discounting it, and inflated ratings of incompetent evaluators), in contrast to the accuracy orientation of task dependency (attention to inconsistency, dispositional inferences to it, lack of discounting negativity, the ability to recognize incompetence).

In another series of studies, romantic dependency showed similar patterns to evaluative dependency, perhaps because in both cases, one is subject to overall, open-ended evaluation – less controllable – instead of evaluation on a specific, concrete task – potentially more controllable. Four experiments (Goodwin, Fiske, Rosen, & Rosenthal, 2002) tested the hypotheses that romantic goals encourage positivity biases on relationship-irrelevant dimensions such as task competence (clouded judgment) and on relationship-relevant dimensions in the absence of information (default positivity). Selective accuracy was expected, given relationship-relevant information. Men and women who had signed up for a dating study showed wishful thinking (clouded judgment and default positivity) when a prospective romantic partner displayed task incompetence. But they showed selective accuracy when the prospective partner displayed social incompetence.

A common theme across evaluative and task outcome dependency is adaptive efforts to use available diagnostic information, but wishful positivity when such potential paths to control are unavailable. In the earlier task-dependency studies, when control was plausible, selective attention to and dispositional processing of inconsistency had been the focal routes to mindreading in efforts to restore control.

Outcome dependency, uncontrollability, and vigilance: Neural substrates of thinking upward

The advent of functional neuroimaging in social psychology allowed us to test this logic by other means. In social cognitive neuroscience generally, the role of the medial prefrontal cortex (MPFC) in thinking about other people, especially their minds, rapidly became evident (Amodio & Frith, 2006; Mitchell, Banaji, & Macrae, 2005). Our lab's contribution to this shared insight came in a preliminary study that varied the established dimensions of dispositional inference – consistency, consensus, distinctiveness (McArthur, 1972) – and observed their neural correlates (Harris, Todorov, & Fiske, 2005). We hypothesized that an action performed consistently and mainly by one actor, regardless of target, would not only be attributed to that actor's disposition, but also activate the MPFC.

Participants read sentences describing behavior (John laughed at the comedian), which had low or high consistency, consensus, and distinctiveness. Of the eight conditions, the predicted combination (high consistency, low consensus, low distinctiveness) elicited both dispositional attributions and MPFC activation. If only John always laughs at this and all comedians, this suggests something about John, rather than the comedian or the circumstances: Both conscious inferences and brain activity respond accordingly.

We followed up these findings about dispositional inference and the MPFC with an outcome-dependency study in the scanner (Ames & Fiske, 2013). The same wind-up toys were enlisted in a within-subjects version of the original outcome-dependency paradigm. Participants met two education-major confederates from a neighboring school, expecting to work with only one on the educational games task. They also received positive expectations about one and negative expectations about the other (counter-balanced with outcome dependency). Then they were scanned as they read teaching evaluations consistent and inconsistent with their expectations about each confederate. This neuroimaging design held constant their timed exposure to this information, but the predicted three-way interaction emerged on the neural area hypothetically focused on dispositional inference. MPFC activation to inconsistent information was indeed lower under outcome independence and higher under outcome dependency. Consistent information showed the reverse pattern.

In short, when people's goals depend on another person, and they have a chance to control their outcomes by learning about that person's unexpected attributes, they show selective vigilance in attention, attributions, and neural activations. All these patterns fit the idea of people trying to attain control, or at least predictability, when they depend on another person because of interdependence.

Outcome dependency, uncontrollability, and vigilance: Talking up the social status hierarchy

People also depend on other people because of societal ranking that makes lower-status groups generally dependent on higher-status groups, because status and power are often correlated. Status carries expectations of competence, so high-status people are thought to have higher knowledge and ability, while lower-status people are expected to have fewer such resources. The Stereotype Content Model (Fiske, 2015; Fiske et al., 2002) finds these meritocratic beliefs around the world (Cuddy et al., 2009; Durante et al., 2013). This means that subordinates must either depend on the alleged competence of those of higher status – or contest it. Our series of studies suggests they do both, but not always in the most obvious ways. When subordinates interact with higher-status others, their own competence is in question, so they might well seek respect in that interaction, more so than the higher-status person, who can assume respect for their presumed competence.

But there's more. When people attempt to convey competence, they may not only emphasize it by self-promoting (Jones & Pittman, 1982). They also emphasize competence by *downplaying* the other major dimension of social cognition, namely warmth (Holoien & Fiske, 2013). Participants instructed to be competent to an unknown audience in an online chat room not only chose more sophisticated (competent) vocabulary but also chose colder, more negative words, a tradeoff compared both to a neutral control and those instructed to convey warmth. Diminishing the opposite, irrelevant dimension (here, warmth) reflects the compensation effect whereby groups and individuals who rate high on either warmth or competence are expected to rate low on the other (Yzerbyt, Kervyn, & Judd, 2008): Warmth and competence trade off, in people's minds. Hence, one can convey either dimension by downplaying the other, relative to the focal dimension (Kervyn, Bergsieker, & Fiske, 2012).

Subordinates trying to be competent also not surprisingly emphasize their own competent traits and – more subtly – de-emphasize their own warm traits (Swencionis & Fiske, unpublished). Upon learning that an interviewer wants efficient workers (rather than team players), online adults role-playing the interviewees not only choose to convey more competence (the obvious strategy), but also choose to convey less warmth (the tradeoff strategy). Social goals shape how people talk upward about themselves when they depend on another.

Mere status creates this talking-up pattern (Swencionis & Fiske, 2016). Told to imagine a workplace initiative in which they are paired with a higher-ranked employee (versus a neutral or lower-ranked one), on-line adults seek to convey both more competence and less warmth about themselves in describing what they would want their partner to know. (Higher-ranked people talking down choose the opposite strategy.)

Subordinates' choice to emphasize their own competence could come either from trying to match the higher-ranked person's supposed competence or from trying to remedy their own supposed lack of competence (Swencionis & Fiske, 2016). Either way, learning that the higher-status person is unexpectedly incompetent (or unexpectedly warm) eliminates the talking-up strategy.

These effects replicate when students come into the lab and learn that they are assigned – based on a bogus test – to be the (lower-ranked) responder to their partner, who will lead the joint task (Swencionis & Fiske, unpublished).

Outcome dependency, uncontrollability, and vigilance: Talking up the racial status hierarchy

Race imitates status in some respects. For example, in our research (Dupree, Obioha, & Fiske, under review), online adults and students show implicit associations between white faces and higher status jobs, as well as black faces and lower-status jobs.

This implicit status hierarchy appears in the interpersonal concerns of black students interacting with white ones (Bergsieker, Shelton, & Richeson, 2010). Black students are concerned with being respected for their competence (whereas whites are concerned with being liked for their nonracist morality). Self-reported goals show these concerns. So do verbal and nonverbal behavior when minorities are talking up to whites, whether in existing relationships or getting-acquainted conversations. Black students talking to whites report wanting to be respected and seen as competent more than wanting to be liked and seen as moral, when these goals appear as choices (endpoints of a single continuum or warmth-competence difference scores). Their verbal and nonverbal behavior likewise reflects self-promotion of competence – mentioning accomplishments, conveying confidence – more than when talking to other minorities. (Whites' verbal and nonverbal behavior talking down to minorities reflects more talking down: ingratiation.) In general, these talking-up effects required the black participants to be engaged in the interaction, but talking up correlated with negative affect.

Further, a related set of studies (Dupree & Fiske, under review) separated warmth and competence goals and examined political views as a moderator, on the grounds that conservatives would support existing status hierarchies and show the talking-up effects most strongly. Indeed, very conservative blacks present more competence to a white partner (talking up), compared to their self-presentation to a black partner. Liberal blacks do not differentiate by race of partner.

Conclusion: Inequality threatens subordinates' well-being

Subordinates carry a burden of vigilance linked to their relative loss of control. Outcome dependency requires subordinates to think harder and to fight for respect in their encounters with higher-status others. These interpersonal encounters fit evidence not only from our lab, but also evidence showing that working-class people's encounters with higher-class others make them experience less control, be more vigilant to threat, develop more communal (less agentic) self-concepts, and show more empathic accuracy (Kraus, Piff, Mendoza-Denton, Rheinschmidt, & Keltner, 2012). All these hypotheses fit the framework developed here, including the role of uncontrollability over resources as an upstream cause of these patterns showing efforts to mind-read, in order to increase control.

This vigilance is a burden. Social-class subordinates carry greater health risks, in part because they have fewer reserves for coping with life events, and the inevitable negative emotions undermine their health (Gallo & Matthews, 2003). The psychophysiology of threat (versus challenge) specifically plays a role in the cardiovascular response to difficult upward comparison (Mendes, Blascovich, Major, & Seery, 2001). Thus, understanding subordinates' efforts to restore a sense of control through mindreading matters for their physical and mental health.

Treating subordinates as passive recipients of their control-deprived situation would be a mistake. Although sometimes subordinates justify the system that disadvantages them (Jost & Banaji, 1994), sometimes they resist as individuals (for example by strategically conveying images of themselves as competent and worthy of respect, as in some of our research). Sometimes subordinates resist collectively, as social identity theory predicts under particular conditions (Ellemers et al., 2002). Some of our work suggests that the possibility of control over the collective that controls one's fate will predict when subordinates bother gathering the information that would prepare for trying to exert control (Dépret & Fiske, 1999). And of course, even subordinates vary in accepting the social dominance of some groups over others (Sidanius & Pratto, 1999).

In opening, we argued that both high and low status are mixed bags, with advantages and disadvantages in the short- and long-term. The operational mechanism is uncontrollability, which afflicts subordinates the most, requiring vigilance, but also bestowing the gift of potential sensitivity and accuracy in their social cognitions. Being on the bottom can be costly, but it is not all bad.

References

Ames, D. L., & Fiske, S. T. (2013). Outcome dependency alters the neural substrates of impression formation. *NeuroImage, 83,* 599–608.

Amodio, D. M., & Frith, C. D. (2006). Meeting of minds: The medial frontal cortex and social cognition. *Nature Reviews Neuroscience, 7*(4), 268–277.

Bergsieker, H. B., Shelton, J. N., & Richeson, J. A. (2010). To be liked versus respected: Divergent goals in interracial interactions. *Journal of Personality and Social Psychology, 99*(2), 248–264.

Crocker, J., & Major, B. (1989). Social stigma and self-esteem: The self-protective properties of stigma. *Psychological Review, 96*(4), 608–630.

Cuddy, A. J. C., Fiske, S. T., Kwan, V. S. Y., Glick, P., Demoulin, S., Leyens, J-Ph., Bond, M. H., Croizet, J-C., Ellemers, N., Sleebos, E., Htun, T. T., Yamamoto, M., Kim, H-J., Maio, G., Perry, J., Petkova, K., Todorov, V., Rodríguez-Bailón, R., Morales, E., Moya, M., Palacios, M., Smith, V., Perez, R., Vala, J., & Ziegler, R. (2009). Stereotype content model across cultures: Towards universal similarities and some differences. *British Journal of Social Psychology, 48*, 1–33.

Dépret, E. F., & Fiske, S. T. (1999). Perceiving the powerful: Intriguing individuals versus threatening groups. *Journal of Experimental Social Psychology, 35*, 461–480.

Dupree, C. H., & Fiske, S. T. (under review). Self-presentation of warmth and competence toward white and black interaction partners.

Dupree, C. H., Obioha, O. A., & Fiske, S. T. (under review). Doctor or dishwasher? Implicit and explicit associations at the intersection of race and status.

Durante, F., Fiske, S. T., Kervyn, N., Cuddy, A. J. C., Akande, A., Adetoun, B. E., Adewuyi, M. F., Tserere, M. M., Al Ramiah, A., Mastor, K. A., Barlow, F. K., Bonn, G., Tafarodi, R. W., Bosak, J., Cairns, E., Doherty, S., Capozza, D., Chandran, A., Chryssochoou1, X., Iatridis, T., Contreras, J. M., Costa-Lopes, R., González, R., Lewis, J. I., Tushabe, G., Leyens, J-Ph., Mayorga, R., Rouhana, N. N., Smith Castro, V., Perez, R., Rodríguez-Bailón, R., Moya, M., Morales Marente, E., Palacios Gálvez, M., Sibley, C. G., Asbrock, F., & Storari, C. C. (2013). Nations' income inequality predicts ambivalence in stereotype content: How societies mind the gap. *British Journal of Social Psychology, 52*, 726–746.

Ellemers, N., Spears, R., & Doosje, B. (2002). Self and social identity. *Annual Review of Psychology, 53*, 161–186.

Erber, R., & Fiske, S. T. (1984). Outcome dependency and attention to inconsistent information. *Journal of Personality and Social Psychology, 47*, 709–726.

Fiske, S. T. (1993). Controlling other people: The impact of power on stereotyping. *American Psychologist, 48*, 621–628.

Fiske, S. T. (2010). Interpersonal stratification: Status, power, and subordination. In S. T. Fiske, D. T. Gilbert, & G. Lindzey (Eds.), *Handbook of social psychology* (5th ed., pp. 941–982). New York: Wiley.

Fiske, S. T. (2015). Intergroup biases: A focus on stereotype content. *Current Opinion in Behavioral Sciences, 3*, 45–50.

Fiske, S. T., & Berdahl, J. (2007). Social power. In A. Kruglanski & E. T. Higgins (Eds.), *Social psychology: Handbook of basic principles* (2nd ed., pp. 678–692). New York: Guilford.

Fiske, S. T., Cuddy, A. J., Glick, P., & Xu, J. (2002). A model of (often mixed) stereotype content: Competence and warmth respectively follow from perceived status and competition. *Journal of Personality and Social Psychology, 82*, 878–902.

French, J. R. P., & Raven, B. (1959). The bases of social power. In D. Cartwright (Ed.), *Studies in social power* (pp. 150–167). Oxford, England: University of Michigan.

Gallo, L. C., & Matthews, K. A. (2003). Understanding the association between socioeconomic status and physical health: Do negative emotions play a role? *Psychological Bulletin, 129*(1), 10–51.

Goffman, E. (1963). *Stigma.* Englewood Cliffs, NJ: Prentice-Hall.

Goodwin, S. A., Fiske, S. T., Rosen, L. D., & Rosenthal, A. M. (2002). The eye of the beholder: Romantic goals and impression biases. *Journal of Experimental Social Psychology, 38*, 232–241.

Guinote, A. (2007). Behaviour variability and the situated focus theory of power. *European Review of Social Psychology, 18*, 256–295.

Harris, L. T., Todorov, A., & Fiske, S. T. (2005). Attributions on the brain: Neuro-imaging dispositional inferences, beyond theory of mind. *NeuroImage, 28*, 763–769.

Holoien, D. S., & Fiske, S. T. (2013). Downplaying positive impressions: Compensation between warmth and competence in impression management. *Journal of Experimental Social Psychology, 49*, 33–41.

Jones, E. E., Farina, A., Hastorf, A. H., Markus, H., Miller, D. T., & Scott, R. A. (1984*). Social stigma: The psychology of marked relationships.* New York: Freeman.

Jones, E. E., & Pittman, T. S. (1982). Toward a general theory of strategic self-presentation. In J. Suls (Ed.), *Psychological perspectives on the self* (pp. 231–262). Hillsdale, NJ: Erlbaum.

Jost, J. T., & Banaji, M. R. (1994). The role of stereotyping in system-justification and the production of false consciousness. *British Journal of Social Psychology, 33*(1), 1–27.

Keltner, D., Gruenfeld, D. H., & Anderson, C. (2003). Power, approach, and inhibition. *Psychological Review, 110*(2), 265–284.

Kervyn, N., Bergsieker, H. B., & Fiske, S. T. (2012). The innuendo effect: Hearing the positive but inferring the negative. *Journal of Experimental Social Psychology, 48*(1), 77–85.

Kraus, M. W., Piff, P. K., Mendoza-Denton, R., Rheinschmidt, M. L., & Keltner, D. (2012). Social class, solipsism, and contextualism: How the rich are different from the poor. *Psychological Review, 119*(3), 546–572.

McArthur, L. A. (1972). The how and what of why: Some determinants and consequences of causal attribution. *Journal of Personality and Social Psychology, 22*(2), 171–193.

Mendes, W. B., Blascovich, J., Major, B., & Seery, M. (2001). Challenge and threat responses during downward and upward social comparisons. *European Journal of Social Psychology, 31*(5), 477–497.

Mitchell, J. P., Banaji, M. R., & Macrae, C. N. (2005). The link between social cognition and self-referential thought in the medial prefrontal cortex. *Journal of Cognitive Neuroscience, 17*(8), 1306–1315.

Neuberg, S. L., & Fiske, S. T. (1987). Motivational influences on impression formation: Outcome dependency, accuracy-driven attention, and individuating processes. *Journal of Personality and Social Psychology, 53*, 431–444.

Ruscher, J. B., & Fiske, S. T. (1990). Interpersonal competition can cause individuating processes. *Journal of Personality and Social Psychology, 58*, 832–843.

Sidanius, J., & Pratto, F. (1999). *Social dominance: An intergroup theory of social hierarchy and oppression.* New York: Cambridge University Press.

Steele, C. M., & Aronson, J. (1995). Stereotype threat and the intellectual test performance of African Americans. *Journal of Personality and Social Psychology, 69*(5), 797–811.

Stevens, L. E., & Fiske, S. T. (2000). Motivated impressions of a powerholder: Accuracy under task dependency and misperception under evaluative dependency. *Personality and Social Psychology Bulletin, 26*, 907–922.

Swencionis, J. K., & Fiske, S. T. (2016). Promote up, ingratiate down: Status comparisons drive warmth-competence tradeoffs in impression management. *Journal of Experimental Social Psychology, 64*, 27–34.

Swencionis, J. K., & Fiske, S. T. (2016). Unpublished data.

Yzerbyt, V. Y., Kervyn, N., & Judd, C. M. (2008). Compensation versus halo: The unique relations between the fundamental dimensions of social judgment. *Personality and Social Psychology Bulletin, 34*(8), 1110–1123.

11

ACCENTUATION OF TENDING AND BEFRIENDING AMONG THE POWERLESS

Ana Guinote and Joris Lammers

This work was supported by a Daedalus Trust grant awarded to Ana Guinote (520180 F67).
Contact: a.guinote@ucl.ac.uk

Considerable research in the past decade has demonstrated that power leads to dis-inhibition and powerlessness to inhibition (Keltner, Gruenfeld, & Anderson, 2003; see also Galinsky, Gruenfeld, & Magee, 2003; Guinote, 2007a; Smith & Bargh, 2008). This association between the powerless and inhibition may have created the false impression that the powerless are inactive, relegated to a passive role in social interactions, and therefore an uninteresting topic of study. Compared to the dynamic powerful, who are actively engaging in action and are leading the way, the powerless seem passive, risk averse, and dull, waiting to follow others. As a consequence, the motivations and strategies of powerless individuals remain largely unknown. In the current chapter, however, we aim to show that the psychological state of powerlessness triggers multifaceted and dynamic social strategies that are designed to enhance the adaptation of individuals. Contrary to common belief, the powerless are an exciting topic of study that offers fruitful avenues for the understanding of human needs and the role of sociality in human adaptation.

Power is often defined as having control over others and valued resources, and powerlessness is defined as being dependent on others to attain valued outcomes (Emerson, 1962; Thibaut & Kelley, 1959; Weber, 1947). Asymmetric power relations are pervasive across varied social contexts, such as within families, in the classroom, or in organizations. A common motivational marker of being powerless is that individuals aim at restoring their sense of control (deCharms, 1968; Fiske & Depret, 1996; Heine, Proulx, & Vohs, 2006; Proulx, Inzlicht, & Harmon-Jones, 2012; Whitson & Galinsky, 2008). In social hierarchies those at the bottom, who typically have low social status (Tajfel, 1974) and lack of control (Kraus, Piff, & Keltner, 2009), tend to strive for upward social mobility. These tendencies can be seen both in humans (see Tajfel, 1974) and nonhuman primates (Boehm & Flack, 2010). The desire for upward mobility and the negative impact of powerlessness on cognitive processes and well-being suggest that people have a core need for control over their outcomes in the context of social relationships. A threat to this need engages cognitive and behavioral strategies that can also be seen, in rudimentary forms, in other species. For example, both powerless humans and other primates are socially attentive and form stronger social bonds compared to their high-rank counterparts, as a way to regain control (see Fritsche et al., 2013; Seyfarth & Cheney, 2003). For example, low-rank monkeys and apes groom more, exhibit appeasing intentions, yield more space, and show less aggression compared to high-rank primates (Sapolsky, 2005; Seyfarth & Cheney, 2003).

In the current chapter we review literature showing the intrapersonal and interpersonal processes by which the powerless seek to restore control. In reviewing this literature, we follow a commonly used analogy between positions of high and low power and different roles in the animal kingdom (e.g. Whitson et al., 2013). Specifically, in this analogy the motivational state of being powerful is compared with that of a predator and the psychological state of the powerlessness with that of a prey. Powerful and powerless humans have advanced multilayered strategies, from attentional processes to social behavior and the creation of shared meaning that nevertheless fit the analogy of a predator and a prey.

A first section is inspired by the notion that where predators have forward-facing eyes, preys have outward-facing eyes that allow them to detect threats and dangers (Campbell, 1947; Land, 1989). We use this analogy to discuss how it occurs in humans through attention and decision-making strategies. A second section is inspired by the notion that predators tend to live either solitary or in small groups, while preys live in larger herds (Fleagle, 2013; Isbell, 1994). We use this analogy to discuss how social representations of powerless people are more strongly driven by their desire to affiliate with others, and in particular by their social group memberships, and how this in turn can affect their behavior. We argue that powerless people use the group as a resource to regain control, similarly to people who are control deprived due to situational causes (see Stollberg, Fritsche, Barth, & Jugert, Chapter 8, this volume). This predator–prey distinction does not only help to review the literature, but it also helps to understand why the powerless are such an interesting group to study. After all, as any biologist will agree, the behavior of preys is as interesting and complex as that of predators. Powerlessness does neither make passive nor uninteresting, but instead leads to highly motivated complex and dynamic behavior.

Outward-facing eyes: Powerlessness and the complexity of cognition and behavior

Predators tend to have forward-facing eyes that allow them to zoom in to one aspect of the environment and focus on their target, while preys have outward-facing eyes that allow them to keep an overview of the wider situation in order to detect threats and dangers and thus allow them to proactively defend themselves against these challenges (Campbell, 1947; Land, 1989). In this first section, we follow this analogy to review part of the literature on how power affects cognition and behavior.

Social attention and accuracy motivation

Hierarchical differences within species create differentials in opportunities and challenges that resonate with the motivational orientation of preys and predators. Dominant animals control more resources and have easier access to mates. To maintain their privileged positions, dominant animals display downward aggression to keep subordinates at bay from valued resources (Cummin, 2005). Subordinates in turn are vigilant and motivated to form accurate social impressions. By observing others, subordinates can more easily detect opportunities to regain control – for example by forming alliances with others – and avoid threats. These attentional strategies have consistently been observed across primate species. For example, in one study male rhesus monkeys sacrificed a reward for the opportunity to view the faces of high-rank monkeys (Deaner, Khera, & Platt, 2005).

In psychology, Fiske and colleagues were among the first to introduce the notion that powerless humans are attentive and motivated to form accurate social impressions of others (see Fiske, 1993; Fiske & Depret, 1996). In a pioneering study participants were dependent on others (vs. not) and read information about their interaction partners (Erber & Fiske, 1984). Participants who were not dependent on others attended primarily to information that was consistent with their expectations and neglected other information. In contrast, dependent participants paid more attention to attributes that contradicted their prior expectations (see also Copeland, 1994; Goodwin, Gubin, Fiske, & Yzerbyt, 2000). Consistent with this notion, a study conducted in the hotel industry asked managers and employees to read stereotype-consistent and -inconsistent information about a white or a black person (Guinote & Phillips, 2010). Subordinates devoted more attention to stereotype-inconsistent information of both targets compared to managers. A similar effect can also be seen in intergroup relations. Members of groups who have less power in society, such as ethnic minorities and women, tend to be more attentive towards outgroup members, and form particularly complex and differentiated perceptions of powerful groups (often reversing the outgroup homogeneity effect; Guinote, 2001; Lorenzi-Cioldi, Eagly, & Stewart, 1995).

Although powerless individuals are particularly motivated to understand their superiors, increased attention often occurs towards targets with the same rank level. Powerless people make more attributions about the behavior of others, as an attempt to understand their dispositions (Fiske & Depret, 1996). In one study participants were assigned to a minority group or a majority group in the laboratory and expected to engage in a group discussion (Guinote, Brown, & Fiske, 2006). Minority members felt more powerless. At the same time, compared to majority group members, they elaborated more about the attributes of the people they expected to interact with. Sense of control in relationships mediated the effect of group size on elaboration.

The motivation to be accurate often (but not always) leads to greater accuracy in person perception. For example, Kraus and colleagues found that individuals from the lower class, who control less resources and have therefore less power, are more accurate in detecting the emotions of their interaction partners (Kraus, Horberg, Goetz, & Keltner, 2011). Participants were asked to tease each other, and then report how they and their partner felt. Low-class participants more accurately reported the hostility of the partner than upper-class participants. Similarly, during negotiations, powerless parties consider more the emotions of their opponents than vice-versa (Van Kleef, De Dreu, & Manstead, 2004). They also ask their opponents more diagnostic and less leading questions (De Dreu & Van Kleef, 2004). Along the same lines, subordinates recall more the non-verbal behavior of superiors than vice versa (Hall, Carter, & Horgan, 2001).

Evidence stems also from studies examining the ability to take the perspective of other people. Galinsky and colleagues demonstrated that the experience of power-lessness (compared to the experience of power) increases the tendency to take other people's perspectives (Galinsky, Magee, Inesi, & Gruenfeld, 2006). For example, in one classic study, participants who first wrote about an experience of powerlessness were more likely (compared to the participants who first recalled an experience of power) to draw an E in an other-oriented manner on their forehead, thus avoiding a common error to fail to consider the others' perspective and draw the E in a self-oriented manner. Demonstrating a similar effect, but in an intergroup jacket, Lammers and colleagues showed that members of powerless groups are more inclined to metastereotype – that is, to consider how their group is stereotypically perceived by more powerful groups (Lammers, Gordijn, & Otten, 2008).

Furthermore, compared to the powerful, the powerless are more strongly influenced by social-comparison information, independent of whether it is upward versus downward or assimilative versus contrastive (Johnson & Lammers, 2012). Whereas the powerful are more inclined to focus on the self and project their own traits, attitudes, and emotions on other people when making judgments, the powerless focus more on the target and its context to arrive at their judgment (Overbeck & Droutman, 2013).

More fundamentally, evidence suggests that powerlessness leads individuals to renounce shortcuts in knowledge, such as reliance on stereotypes and the tendency to anchor information-processing too heavily on the self. For example, powerless individuals rely less on their dispositions and enduring attitudes compared to those who have power (Guinote, Weick, & Cai, 2012). Powerless individuals are motivated to process information in a bottom-up, piecemeal manner (Fiske, 1993; Fiske & Depret, 1996).

Both previously discussed effects – that the powerless are less self-centered and that they avoid short cuts – can also be seen with regard to the use of gut feelings and subjective experiences that arise during thought processes in the construction of judgments. For instance, Weick and Guinote (2008) asked powerful and powerless participants to retrieve many or few differences between men and women, and subsequently to describe men and women along several attributes stereotypic of men (e.g., courageous, assertive) and women (e.g., gentle, unassertive). Recalling many instances of leisure time is more difficult than recalling few instances. If it is easier to recall differences between men and women, then one can infer that the gender groups are different from one another and rely on stereotypes. Feelings of power magnified this tendency. Similar results were obtained with actual managers and employees in the industry, regarding their perceptions of work-life balance.

Even though we have argued that powerful people often use the self as reference, and use shortcuts in person perception, this is not to say they are always less capable of paying attention to others and being accurate in social impressions than those with less power (Gordon & Chen, 2013; Overbeck & Park, 2001; Schmid Mast, Jonas, & Hall, 2009). Rather, the powerless are more unconditionally socially attentive, displaying increased attention irrespective of the situation. In contrast, the degree to which the powerful pay attention to others is more flexible and depends on their current states and goals (Guinote, 2007b). This notion is supported by research testing the link between power(lessness) and attention to those aspects of another person that are relevant for one's own goals. Several studies showed that people who were primed with power paid close attention to others only when this was instrumental to attaining their goals, whereas this was not the case for powerless individuals (Gruenfeld, Inesi, Magee, & Galinsky, 2008; Overbeck & Park, 2006). Again, parallel effects have been found in intergroup relations. Various findings converge to show that those who feel powerful focus selectively on those aspects of other groups that are relevant for their own goals and ignore irrelevant aspects, whereas those who feel powerless devote their attention to the other group more unconditionally (Guinote, 2008; Gwinn, Judd, & Park, 2013; Lammers & Stapel, 2011).

Careful decision making and multiple-goal focus

Being powerless activates the goal of understanding the social environment, but it also affects strategies during the pursuit of non-social goals. With increased constraints, powerless individuals need to ponder carefully before making decisions and engage less in automatic decision-making (Keltner et al., 2003). Powerless people consider alternatives before making decisions, and weigh different sources of information and courses of action, which are often deemed as equally important (Guinote, 2007b).

Powerless individuals have their attention divided between social concerns and the tasks at hand, which creates complex motivational constellations and reduces the availability of cognitive resources. Research has shown that compared to powerful individuals, powerless individuals consider more information before setting a goal and take longer to initiate goal-directed action (Guinote, 2007a). They consider multiple goals as equally important, whereas those who have power tend to prioritize one goal over the other. For example, in one study (Guinote, 2008) participants were given a work goal or a social leisure goal. Specifically, they were asked to describe a day at work or a day when a friend had visited them. Powerful participants focused their activities on work, when pursuing a work goal, and on leisure, when pursing a social goal. In contrast, powerless participants engaged in both types of activities at the same time. They worked less when at work, and continued to think of work when in leisure. Furthermore, participants' attention strategies were consistent with their prioritization strategies. In a reading task, powerful participants processed more extensively goal-relevant (vs. -irrelevant) information, whereas the powerless attended more equally to goal-relevant and -irrelevant information.

Powerless individuals also show reduced accessibility of their focal goals during goal striving (Slabu & Guinote 2010). Furthermore, during the pursuit of multiple goals, powerful individuals complete one goal at a time, whereas powerless individuals prefer to multitask (Cai & Guinote, 2015).

One consequence of the complex motivational system of powerless individuals, and its excess demands, is that they have less working memory capacity and have difficulty controlling attention. Powerless individuals have difficulty ignoring task-irrelevant information, and underperform on tasks that measure executive functions – that is, cognitive functions that coordinate and manage information necessary for appropriate actions and planning (Baddeley, 1996; Guinote, 2007b; Smith, Jostmann, Galinsky, & van Dijk, 2008).

Noteworthy is the fact that powerless individuals prefer to consider multiple sources of information as equally important even when attentional demands are low. For example, the studies mentioned above by Erber and Fiske (1984) or Guinote and Phillips (2010) suggest that when people are dependent on others they are intrinsically motivated to gather information that is against their expectations. Therefore, increased attention to goal-irrelevant information does not merely derive from cognitive deficits. Instead it reflects the motivational orientation of powerless individuals.

In summary, much like preys have outward-facing eyes that allow them to keep an overview of the wider situation in order to detect threats, research examining the cognitive strategies of powerless individuals shows that these individuals prioritize the understanding of their social environment, in particular of power holders. They renounce prior knowledge structures, such as stereotypes and expectancies, and attend to information in a more bottom-up manner. Powerless individuals also anchor their judgments less strongly on information associated with the self, such as subjective experiences, and engage less in shortcuts to make judgments. Powerless individuals reason more and make more dispositional attributions about their interaction partners compared to other individuals. During the pursuit of goals, powerless individuals more equally weigh different courses of action, have less clear priorities, and have more difficulty in controlling attention at the service of their goals.

Turning toward the herd: Powerlessness and communal focus

The attempts by the powerless to restore control are not limited to the cognitive strategies discussed in the previous section, but also extend to interpersonal behavior. The risks associated with being predated force prey animals to seek closeness of others. To defend against predators, they turn to other members of their species and seek to restore control by joining the herd (Fleagle, 2013; Isbell, 1994). Similarly, within species dominance-subordination relationships lead to an imbalance in opportunities and challenges that have similar effects as the predator-prey relationship. In the current section, we propose that powerlessness similarly leads people to seek closeness to others and that this link between powerlessness and increased social closeness may even be one of the most defining strategies of how people cope with powerlessness. We propose that, similarly to people who are control deprived in other contexts (Fritsche et al., 2013; Fritsche, Jonas, & Fankhänel, 2008), the powerless turn to others to regain a sense of control and deal with threat. We first discuss how powerlessness increases social-closeness motivation. Then we discuss how powerlessness-induced closeness leads people in a low-power state to further increase synchrony and coordination by attuning their behavior more to others, and showing generosity and help. Finally, we discuss how this increased social closeness connects to the powerless' strategy to restore control by seeking, building, and strengthening coalitions to help each other and defend against outsiders.

Powerlessness and social closeness

David Kipnis was one of the first experimental psychologists to ask the question how having power affects human behavior. In one experiment, he showed that people who had a manager role with more power were more inclined to keep distance compared to managers with less power, indeed suggesting a negative link between power and closeness (Kipnis, 1972). More recent research by Lammers and colleagues extended these results by also including powerless conditions. Specifically, students were told that they would complete a series of puzzles and were asked whether they preferred to do so alone or instead work on the puzzles with co-students. Compared to students who prior to being asked this question first recalled an experience of power, those students who wrote about an experience of powerlessness were more likely to prefer working together with their co-student (Lammers, Galinsky, Gordijn, & Otten, 2012). Other findings showed that low-power (compared to high-power) manipulation made students more likely to prefer playing multi-player over playing single-player computer games. Much in line, recent research by Case and others showed that participants who recalled an experience of powerlessness were more likely to join a fictitious student service designed to connect students and form friendships (Case, Conlon, & Maner, 2015). These findings converge to show that people in a powerless position are particularly inclined to turn to others and form stronger bonds. This makes sense given that seeking such connections can restore the sense of control that they lack.

Further converging evidence for this link between lacking power and increased social closeness is offered by a variety of findings showing that variables that are associated with powerlessness similarly increase social closeness. For example, although power and status are conceptually different and it is important to distinguish the two in research, both are important expressions of social hierarchy and in practice often go hand in hand (Blader & Chen, 2014). Consistent with the idea that powerlessness increases social closeness, lacking status has a parallel effect. Specifically, research by Guinote and colleagues shows that reducing people's sense of status by giving them false feedback on their group's relative poor standing toward other groups increases people's communal focus and leads to more prosocial behavior (Guinote, Cotzia, Sandhu, & Siwa, 2015). In summary, a variety of findings associate powerlessness and variables associated with lacking power with increased social closeness.

Appeasing behavior and conformity

Powerless people do not only show increased closeness to others, but they are also more likely to appease and conform to others. Several findings indicate that when individuals lack power they tend to behaviorally fit in with the expectations of others, in particular of the power holders. In a seminal study Copeland (1994) gave half of the participants power, by letting them choose an interaction partner. Copeland provided participants also with information about the target (e.g., the target was introvert or extrovert). Subsequently, participants interacted with one another and completed questionnaires about their impressions of their partners. Consistent with the effects of power on social attention, those with power, but not those who lacked power, perceived the targets in line with their expectations. Importantly, external naïve judges found that powerless partners behaved in ways that confirmed the expectations of the powerful partner (i.e., showing *behavioral confirmation*).

The readiness of powerless individuals to change in line with social influences can be seen also at the more basic level of memory for events and people. Memory is malleable and susceptible to influences that occur after the initial information has been encoded (Schacter, Norman, & Koutstaal, 1998). This often happens when people recall events together, as they influence each other's recollections – a phenomenon called *memory conformity*. In a study by Skagerberg and Wright (2008) participants first saw 50 pictures of faces, and were then asked to engage in a powerful or powerless role, in pairs. Subsequently, participants completed a face-recognition test, and one partner responded before the other. Powerless participants were more influenced by their partners' responses compared with powerful participants. Thus, the powerless show more memory conformity than the powerful.

It is known that in romantic and friendship relations partners become more similar to one another in their emotional responses over the course of time (Anderson, Keltner, & John, 2003). However, those who have less power in the relationship tend to change more than those who have more power, again suggesting that those who lack power more strongly change the self to conform to others. An examination of the identity of subordinate group members found that they tend to perceive themselves more in line with attributes that define their groups (e.g., they engage in self-categorization) rather than in terms of their individuating attributes (Guinote, 2001; Simon & Hamilton, 1994).

Closer observance of norms

If the powerless seek social closeness to others to restore their sense of control, then this effect should not be limited to conformity and group identification but should be reflected also in a more general tendency to follow social norms. Again turning to the predator and prey analogy, birds flying together in flocks move in a highly synchronic manner and do so to allow the group to act in a coordinated manner and to successfully evade predators (Caraco, Martindale, & Pulmeliam, 1980; Treisman, 1975). If the powerless seek contact with a group to restore their sense of control, then they should also be particularly likely to move in a coordinated manner. One particularly important way in which people coordinate their behavior is by following norms (Trivers, 1985). By restraining the choices of individuals, norms help the group to function as a collective and thus increase collective outcomes (Frank, 1988). Therefore, if the powerless gain control by forming more coherent groups, then they should more closely follow any existing or emerging social norm demonstrated by that group.

Initial evidence for this idea comes from research by Guinote, Judd, and Brauer (2002), who studied variability of behavior by having ten groups of eight participants interact, after half were assigned to a high-power and the other half to a low-power role, and videotaping that interaction. Next, a third group of participants rated the behavior of each of the eight participants in a session on ten traits. Results showed that the behavior of participants in a high-power role was seen as more variable than that of low-power participants, suggesting that the powerless followed emerging norms in the group more closely. Importantly, this effect was even found without the raters' knowing who was assigned to what role or even knowing that participants were assigned to different power roles at all, strongly suggesting that these effects are due to actual differences in the degree to which people follow norms.

More direct evidence for the idea that the powerless follow social norms more closely comes from research by Galinsky and colleagues (2008), in which the effect of power and the influence of the social situation were manipulated independently. For example, in one study participants were asked to draw an alien and were either provided with an example picture of an alien with huge wings, supposedly drawn by an earlier participant, or they were not shown that picture. The researchers were interested in whether participants would follow the example and also draw a winged alien, if exposed to that earlier example. Results showed that if participants were first asked to recall an experience of powerlessness, the likelihood that participants followed that example was tripled, suggesting that people who feel powerless are more inclined to follow emerging norms (Galinsky, Magee, Gruenfeld, Whitson, & Liljenquist, 2008).

Related evidence comes from findings by Rucker and Galinsky (2009), who found that powerlessness leads to the consumption of branded products with highly visible logos. Although the authors explain this by noting that purchasing such products are a form of conspicuous consumption that helps people to regain status, these effects can also be explained by the notion that such branded products help young people to reaffirm norms on what clothing fits with the group and what does not.

Particularly strong evidence for the idea that powerlessness increases the tendency to follow existing social norms comes from a series of findings testing the effects of power on the observance of moral guidelines. For example, in one study, participants were first exposed to a low-power or high-power prime and then were given the opportunity to roll a set of dice and claim lottery tickets based on their roll. In this case, the relevant norm is clearly not to lie and instead to truthfully report the outcome of the roll (and associated number of tickets). Results showed that although participants in both conditions disregarded the norm somewhat, those in the low-power condition were less inclined to do so and instead followed the norm to accurately report the number of tickets (Lammers, Stapel, & Galinsky, 2010).

A conceptually similar effect was found by Yap and colleagues, who instead used an embodied perspective on power. Participants adopted either an expansive bodily position, associated with power, or a contractive bodily position, associated with powerlessness. For example, in one study participants were seated in a car seat that required a more contracted or a more expansive seating position. Sitting in the contracted, low-power position caused participants to observe driving norms more closely (causing less accidents) and also led them to more closely follow additional instructions, compared to when sitting in an expansive, high-power position (Yap, Wazlawek, Lucas, Cuddy, & Carney, 2013).

Among the most important moral norms in most societies – including our own – are those norms that regulate sexual behavior. If the powerless observe norms more closely, then they should also be more restrictive in their sexual behavior. In support of that idea, a series of findings have shown that powerlessness is negatively associated with sexual permissiveness and deviance. For example, people who hold a relatively powerless position at work are less inclined to betray their romantic partner (Lammers, Stoker, Jordan, Pollmann, & Stapel, 2011; for replications, see Lammers & Maner, 2015; Trautmann, Van de Kuilen, & Zeckhauser, 2013) and are less inclined to engage in sexually deviant behaviors such as sadomasochism (Lammers & Imhoff, 2016).

Finally, to help a collective in behaving in a coordinated and synchronous manner, the members of that collective should not only observe each other and follow any emerging norms, but they should also be more strongly inclined to punish those who violate norms and be disinclined to excuse others. Indeed, research shows that when confronted with deviants, the powerless are less likely to forgive than the powerful, especially when strongly committed to a relationship (Karremans & Smith, 2010).

One exception to consider here, however, is that we have presented norms mainly as a strategy where the powerless observe social norms more strictly in order to gain from it, by maximizing cooperation and curtailing the discretion of the powerful. Alternatively, the powerful may instill norms to enforce collaboration from the powerless, even in the absence of direct supervision. In fact, the internalization of such norms by the powerless is considered one of the most effective forms of power exercise (Foucault, 1975/1979). Similarly, in research on non-human primates, it has been argued that alpha members set norms on the proper ways to occupy space, on mating, and on eating, in order to exercise control over lower-ranked members (e.g., Cummins, 2005). This suggests that the powerful also may sometimes be stricter in enforcing moral norms. Indeed some research shows that the powerful may also be stricter in their interpretation of norms, and be less flexible in allowing exceptions (Lammers & Stapel, 2009; Van Prooijen, Coffeng, & Vermeer, 2014).

In summary, a variety of findings show that the powerless do not only seek more social closeness to others and pay more attention to others, but that they are also typically stricter in following emerging and existing moral norms.

Generosity and helping

Another behavioral tendency associated with powerlessness that may help in regaining control is that powerless individuals act in agreeable ways during interactions (Copeland, 1994) and try to get along (Snyder & Kiviniemi, 2001). For example, in a study by Hecht and LaFrance (1998) participants were assigned to a powerful, a control, or a powerless condition, interacted in dyads and were videotaped. A coding of smiles revealed that, for powerful and control participants, smiling was correlated with their positive affective states. This was, however, not the case for powerless participants, who *felt obliged to smile*. Furthermore, in interactions, powerless speakers are more polite than their powerful counterparts (Holtgraves, 2010; Ng & Bradac, 1993). For example, they make less direct requests and assert themselves less forcefully. These actions accommodate the power holders and decrease potential conflict, which powerless people cannot afford.

Those who experience a sense of powerlessness are generally inclined to cooperate and help. A classic study by Sachdev and Bourhis (1991) found that members of minimal groups who had a subordinate position in an experimental setting were more parity oriented and less discriminatory against the outgroup members compared to dominant group members. Similarly, Lammers and colleagues (2012) found that participants who first completed a low-power priming manipulation were more inclined to cooperate in an economic dilemma, where they sacrificed their personal interests in favor of the greater good. Other studies found that the powerless used less deceptive tactics, such as promising to cooperate and then competing with their partners to increase their gains (Haney, Banks, & Zimbardo, 1973).

Other findings have shown that the powerless are more inclined to spend money on others and less on the self. For example, participants who first imagined holding a low-power employee role bought more chocolates (at 5¢ per piece) to give to another person, compared to participants who first imagined holding a powerful manager role (Rucker, Dubois, & Galinsky, 2011). Similarly, five-year-old children who were in a subordinate position gave more of their stickers to a child in need compared to dominant children, and this occurred regardless of whether the hierarchical positions were driven by personal dominance or were experimentally induced (Guinote et al., 2015).

The powerless are not only more likely to help others, but they are also more likely to reciprocate other people's help. One reason for this is that the powerless are more likely to believe that the help and generosity offered to them by others is genuine and earnest and they are less likely to infer strategic intentions. For example, Inesi and colleagues found that if one colleague did another colleague a favor, those with less power were more likely to believe that this favor reflected a sincere desire to help them and were less likely to make the cynical attribution that such help merely reflected a strategic decision to help the self (Inesi, Gruenfeld, & Galinsky, 2012).

This increased helping behavior even extends to immoral forms of helping. That is, where the powerful are more likely to cheat for selfish reasons, the powerless are more likely to cheat for pro-social reasons. For example, in one study reported by Dubois, Rucker, and Galinsky (2015), people were asked to imagine working in a restaurant and were then either asked whether they would take food without paying to satisfy their own hunger or give a hungry friend food without paying for it. People low in chronic sense of power were less likely to take food to satisfy their own hunger, but more likely to steal food to give to their friend. Such results demonstrate one strategic effect of powerlessness-induced closeness, where the powerless form a tighter coalition to help each other.

Powerlessness-induced closeness does not only lead the powerless to help each other in getting what they want, but tentative evidence suggests that it can also help them in assisting each other to defend against external threats – in particular against more powerful others. One of the mechanisms through which this operates may be gossip. Although often viewed as a sin, gossiping can also serve pro-social goals by helping a group detect and undermine deviants, by damaging their reputation (Beersma & Van Kleef, 2011; Feinberg, Willer, Stellar, & Keltner, 2012). Gossiping is a particularly effective tool for the powerless because it allows low-power members to covertly undermine the power base of the powerful (Keltner, Van Kleef, Chen, & Kraus, 2008). Furthermore, where the powerless may actively use their social closeness to undermine the position of the powerful through gossip, the powerful tend to be barred from participating in such interaction. As a result, the powerful may miss many signs about the instability of their position. This can even lead to an illusion of alliance, where the powerful believe that their relations with others are stronger than they actually are (Brion & Anderson, 2013). Helped by their connections, the powerless may form more pessimistic but accurate estimations of their position that help them to operate more carefully.

Conclusion

In the current chapter, we have aimed to show that the psychological state of powerlessness fundamentally changes how individuals think, feel, and act. Viewing the powerless as simply inhibited and only lacking behavioral approach misses a large number of interesting motivational strategies used by disempowered individuals to regain control, which converge in increased complex cognition and in an increased communal focus. We propose that the core priorities of the powerless are to achieve a more detailed understanding of the social world, to fit in with that social world, to help others, and to create socially shared beliefs that ensure fairness. At the cognitive level, we propose that powerless individuals use vigilant cognitive processes and careful decision-making, even if the excessive demands that this entails can compromise the cognitive abilities of powerless individuals. At the social level, we propose that powerless individuals maximize closeness, even if the increased appeasement, generosity, and adherence to norms may reduce any individual benefits. We believe that, because the psychological state of the powerless is characterized by these two seeming inconsistencies, studying the powerless is as interesting as studying the powerful. It unravels how and when individuals rely on agency and individuality and when they rely on communion and social coordination as a control mechanism. Crucially, as we have seen, individuals are highly responsive to temporary threats to social control, some of which were induced experimentally. This suggests that individuals possess motivational and cognitive programs (see Kenrick, 2002) that they deploy flexibly as they navigate complex social relations of varied levels of social control.

References

Anderson, C., Keltner, D., & John, O. (2003). Emotional convergence between people over time. *Journal of Personality and Social Psychology, 84*, 1054–1068. doi:10.1037/0022-3514.84.5.1054

Baddeley, A. D. (1996). Exploring the central executive. *Quarterly Journal of Experimental Psychology, 49*, 5–28.

Beersma, B., & van Kleef, G. A. (2011). How the grapevine keeps you in line: Gossip increases contributions to the group. *Social Psychological and Personality Science, 2*, 642–649. doi:10.1177/1948550611405073

Blader, S. L., & Chen, Y. R. (2014). What's in a name? Status, power, and other forms of social hierarchy. In J. T. Cheng, J. L. Tracy, & C. Anderson (Eds.), *The psychology of social status* (pp. 71–95). New York: Springer.

Boehm, C., Flack, J. (2010). The emergence of simple and complex power structures through social niche construction. In A. Guinote (Ed.). *The Social Psychology of Power*, pp. 46-87. London: Guilford.

Brion, S., & Anderson, C. (2013). The loss of power: How illusions of alliance contribute to powerholders' downfall. *Organizational Behavior and Human Decision, 121*, 129–139. doi:10.1016/j.obhdp.2013.01.005

Cai, A., & Guinote, A. (2015). *Lack of power increases multitasking but decreases multitasking ability.* Manuscript submitted for publication. University College London.

Campbell, D. (1947). Binocular vision. *The British Journal of Ophthalmology, 31*, 321–336.

Caraco, T., Martindale, S., & Pulliam, H. R. (1980). Avian flocking in the presence of a preda-tor. *Nature, 285*, 400–401.

Case, C. R., Conlon, K. E., & Maner, J. K. (2015). Affiliation-seeking among the powerless: Lacking power increases social affiliative motivation. *European Journal of Social Psychology, 45*, 378–385. doi:10.1002/ejsp.2089

Copeland, J. T. (1994). Prophecies of power: Motivational implications of social power for behavioral confirmation. *Journal of Personality and Social Psychology, 67*, 264–277.

Cummins, D. (2005). Dominance, status, and social hierarchies. In Buss, D.M. (Ed.) *The hand-book of evolutionary psychology* (pp. 676-697). Hoboken, NJ: Wiley.

Deaner, R. O., Khera, A.V., & Platt, M. L. (2005). Monkeys pay per view: Adaptive valuation of social images by rhesus macaques. *Current Biology, 15*, 543–548.

deCharms, R. (1968). *Personal causation*. New York: Academic.

De Dreu, C. K., & Van Kleef, G. A. (2004). The influence of power on the information search, impression formation, and demands in negotiation. *Journal of Experimental Social Psychol-ogy, 40*, 303–319.

Dubois, D., Rucker, D. D., & Galinsky, A. D. (2015). Social class, power, and selfishness: When and why upper and lower class individuals behave unethically. *Journal of Personality and Social Psychology, 108*, 436–449.

Emerson, R. M. (1962). Power-dependence relations. *American Sociological Review, 27*, 31–41.

Erber, R., & Fiske, S. T. (1984). Outcome dependency and attention to inconsistent informa-tion. *Journal of Personality and Social Psychology, 47*, 709–726.

Feinberg, M., Willer, R., Stellar, J., & Keltner, D. (2012). The virtues of gossip: Reputational information sharing as prosocial behavior. *Journal of Personality and Social Psychology, 102*, 1015–1030. doi:10.1037/a0026650

Fiske, S. (1993). Controlling other people: The impact of power on stereotyping. *American Psychologist, 48*, 621–621.

Fiske, S. T., & Dépret, E. (1996). Control, interdependence and power: Understanding social cognition in its social context. *European Review of Social Psychology, 7*, 31–61.

Fleagle, J. G. (2013). *Primate adaptation and evolution* (3rd Edn). London: Academic Press.

Foucault, M. (1979). *Discipline and punish*. Trans. Alan Sheridan. Original published 1975, Surveiller et punir, New York: Vintage.

Frank, R. H. (1988). *Passions within reason: The strategic role of the emotions.* New York: Norton.

Fritsche, I., Jonas, E., Ablasser, C., Beyer, M., Kuban, J., Manger, A.-M., & Schultz, M. (2013). The power of we: Evidence for group-based control restoration. *Journal of Experi-mental Social Psychology, 49*, 19–32.

Fritsche, I., Jonas, E., & Fankhänel, T. (2008). The role of control motivation in mortality salience effects on ingroup support and defense. *Journal of Personality and Social Psychology, 95*, 524–541.

Galinsky, A. D., Gruenfeld, D. H., & Magee, J. C. (2003). From power to action. *Journal of Personality and Social Psychology, 85*, 453–466. doi:10.1037/0022-3514.85.3.453

Galinsky, A. D., Magee, J. C., Ena Inesi, M., & Gruenfeld, D. H. (2006). Power and perspec-tives not taken. *Psychological Science, 17*, 1068–1074.

Galinsky, A. D., Magee, J. C., Gruenfeld, D. H., Whitson, J. A., & Liljenquist, K. (2008). Power reduces the press of the situation: Implications for creativity, conformity, and dissonance. *Journal of Personality and Social Psychology, 95*, 1450–1466. doi:10.1037/a0012633

Goodwin, S., Gubin, A., Fiske, S., & Yzerbyt, V.Y. (2000). Power can bias impression processes: Stereotyping subordinates by default and by design. *Group Processes and Intergroup Rela-tions, 3*, 227–256. doi:10.1177/1368430200003003001

Gordon, A. M., & Chen, S. (2013). Does power help or hurt? The moderating role of self-other focus on power and perspective-taking in romantic relationships. *Personality and Social Psychology Bulletin, 39*, 1097–1110. doi:10.1177/0146167213490031

Gruenfeld, D. H., Ena Inesi, M., Magee, J. C., & Galinsky, A. D. (2008). Power and the objectification of social targets. *Journal of Personality and Social Psychology, 95*, 111–127. doi:10.1037/0022-3514.95.1.111

Guinote, A. (2001). The perception of group variability in a non-minority and a minority context: When adaptation leads to out-group differentiation. *British Journal of Social Psychology, 40*, 117–132.

Guinote, A. (2007a). Power and goal pursuit. *Personality and Social Psychology Bulletin, 33*, 1076–1087. doi:10.1177/0146167207301011

Guinote, A. (2007b). Power affects basic cognition: Increased attentional inhibition and flexibility. *Journal of Experimental Social Psychology, 43*, 685–697–697.

Guinote, A. (2008). Power and affordances: when the situation has more power over powerful than powerless individuals. *Journal of Personality and Social Psychology, 95*, 237–252.

Guinote, A., Brown, M., & Fiske, S. T. (2006). Minority status decreases sense of control and increases interpretive processing. *Social Cognition, 24*, 169–186.

Guinote, A., Cotzia, I., Sandhu, S., & Siwa, P. (2015). Social status modulates prosocial behavior and egalitarianism in preschool children and adults. *PNAS, 112*, 731–736. doi:10.1073/pnas.1414550112

Guinote, A., Judd, C., & Brauer, M. (2002). Effects of power on perceived and objective group variability: Evidence that more powerful groups are more variable. *Journal of Personality and Social Psychology, 82*, 708–721.

Guinote, A., & Phillips, A. (2010). Power can increase stereotyping. *Social Psychology, 41*, 3–9.

Guinote, A., Weick, M., & Cai, A. (2012). Does power magnify the expression of dispositions? *Psychological Science, 23*, 475–482. doi:10.1177/0956797611428472

Gwinn, J. D., Judd, C. M., & Park, B. (2013). Less power = less human? Effects of power differentials on dehumanization. *Journal of Experimental Social Psychology, 49*, 464–470. doi:10.1016/j.jesp.2013.01.005

Hall, J. A., Carter, J. D., & Horgan, T. G. (2001). Status roles and recall of nonverbal cues. *Journal of Nonverbal Behavior, 25*, 79–100.

Haney, C., Banks, W. C., & Zimbardo, P. G. (1973). Study of prisoners and guards in a simulated prison. *Naval Research Reviews, 9*, 1–17.

Hecht, M. A., & LaFrance, M. (1998). License or obligation to smile: The effect of power and sex on amount and type of smiling. *Personality and Social Psychology Bulletin, 24*, 1332–1342.

Heine, S. J., Proulx, T., & Vohs, K. D. (2006). The meaning maintenance model: On the coherence of social motivations. *Personality and Social Psychology Review, 10*, 88–110.

Holtgraves, T. (2010). Social psychology and language: Words, utterances and conversations. In S. Fiske, D. Gilbert, & G. Lindzey (Eds.), *Handbook of social psychology* (5th ed, pp. 1386–1422). Hoboken, NJ: Wiley and Sons.

Inesi, M. E., Gruenfeld, D. H., & Galinsky, A. D. (2012). How power corrupts relationships: Cynical attributions for others' generous acts. *Journal of Experimental Social Psychology, 48*, 795–803. doi:10.1016/j.jesp.2012.01.008

Isbell, L. A. (1994). Predation on primates: Ecological patterns and evolutionary consequences. *Evolutionary Anthropology: Issues, News, and Reviews, 3*, 61–71.

Johnson, C. S., & Lammers, J. (2012). The powerful disregard social comparison information. *Journal of Experimental Social Psychology, 48*, 329–334. doi:10.1016/j.jesp.2011.10.010

Karremans, J. C., & Smith, P. K. (2010). Having the power to forgive: When the experience of power increases interpersonal forgiveness. *Personality and Social Psychology Bulletin, 36*, 1010–1023.

Keltner, D., Gruenfeld, D. H., & Anderson, C. (2003). Power, approach, and inhibition. *Psychological Review, 110*, 265–284. doi:10.1037/0033-295X.110.2.265

Keltner, D., van Kleef, G. A., Chen, S., & Kraus, M. (2008). A reciprocal influence model of social power: Emerging principles and lines of inquiry. *Advances in Experimental Social Psychology, 40*, 151–192.

Kenrick, D. T., Maner, J. K., Butner, J., Li, N. P., Becker, D. V., & Schaller, M. (2002). Dynamical evolutionary psychology: Mapping the domains of the new interactionist paradigm. *Personality and Social Psychology Review, 6*, 347–356.

Kipnis, D. (1972). Does power corrupt? *Journal of Personality and Social Psychology, 24*, 33–41.

Kraus, M. W., Horberg, E. J., Goetz, J. L., & Keltner, D. (2011). Social class rank, threat vigilance, and hostile reactivity. *Personality and Social Psychology Bulletin*, 0146167211410987.

Kraus, M. W., Piff, P. K., & Keltner, D. (2009). Social class, sense of control, and social explanation. *Journal of Personality and Social Psychology, 97*, 992–1004.

Lammers, J., Galinsky, A. D., Gordijn, E. H., & Otten, S. (2012). Power increases social distance. *Social Psychological and Personality Science, 3*, 282–290.

Lammers, J., Gordijn, E. H., & Otten, S. (2008). Looking through the eyes of the powerful. *Journal of Experimental Social Psychology, 44*, 1229–1238. doi:10.1016/j.jesp.2008.03.015

Lammers, J., & Imhoff, R. (2016). Power and sadomasochism: Understanding the antecedents of a knotty relationship. *Social Psychological and Personality Science, 7*, 142-148.

Lammers, J., & Maner, J. (2015). Power and attraction to the counternormative aspects of infidelity. *Journal of Sex Research, 53*, 54–63. doi:10.1080/00224499.2014.989483

Lammers, J., & Stapel, D. A. (2009). How power influences moral thinking. *Journal of Personality and Social Psychology, 97*, 279–289. doi:10.1037/a0015437

Lammers, J., & Stapel, D. A. (2011). Power increases dehumanization. *Group Processes and Intergroup Relations, 14*, 113–126. doi:10.1177/1368430210370042

Lammers, J., Stapel, D. A., & Galinsky, A. D. (2010). Power increases hypocrisy: Moralizing in reasoning, immorality in behavior. *Psychological Science, 21*, 737–744. doi:10.1177/0956797610368810

Lammers, J., Stoker, J. I., Jordan, J., Pollmann, M., & Stapel, D. A. (2011). Power increases infidelity among men and women. *Psychological Science, 22*, 1191–1197. doi:10.1177/0956797611416252

Land, M. F. (1989). Variations in the structure and design of compound eyes. In D. G. Stavenga & R. C. Hardie (Eds.), *Facets of vision* (pp. 90–111). Berlin: Springer.

Lorenzi-Cioldi, F., Eagly, A. H., & Stewart, T. L. (1995). Homogeneity of gender groups in memory. *Journal of Experimental Social Psychology, 31*, 193–217.

Ng, S. H., & Bradac, J. J. (1993). *Power in language: Verbal communication and social influence.* New York: Sage Publications, Inc.

Overbeck, J. R., & Droutman, V. (2013). One for all: Social power increases self-anchoring of traits, attitudes, and emotions. *Psychological Science, 24*, 1466–1476. doi:10.1177/0956797612474671

Overbeck, J., & Park, B. (2001). When power does not corrupt: Superior individuation processes among powerful perceivers. *Journal of Personality and Social Psychology, 81*, 549–565.

Overbeck, J., & Park, B. (2006). Powerful perceivers, powerless objects: Flexibility of powerholders' social attention. *Organizational Behavior and Human Decision Processes, 99*, 227–243.

Proulx, T., Inzlicht, M., & Harmon-Jones, E. (2012). Understanding all inconsistency compensation as a palliative response to violated expectations. *Trends in Cognitive Sciences, 16*, 285–291. doi:10.1016/j.tics.2012.04.002

Rucker, D. R. D., Dubois, D., & Galinsky, A. D. (2011). Generous paupers and stingy princes: Power drives consumer spending on self versus others. *The Journal of Consumer Research, 37*, 1015–1029. doi:10.1086/657162

Rucker, D. R. D., & Galinsky, A. D. (2009). Conspicuous consumption versus utilitarian ideals: How different levels of power shape consumer behavior. *Journal of Experimental Social Psychology, 45*, 549–555. doi:10.1016/j.jesp.2009.01.005

Sachdev, I., & Bourhis, R. Y. (1991). Power and status differentials in minority and majority group relations. *European Journal of Social Psychology, 21*, 1–24.

Sapolsky, R. M. (2005). The influence of social hierarchy on primate health. *Science, 308*, 648–652.

Schacter, D. L., Norman, K. A., & Koutstaal, W. (1998). The cognitive neuroscience of constructive memory. *Annual Review of Psychology, 49*, 289–318.

Schmid Mast, M., Jonas, K., & Hall, J. A. (2009). Give a person power and he or she will show interpersonal sensitivity: The phenomenon and its why and when. *Journal of Personality and Social Psychology, 97*, 835–850. doi:10.1037/a0016234

Seyfarth, R. M., & Cheney, D. L. (2003). Signallers and receivers in animal communication. *Annual Review of Psychology, 54*, 145–173.

Simon, B., & Hamilton, D. L. (1994). Self-stereotyping and social context: The effects of relative in-group size and in-group status. *Journal of Personality and Social Psychology, 66*, 699–711.

Skagerberg, E. M., & Wright, D. B. (2008). The prevalence of co-witnesses and co-witness discussions in real eyewitnesses. *Psychology, Crime & Law, 14*, 513–521.

Slabu, L., & Guinote, A. (2010). Getting what you want: Power increases the accessibility of active goals. *Journal of Experimental Social Psychology, 46*, 344–349. doi:10.1016/j.jesp.2009.10.013

Smith, P. K., & Bargh, J. (2008). Nonconscious effects of power on basic approach and avoidance tendencies. *Social Cognition, 26*, 1–24.

Smith, P. K., Jostmann, N. B., Galinsky, A. D., & van Dijk, W. W. (2008). Lacking power impairs executive functions. *Psychological Science, 19*(5), 441–447.

Snyder, M., & Kiviniemi, M. T. (2001). Getting what they came for: How power influences the dynamics and outcomes of interpersonal interaction. In A. Y. Lee-Chai & J. A. Bargh (Eds.), *The use and abuse of power: Multiple perspectives on the causes of corruption* (pp. 133–155). New York: Psychology Press.

Tajfel, H. (1974). Social identity and intergroup behaviour. *Social Science Information/sur les sciences sociales*, 13, 65–93.

Thibaut, J. W., & Kelley, H. H. (1959). *The social psychology of groups*. New York: Wiley.

Trautmann, S. T., van de Kuilen, G., & Zeckhauser, R. J. (2013). Social class and (un)ethical behavior: A framework, with evidence from a large population sample. *Perspectives on Psychological Science, 8*, 487–497. doi:10.1177/1745691613491272

Treisman, M. (1975). Predation and the evolution of gregariousness. I. Models for concealment and evasion. *Animal Behaviour, 23*, 779–800.

Trivers, R. L. (1985). *Social evolution*. Menlo Park, CA: Benjamin/ Cummings.

Van Kleef, G. A., De Dreu, C. K., & Manstead, A. S. (2004). The interpersonal effects of anger and happiness in negotiations. *Journal of Personality and Social Psychology, 86*, 57–76.

Van Prooijen, J. W., Coffeng, J., & Vermeer, M. (2014). Power and retributive justice: How trait information influences the fairness of punishment among power holders. *Journal of Experimental Social Psychology, 50*, 190–201.

Weber, M. (1947). *The theory of social and economic organization*. (Trans. A. M. Henderson & T. Parsons). New York: Oxford University Press.

Weick, M., & Guinote, A. (2008). When subjective experiences matter: Power increases reliance on ease of retrieval. *Journal of Personality and Social Psychology, 94*, 956–970.

Whitson, J. A., & Galinsky, A. D. (2008). Lacking control increases illusory pattern perception. *Science, 322*, 115–117. doi:10.1126/science.1159845

Whitson, J. A., Liljenquist, K. A., Galinsky, A. D., Magee, J. C., Gruenfeld, D. H., & Cadena, B. (2013). The blind leading: Power reduces awareness of constraints. *Journal of Experimental Social Psychology, 49*, 579–582. doi:10.1016/j.jesp.2012.10.009

Yap, A. J., Wazlawek, A. S., Lucas, B. J., Cuddy, A. J. C., & Carney, D. R. (2013). The ergonomics of dishonesty: The effect of incidental posture on stealing, cheating, and traffic violations. *Psychological Science, 24*, 2281–2289. doi:10.1177/0956797613492425

12

THE EMOTIONAL SIDE OF POWER(LESSNESS)

Katerina Petkanopoulou, Guillermo B. Willis, and Rosa Rodríguez-Bailón

Author note

Correspondence concerning this article should be addressed to Katerina Petkanopoulou, Centro de Investigación Mente Cerebro y Comportamiento, University of Granada, Campus Cartuja S/N 18071, Granada, Spain. E-mail: pkaterina@ugr.es

Power differences are a pervasive phenomenon of social life. Power has been considered to have different bases (French & Raven, 1959; Overbeck, 2010; Schmid Mast, 2010) and has been commonly defined as the capacity to influence and control others and to administer rewards and punishments (Fiske, 1993; Keltner, Gruenfeld, & Anderson, 2003; Turner, 2005). At an interpersonal level of analysis – which is the main focus of this chapter – social power changes how individuals think, feel, and act during their interactions with one or more partners (Anderson & Berdahl, 2002; Galinsky, Gruenfeld, & Magee, 2003; Guinote & Vescio, 2010; Schmid Mast, 2010). However, although considerable research has been performed on the effects of social power on behavioral and cognitive processes (Galinsky et al., 2003; Guinote, 2007a; P. K. Smith, Jostmann, Galinsky, & van Dijk, 2008; Willis, Rodríguez-Bailón, & Lupiáñez, 2011), its emotional consequences have been less explored and the existing literature shows less conclusive results.

Our aim with this chapter is threefold. First, we will summarize research findings on how possessing or lacking social power affects individuals' moods and emotional states. Second, we will review the literature on the relation between social power, social motives, and specific emotions. We will argue that applying a perspective based on the social functions of discrete emotions, rather than a valence-based perspective, can provide clearer and more informative results about powerful and powerless individuals' emotional expression as well as about the motives that underlie this expression (i.e., social distancing vs. affiliative motives). Third, we will closely discuss the case of anger in order to show an example of how power shapes emotional expression. We will argue that although this emotion is often associated with high power, powerless individuals also express it, but they do it in an indirect way. Finally, we will discuss some possible moderators (e.g., legitimacy) of the effect of power on emotional processes and open up possibilities for new predictions on the effects of social power on other emotions.

It should be noted that throughout this chapter we mention findings on both power and status differences. Given that these constructs are strongly correlated (Spears, Greenwood, de Lemus, & Sweetman, 2010) we think that existing findings on how status hierarchies affect emotion could be taken as a valuable framework for researchers dealing with the emotional effects of power. However, this does not mean that we consider power and status as equivalent constructs (Fiske & Berdahl, 2007; Fragale, Overbeck, & Neale, 2011). Rather, it should be taken as an invitation to test the similarities and differences of power and status effects on emotion.

Power and positive-negative affect

The approach/inhibition theory of power proposes that both power and powerlessness influence affective processes (Keltner et al., 2003). It states that low-power individuals are more exposed to environmental constraints and threats, which leads them to develop more negative mood and greater experience and expression of negative emotions. By contrast, powerful individuals, who are more exposed to opportunities and environmental rewards, tend to show more positive affect (Keltner et al., 2003). However, empirical evidence supporting these predictions is not so clear, especially regarding the association between powerlessness and negative emotions.

Trait dominance has been found to be negatively correlated with the experience of negative affect and positively correlated with positive affect, supporting the claims of the approach/inhibition theory (Anderson & Berdahl, 2002). However, priming participants with power or powerlessness has not been found to influence individuals' positive or negative affect (Galinsky et al., 2003; P. K. Smith & Bargh, 2008). By contrast, using interaction paradigms in which participants are randomly assigned to powerful and powerless roles has been found to support the predicted effects of power on positive affect, but has not shown that powerlessness leads to negative affect (e.g., Berdahl & Martorana, 2006; Langner & Keltner, 2008).

Berdahl and Martorana (2006) asked their participants to discuss a controversial topic, such as poverty, in groups composed of one leader and two subordinates. Leaders, in comparison to subordinates, were found not only to experience but also to express more positive emotions. However, as it has been said, the association between powerlessness and increased experience and expression of negative emotions was not confirmed, as powerless participants did not differ from powerful participants in the experience and expression of negative emotions.

Later, Langner and Keltner (2008) asked powerful and powerless participants to tease each other and measured positive and negative affect during this interaction. Their results revealed that individuals' influence within a romantic relationship as well as participants' perceived power after the experimental role assignment were positively correlated with the degree of positive affect but was not correlated with the degree of negative affect.

Taken together, these results suggest that social power increases positive affect but it should be measured during meaningful interactions (e.g., teasing interaction, controversial discussion) between powerful and powerless individuals that leave space for intense emotions to be raised (Berdahl & Martorana, 2006; Langner & Keltner, 2008). Yet, the causal effect of powerlessness on negative affect has not received the same degree of support (Berdahl & Martorana, 2006; Langner & Keltner, 2008; Petkanopoulou, Willis, & Rodríguez-Bailón, 2012; P. K. Smith & Bargh, 2008).

Although the experience and expression are two components of emotion that tend to be correlated, this is not always the case (Gross, John, & Richards, 2000). For instance, it has been suggested that powerless individuals are more limited by social norms and their emotion expression – especially when they interact with a powerful target – does not always correspond to their internal moods and states (Hecht & LaFrance, 1998). Therefore, considering the emotion expression as the observable outcome of individuals' real inner feelings could lead to misleading conclusions about the emotional effects of powerlessness.

A second possible reason for the unclear effects of powerlessness on negative emotions could be that they were studied from a valence-based perspective. In the same line of other authors who also highlighted the informative value of specific emotions rather than moods and states (Van Kleef, De Dreu, & Manstead, 2010), we claim that a discrete emotion approach seems more useful to have a better understanding of the emotional effects of having or lacking social power. This is because discrete negative emotions are accompanied by different appraisals and action tendencies (Frijda, Kuipers, & ter Schure, 1989; Lazarus, 1991) and serve different social goals related to cooperation or competition (Fischer & Manstead, 2008; Van Kleef et al., 2010). Therefore, given that powerful and powerless individuals differ in the goals they pursue, they may express different emotions such as anger and sadness differently.

Thus, we will next review findings of two different lines of research. On the one hand, we will provide evidence that shows that social power influences social motives and goals (Case, Conlon, & Maner, 2015; Lammers, Galinsky, Gordijn, & Otten, 2012; Van Kleef et al., 2008). On the other hand, we will follow a social-functional perspective of emotions and show that specific social functions and goals are accomplished with the expression of some discrete emotions (Fischer & Manstead, 2008; Van Kleef et al., 2010). Although a direct relationship between power – or powerlessness – and specific emotions has not been clearly proven yet (for exceptions, see Schmid Mast, Jonas, & Hall, 2009; Van Kleef et al., 2008), we believe that considering these two different lines of research can improve our understanding about the relation between power and affective processes.

Social power motives and discrete emotions

It has been established that social power affects individuals' motives and goals (Fiske, 1993; Guinote, 2007b). The better objective circumstances of powerful individuals make such individuals more biased towards goals that serve to enhance and maintain their privileged position (Willis & Guinote, 2011), such as self-serving goals (Kipnis, 1976; Winter, 1973). Along these lines, Keltner, Gruenfeld, Galinsky, and Kraus (2010) argued that power-holders choose to pursue personal goals rather than goals that serve their subordinates, and Gruenfeld, Inesi, Magee, and Galinsky (2008) showed that the powerful think more of what others can do for them than of what they can do for others.

Similarly, given that the powerful have greater control over their own and others' outcomes (Fiske, 1993), they have a greater sense of independence and self-sufficiency (Guinote, 2007b; Lammers et al., 2012). This in turn may increase social distance toward others, making such individuals less motivated to maintain close relationships and less likely to incorporate others in the way they define their self (Magee & P. K. Smith, 2011; P. K. Smith & Trope, 2006; Voyer & McIntosh, 2013). This idea is consistent with the finding that powerful individuals prefer working alone rather than in teams and are less willing to make decisions that favor communal welfare (Lammers et al., 2012).

Conversely, powerless individuals are more motivated to affiliate with others and aim to increase closeness and cohesion in their relationships (Case et al., 2015; Guinote & Lammers, Chapter 11, this volume). Partners who reported having lower power in their romantic relationship have been found to try to adjust to the emotional experience of high power individuals (Anderson, Keltner, & John, 2003). Moreover, studies that explicitly measured affiliative motivation have confirmed that powerless individuals' greater willingness to connect with others led them to generate greater reciprocal and complementary responses to other people's distress (Van Kleef et al., 2008).

In short, this line of research suggests that high power promotes the development of an independent self-construal and increases social distance motives whereas low power is associated with an interdependent self-construal and social affiliative motives (Case et al., 2015; Lammers et al., 2012; Lee & Tiedens, 2001; Magee & Smith, 2011; Voyer & McIntosh, 2013). Consequently, from a social functional perspective (Fischer & Manstead, 2008; Van Kleef et al., 2010), the powerful and the powerless should be more prone to express the emotions that help them satisfy such motives.

Fischer and Manstead (2008) argued that emotions mainly serve two broad social functions that are crucial for people's interactions: an affiliative and a social distancing function. Thus, some emotions such as sadness, shame, and guilt help people to get closer to others and affiliate with them; other emotions such as anger and pride create social distance and promote competition for status (Fischer & Manstead, 2008). In the same vein, Kitayama, Markus, and Kurokawa (2000) suggested using the terms *engaging* and *disengaging* emotions. The experience of the former motivates people to establish harmonious social relationships and perceive themselves as interdependent and connected to others. By contrast, disengaging emotions motivate people to perceive themselves as independent and disengaged from others (Kitayama et al., 2000).

Emotions such as sadness and disappointment are elicited when people face a loss or a threat and are associated with appraisals of lack of control and withdrawal action tendencies (Ellsworth & C.A. Smith, 1988; Frijda, 1986; Frijda et al., 1989; Lazarus, 1991). The expression of these emotions, by conveying signals of vulnerability and neediness, triggers empathetic emotional responses and invites the recipient to attend to and support the person who expresses them. Therefore, expressing sadness and disappointment serves people's affiliative goals (Clark & Taraban, 1991; Fischer & Manstead, 2008; Van Kleef et al., 2010). The same type of goals can be achieved with the expression of the "moral emotions" of shame and guilt, which are associated with a motivation to repair the damage caused and convey signs of appeasement to the receiver (Baumeister, Stillwell, & Heatherton, 1994; Gausel & Leach, 2011; Shariff & Tracy, 2011; Van Kleef et al., 2010). Moreover, affiliative emotions are usually associated with displays of low status and powerlessness (Fischer, Rodriguez Mosquera, van Vianen, & Manstead, 2004; Timmers, Fischer, & Manstead, 1998), and it has been found that individuals are assessed as being less dominant when they express these emotions (Hareli, Shomrat, & Hess, 2009).

By contrast, anger has been characterized as the most prototypical "powerful emotion" (Fischer et al., 2004; Timmers et al., 1998). Anger is elicited by appraisals of goal blockage and is associated with high coping potential, approach, and even aggressive action tendencies (Averill, 1983; Berkowitz, 1993; Frijda, 1986). Although some studies have shown that anger can help people to get closer in the long term, it seems that this emotion serves a social distancing function in the short term (Fischer & Manstead, 2008; Fischer & Roseman, 2007). By expressing anger people convey signs of toughness, high status, and dominance (Knutson, 1996; Sinaceur & Tiedens, 2006; Tiedens, 2001) and aim to control the behavior of the person they are angry at (Fischer & Evers, 2011; Sinaceur & Tiedens, 2006).

Another social distancing emotion is pride (Fischer & Manstead, 2008). Pride is accompanied by a high coping potential, personal agency about positive outcomes, and a positive self-evaluation (Ellsworth & C. A. Smith, 1988; K. M. Lewis, 2000; Tracy & Robins, 2007). Participants who were induced to feel proud, in comparison with a neutral state, showed more dominant behavior and their counterparts also perceived them as such during a group problem-solving task (Williams & Desteno, 2009). Furthermore, studies have found a strong implicit association between displays of pride and high status. This association has been found to be stronger than the association between other emotions (e.g., happiness, anger) and status (Shariff, Tracy, & Markusoff, 2012; Shariff & Tracy, 2009).

The relation between status and discrete emotions has been found to be bidirectional (Tiedens, Ellsworth, & Mesquita, 2000). Participants not only attributed high status to characters who were presented as being proud and angry, and low status to characters who were presented as being appreciative, sad, and guilty, but also the other way round. That is, participants expected high-status individuals to respond with pride and low-status individuals to respond with appreciation when positive outcomes occurred. As a way to cope with negative results, participants expected low-status individuals to feel sad and guilty and high-status individuals to feel angry (Tiedens et al., 2000).

Given that power increases social distance motives, whereas powerlessness increases social affiliative motives, the powerful should be more likely to express emotions such as anger and pride, whereas the powerless should be more likely to express emotions such as sadness, shame, and guilt, confirming the existing stereotypes mentioned above (Tiedens et al., 2000).

However, for several reasons such results may not be as straightforward as predicted. First, various factors related to the social context in which the emotions appear, or related with how power is perceived or operationalized, may act separately or jointly as moderators of the effect of power on individuals' motivation and consequently on their emotional expression. Second, the social motives that underlie individuals' emotional expression are often mixed and even contradictory. For example, in a given situation individuals may be motivated to distance themselves from others and gain relative status over them, but at the same time they may be motivated to act in accordance with social rules and maintain harmonious relationships. Thus, individuals' emotional expression may be the outcome of the balance between different and even competing social motives.

Finally, individuals' emotional expression depends not only on the evaluation of the emotion-eliciting situation or on their own social motives. It also depends on the anticipated consequences related to the reactions of others to one's own emotional expression, that is, on people's social appraisals (Evers, Fischer, Mosquera, & Manstead, 2005; Manstead & Fischer, 2001). Although various types of motives may induce people to express certain emotions, they may finally avoid expressing them directly if they anticipate that this expression could lead to detrimental consequences (i.e., negative social appraisal; see Evers et al., 2005).

The best example to further understand these processes might be anger, which is considered to be a "powerful" emotion. Given that expressing anger may have important implications for maintaining or changing the hierarchy, this emotion has caught the interest of many scholars who study emotions in an intergroup domain and have compared the emotional experience and expression of members of powerful and powerless groups (Mackie, Devos, & Smith, 2000; Van Zomeren, Leach, & Spears, 2012; Van Zomeren, Spears, Fischer, & Leach, 2004). However, evidences about the expression of this emotion in an interpersonal domain are more scarce and less clear (Berdahl & Martorana, 2006; Tiedens et al., 2000). In the next section we will further discuss the effect of power on anger expression, as well as the social factors that may moderate either the relation between power and social motives, or the relation between social motives and emotional expression.

When powerless individuals express "powerful" emotions: The case of anger

As stated above, the expression of anger is aimed at changing the behavior of and controlling the person toward whom it is addressed and helps people gain social distance and relative status (Fischer & Manstead, 2008; Fischer & Roseman, 2007). Therefore, this emotion has been considered appropriate for powerful individuals. For example, it has been claimed that anger has an "authority entry requirement", as individuals who have power and authority are more entitled or licensed to express this emotion (Averill, 1997). Other authors have described anger as a privilege possessed by people with a superior social and structural position (Taylor & Risman, 2006).

However, in other cases, empirical evidence has contradicted this positive association between power and anger, demonstrating that powerless and low-status individuals express more anger than powerful individuals. For instance, Berdahl and Martorana (2006) showed that powerless (and not powerful) participants were the ones who experienced and expressed more anger during a group discussion.

These apparently contradictory results might be explained by the fact that although low power and status are related to an affiliative motivation, this motivation is not stable. Various factors, such as the way that power is construed in a given social context, or individuals' perceived illegitimacy or stability of power, could play an important moderating role by affecting the social motives of powerful and powerless individuals.

It has been argued that social power may activate different goals depending on the social context or on individuals' dispositions and traits. Thus, in some cases power is perceived in terms of self-interest and opportunity, whereas in others it may activate communal goals and be construed as a responsibility (Chen, Lee-Chai, & Bargh, 2001; Sassenberg, Ellemers, & Scheepers, 2012). In this second case, high power increases interpersonal sensitivity as well as individuals' tendency to behave in socially desirable ways (Chen et al., 2001; Schmid Mast et al., 2009). In a similar vein, it could be expected that when power is operationalized as responsibility and activates the idea of *noblesse oblige,* powerful individuals would be less motivated to distance themselves from others and more reluctant to express anger than powerless individuals.

Another factor that may influence powerless individuals' motives to express anger is the evaluation of their powerless situation as being legitimate or not. Although powerful individuals are motivated to maintain their power and reinforce the status quo, individuals who lack power may also be motivated to restore their power and enhance their status (Fiske & Dépret, 1996). Especially when individuals think that they deserve power but lack it, they tend to perceive their situation as illegitimate and are more resistant to the loss of their power and more motivated to regain it and to increase the social distance between themselves and others (Lammers et al., 2012; Willis, Guinote, & Rodríguez-Bailón, 2010). Such individuals may therefore express anger for this purpose.

Summing up, these results reveal that although anger expression is associated with elevated power, under certain conditions this effect may be inverted and powerless individuals may be more willing to express it. However, it has been emphasized that, although emotions are functional, they do not always fulfill the goals that they are supposed to serve (Fischer & Manstead, 2008). For example, the fact that anger expression aims to distance oneself from others and gain relative power over them does not mean that this goal is always achieved. Thus, when powerless individuals express anger toward a powerful counterpart they may fail to accomplish their goal (Fischer & Manstead, 2008) because they are constrained by their counterpart's higher ability to administer punishment (Keltner et al., 2003).

Results obtained in the context of negotiations where both opponents are instigated by a competitive motivation and therefore aim to force a desirable change on the other individual's behavior have revealed that expressing anger helps powerful negotiators to fulfill this goal, but that this is not the case for powerless negotiators (Van Kleef et al., 2010). Anger expressed by a powerful negotiator toward a powerless opponent has been found to elicit complementary fear responses in the recipient that lead to a favorable subsequent offer (Lelieveld, Van Dijk, Van Beest, & Van Kleef, 2012). However, opponents with good alternatives (i.e., high bargaining power) have been found at best to remain unaffected by their opponent's emotional expression, and in some cases even to react with reciprocal anger responses to their powerless counterparts' anger and consequently with detrimental behavioral reactions (Lelieveld et al., 2012; Sinaceur & Tiedens, 2006; Van Kleef, De Dreu, & Manstead, 2004; Van Kleef, De Dreu, Pietroni, & Manstead, 2006).

This illustrates that the effectiveness of anger expression depends on individuals' ability to assess their own goals together with the goals and appraisals of others, and accurately anticipate their reactions (Fischer & Manstead, 2008; Manstead & Fischer, 2001). Therefore, there are situations in which, despite being motivated to express anger, powerless individuals may anticipate that by doing so they could get in trouble and thus strategically avoid expressing this emotion directly toward a powerful target. In a study, Dutch women involved in traditional relationships, in which power differences were salient, were found to anticipate more negative consequences (i.e., negative social appraisals) than men as a result of expressing anger. These negative social appraisals led them to express less direct anger than men, although they reported being angrier than them (Fischer & Evers, 2011).

However, expressing anger directly toward the person someone is angry at is not the only way to cope with this emotion. It has been suggested that people can address this emotion in more indirect and subtle ways (Linden et al., 2003). Timmers et al. (1998) manipulated the object-target relationship, where the object is the person who caused the anger and the target is the person toward whom the anger is expressed. They showed that women, compared to men, expressed less anger directly toward the person they were angry at (object-target same), but they expressed more anger in a context in which the object of their anger was not present (object-target different), a type of indirect anger expression (Timmers et al., 1998). Although this study did not directly deal with the emotional effects of power, it has been suggested that gender differences in anger expression could be explained by the differences in power and status held by men and women (Fischer & Evers, 2011; Schmid Mast, 2010; Timmers et al., 1998).

Along the same lines, it has been found that people express their anger in a more overt and direct way toward low-status individuals, but when their anger is directed toward a high-status individual, they either suppress it or choose to express it indirectly by sharing it with others (P. Kuppens, Van Mechelen, & Meulders, 2004).

It has been supported that emotional sharing has beneficial effects for relationships, as it brings people closer and strengthens the bonds between them (Rime, 2009; Rimé & Zech, 2001). It is also worth noting that in some cases sharing emotionally relevant situations elicits group-based appraisal and emotions as well as a sense of a common group identity and helps people to form coalitions and coordinate their actions (T. Kuppens, Yzerbyt, Dandache, Fischer, & van der Schalk, 2013; Livingstone, Spears, Manstead, Bruder, & Shepherd, 2011; Peters & Kashima, 2007; Yzerbyt & T. Kuppens, 2012). Thus, expressing anger indirectly through social sharing seems to play a double function for powerless individuals: on the one hand, it may trigger nurturing responses in others and satisfy their need to affiliate (P. Kuppens et al., 2004; Rimé & Zech, 2001; Rime, 2009); on the other hand, it may give rise to group processes (Peters & Kashima, 2007; Yzerbyt & Kuppens, 2012) that may help powerless individuals to counter their disadvantage and restore their power and control. This idea is in line with findings showing that the lack of personal control motivates individuals to restore such control through their groups – they strive for group-based control (Fritsche et al., 2013).

In sum, all these results suggest that powerless individuals are aware that expressing anger directly may imply negative consequences for them (Fischer & Evers, 2011). However, this does not prevent them from expressing anger at all; they instead choose to do so in an indirect way by sharing their anger with others or venting their anger with them in the absence of the powerful object of their anger (P. Kuppens et al., 2004; Timmers et al., 1998). In other words, powerless individuals express their anger in such a way that they can guarantee the functionality of this emotion.

Conclusions

In this chapter we have attempted to provide an overview of the literature that deals with the relation between social power and emotion. We first reviewed the studies that aimed to verify the statements of the approach/inhibition theory that associate powerlessness with the experience and expression of negative emotions and the decreased experience and expression of positive ones (Keltner et al., 2003). We concluded that, although the latter has received considerable support, the former is still uncertain (Berdahl & Martorana, 2006; Langner & Keltner, 2008). We recognize the relevance of the empirical evidence provided through the approach/ inhibition theory, and the contribution of researchers that examined the effect of power on individuals' moods and states. However, we consider that following the notion based on specific emotions and their functions (Fischer & Manstead, 2008; Van Kleef et al., 2010) may be useful to clear up ambiguities on the emotional effects of power. This is because it can provide additional information about the motives and goals that instigate powerful and powerless individuals' emotional responses.

We adopted a social functional perspective that is based on the idea that specific emotions help people to either affiliate or distance themselves from others and gain relative status and power over them (Fischer & Manstead, 2008) and we reviewed the evidence that associates low power with the experience and expression of affiliative emotions, such as sadness and guilt, and high power with social distancing emotions, such as anger and pride (e.g., Schmid Mast et al., 2009; Tiedens et al., 2000; Van Kleef et al., 2008).

Finally, we explored in greater depth the effect of power on anger, considered as a typical powerful emotion, and we showed some evidence supporting the argument that this emotion is also associated with powerless individuals (Berdahl & Martorana, 2006). We argued that when the context favors competition (e.g., negotiation), or when powerless individuals perceive their disadvantaged position as illegitimate, such individuals are also motivated to increase the distance with others and gain relative power and status.

However, studies mainly conducted in the context of social negotiations have provided good explanations to understand why expressing anger directly in some cases may be ineffective for powerless individuals, who seem to be aware of this (e.g., Lelieveld et al., 2012). In this regard, we think that social appraisals (Manstead & Fischer, 2001) could determine the way powerless individuals cope with their anger. We also reviewed empirical evidence that demonstrated that avoiding a direct expression of anger does not mean being passive since anger can be expressed using indirect ways that may be more effective to fulfill powerless individuals' goals (P. Kuppens et al., 2004).

In summary, as it can been seen in Figure 12.1, based on the research reviewed in this chapter, we suggested powerful and powerless individuals' affiliative and social distancing motives respectively, as well as their social appraisals, as possible mediators of the effect of power on emotion expression. We also proposed that the different ways that power and powerlessness are construed and experienced are possible moderators of this effect.

Although an important part of this chapter is devoted to anger, we consider that the effects of power on other specific emotions also deserve further study. We dealt with anger in detail because this allowed us to fulfill two goals: first, to show that the motivation of powerless individuals to affiliate (with the powerful) is not unconditional and stable but rather is influenced by contextual features and by powerless individuals' evaluation of their position (i.e., as legitimate or illegitimate); second, to highlight the need to go beyond the expression-suppression dualism and consider

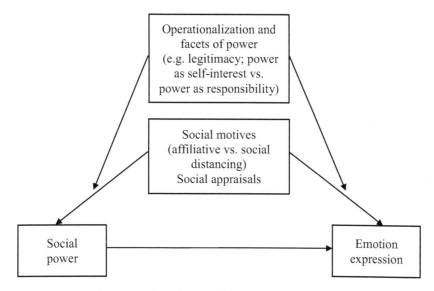

FIGURE 12.1   Moderators and mediators of the relation between power and emotion expression.

a broader spectrum of emotion-related responses in order to better understand the emotional side of powerlessness.

We consider that similar processes may take place with other emotions. For instance, sadness is an affiliative emotion and a signal of weakness (Van Kleef et al., 2010), and we could expect powerless individuals to express this emotion more than powerful ones. However, powerless individuals who perceive their position as illegitimate may be more motivated to distance themselves from their powerful counterparts rather than affiliate with them. Therefore, they may suppress sadness and similar emotions in front of their illegitimate powerful counterparts as a way of avoiding presenting themselves as vulnerable.

In this chapter we suggested that the social distancing and affiliative motivations might act as potential mediators of the emotional effects of power. However, exploring the explicative value of other factors could be also helpful in order to understand better how the possession or the lack of power shapes individuals' emotion expression. For instance, powerless individuals' need for control restoration (see Bukowski & Kofta, Chapter 1, this volume) could lead them to express emotions that help them to enhance their sense of control.

Finally it is noteworthy that the effects of social power can be studied at different levels of analysis (i.e., intrapersonal, interpersonal, intergroup, and ideological; Brauer & Bourhis, 2006). Belonging to either a structurally advantaged or a disadvantaged group also affects individuals' group-based emotions (i.e., emotions that people experience and express on behalf of their group; Smith, Seger, & Mackie, 2007). Given the main focus of this chapter, we did not refer to the emotional effects of power and powerlessness at an intergroup level. Literature on this field suggests that there could be some similarities between these effects of power at both interpersonal and intergroup levels. In this chapter we suggested that in interpersonal relationships the expression of anger is associated with powerful individuals; however, we argued that perceived illegitimacy may reverse this effect. In a similar vein, at an intergroup level it was found that perceiving the in-group as stronger predicts the expression of anger toward the out-group (Mackie et al., 2000). However, this emotion is also experienced and expressed by members of minority or structurally disadvantaged groups who perceive their situation as illegitimate (Van Zomeren et al., 2012, 2004).

However, despite possible similarities, there are several reasons why we consider that the emotional effects of power and powerlessness at an intergroup and at an interpersonal level should be treated separately. First, emotions may serve different social functions at each level (Fischer & Manstead, 2008). For example, at an intergroup level the experience of the affiliative emotions of guilt and pity by members of advantaged groups may be accompanied by benevolent reactions and finally help them to maintain their superiority (Leach, Iyer, & Pedersen, 2006; Thomas, McGarty, & Mavor, 2009). Furthermore, there are several factors that are not applicable to interpersonal relationships and that could be important moderators or mediators of the emotional effects of power at an intergroup level, such as group-identification or perceived identity threat (Livingstone, Spears, Manstead, & Bruder, 2009; E. R. Smith et al., 2007). For those reasons we delimited the literature reviewed in this chapter to the interpersonal level of power.

In conclusion, we aimed to provide an overview of the main studies so far on the relation between social power and emotion and to raise new questions for future research on this topic. For these purposes, we considered literature on the social functions of emotions, the social motives related to power, and appraisal processes. We are convinced that bringing together insights from these different research areas can open possibilities for new predictions and contribute to a better and more complete understanding of the effect of power on emotion.

References

Anderson, C., & Berdahl, J. L. (2002). The experience of power: Examining the effects of power on approach and inhibition tendencies. *Journal of Personality and Social Psychology, 83*, 1362–1377. doi:10.1037/0022-3514.83.6.1362

Anderson, C., Keltner, D., & John, O. P. (2003). Emotional convergence between people over time. *Journal of Personality and Social Psychology, 84*, 1054–1068. doi:10.1037/0022-3514.84.5.1054

Averill, J. R. (1983). Studies on anger and aggression. Implications for theories of emotion. *The American Psychologist, 38*, 1145–1160. doi:10.1037/0003-066X.38.11.1145

Averill, J. R. (1997). The emotions: An integrative approach. In R. Hogan, J. A. Johnson, & S. R. Briggs (Eds.), *Handbook of personality psychology* (pp. 513–541). San Diego: Academic Press.

Baumeister, R. F., Stillwell, A. M., & Heatherton, T. F. (1994). Guilt: An interpersonal approach. *Psychological Bulletin, 115*, 243–267. doi:10.1037/0033-2909.115.2.243

Berdahl, J. L., & Martorana, P. (2006). Effects of power on emotion and expression during a controverial group discussion. *European Journal of Social Psychology, 36*, 497–509. doi:10.1002/ejsp.354

Berkowitz, L. (1993). *Aggression: Its causes, consequences, and control.* New York: McGraw-Hill.

Brauer, M., & Bourhis, R. Y. (2006). Social power. *European Journal of Social Psychology, 36*, 601–616. doi:10.1002/ejsp.355

Case, C. R., Conlon, K. E., & Maner, K. (2015). Affiliation-seeking among the powerless: Lacking power increases social affiliative motivation. *European Journal of Social Psychology, 45*, 378–385. doi:10.1002/ejsp.2089

Chen, S., Lee-Chai, A. Y., & Bargh, J. A. (2001). Relationship orientation as a moderator of the effects of social power. *Journal of Personality and Social Psychology, 80*, 173–187. doi:10. 1037//0022-3514.80.2.173

Clark, M. S., & Taraban, C. (1991). Reactions to and willingness to express emotion in communal and exchange relationships. *Journal of Experimental Social Psychology, 27*, 324–336. doi:10.1016/0022-1031(91)90029-6

Ellsworth, P. C., & Smith, C. A. (1988). From appraisal to emotion: Differences among unpleasant feelings. *Motivation and Emotion, 12*, 271–302. doi:10.1007/BF00993115

Evers, C., Fischer, A. H., Rodríguez Mosquera, P. M., & Manstead, A. S. R. (2005). Anger and social appraisal: A "spicy" sex difference? *Emotion, 5*, 258–266. doi:10.1037/1528-3542.5.3.258

Fischer, A. H., & Evers, C. (2011). The social costs and benefits of anger as a function of gender and relationship context. *Sex Roles, 65*, 23–34. doi:10.1007/s11199-011-9956-x

Fischer, A. H., & Manstead, A. S. R. (2008). Social functions of emotion. In M. Lewis, J. Haviland-Jones, & L. Feldman Barrett (Eds.), *Handbook of emotions* (3rd ed., pp. 456–468). New York: Guilford Press.

Fischer, A. H., Rodriguez Mosquera, P. M., van Vianen, A. E. M., & Manstead, A. S. R. (2004). Gender and culture differences in emotion. *Emotion, 4*, 87–94. doi:10.1037/ 1528-3542.4.1.87

Fischer, A. H., & Roseman, I. J. (2007). Beat them or ban them: The characteristics and social functions of anger and contempt. *Journal of Personality and Social Psychology, 93*, 103–115. doi:10.1037/0022-3514.93.1.103

Fiske, S. T. (1993). Controlling other people: The impact of power on stereotyping. *American Psychologist, 48*, 621–628. doi:10.1037/0003-066X.48.6.621

Fiske, S. T., & Berdahl, J. L. (2007). Social power. In A. Kruglanski & T. Higgins (Eds.), *Social psychology: A handbook of basic principles* (2nd ed.), 678-692. New York: Guildford.

Fiske, S. T., & Dépret, E. (1996). Control, interdependence and power: Understanding Social cognition in its social context. *European Review of Social Psychology, 7*, 31–61. doi:10.1080/14792779443000094

Fragale, A. R., Overbeck, J. R., & Neale, M. A. (2011). Resources versus respect: Social judgments based on targets' power and status positions. *Journal of Experimental Social Psychology, 47*, 767–775. doi:10.1016/j.jesp.2011.03.006

French, J., & Raven, B. H. (1959). The bases of social power. In D. Cartwright (Ed.), *Studies in social power* (pp. 150–167). Ann Arbor, MI: Institute for social Research.

Frijda, N. H. (1986). T*he emotion.* London: Cambridge University Press.

Frijda, N. H., Kuipers, P., & Ter Schure, E. (1989). Relations among emotion, appraisal, and emotional action readiness. *Journal of Personality and Social Psychology, 52*, 212–228. doi:10.1037/0022-3514.57.2.212

Fritsche, I., Jonas, E., Ablasser, C., Beyer, M., Kuban, J., Manger, A., & Schultz, M. (2013). The power of we : Evidence for group-based control. *Journal of Experimental Social Psychology, 49*, 19–32. doi:10.1016/j.jesp.2012.07.014

Galinsky, A. D., Gruenfeld, D. H., & Magee, J. C. (2003). From power to action. *Journal of Personality and Social Psychology, 85*, 453–466. doi:10.1037/0022-3514.85.3.453

Gausel, N., & Leach, C. W. (2011). Concern for self-image and social image in the management of moral failure: Rethinking shame. *European Journal of Social Psychology, 41*, 468–478. doi:10.1002/ejsp.803

Gross, J. J., John, O. P., & Richards, J. M. (2000). The dissociation of emotion expression from emotion experience: A personality perspective. *Personality and Social Psychology Bulletin, 26*, 712–726. doi:10.1177/0146167200268006

Gruenfeld, D. H., Inesi, M. E., Magee, J. C., & Galinsky, A. D. (2008). Power and the objectification of social targets. *Journal of Personality and Social Psychology, 95*, 111–127. doi:10.1037/0022-3514.95.1.111

Guinote, A. (2007a). Power affects basic cognition: Increased attentional inhibition and flexibility. *Journal of Experimental Social Psychology, 43*, 685–697. doi:10.1016/j.jesp.2006.06.008

Guinote, A. (2007b). Power and goal pursuit. *Personality and Social Psychology Bulletin, 33*, 1076–1087. doi:10.1177/0146167207301011

Guinote, A., & Vescio, T. K. (2010). *The social psychology of power*. New York: Guilford Press.

Hareli, S., Shomrat, N., & Hess, U. (2009). Emotional versus neutral expressions and perceptions of social dominance and submissiveness. *Emotion, 9*, 378–384. doi:10.1037/a0015958

Hecht, M. A., & LaFrance, M. (1998). License or obligation to smile: The effect of power and sex on amount and type of smiling. *Personality and Social Psychology Bulletin, 24*, 1332–1342. doi:10.1177/01461672982412007

Keltner, D., Gruenfeld, D. H., & Anderson, C. (2003). Power, approach and inhibition. *Psychological Review, 110*, 265–284. doi:10.1037/0033-295X.110.2.265

Keltner, D., Gruenfeld, D. H., Galinsky, A. D., & Kraus, M. W. (2010). Paradoxes of power: Dynamics of the acquisition, experience, and social regulation of social power. In A. Guinote & T. K. Vescio (Eds.), *The social psychology of power* (pp. 177–208). New York: Guilford Press.

Kipnis, D. (1976). *The powerholders*. Chicago: University of Chicago Press.

Kitayama, S., Markus, H. R., & Kurokawa, M. (2000). Culture, emotion, and well-being: Good feelings in Japan and the United States. *Cognition & Emotion, 14*, 93–124. doi:10.1080/026999300379003

Knutson, B. (1996). Facial expressions of emotion influence interpersonal trait inferences. *Journal of Nonverbal Behavior, 20*, 165–182. doi:10.1007/BF02281954

Kuppens, P., Van Mechelen, I., & Meulders, M. (2004). Every cloud has a silver lining: Interpersonal and individual differences determinants of anger-related behaviors. *Personality and Social Psychology Bulletin, 30*, 1550–1564. doi:10.1177/0146167204271176

Kuppens, T., Yzerbyt, V. Y., Dandache, S., Fischer, A. H., & van der Schalk, J. (2013). Social identity salience shapes group-based emotions through group-based appraisals. *Cognition and Emotion, 27*, 1359–1377. doi:10.1080/02699931.2013.785387

Lammers, J., Galinsky, A. D., Gordijn, E. H., & Otten, S. (2012). Power increases social distance. *Social Psychological and Personality Science, 3*, 282–290. doi:10.1177/1948550611418679

Langner, C. A., & Keltner, D. (2008). Social power and emotional experience: Actor and partner effects within dyadic interactions. *Journal of Experimental Social Psychology, 44*, 848–856. doi:10.1016/j.jesp.2007.08.002

Lazarus, R. S. (1991). *Emotion and adaptation*. New York: Oxford University Press.

Leach, C. W., Iyer, A., & Pedersen, A. (2006). Anger and guilt about ingroup advantage explain the willingness for political action. *Personality and Social Psychology Bulletin, 32*, 1232–1245. doi:10.1177/0146167206289729

Lee, F., & Tiedens, L. Z. (2001). Is it lonely at the top?: The independence and interdependence of power holders. In B. Staw & R. Sutton (Eds.), *Research in organizational behavior* (Vol. 23, pp. 43–91). Greenwich, CT: JAI Press.

Lelieveld, G. J., Van Dijk, E., Van Beest, I., & Van Kleef, G. A. (2012). Why anger and disappointment affect other's bargaining behavior differently: The moderating role of power and the mediating role of reciprocal and complementary emotions. *Personality and Social Psychology Bulletin, 38*, 1209–1221. doi:10.1177/0146167212446938

Lewis, K. M. (2000). When leaders display emotion: How followers respond to negative emotional expression of male and female leaders. *Journal of Organizational Behavior, 21*, 221–234. doi:10.1002/(SICI)1099-1379(200003)21:2<221::AID-JOB36>3.0.CO;2-0

Linden, W., Hogan, B. E., Rutledge, T., Chawla, A., Lenz, J. W., & Leung, D. (2003). There is more to anger coping than "in" or "out". *Emotion, 3*, 12–29. doi:10.1037/1528-3542.3.1.12

Livingstone, A. G., Spears, R., Manstead, A. S. R. and Bruder, M. (2009). Illegitimacy and identity threat in (inter)action: predicting intergroup orientations among minority group members. *British Journal of Social Psychology, 48*, 755–775.

Livingstone, A. G., Spears, R., Manstead, A. S. R., Bruder, M., & Shepherd, L. (2011). We feel, therefore we are: Emotion as a basis for self-categorization and social action. *Emotion, 11*, 754–767. doi:10.1037/a0023223

Mackie, D. M., Devos, T., & Smith, E. R. (2000). Intergroup emotions: Explaining offensive action tendencies in an intergroup context. *Journal of Personality and Social Psychology, 79*, 602–616. doi:10.1037/0022-3514.79.4.602

Magee, J. C., & Smith, P. K. (2011, June). *What drives the psychological effects of power? A comparison of the approach/inhibition and social distance theories.* Paper presented at the 24th annual conference of the International Association for Conflict Management. Retrieved from: http://ssrn.com/abstract=1872175

Manstead, A. S. R., & Fischer, A. H. (2001). Social appraisals: The social word as object of and influence on appraisal processes. In K. Scherer, A. Schorr, & T. Johnstone (Eds.), *Appraisals processes in emotion: Theory, method, research* (pp. 221–232). New York: Oxford University Press.

Overbeck, J. R. (2010). Concepts and historical perspectives on power. In A. Guinote & T. Vescio (Eds.), *The social psychology of power* (pp. 19–45). New York: Guilford Press.

Peters, K., & Kashima, Y. (2007). From social talk to social action: Shaping the social triad with emotion sharing. *Journal of Personality and Social Psychology, 93*, 780–797. doi:10.1037/0022-3514.93.5.780

Petkanopoulou, K., Willis, G. B., & Rodríguez-Bailón, R. (2012). Controlling others and controlling oneself: Social power and emotion suppression. *Revista de Psicología Social, 27*, 305–316. doi:10.1174/021347412802845586

Rime, B. (2009). Emotion elicits the social sharing of emotion: Theory and empirical review. *Emotion Review, 1*, 60–85. doi:10.1177/1754073908097189

Rimé, B., & Zech, E. (2001). The social sharing of emotion: Interpersonal and collective dimensions. *Boletin de Psicología, 70*, 97–108. Retrieved from: http://hdl.handle.net/2078.1/92733

Sassenberg, K., Ellemers, N., & Scheepers, D. (2012). The attraction of social power: The influence of construing power as opportunity versus responsibility. *Journal of Experimental Social Psychology, 48*, 550–555. doi:10.1016/j.jesp.2011.11.008

Schmid Mast, M. (2010). Interpersonal behaviour and social perception in a hierarchy: The interpersonal power and behaviour model. *European Review of Social Psychology, 21*, 1–33. doi:10.1080/10463283.2010.486942

Schmid Mast, M., Jonas, K., & Hall, J. A. (2009). Give a person power and he or she will show interpersonal sensitivity: The phenomenon and its why and when. *Journal of Personality and Social Psychology, 97*, 835–850. doi:10.1037/a0016234

Shariff, A. F., & Tracy, J. L. (2009). Knowing who's boss: Implicit perceptions of status from the nonverbal expression of pride. *Emotion, 9*, 631–639. doi:10.1037/a0017089

Shariff, A. F., & Tracy, J. L. (2011). What are emotion expressions for? *Current Directions in Psychological Science, 20*, 395–399. doi:10.1177/0963721411424739

Shariff, A. F., Tracy, J. L., & Markusoff, J. L. (2012). (Implicitly) Judging a book by its cover: The power of pride and shame expressions in shaping judgments of social status. *Personality and Social Psychology Bulletin, 38*, 1178–1193. doi:10.1177/0146167212446834

Sinaceur, M., & Tiedens, L. Z. (2006). Get mad and get more than even: When and why anger expression is effective in negotiations. *Journal of Experimental Social Psychology, 42*, 314–322. doi:10.1016/j.jesp.2005.05.002

Smith, E. R., Seger, C. R., & Mackie, D. M. (2007). Can emotions be truly group level? Evidence regarding four conceptual criteria. *Journal of Personality and Social Psychology, 93*, 431–446. http://doi.org/10.1037/0022-3514.93.3.431

Smith, P. K., & Bargh, J. A. (2008). Nonconscious effects of power on basic approach and avoidance tendencies. *Social Cognition, 26*, 1–24. doi:10.1521/soco.2008.26.1.1

Smith, P. K., Jostmann, N. B., Galinsky, A. D., & van Dijk, W. W. (2008). Lacking power inpairs executive functions. *Psychological Science, 19*, 441–447. doi:10.1111/j.1467-9280.2008.02107.x

Smith, P. K., & Trope, Y. (2006). You focus on the forest when you're in charge of the trees: Power priming and abstract information processing. *Journal of Personality and Social Psychology, 90*, 578–596. doi:10.1037/0022-3514.90.4.578

Spears, R., Greenwood, R., de Lemus, S., & Sweetman, J. (2010). Legitimacy, social identity, and power. In A. Guinote & T. K. Vescio (Eds.), *The social psychology of power* (pp. 251–383). New York: Guilford Press.

Taylor, T., & Risman, B. J. (2006). Doing deference or speaking up: Deconstructing the experience and expression of anger. *Race, Gender & Class, 13*, 60–80.

Thomas, E. F., McGarty, C., & Mavor, K. I. (2009). Transforming "apathy into movement": The role of prosocial emotions in motivating action for social change. *Personality and Social Psychology Review, 13*, 310–333. doi:10.1177/1088868309343290

Tiedens, L. Z. (2001). Anger and advancement versus sadness and subjugation: The effect of negative emotion expressions on social status conferral. *Journal of Personality and Social Psychology, 80*, 86–94. doi:10.1037//0022-351480.1.86

Tiedens, L. Z., Ellsworth, P. C., & Mesquita, B. (2000). Sentimental stereotypes: Emotional expectations for high-and low-status group members. *Personality and Social Psychology Bulletin, 26*, 560–575. doi:10.1177/0146167200267004

Timmers, M., Fischer, A. H., & Manstead, A. S. R. (1998). Gender differences in motives for regulating emotions. *Personality and Social Psychology Bulletin, 9*, 974–985. doi:10.1177/0146167298249005

Tracy, J. L., & Robins, R. W. (2007). Emerging insights into the nature and function of pride. *Current Directions in Psychological Science, 16*, 147–150.

Turner, J. C. (2005). Explaining the nature of power: A three-process theory. *European Journal of Social Psychology, 35*, 1–22. doi:10.1002/ejsp.244

Van Kleef, G. A., De Dreu, C. K. W., & Manstead, A. S. R. (2004). The interpersonal effects of emotions in negotiations: A motivated information processing approach. *Journal of Personality and Social Psychology, 87*, 510–528. doi:10.1037/0022-3514.87.4.510

Van Kleef, G. A., De Dreu, C. K. W., & Manstead, A. S. R. (2010). An interpersonal approach to emotion in social decision making: The emotions as social information model. *Advances in Experimental Social Psychology, 42*, 45–96. doi:10.1016/S0065-2601(10)42002-X

Van Kleef, G. A., De Dreu, C. K. W., Pietroni, D., & Manstead, A. S. R. (2006). Power and emotion in negotiation: Power moderates the interpersonal effects of anger and happiness on concession making. *European Journal of Social Psychology, 36*, 557–581. doi:10.1002/ejsp.320

Van Kleef, G. A., Oveis, C., Van Der Löwe, I., Luokogan, A., Goetz, J., & Keltner, D. (2008). Power, distress, and compassion: Turning a blind eye to the suffering of others. *Psychological Science, 19*, 1315–1322. doi:10.1111/j.1467-9280.2008.02241.x

Van Zomeren, M., Leach, C. W., & Spears, R. (2012). Protesters as "passionate economists": A dynamic dual pathway model of approach coping with collective disadvantage. *Personality and Social Psychology Review, 16*, 180–199. doi:10.1177/1088868311430835

Van Zomeren, M., Spears, R., Fischer, A. H., & Leach, C. W. (2004). Put your money where your mouth is! Explaining collective action tendencies through group-based anger and group efficacy. *Journal of Personality and Social Psychology, 87*, 649–664. doi:10.1037/0022-3514.87.5.649

Voyer, B. G., & McIntosh, B. (2013). The psychological consequences of power on self-perception: Implications for leadership. *Leadership & Organization Development Journal 34*, 639–660. doi:10.1108/LODJ-10-2011-0104

Williams, L. A., & Desteno, D. (2009). Pride: Adaptive social emotion or seventh sin? *Psychological Science, 20*, 284–288. doi:10.1111/j.1467-9280.2009.02292.x

Willis, G. B., & Guinote, A. (2011). The effects of social power on goal content and goal striving: A situated perspective. *Social and Personality Psychology Compass, 5*, 706–719. doi:10.1111/j.1751-9004.2011.00382.x

Willis, G. B., Guinote, A., & Rodríguez-Bailón, R. (2010). Illegitimacy improves goal pursuit in powerless individuals. *Journal of Experimental Social Psychology, 46*, 416–419. doi:10.1016/j.jesp.2009.10.009

Willis, G. B., Rodríguez-Bailón, R., & Lupiáñez, J. (2011). The boss is paying attention: Power affects the functioning of the attentional networks. *Social Cognition, 29*, 166–181. doi:10.1521/soco.2011.29.2.166

Winter, D. G. (1973). *The power motive*. New York, NY, US: Free Press.

Yzerbyt, V. Y., & Kuppens, T. (2012). From group-based appraisals to group-based emotions. The role of communication and social sharing. In D. Hermans, B. Rimé, & B. Mesquita (Eds.), *Changing emotions* (pp. 97–104). New York: Psychology Press.

13

UNCONTROLLABILITY, REACTANCE, AND POWER

Power as a resource to regain control after freedom threats

Christina Mühlberger, Eva Jonas, and Sandra Sittenthaler
UNIVERSITY OF SALZBURG

Correspondence: Christina Mühlberger, University of Salzburg, Psychology, Social Psychology, Salzburg, 5020, Austria. Email: christina.muehlberger@sbg.ac.at

Having control, that is, being able to produce desired outcomes through one's own actions (e.g., Baumeister, 1999; Pittman & D'Agostino, 1985), is a basic psychological need (Fiske & Dépret, 1996; Pittman & Zeigler, 2007; Skinner, 1995). If individuals are not allowed to act as they wish, their control of their own behaviors and of the desired behaviors' outcomes is threatened. This is exactly what happens in the case of a freedom threat, i.e., when people are forced to behave in a specific way or not allowed to behave in a desired way. According to reactance theory (Brehm, 1966), people then experience psychological reactance, a motivation to fight for and regain freedom. Imagine Steph, a doctoral student in her second year. During her first year she attended a few conferences and thereby established contact with renowned professors. In her second year, Steph wants to further expand her social network (desired outcome). Thus, she eagerly registers for diverse conferences, workshops, and meetings (own actions). She feels able to achieve her desired outcome through her own actions. Now imagine that her supervisor is not content with Steph attending so many conferences and instead wants Steph to focus on writing articles for her doctoral thesis. Therefore, the supervisor restricts Steph's freedom to go to conferences, workshops, and meetings during the second year of her doctoral studies. As Steph is not allowed to attend any more conferences, she is not able to achieve her desired outcome of expanding her social network. The supervisor's prohibition poses a threat to Steph's freedom to attend conferences and thereby to her control over her desired outcome.

But why and how does a threat to freedom threaten people's control, and what exactly is control? What is the consequence of this threat, and what will Steph do to restore control? We address these questions by first defining and describing the construct of control. Then, we give an overview on how freedom threats lead to a motivational arousal state called psychological reactance and consider its connection to the perception of control. Next, we will review evidence supporting the notion that power is a resource to deal with threats.

Control

Having actual control means that control is actually present in the context and the person. Having a perception or sense of control is an individual's belief to possess control, i.e., the belief in being able to produce desired outcomes through one's own actions (e.g., Baumeister, 1999; Pittman & D'Agostino, 1985; Skinner, 1995, 1996). Skinner (1996) distinguished between different control relations, the agent-means-ends relations: The *agent–ends* relation refers to the extent to which a person is able or simply believes he or she is able to attain desired outcomes (Steph believes in expanding her social network). If individuals perceive themselves as capable of producing desirable and preventing undesirable outcomes, they have an expectation of agent–ends control. The *agent–means* relation refers to the extent to which a person is able or believes he or she is able to perform a certain behavior (Steph attends conferences). If individuals feel capable of exerting the behavior, they have an expectation of agent–means control. The *means–ends* relation refers to the extent to which a certain behavior causes or can cause an outcome (attending conferences to expand one's social network). The agent-means-ends relations refer to objective control, the extent to which people can indeed produce outcomes through their own actions, as well as perceived control, the extent to which people believe that they can produce outcomes through their own actions (Skinner, 1996).

In the example of Steph, the agent–means relation and thus also the means–ends relation are interrupted. She is not allowed to attend any more conferences and thus cannot use them to expand her social network, either. She experiences a threat to her freedom to attend conferences. What will Steph do now? There are two possibilities for her: she can accept and thus comply with the supervisor's prohibition, or she can refuse to accept and fight against the supervisor's prohibition in order to reestablish her control. The latter can be derived from the theory of psychological reactance (Brehm, 1966; Brehm & Brehm, 1981; Miron & Brehm, 2006; for a recent overview of reactance theory see Steindl, Jonas, Sittenthaler, Traut-Mattausch, & Greenberg, 2015).

Reactance theory

Reactance theory (Brehm, 1966; Brehm & Brehm, 1981) attempts to explain people's reactions to a perceived or actual threat to their freedoms. In the theory, freedom is defined ". . .as an individual's belief that he or she can engage in a particular behavior. The freedom can pertain to what one does, how one does it, or when one does it. . ." (Brehm & Brehm, 1981, p. 358). Individuals take certain freedoms for granted, meaning people are confident that they have the freedom to perform and the freedom not to perform certain behaviors. Thus, freedom refers to one's choice between performing or not performing a behavior (Brehm & Brehm, 1981). Although the expectation of control seems to be very similar and is sometimes described as theoretically equivalent to having a freedom (e.g., Wortman & Brehm, 1975), control refers to people's perception that they are capable of performing a behavior (e.g., Baumeister, 1999; Pittman & D'Agostino, 1985). Thus, while control seems to be about one's perception of being able to do something, freedom seems to be about choosing to do something. For example, people implicitly assume they are free to buy a certain brand of milk in the grocery store, to voice their own opinion on quotas of women in companies, or to organize their vacations according to their own wishes.

If these free behaviors are threatened or lost, people perceive "that some event has increased the difficulty of exercising the freedom in question" (Brehm & Brehm, 1981, p. 35). It implies an interruption of the relation between the agent and his or her free behaviors (means) to produce the desired goal (ends). In the example of Steph, this means that due to her supervisor's prohibition, attending conferences becomes more difficult for her. This perception can arouse reactance, a motivational state focused on restoring or securing the threatened freedom.

Reactance is manifested in (a) *reactance motivation*, an increased subjective desire to engage in behaviors to restore freedom, and (b) *reactance striving*, actual behavioral attempts to restore freedom (Brehm, 1966; Brehm & Brehm, 1981; Wright, Agtarap, & Mlynski, 2015). The strength of the reactance motivation depends on people's initial confidence in the freedom, the subjective importance of the threatened freedom, and the perceived magnitude of the threat (Brehm, 1966; Brehm & Brehm, 1981; Wright et al., 2015). If Steph had been sure she possessed the freedom to attend conferences, if attending conferences is in general very important to her, and if she perceived the supervisor's prohibition as highly threatening, reactance motivation would be very strong. This increased desire to reestablish the threatened freedom is accompanied by subjective reactions, such as an increased attractiveness of the threatened outcome, hostility or diffuse aggression toward the agent who has threatened the freedom, and an increased perception of self-direction, meaning that individuals are aware of their own desires and goals and know that they are their own director of behavior (Brehm, 1966; Brehm & Brehm, 1981).

Reactance motivation leads to reactance striving. Threatened people can directly or indirectly reestablish their freedom by exerting the restricted behavior or by performing related behaviors. They can also aggressively force the threatening agent to remove the threat (Brehm, 1966; Brehm & Brehm, 1981). By using these strategies, people may again be able to achieve their desired goals and thereby reestablish control in the sense of agent–means–ends.

Reestablishing control

The most effective way to reestablish one's control is direct reactance striving. Directly exerting the threatened behavior may help one regain one's agent–means control. For instance, as a reaction to antismoking messages, graphic cigarette warnings, or requests to abandon this bad health habit, people increase their smoking intentions (Erceg-Hurn & Steed, 2011; Grandpre, Alvaro, Burgoon, Miller, & Hall, 2003; Shoham, Trost, & Rohrbaugh, 2004). Moreover, if a received favor arouses pressure to return a favor, people are unlikely to perform a favor in return (Brehm & Cole, 1966). They are also less willing to help others if they experienced reactance following a request for help (Jonas et al., 2009). This boomerang effect has been well investigated in numerous empirical studies. It may serve to restore the relation between the agent and his or her means (e.g., smoking) in order to achieve the desired outcome (e.g., relaxation).

Other possible strategies that restore control operate in an indirect manner (Brehm, 1966; Brehm & Brehm, 1981). For example, a person who observes another one performing the threatened behavior also observes that the means-ends relation works and thus, may experience a means-ends control. Another example is the realization of a similar behavior, i.e., using other means, which would serve to build an agent-means relation. These indirect restoration strategies do not restore actual control between the agent and the means that were threatened but provide people with a perception of control. Similarly, by aggressing toward the threatening agent (Smith, 1977; Worchel & Brehm, 1971), an individual might experience a sense of control, as well. Aggressively forcing the threatening person to remove the threat may lead to a stronger experience of the agent-means relation because one is capable of influencing the threatening person. Reactance effects that accompany but do not directly restore control are subjective reactions, such as an increased desire for the threatened freedom (e.g., Bijvank, Konijn, Bushman, & Roelofsma, 2009; Brehm, 1966; Brehm & Brehm, 1981; Dillard & Shen, 2005; Rains, 2013), which means an increase in the attractiveness of the means and/or ends.

To illustrate with our example, Steph has learned that her supervisor does not want her to participate in conferences. Her agent–means relation is interrupted. To regain control, Steph could secretly attend a conference while pretending to write a paper (direct restoration). Thus, Steph would be able to fulfill her desired outcome of expanding her social network. Instead of attending a conference specific to her field of study, Steph could attend a conference related to another discipline to widen her circle of contacts (indirect restoration). Another strategy would be to react with aggression to the prohibition, forcing her supervisor to remove the threat (indirect restoration). Steph would again be able to achieve her goal of expanding her social network. These strategies either directly restore Steph's control over her means to achieve her desired outcome or indirectly restore control by achieving the desired outcome through other means.

But do people always invest in restoration attempts, or are there also situations in which they do not even try? Here, the difficulty of the required behavior plays an important role (Wright et al., 2015). To provide a more thorough understanding of the emergence of reactance striving, we present an expansion of reactance theory called motivation intensity theory.

Motivation intensity theory

The original theory of psychological reactance (Brehm, 1966; Brehm & Brehm, 1981) posits a subjective and a behavioral manifestation of reactance: reactance motivation, which is the increased desire to exercise the threatened freedom (subjective), and reactance striving, which is the increased tendency to exercise the threatened freedom (behavioral). However, the original theory does not say anything about the intensity of reactance striving, i.e., the intensity of behavior, and how it is related to reactance motivation. As originally formulated, the theory assumes that high reactance motivation causes high reactance striving. In an attempt to elaborate on this issue, Wright et al. (2015) link Brehm's reactance theory and Brehm's Motivation intensity theory (MIT; Brehm & Self, 1989; Wright & Brehm, 1989). Motivational intensity is the actual amount of effort people expend to satisfy their motives. According to MIT, this intensity depends on the difficulty of satisfying the motives and on people's performance capacity (Brehm & Self, 1989; Wright, 2008; Wright et al., 2015; Wright & Brehm, 1989). If difficulty increases, motivational intensity also increases but only up to the point where success seems impossible. Moreover, people's capacity (ability or efficacy, see Wright et al., 2015) to perform a behavior also influences motivational intensity.

According to Wright et al. (2015), first, reactant striving is determined by the factors of MIT – the difficulty of restoring the freedom and people's performance capacity. The more difficult the behavior, the more effort people expend up to the point where success seems impossible or where the costs of reactance striving exceed the benefits. Reactance striving also depends on people's actual or perceived performance capacity (being able to restore freedom). Low-capacity performers should give up earlier than high-capacity performers. Second, reactance motivation, and not reactant striving, is determined by the traditional determinants of reactance, that is, initial confidence in the freedom, subjective importance of the freedom, and perceived magnitude of the threat. Moreover, reactance motivation should also be determined by the outcome's *incentive value*, i.e., the attractiveness of the outcome for the person, and the *outcome expectancy*, i.e., the person's belief that his or her own actions can indeed secure the outcome (Wright et al., 2015).

Integrating the components of MIT and reactance in our example, for Steph, attending conferences has an incentive value because she can expand her social network, and she believes that attending conferences indeed leads to an expansion of her social network (outcome expectancy). This would lead to a strong reactance motivation. If attending a conference is easy for Steph (e.g., if her supervisor has a laissez-faire management style and does not set deadlines for writing her thesis), she might not have to deploy a lot of effort to convince her supervisor (low reactant striving). If attending conferences is very difficult for Steph (e.g., if her supervisor is very strict and wants her to submit the final version of her thesis within six months), reactant striving should also be low because she might think that convincing her supervisor is impossible. She might also perceive the costs of convincing her supervisor as higher than the benefits of attending conferences. However, if attending conferences is moderately difficult for Steph (e.g., if her supervisor wants her to submit only a first version of her thesis within 6 months), she might deploy a lot of effort to convince her supervisor that she should attend a conference (high reactant striving). Here, Steph may try harder to convince her supervisor if she is or believes that she is a capable speaker (high performance capacity). If she is not convinced of her capacity to restore freedom, she would give up.

This conviction of performance capacity resembles the concept of a general belief in one's ability to alter a situation, that is, a general expectation of control. If this expectation is not present, people display symptoms of helplessness. They passively endure the threat or even withdraw from it (Mikulincer, 1988; Pittman & Pittman, 1979; Seligman, 1975; Wortman & Brehm, 1975). This state of giving up is the opposite of psychological reactance, a state that only occurs if people feel capable of restoring their freedom. This was found in a study on stereotype threat and negotiation by Kray, Reb, Galinsky, and Thompson (2004). An explicit expectation that men are better at negotiating led to the exact opposite behavior in women, namely, higher performance. However, such behavior occurred only if women had sufficient power to act. This is in line with the idea that reactance develops only if people feel capable of changing the current situation (Mikulincer, 1988; Pittman & Pittman, 1979; Wortman & Brehm, 1975). In this state, people experience a general sense of control (Mikulincer, 1988; Pittman & Pittman, 1979; Wortman & Brehm, 1975). A high sense of control can be observed in people feeling powerful.

Power

A feeling of power provides people with access to material resources such as food, money, or economic opportunities, and social resources such as knowledge, praise, or positive attention (Keltner, Gruenfeld, & Anderson, 2003). It also makes one aware that he or she is free from constraints, which means that one is able to act without interference from others and without serious consequences (Keltner et al., 2003). The decreased dependence from others, rather than general power over other people, seems to be the primary motive lying behind power and comes along with a heightened feeling of control over own outcomes (van Dijke & Poppe, 2006). Although power and control have similar definitions, they have been shown to act more as an independent and dependent variable. While power is often defined as the experience of being able to influence others or control others' outcomes (e.g., Guinote, 2007a; van Dijke & Poppe, 2006; Vescio, Snyder, & Butz, 2003), control is the experience of being able to produce desired outcomes through one's own actions (e.g., Pittman & D'Agostino, 1989; Skinner, 1996). A sense of power acts as an independent variable leading people to experience a sense of control (Guinote, 2007a; Guinote, Brown, & Fiske, 2006). Guinote et al. (2006) concluded that control as a basic need is the driving mechanism behind power that affects how individuals process information (also see Guinote, 2007a; van Dijke & Poppe, 2006). Thus, power might not only bring along resources, such as money or opportunities; it might be a psychological resource itself.

In general, resources can be broadly defined as means to attain ends (e.g. money, food, opportunities) or as entities that "are centrally valued in their own right (e.g., self-esteem, close attachments, health, and inner peace)" (Hobfoll, 2002, p. 307). Power can have a real base, such as material and social resources (objective power) but can also refer to the subjective sense of power (see Anderson & Berdahl, 2002; compare Skinner, 1996) that entails the sense of control (see Guinote, 2007a; Guinote et al., 2006; van Dijke & Poppe, 2006). It can be seen as a psychological resource similar to other psychological resources, such as self-esteem, self-efficacy, optimism, or hope (Harber, Yeung, & Iacovelli, 2011). Such resources can attenuate reactions to threat and provide effective coping strategies (Harber et al., 2011; Hobfoll, 2002).

Possessing resources and being unconstrained by others or by the actions' consequences, powerful people are less sensitive to threats and punishment compared to powerless people (for an overview, see Keltner et al., 2003). Supporting this statement, Scheepers, de Wit, Ellemers, and Sassenberg (2012) found that during a stressful situation, people feeling powerful show an efficient cardiovascular pattern indicative of a challenge response. This state occurs when people's resources meet or even exceed evaluated demands of a situation. It enables people to better mobilize their bodily resources. By contrast, people feeling powerless show an inefficient cardiovascular pattern indicative of a threat response which occurs when people's resources do not meet the demands (Blascovich & Tomaka, 1996).

Given that powerful people are free from constraints, what are the implications for the experience and reactions to constraints? A common notion is that power provides individuals freedom from constraints (Keltner et al., 2003), so constraints may in general be unexpected for or even overseen by these individuals. They may feel less threatened when confronted with constraints. But how exactly do powerful people react when they are threatened in their freedom?

Power and threats

Research on power and reactance provides evidence for different physiological reactions for high- and low-power individuals. In a pilot study measuring heart rate (Sittenthaler, Jonas, & Steindl, 2011), people were primed with power by counting money. The control group counted pieces of paper (Zhou, Vohs, & Baumeister, 2009). Afterwards, a classic freedom threat was employed by restricting the third most attractive choice out of seven possible choices (e.g., Brehm, Stires, Sensenig, & Shaban, 1966). First analyses replicated previous research showing that the freedom threat increases heart rate compared to a control group (Sittenthaler, Jonas, & Traut-Mattausch, in press; Sittenthaler, Steindl, & Jonas, 2015). Interestingly, this effect was qualified by an interaction between freedom threat and power such that only people counting papers showed an increase in heart rate. For people primed with power, heart rate remained the same, no matter if they were or were not restricted in their freedom. This result might imply that power leads people to stay calm when a threat happens. Studies investigating the effect of power on the subjective experience of reactance (Sittenthaler et al., 2011; Steindl & Jonas, 2015) used items assessing participants' perception of the freedom threat and their emotional experience (see Sittenthaler, Traut-Mattausch, Steindl, & Jonas, 2015; also see Steindl et al., 2015). In these studies, it was found that high- vs. low-power participants reported about the same amount of reactance when they had been restricted in their freedom. Thus, both high- and low-power individuals seem to perceive the threat but high-power individuals do not seem to feel threatened. With regard to their physiological response, they remain calm. Power seems to possess a buffering function against the physiological stress responses that threats create.

Yet, according to studies demonstrating that high- and low-power people differ in their behaviors, such that for example high-power people show higher action orientation, maybe they also differ with regard to their restoration behaviors when confronted with freedom threats?

Power induces flexibility

According to the situated focus theory of power (Guinote, 2007a), individuals who feel powerful are more flexible in processing information that is relevant to their goals, allowing them to cognitively adapt to the situation. They act in a goal-consistent manner, i.e., they show behaviors consistent with desired end states (Galinsky, Gruenfeld, & Magee, 2003; Guinote, 2007b) and are flexible in attempting different means to attain their desired end states (Guinote, 2007b). Regarding goal-consistent behavior, for example, Galinsky et al. (2003, experiment 2) found that individuals primed with high power were more likely to remove an annoying fan than individuals primed with low power which satisfied individuals' goal of reducing discomfort. Regarding flexibility, Guinote (2007b, study 3) demonstrated that participants in powerful roles made more new attempts to find a solution for a problem-solving task than participants in powerless roles. When processing information, they respond in line with the demands of the situation and focus on the objective information provided (Guinote, 2007b; Guinote et al., 2006). Guinote et al. (2006) manipulated power by assigning participants to a majority or minority group and assessed how information of an anticipated interaction partner was processed. Results revealed that compared to minority members, majority members based their reasoning more on the objective information which was provided than on subjective interpretations. This result was fully mediated by the majority member's sense of control. Members of the majority group felt more in control than members of the minority group. This result indicates that control is the driving factor for flexible information processing. Guinote (2007a) argued that "power increases the ability to utilise executive control in line with situational demands, thereby inducing flexibility in the ways information is processed" (p. 267). Powerful people are better able than powerless people to consider higher-order goals for effective cognitive processing (Guinote, 2007a). Together, these findings suggest that power allows people to engage in behaviors relevant for attaining their goals.

Power induces flexibility in threatening situations

Incorporating the situated focus theory of power (Guinote, 2007a) into the theory of psychological reactance (Brehm, 1966), we argue that threatened individuals who experience themselves as powerful are better able to engage in processes relevant to their desired goal. Having enough resources and being free from constraints (Keltner et al., 2003) would allow them to focus on the higher-order goal, that is, their desired overarching goal that has been blocked by the threat. They should be less sensitive to the threat but more sensitive to rewards and strategies that help them to obtain goals related to these rewards (Keltner et al., 2003; Zander & Forward, 1968). Thus, individuals who feel powerful may free themselves more quickly from the threat and manage to reorient themselves.

Therefore, referring to the classic reactance effects, although anti-smoking messages and graphic cigarette warnings would arouse reactance in powerful people, such people would focus on their overarching goal (e.g., relaxation) associated with smoking. They could, for instance, desist from smoking but engage in yoga classes in order to achieve their goal of relaxation. In the language of control theories, this would mean that agent–ends control is reestablished by employing alternative means. If Steph is told to refrain from attending conferences and does not feel powerful enough to effectively deal with this prohibition, that is, if she does not possess enough resources to focus on her overarching goal, she may try everything possible to convince her supervisor to allow her to attend a conference. She sticks to the threatened behavior, which she sees as the only possible way to achieve her goal. But if Steph is told to refrain from attending conferences and has enough resources to deal with this prohibition in an efficient way, she may try everything possible to achieve her goal of expanding her social network, rather than persevere in her goal of attending the threatened conferences. For example, she might organize a meeting for doctoral students in her department or ask colleagues from the same department to collaborate with her on an article. Thus, she might reinterpret the supervisor's prohibition as a challenge to find other ways to achieve her goal. Either way, control is restored, but for high-power people this is achieved by charting a different way to reach their desired outcome.

In two studies on information search (Steindl & Jonas, 2015), we tested the hypothesis that high-power people whose own decision has been restricted do not prefer information supporting this decision but prefer information supporting alternative decisions that also serve to attain a relevant goal. In both studies, participants' goal was to choose one out of three different vacations. The preferred choice either was or was not restricted. In the first study, we measured participants' sense of power[1] (strong, proud, determined) regarding the vacation situation after the restriction, and in the second study, before the restriction we primed participants with high power or low power (see Galinsky et al., 2003), or we did not prime them (control group). Then we presented participants with 24 statements either emphasizing the three vacations' advantages or their disadvantages (see Jonas, Graupmann, & Frey, 2006). Participants were asked to pick the ones most relevant for their final decision for a vacation and that they wanted to read about in more detail. To analyze this information search, we built a score that indicated their preference for information supporting their initial decision (advantages of the chosen vacation and disadvantages of the non-chosen vacations) over information supporting alternative decisions (advantages of the nonchosen vacations and disadvantages of the chosen vacation; see "confirmation bias"; Jonas, Schulz-Hardt, Frey, & Thelen, 2001, p. 557). Analyses in both studies revealed that threatened but high-power individuals (power was assessed either by measuring power or by priming power) preferred information supporting alternatives – they were especially interested in advantages of the remaining non-restricted vacations, but they were also interested in disadvantages of the chosen vacation (Figure 13.1 and 13.2). This would mean that threatened but powerful individuals were more open-minded about alternatives, probably having in mind their overarching goal of taking a vacation. Threatened individuals who experienced low power or no power (control group) were equally interested in supporting their initial decision and in supporting alternatives, i.e., they searched for information in a more balanced way.

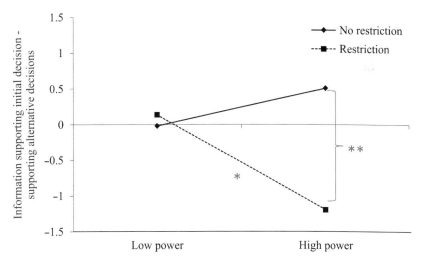

FIGURE 13.1   The effect of restriction and power on participants' information search. Positive values indicate a preference for supporting their initial decision and negative values indicate a preference for supporting alternative decisions (=confirmation bias). Plotted values reflect the confirmation bias below and above the mean of feeling powerful. Restriction × Power interaction: $b = -1.02$, $SE = 0.50$, $t(156) = -2.07$, $p = .041$; $^{\star}p < .05$, $^{\star\star}p < .01$.

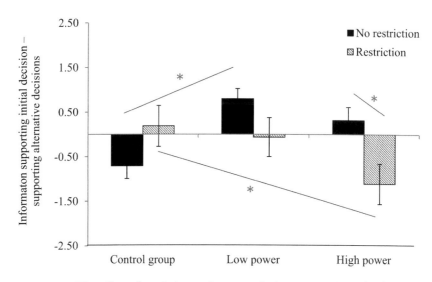

FIGURE 13.2 The effect of restriction and power priming on participants' information search. Positive values indicate a preference for supporting their initial decision and negative values indicate a preference for supporting alternative decisions (=confirmation bias). Restriction × Power interaction: $F(2, 95) = 3.56, p = .032, \eta^2 = .07; {}^{\star}p < .05$.

Our results are in line with research demonstrating that compared to powerless individuals, powerful individuals respond in more flexible ways when they face difficulties in pursuing their goals, i.e., they try new strategies to pursue the goal (Guinote, 2007b). Furthermore, in line with studies indicating that power leads to overconfidence in decision-making (Fast, Sivanathan, Mayer, & Galinsky, 2012), we found that participants who were primed with power but who were not threatened in their freedom indicated a confirmation bias, i.e., they preferred information supporting their initial decision. In both studies, the threatened group reported more experience of reactance than the control group but interestingly, low-power and high-power participants reported about the same amount of reactance, indicating that people's different information search cannot be due to a difference in the subjective experience of reactance.

Both studies provide evidence for power playing a crucial role in information processing after threats. When individuals were socially influenced not to pick an initially preferred option but were feeling powerful, they were more open-minded to alternative vacations. One could argue that this contrasts with studies showing that high-power individuals are less influenced by situational information than low-power individuals (Galinsky, Magee, Gruenfeld, Whitson, & Liljenquist, 2008; Skagerberg & Wright, 2008). However, as our results suggest, the important question may not be whether power leads to resisting social influence attempts or not, but what the overarching goal is. This suggests that powerful individuals always keep their higher-order goal in mind when dealing with threats. In some cases it may be necessary to resist influence and in others not. This interpretation is in line with the situated focus theory of power (Guinote, 2007a), which argues that powerful individuals possess the necessary resources for flexible cognitive processing to focus on their higher-order goal.

Concluding thoughts

In an effort to connect the theories of control, reactance, motivation intensity, and power, we outlined that power plays a crucial role in information processing after one's freedom has been threatened. Presumably this is due to high-power individuals' increased resources to regain control. High-power people have the necessary resources to act in a goal-consistent manner. Therefore, keeping in mind the important overarching goals, a powerful individual selectively processes information relevant to the pursuit of those goals. We illustrated how perceiving oneself as powerful leads people to process information in a more open-minded way. Results show that the classic reactance effects that lead to a restoration of control and by which people more strongly stick to the threatened means (boomerang behaviors, derogation of the threatening agent, hostility, and aggression) are not the only possible options. These classic reactance effects have mainly been considered undesirable and as shown by numerous studies, reactance often results in such undesirable consequences.

Interestingly, research on reactance has also found desirable consequences. For example, reactance is associated not just with negative affect, such as anger, but also with activating positive affect, such as feeling strong and determined (Sittenthaler, Steindl et al., 2015). Indeed, the experience of reactance also elicited heightened achievement motivation (Steindl & Jonas, 2014). Moreover, in studies using electroencephalography (EEG), reactance was accompanied by increased left frontal alpha asymmetry (Steindl, Jonas, Klackl, Sittenthaler, & Hekele, 2016). This is thought to be an indicator of approach motivation, a state that motivates people to move toward something (Harmon-Jones, 2003; Harmon-Jones & Allen, 1998; Harmon-Jones, Harmon-Jones & Price, 2013). Similar to reactance, approach motivation is elicited only when people feel able to cope with a situation (Harmon-Jones, Lueck, Fearn, & Harmon-Jones, 2006; Harmon-Jones, Sigelman, Bohlig, & Harmon-Jones, 2003).

Although people feeling powerful seem to effectively deal with freedom threats, what would happen if the freedom threat concerns their power? Speaking in terms of control, in this case, the agent and therefore also his or her relations to means and ends would be interrupted. In a study by Rodrigues-Bailon, Moya, and Yzerbyt (2000), power holders with a threatened position processed information in a more biased and heuristic way. They devoted more attention to negative stereotypic information about a subordinate. The authors concluded that whenever power is questioned, powerholders may feel threatened and may try everything possible to increase the legitimacy of their position. Thus, if one's power is threatened, the function of power to process information in a more flexible way might not work anymore. Research is needed to investigate this issue in more detail.

Another question that arises is whether the reorientation of powerful people is indeed due to more flexibility in cognitive processing or to heightened attentional vigilance. Heightened attentional vigilance is produced by the Behavioral Inhibition System (BIS; Gray, 1982, 1990; McNaughton & Corr, 2004), a motivational system which inhibits all ongoing behaviors and arouses vigilance in order to orient people toward the information relevant for solving a specific threatening situation (Jonas et al., 2014). In the studies by Steindl and Jonas (2015), powerful people may experience heightened vigilance due to the freedom threat. This might explain why they reorient by paying special attention to the non-threatened remaining vacations. Keeping in mind their overarching goal of spending a vacation, they focus on the information relevant for achieving their goal. However, it is also possible that people feeling powerful terminate the BIS phase very quickly. According to the model by Jonas et al. (2014), BIS activation can be attenuated by activation of the behavioral approach system (BAS; Gray, 1982, 1990; McNaughton & Corr, 2004). In BAS mode, threatened individuals approach alternative, unimpeded goals. People high on approach motivation reach the BAS state more quickly. Thus, power which activates approach-related affect, cognition, and behavior (Keltner et al., 2003) may lead people to succeed in flipping to the BAS more rapidly because they perceive the freedom threat more as a challenge than a threat (Scheepers et al., 2012). In BAS mode, they perform approach-oriented behaviors in order to pursue their overarching goals. Research is needed in order to address the specific mechanisms that are underlying the effects of power and threats.

The current chapter provides evidence that freedom threats do not necessarily cause undesirable effects to restore one's freedom. Rather, freedom threats can result in behaviors other than derogating the threatening agent or behaving in a hostile and aggressive way. If people feel powerful and thus, possess the necessary resources to act according to their goals, they do not stick to the threatened freedom but adapt to the new situation in a flexible way.

Acknowledgments

The first author of this article was financially supported by the Doctoral College "Imaging the Mind" of the Austrian Science Fund (FWF-W1233).

Note

1 Note that the German word for "powerful" is "strong"

References

Anderson, C., & Berdahl, J. L. (2002). The experience of power: Examining the effects of power on approach and inhibition tendencies. *Journal of Personality and Social Psychology, 83*, 1362–1377. http://doi.org/10.1037//0022–3514.83.6.1362

Baumeister, R. F. (1999). The nature and structure of the self: An overview. In R. F. Baumeister (Ed.), *The self in social psychology* (pp. 1–20). Philadelphia: Psychology Science.

Bijvank, M. N., Konijn, E. A., Bushman, B. J., & Roelofsma, P. H. M. P. (2009). Age and violent-content labels make video games forbidden fruits for youth. *Pediatrics, 123*, 870–876. doi:10.1542/peds.2008-0601

Blascovich, J., & Tomaka, J. (1996). The biopsychosocial model of arousal regulation. *Advances in Experimental Social Psychology, 28*, 1–51. http://dx.doi.org/10.1016/S0065–2601(08)60235-X

Brehm, J. W. (1966). *A theory of psychological reactance.* New York: Academic Press.

Brehm, J. W., & Brehm, S. S. (1981). *Psychological reactance – A theory of freedom and control.* New York: Academic Press.

Brehm, J. W., & Cole, A. H. (1966). Effect of a favor which reduces freedom. *Journal of Personality and Social Psychology, 3*, 420–426. http://dx.doi.org/10.1037/h0023034

Brehm, J. W., & Self, E. A. (1989). The intensity of motivation. *Annual Review of Psychology, 40*, 109–131. http://dx.doi.org/10.1146/annurev.ps.40.020189.000545

Brehm, J. W., Stires, L. K., Sensenig, J., & Shaban, J. (1966). The attractiveness of an eliminated choice alternative. *Journal of Experimental Social Psychology, 2*, 301–313. http://doi.org/10.1016/0022–1031(66)90086–2

Dillard, J. P., & Shen, L. (2005). On the nature of reactance and its role in persuasive health communication. *Communication Monographs, 72*, 144–168. doi:10.1080/03637750500111815

Erceg-Hurn, D. M., & Steed, L. G. (2011). Does exposure to cigarette health warnings elicit psychological reactance in smokers? *Journal of Applied Social Psychology, 41*, 219–237. http://doi.org/10.1111/j.1559–1816.2010.00710.x

Fast, N. J., Sivanathan, N., Mayer, N. D., & Galinsky, A. D. (2012). Power and overconfident decision-making. *Organizational Behavior and Human Decision Processes, 117*, 249–260. http://doi.org/10.1016/j.obhdp.2011.11.009

Fiske, S. T., & Dépret, E. (1996). Control, interdependence and power: Understanding social cognition in its social context. *European Review of Social Psychology, 7*, 31–61. http://doi.org/10.1080/14792779443000094

Galinsky, A. D., Gruenfeld, D. H., & Magee, J. C. (2003). From power to action. *Journal of Personality and Social Psychology, 85*, 453–466. http://doi.org/10.1037/0022–3514.85.3.453

Galinsky, A. D., Magee, J. C., Gruenfeld, D. H., Whitson, J. A., & Liljenquist, K. A. (2008). Power reduces the press of the situation: Implications for creativity, conformity, and dissonance. *Journal of Personality and Social Psychology, 95*, 1450–1466. http://doi.org/10.1037/a0012633

Grandpre, J., Alvaro, E. M., Burgoon, M., Miller, C. H., & Hall, J. R. (2003). Adolescent reactance and anti-smoking campaigns: A theoretical approach. *Health Communication, 15*, 349–366. http://doi.org/10.1207/S15327027HC1503_6

Gray, J. A. (1982). *The neuropsychology of anxiety.* New York: Oxford University Press.

Gray, J. A. (1990). Brain systems that mediate both emotion and cognition. *Cognition and Emotion, 4*, 269–288. http://dx.doi.org/10.1080/02699939008410799

Guinote, A. (2007a). Behaviour variability and the situated focus theory of power. *European Review of Social Psychology, 18*, 256–295. http://doi.org/10.1080/10463280701692813

Guinote, A. (2007b). Power and goal pursuit. *Personality and Social Psychology Bulletin, 33*, 1076–1087. http://doi.org/10.1177/0146167207301011

Guinote, A., Brown, M., & Fiske, S. T. (2006). Minority status decreases sense of control and increases interpretive processing. *Social Cognition, 24*, 169–186. http://doi.org/10.1521/soco.2006.24.2.169

Harber, K. D., Yeung, D., & Iacovelli, A. (2011). Psychosocial resources, threat, and the perception of distance and height: Support for the resources and perception model. *Emotion, 11*, 1080–1090. http://doi.org/10.1037/a0023995

Harmon-Jones, E. (2003). Clarifying the emotive functions of asymmetrical frontal cortical activity. *Psychophysiology, 40*, 838–848. http://doi.org/10.1111/1469–8986.00121

Harmon-Jones, E., & Allen, J. J. B. (1998). Anger and frontal brain activity: EEG asymmetry consistent with approach motivation despite negative affective valence. *Journal of Personality and Social Psychology, 74*, 1310–1316. http://dx.doi.org/10.1037/0022–3514.74.5.1310

Harmon-Jones, E., Harmon-Jones, C., & Price, T. F. (2013). What is approach motivation? *Emotion Review, 5*, 291–295. http://doi.org/10.1177/1754073913477509

Harmon-Jones, E., Lueck, L., Fearn, M., & Harmon-Jones, C. (2006). The effect of personal relevance and approach-related action expectation on relative left frontal cortical activity. *Psychological Science, 17*, 434–440. http://doi.org/10.1111/j.1467–9280.2006.01724.x

Harmon-Jones, E., Sigelman, J. D., Bohlig, A., & Harmon-Jones, C. (2003). Anger, coping, and frontal cortical activity: The effect of coping potential on anger-induced left frontal activity. *Cognition and Emotion, 17*, 1–24. http://dx.doi.org/10.1080/02699930302278

Hobfoll, S. E. (2002). Social and psychological resources and adaptation. *Review of General Psychology, 6*, 307–324. http://doi.org/10.1037/1089–2680.6.4.307

Jonas, E., Graupmann, V., & Frey, D. (2006). The influence of mood on the search for supporting vs. conflicting information. *Personality and Social Psychology Bulletin, 32*, 3–15. http://dx.doi.org/10.1177/0146167205276118

Jonas, E., Graupmann, V., Kayser, D. N., Zanna, M., Traut-Mattausch, E., & Frey, D. (2009). Culture, self, and the emergence of reactance: Is there a "universal" freedom? *Journal of Experimental Social Psychology, 45*, 1068–1080. doi:10.1016/j.jesp.2009.06.005

Jonas, E., McGregor, I., Klackl, J., Agroskin, D., Fritsche, I., Holbrook, C., Nash, K., Proulx, T., & Quirin, M. (2014). Threat and defense: From anxiety to approach. In J. M. Olson and M. P. Zanna (Eds.), *Advances in experimental social psychology* (Vol. 49, pp. 219–286). San Diego, CA: Academic Press. http://dx.doi.org/10.1016/b978–0–12–800052–6.00004–4

Jonas, E., Schulz-Hardt, S., Frey, D., & Thelen, N. (2001). Confirmation bias in sequential information search after preliminary decisions: An expansion of dissonance theoretical research on selective exposure to information. *Journal of Personality and Social Psychology, 80*, 557–571. http://dx.doi.org/10.1037/0022–3514.80.4.557

Keltner, D., Gruenfeld, D. H., & Anderson, C. (2003). Power, approach, and inhibition. *Psychological Review, 110*, 265–284. http://doi.org/10.1037/0033–295X.110.2.265

Kray, L. J., Reb, J., Galinsky, A. D., & Thompson, L. (2004). Stereotype reactance at the bargaining table: The effect of stereotype activation and power on claiming and creating value. *Personality and Social Psychology Bulletin, 30*, 399–411. http://doi.org/10.1177/0146167203261884

McNaughton, N., & Corr, P. J. (2004). A two-dimensional neuropsychology of defense: Fear/anxiety and defensive distance. *Neuroscience and Biobehavioral Reviews, 28*, 285–305. http://dx.doi.org/10.1016/j.neubiorev.2004.03.005

Mikulincer, M. (1988). Reactance and helplessness following exposure to unsolvable problems: The effects of attributional style. *Journal of Personality and Social Psychology, 54*, 679–686. http://dx.doi.org/10.1037/0022–3514.54.4.679

Miron, A. M., & Brehm, J. W. (2006). Reactance theory-40 years later. *Zeitschrift für Sozialpsychologie, 37*, 9–18. http://dx.doi.org/10.1024/0044–3514.37.1.9

Pittman, N. L., & Pittman, T. S. (1979). Effects of amount of helplessness training and internal-external locus of control on mood and performance. *Journal of Personality and Social Psychology, 37*, 39–47. http://dx.doi.org/10.1037/0022–3514.37.1.39

Pittman, T. S., & D'Agostino, P. R. (1985). Motivation and attribution: The effects of control deprivation on subsequent information processing. In J. H. Harvey & G. Weary (Eds.), *Attribution: Basic and applied issues* (pp. 117–142). New York: Academic Press.

Pittman, T. S., & Zeigler, K. R. (2007). Basic human needs. In A. Kruglanski & E. T. Higgins (Eds.), *Social psychology: Handbook of basic principles* (2nd ed., pp. 473–489). New York: Guilford.

Rains, S. A. (2013). The nature of psychological reactance revisited: A meta-analytic review. *Human Communication Research, 39*, 47–73. doi:10.1111/j.1468-2958.2012.01443.x

Rodrigues-Bailon, R., Moya, M., & Yzerbyt, V. (2000). Why do superiors attend to negative stereotypic information about their subordinates? Effects of power legitimacy on social perception. *European Journal of Social Psychology, 30*, 651–671. http://dx.doi.org/10.1002/1099–0992(200009/10)30:5<651::AID-EJSP13>3.0.CO;2-O

Scheepers, D., de Wit, F., Ellemers, N., & Sassenberg, K. (2012). Social power makes the heart work more efficiently: Evidence from cardiovascular markers of challenge and threat. *Journal of Experimental Social Psychology, 48*, 371–374. http://doi.org/10.1016/j.jesp.2011.06.014

Seligman, M. E. P. (1975). *Helplessness. On depression, development and death.* San Francisco, CA: Freeman.

Shoham, V., Trost, S., & Rohrbaugh, M. (2004). From state to trait and back again: Reactance theory goes clinical. In R. A. Wright, J. Greenberg, & S. S. Brehm (Eds.), *Motivational analyses of social behavior: Building on Jack Brehm's contributions to psychology* (pp. 167–185). Mahwah: Lawrence Erlbaum Associates.

Sittenthaler, S., Jonas, E., & Steindl, C. (2011). *Power, reactance, and its underlying physiology.* Unpublished raw data, University of Salzburg, Austria.

Sittenthaler, S., Jonas, E., & Traut-Mattausch, E. (2016). Explaining self and vicarious reactance: A process model approach. *Personality and Social Psychology Bulletin, 42*, 458–470.

Sittenthaler, S., Steindl, C., & Jonas, E. (2015). Legitimate vs. illegitimate restrictions – A motivational and physiological approach investigating reactance processes. *Frontiers in Psychology, 6*(632), 1–11. http://dx.doi.org/10.3389/fpsyg.2015.00632

Sittenthaler, S., Traut-Mattausch, E., Steindl, C., & Jonas, E. (2015). Salzburger State Reactance Scale (SSR Scale): Validation of a scale measuring state reactance. *Zeitschrift Für Psychologie, 223*, 257–266. http://doi.org/10.1027/ 2151–2604/a000228

Skagerberg, E. M., & Wright, D. B. (2008). Manipulating power can affect memory conformity. *Applied Cognitive Psychology, 22*, 207–216. http://doi.org/10.1002/acp.1353

Skinner, E. A. (1995). *Perceived control, motivation, and coping.* London: Sage Publications. http://dx.doi.org/10.4135/9781483327198

Skinner, E. A. (1996). A guide to constructs of control. *Journal of Personality and Social Psychology, 71*, 549–570. http://doi.org/10.1037/0022–3514.71.3.549

Smith, M. J. (1977). The effects of threats to attitudinal freedom as a function of message quality and initial receiver attitude. *Communication Monographs, 44*, 196–206. http://doi.org/10.1080/03637757709390131

Steindl, C., & Jonas, E. (2014). *Reactance and achievement motivation.* Unpublished raw data, University of Salzburg, Austria.

Steindl, C., & Jonas, E. (2015). *Reactance, power, and information search.* Unpublished raw data, University of Salzburg, Austria.

Steindl, C., Jonas, E., Klackl, J., Sittenthaler, S., & Hekele, F. (2016). *Psychological reactance increases relative left frontal cortical activation.* Manuscript in preparation.

Steindl, C., Jonas, E., Sittenthaler, S., Traut-Mattausch, E., & Greenberg, J. (2015). Understanding psychological reactance: New developments and findings. *Zeitschrift für Psychologie, 223*, 205–2014. http://dx.doi.org/10.1027/2151–2604/a000222

Van Dijke, M., & Poppe, M. (2006). Striving for personal power as a basis for social power dynamics. *European Journal of Social Psychology, 36*, 537–556. http://doi.org/10.1002/ejsp.351

Vescio, T. K., Snyder, M., & Butz, D. A. (2003). Power in stereotypically masculine domains: A social influence strategy X stereotype match model. *Journal of Personality and Social Psychology, 85*, 1062–1078. http://doi.org/10.1037/0022–3514.85.6.1062

Worchel, S., & Brehm, J. W. (1971). Direct and implied social restoration of freedom. *Journal of Personality and Social Psychology, 18*, 294–304. http://doi.org/10.1037/h0031000

Wortman, C. B., & Brehm, J. W. (1975). Responses to uncontrollable outcomes: An integration of reactance theory and the learned helplessness model. In L. Berkowitz (Ed.), *Advances in experimental social psychology* (Vol. 8, pp. 277–336). New York, NY: Academic Press.

Wright, R. A. (2008). Refining the prediction of effort: Brehm's distinction between potential motivation and motivation intensity. *Social and Personality Psychology Compass, 2*, 682–701. http://doi.org/10.1111/j.1751–9004.2008.00093.x

Wright, R. A., Agtarap, S. D., & Mlynski, C. (2015). Conversion of reactance motives into effortful goal pursuit: Implications of Brehm's theory of motivation intensity. *Zeitschrift für Psychologie, 223*, 267–276. http://dx.doi.org/10.1027/2151–2604/a000228

Wright, R. A., & Brehm, J. W. (1989). Energization and goal attractiveness. In L. A. Pervin (Ed.), *Goal concepts in personality and social psychology* (pp.169-210). Hillsdale, NJ: Erlbaum.

Zander, A., & Forward, J. (1968). Position in group, achievement motivation, and group aspirations. *Journal of Personality and Social Psychology, 8*, 282–288. http://dx.doi.org/10.1037/h0025595

Zhou, X., Vohs, K. D., & Baumeister, R. F. (2009). The symbolic power of money: Reminders of money alter social distress and physical pain. *Psychological Science, 20*, 700–706. http://doi.org/10.1111/j.1467-9280.2009.02353.x

INDEX